Introduction to

Java™

Programming

Second Edition

Y. Daniel Liang

Bob,

Thanks for your mentoring and support.

Daniel

que
E&T

An Imprint of Macmillan Computer Publishing
201 W. 103rd St., Indianapolis, IN 46290

INTRODUCTION TO JAVA PROGRAMMING, SECOND EDITION

Library of Congress Catalog No.: 98-88887

ISBN: 1-58076-255-7

02 01 00 99   4 3 2 1

Interpretation of the printing code: the rightmost double-digit number is the year of the book's printing; the rightmost single-digit number, the number of the book's printing. For example, a printing code of 99-1 shows that the first printing of the book occurred in 1999.

Composed in *AGaramond* and *MCPdigital* by Que® Education and Training.

Trademark Acknowledgments

PUBLISHER:
Robert Linsky

EXECUTIVE EDITOR:
Randy Haubner

DIRECTOR OF PRODUCT MARKETING:
Susan L. Kindel

OPERATIONS MANAGER:
Christine Moos

DEVELOPMENT EDITOR:
Songlin Qiu

PROJECT EDITOR:
Tim Tate

COPY EDITOR:
Carolyn Linn

TECHNICAL EDITOR:
Alfonso Hermida

SOFTWARE SPECIALIST:
Angela Denny

COVER DESIGNER:
Nathan Clement

BOOK DESIGNER:
Louisa Klucznik

INDEXER:
Chris Barrick

PROOFREADER:
John Etchison

LAYOUT TECHNICIAN:
Eric S. Miller

ABOUT THE AUTHOR

Y. Daniel Liang holds B.S. and M.S. degrees in computer science from Fudan University in Shanghai and a Ph.D. degree in computer science from the University of Oklahoma. He has published numerous papers in international journals and has taught Java courses nationally and internationally. He has consulted in the areas of algorithm design, client/server computing, and database management.

Dr. Liang is currently an associate professor in the Department of Computer Science at Indiana University-Purdue University at Fort Wayne, where he twice received the Excellence in Research Award from the School of Engineering, Technology, and Computer Science. He can be reached via the Internet at **liangy@ipfw.edu**.

ACKNOWLEDGMENTS

I am grateful to the readers of the first edition who offered comments, suggestions, bug reports, and praise. Their enthusiastic support prompted the second edition, which incorporates many of their fine contributions.

Many students helped to prepare this book. Hao Wu drew all the diagrams in the early draft and helped test some examples. Michael Willig, Russell Minnich, Balaram Nair, and Ben Stonebraker helped to correct many typos and errors for the first edition. Mike Sunderman of Raytheon Systems offered several corrections for the second edition.

Dr. Fen English, Dr. James Silver, and many colleagues in the Department of Computer Science have supported this project and offered valuable suggestions and assistance. It was a pleasure to teach the introductory Java course with Mark Temte and Bob Sanders.

I was fortunate to work with an excellent team at Que Education & Training, whose contributions greatly improved the content and presentation of this book. For the first edition, I learned many valuable tips from Marta Partington, Development Editor, who guided me through the revision of the text, and Tom Cirtin, who did a super job as Production Editor. For the second edition, Songlin Qiu, the Development Editor, coordinated the entire development and production process and offered good advice to improve and enhance the text. Tim Tate, the Project Editor, helped in producing the book. Carolyn Linn, the Copy Editor, helped polish my English. Alfonso Hermida was the Technical Editor for both editions; he reviewed all source code and offered good suggestions. Once again, the entire development and production teams for both editions have my thanks for developing and producing the finished product.

I would also like to thank Randy Haubner, the Executive Editor, who organized and oversaw the project; Robin Drake, who helped develop the instructor's manual for the first edition; and Betsy Brown and Susan Kindel for their support of the project.

As always, I am indebted to my wife, Samantha, for love, support, and encouragement.

*To Samantha, Michael, and Michelle,
with love*

INTRODUCTION

To the Student

There is nothing more important to the future of computing than the Internet. There is nothing more exciting on the Internet than Java. A revolutionary programming language developed by Sun Microsystems, Java has become the de facto standard for cross-platform applications and programming on the World Wide Web since its inception in May 1995.

Before Java, the Web was used primarily for viewing static information on the Internet using HTML, a script language for document layout and for linking documents over the Internet. Java programs can be embedded in an HTML page and downloaded by Web browsers to bring live animation and interactive applications to Web clients.

Java is a full-featured, general-purpose programming language, which is capable of developing robust and mission-critical applications. In the last three years, Java has gained enormous popularity and has quickly become the most popular and successful programming language. Today, Java is used not only for Web programming, but also to develop standalone applications. Many companies that considered Java to be more hype than substance before are now using Java to create distributed applications accessed by customers and partners across the Internet. For every new project being developed today, companies are asking how Java could be used to make their work easier.

Java's Design and Advantages

Java is an object-oriented programming language. Object-oriented programming is a favored programming approach today that replaces the traditional procedure-based programming techniques. An object-oriented language uses abstraction, encapsulation, inheritance, and polymorphism to provide great flexibility, modularity, and reusability for developing software.

Java is platform independent. Java programs can run on any machine with any operating system that supports the Java Virtual Machine, a software component that interprets Java instructions and carries out associated actions.

Java is distributed. Networking is inherently built-in. Simultaneous processing can occur on multiple computers on the Internet. Writing network programs is treated as simple data input and output in Java.

Java is multithreaded. Multithreading is the capability of a program to perform several tasks simultaneously; for example, a program can download a video file while playing the video at the same time. Multithreading is particularly useful in graphical user interface (GUI) and network programming. Multithread programming is smoothly integrated in Java. In other languages, you have to call procedures that are specific to the operating system to enable multithreading.

Java is secure. Computers become vulnerable when they are connected with others. Viruses and malicious programs can damage your computer. Java is designed with multiple layers of security that ensure proper access of private data and restrict access to disk files.

Java's Versatility

Stimulated by the promise of writing programs once and running them anywhere, the computer industry gave Java unqualified endorsement. IBM, Sun, Apple, Microsoft, and many other vendors are working to integrate the Java Virtual Machine with their operating systems so that Java programs can run directly and efficiently on the native machine. Java programs run not only on full-featured computers, but also on consumer electronics and appliances.

There is a great potential for Java to unite existing legacy applications written on different platforms to run together. Java has been perceived as a universal front end for the enterprise database. The leading database companies, such as IBM, Oracle, Sybase, and Informix, have extended their commitment to Java by integrating Java into their products. Oracle, for example, plans to enable native Java applications to run on its server, and to deliver a complete set of Java-based development tools supporting the integration of current applications with the Web.

Learning Java

The key to developing software is applying the concept of abstraction in the design and implementation of the software project. The overriding objective of this book is, therefore, to teach how to solve problems using many levels of abstraction, and to teach how to see problems in small and in large.

Students were the source of inspiration for this book. I learned to teach programming from my students. Students told me they wanted a book that uses easy-to-follow examples to teach programming concepts. In the summer of 1996, I was looking for a Java text. I encountered many reference books and several books converted from C and C++ texts on the market. I could not find the kind of book that I was looking for, so the idea was born to write a book to teach basic Java concepts using good examples.

This book covers major topics in Java programming, including programming structures, methods, objects, classes, inheritance, AWT, applets, exception handling, multithreading, multimedia, I/O, and networking. For students new to object-oriented programming, it takes some time to become familiar with the concept of objects and classes. Once you master the principles, programming in Java is easy and productive. For students who know object-oriented programming languages, such as C++ and Smalltalk, learning Java is easier. In fact, Java is simpler than C++ and Smalltalk in many aspects.

The book is completely based on JDK 1.1 and is compatible with JDK 1.2. All the examples were tested using JDK 1.1 and JDK 1.2 on Windows 95 and on Sun Solaris using no deprecated API. The companion CD-ROM contains the JDK 1.2

beta 4 and the source code of all the examples in the text. You can download the latest version of JDK 1.2 from JavaSoft at **www.javasoft.com**.

Coming soon are *Introduction to Java Programming with Visual J++ 6.0* and *Introduction to Java Programming with JBuilder 2*. Both books are written by Y. Daniel Liang and will be published by Que Education and Training.

To the Instructor

There are three popular strategies in teaching Java. The first strategy is to mix Java applets and graphics programming with object-oriented programming concepts. The second strategy is to introduce object-oriented programming from the start. The third strategy is a step-by-step approach, first laying a sound foundation on programming elements, control structures, and methods, and then moving on to the graphical user interface, applets, multithreading, multimedia, I/O, and networking.

The first strategy, starting with GUI and applets, seems attractive, but requires substantial knowledge of OOP and full understanding of the JDK event-handling model; thus, students may never fully understand what they are doing. The second strategy is based on the perception that the objects should be introduced first because Java is an object-oriented programming language. That perception, however, does not strike a chord with the students. From more than 20 Java courses I taught in the past, I found that introducing primitive data types, control structures, and methods helps prepare students to learn object-oriented programming. Therefore, this text adopts the third strategy, proceeding at a steady pace through all necessary and important basic concepts first, then quickly moving to object-oriented programming and then to building interesting GUI applications and applets with multimedia and networking using the object-oriented approach.

This book is primarily intended for introductory programming courses; however, it can also be used for teaching Java as a second language, or for a short training course for experienced programmers. The book contains more material than can be covered in a single semester. You can cover the first 12 chapters, then use the remaining chapters as time permits.

The *Instructor's Resource* CD-ROM is available for adopters of this book. It contains the following resources:

- Lecture notes with suggested teaching strategies and activities

- Microsoft PowerPoint slides for lectures

- Answers to chapter reviews

- Solutions to programming exercises

- Over 400 multiple choice and true or false questions and answers covering all of the chapters of this book in sequence

To receive the Instructor's CD-ROM, contact your Macmillan sales representative.

Key Features of This Book

Introduction to Java Programming, Second Edition uses the following elements to get the most out of the material:

- **Objectives** lists what students learn from the chapter. This helps students to determine whether they have met these objectives after completing the chapter.

- **Introduction** opens the discussion with a brief overview of what to expect from the chapter.

- Programming concepts are taught by representative **Examples**, carefully chosen and presented in an easy-to-follow style. Each example is described, and includes the source code, a sample run, and an Example Review. The source code of the examples is contained in the companion CD-ROM.

  Each program is complete and ready to be compiled and executed. The sample run of the program is captured from the screen to give students a live presentation of the example. Reading these examples is much like entering and running them on a computer.

- **Chapter Summary** reviews the important subjects that students should understand and remember. It also helps students reinforce the key concepts they have learned in the current chapter.

- **Chapter Review** helps students to track progress and evaluate learning.

- **Programming Exercises** at the end of each chapter provide students opportunities to apply the skills on their own. The trick of learning programming is practice, practice, and practice. To that end, this book provides a large number of exercises.

- **Notes**, **Tips**, and **Cautions** are inserted throughout the text to offer students valuable advice and insight on important aspects of program development:

NOTE

Provides additional information on the subject and reinforces important concepts.

TIP

Teaches good programming style and practice.

CAUTION

Helps students steer away from the pitfalls of programming errors.

What's New in the Second Edition

The second edition expands and improves upon the first edition. The major changes are as follows:

- The text has been updated to conform to the JDK 1.2 standards. All the source code can compile and run in JDK 1.2 with no deprecated methods.

- A new section on inner classes was added in Chapter 7, "Class Inheritance." A new section on using `Scrollbar` was added in Chapter 9, "Creating User Interfaces." A new section on using `FileDialog` was added in Chapter 14, "Input and Output."

- New naming conventions for AWT objects are introduced and used consistently to improve code readability.

- A new appendix, E, titled "An HTML Tutorial," was added to introduce basics of writing HTML pages. A new appendix, F, titled "Using the Companion CD-ROM," was added to guide the students in installing JDK 1.2 and in using the source code in the text.

- A new glossary is provided to summarize key terms and definitions used in the text.

- The appendixes on JBuilder in the first edition were removed. Interested readers should refer to the author's new book, *Introduction to Java Programming with JBuilder 2.*

Organization of This Book

This book is divided into four Parts that, taken together, form a comprehensive course on Java programming. Because knowledge is cumulative, the early chapters provide the conceptual basis for understanding Java and guide students through simple examples and exercises; subsequent chapters progressively present Java programming in detail and culminate in teaching the development of comprehensive Java applications. The appendixes contain a mixed bag of topics that include an HTML tutorial.

Part I: Fundamentals of Java Programming

This Part is a steppingstone to prepare you to embark on the journey of learning Java. You will start to know Java and learn to write simple Java programs with primitive data types, control structures, and methods.

Chapter 1, "Introduction to Java," gives an overview of the major features of Java: object-oriented programming, platform independence, Java bytecode, security, performance, multithreading, and networking. This chapter also gives a brief introduction to Java applications and applets, and discusses their similarities and differences. Simple examples for writing applications and applets are provided, along with a brief anatomy of programming structures.

Chapter 2, "Java Building Elements," introduces primitive data types, operators, and expressions. Important topics include identifiers, variables, constants, assignment statements, primitive data types, operators, and shortcut operators. Java programming style and documentation are also addressed.

Chapter 3, "Control Structures," introduces decision and repetition statements. The Java decision statements include various forms of if statements, the switch statement, and the shortcut if statement. The repetition statements include the for loop, the while loop, and the do loop. Students will also learn the role of the keywords break and continue, which are used in the control structures.

Chapter 4, "Methods," introduces method creation, calling methods, passing parameters, returning values, method overloading, and recursion. The key to developing software is applying the concept of abstraction. This chapter also introduces the concept of method abstraction in problem solving.

Part II: Object-Oriented Programming

This Part introduces object-oriented programming. Java is a class-centric, object-oriented programming language that uses abstraction, encapsulation, inheritance, and polymorphism to provide great flexibility, modularity, and reusability for developing software. You will learn programming with objects and classes, arrays and strings, and class inheritance.

Chapter 5, "Programming with Objects and Classes," begins with objects and classes. The important topics include defining classes, creating objects, using constructors, passing objects to methods, instance and class variables, and instance and class methods. Many examples are provided to demonstrate the power of the object-oriented programming approach. Students will learn the benefits (abstraction, encapsulation, and modularity) of object-oriented programming from these examples. There are more than 500 predefined Java classes grouped in several packages. Starting with this chapter, students will gradually learn to use Java classes to develop their own programs. The Math class for performing basic math operations is introduced in this chapter.

Chapter 6, "Arrays and Strings," explores two important structures: arrays for processing data in lists and tables, and strings using the String, StringBuffer, and StringTokenizer classes. Arrays are treated as objects in Java. Strings are treated as a special kind of array in many high-level languages, but strings are not related to arrays in Java. Strings and arrays are used very differently in Java.

Chapter 7, "Class Inheritance," teaches how to extend an existing class and modify it as needed. Inheritance is an extremely powerful programming technique, further extending software reusability. Java programs are all built by extending predefined Java classes. The major topics include defining subclasses, using the keywords super and this, using the modifiers final and abstract, and casting objects and interfaces. This chapter introduces the Object class, which is the root of all Java classes. Students will learn primitive data type wrapper classes to encapsulate primitive data type values in objects and learn Date, Calendar, TimeZone, Locale, and DateFormat and their subclasses to process dates and times.

Part III: Graphics Programming

This Part introduces Java graphics programming. Major topics include event-driven programming, creating graphical user interfaces, and writing applets. You will learn the architecture of Java graphics programming API and use the user interface components to develop graphics applications and applets.

Chapter 8, "Getting Started with Graphics Programming," introduces the concepts of Java graphics programming using the AWT (Abstract Window Toolkit). Topics include the AWT class hierarchy, event-driven programming, frames, panels, canvases, and simple layout managers (FlowLayout, GridLayout, and BorderLayout). This chapter also introduces drawing geometric figures in the graphics context.

Chapter 9, "Creating User Interfaces," introduces the user interface components, including buttons, labels, text fields, text areas, choices, lists, check boxes, check box groups, menus and scrollbars. Today's client/server and Web-based applications use a graphical user interface (GUI, pronounced "goo-ee"). Java has a rich set of classes to help you build GUIs.

Chapter 10, "Applets and Advanced Graphics," takes an in-depth look at applets, and discusses applet behaviors and an applet's relationship with other AWT classes. Applets are a special kind of Java class that can be executed from the Web browser. Students will learn to convert applications to applets and vice versa, and learn to run programs both as applications and as applets. This chapter also introduces two advanced layout managers (CardLayout and GridBagLayout) and the use of no layout. Advanced examples on handling mouse and keyboard events are also provided.

Part IV: Developing Comprehensive Projects

This Part is devoted to several advanced features of Java programming. You will learn to develop comprehensive programs using these features, such as using exception handling to make your program robust, using multithreading to make your program more responsive and interactive, incorporating sound and images to make your program user friendly, using input and output to manage and process a large quantity of data, and creating client/server applications with Java networking support.

Chapter 11, "Exception Handling," teaches students how to define exceptions, throw exceptions, and handle exceptions so that the programs can continue to run or terminate gracefully in the event of runtime errors. The chapter discusses predefined exception classes, and gives examples for creating user-defined exception classes.

Chapter 12, "Multithreading," introduces threads, which enable the running of multiple tasks simultaneously in one program. Students will learn to use the Thread class and the Runnable interface to launch separate threads. The chapter also discusses thread states, thread priority, thread groups, and the synchronization of conflicting threads.

Chapter 13, "Multimedia," teaches students to incorporate sound and images to bring live animation to Java programs. The chapter also discusses various techniques for smoothing animation.

Chapter 14, "Input and Output," introduces input and output streams. Students will learn the class structures of I/O streams, byte and character streams, file I/O streams, data I/O streams, print streams, delimited I/O, random file access, and interactive I/O.

Chapter 15, "Networking," introduces network programming. Students will learn the concepts of network communication, stream sockets, client/server programming, and reading data files from the Web server.

Appendixes

This section covers a mixed bag of topics. Appendix A lists Java keywords. Appendix B gives tables of ASCII characters and their associated codes in decimal and in hex. Appendix C shows the operator precedence. Appendix D summarizes Java modifiers and their usage. Appendix E introduces HTML. Appendix F contains information for using the companion CD-ROM. Finally, Appendix G provides a glossary of key terms found in the text.

What's on the Companion CD-ROM

The companion CD-ROM contains JDK 1.2 beta 4 for Windows 95, 98, and NT, and the source code for all the examples in the text. Please refer to Appendix F, "Using the Companion CD-ROM," for instructions on installing JDK 1.2 and using the example source code.

CONTENTS AT A GLANCE

TABLE OF CONTENTS

FUNDAMENTALS OF JAVA PROGRAMMING

You have heard a lot about Java. You are anxious to start writing Java programs. This Part is a steppingstone to prepare you to embark on the journey of learning Java. You will start to know Java and learn to write simple Java programs with primitive data types, control structures, and methods.

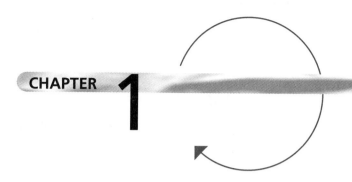

CHAPTER 1

INTRODUCTION TO JAVA

Objectives

- Learn about Java and its history.
- Understand the relationship between Java and the World Wide Web.
- Find Java resources on the Web.
- Become familiar with Java development tools.
- Understand the Java running environment.
- Write a simple Java application.
- Write a simple Java applet.
- Compile and run Java applications and applets.

Introduction

By now, you have probably heard about the exciting programming language Java. It might seem that Java is everywhere! Java books are in your local bookstores. Major newspapers and magazines run articles about Java. It is impossible to read a computer magazine without seeing this magic word *Java*. So why is it so hot? Java's main distinguishing characteristic is that it enables the user to deploy applications on the Internet. The future of computing is highly influenced by the Internet, and Java promises to remain a big part of that future. Java is *the* Internet programming language.

You are about to begin an exciting journey, learning a powerful programming language. Java is cross-platform, object-oriented, network-based, and multimedia-ready. After its inception in May 1995, Java quickly became a mature language for deploying mission-critical applications. This chapter begins with a brief history of Java and its programming features, followed by simple examples of Java applications and applets.

The History of Java

Java was developed by a team led by James Gosling at Sun Microsystems, a company best known for its workstations. Originally called Oak, Java was designed for use in embedded consumer electronic applications in 1991. It was redesigned for developing Internet applications and renamed Java in 1995. Java programs can be embedded in HTML pages and downloaded by Web browsers to bring live animation and interaction to Web clients.

The power of Java is not limited to Web applications. Java is a general-purpose programming language. It has full programming features and can be used to develop stand-alone applications. Java is inherently object oriented. Although many object-oriented languages began strictly as procedural languages, Java was designed to be object oriented from the start. Object-oriented programming (OOP) is currently a popular programming approach that replaces the traditional procedural programming techniques.

NOTE
One of the central issues in software development is how to reuse code. Object-oriented programming provides great flexibility, modularity, clarity, and reusability through method abstraction, class abstraction, and class inheritance—all of which you'll learn about in this book.

Characteristics of Java

Java has gained enormous popularity. Its rapid ascension and wide acceptance can be traced to its design and programming features, particularly its promise that you can write a program once and run the program anywhere. Java was chosen as the language for *network computers* (NC) and has been perceived as a universal front end for the enterprise database. As stated in the Java language white paper by Sun, Java is *simple, object oriented, distributed, interpreted, robust, secure, architecture neutral, portable, high performance, multithreaded,* and *dynamic.* Let's analyze those often-used buzzwords.

Java Is Simple

No language is simple, but Java is a bit easier than the popular object-oriented programming language C++, which had been the dominant software development language before Java. Java is partially modeled after C++, but greatly simplified and improved. For instance, pointers and multiple inheritance often make programming complicated. Java replaced multiple inheritance in C++ with a simple structure called *interface*, and eliminated pointers.

Java uses automatic memory allocation and garbage collection, while C++ requires the programmer to allocate memory and to collect garbage. Also, the number of language constructs is small for such a powerful language. The clean syntax makes Java programs easy to write and read. Some people refer to Java as "C++−−" because it is like C++, but with more functionality and fewer negative aspects.

Java Is Object Oriented

Object-oriented programming models the real world. Everything in the world can be modeled as an object. A circle is an object, a person is an object, and a window's icon is an object. Even a mortgage can be perceived as an object. A Java program is called object oriented because programming in Java is centered on creating objects, manipulating objects, and making objects working together.

An object has *properties* and *behaviors.* Properties are described by using *data*, and behaviors are defined by using *methods.* Objects are defined by using classes in Java. A class is like a template for the objects. An object is a concrete realization of a class description. The process of creating an object of the class is called *instantiation.* For example, you can define the class `Circle` by which to model all `Circle` objects (see Figure 1.1), with `radius` as the property and `findArea` as the method to find the area of the circle. You can create a `Circle` object by instantiating the class with a particular radius. You can create a circle with radius 2, and another circle with radius 5. You can then find the area of the respective circles by using the `findArea` method.

A Java program consists of one or more classes. Classes are arranged in a treelike hierarchy, so that a child class can inherit properties and behaviors from its parent class. Java comes with an extensive set of predefined classes, grouped in packages. You can use them in your programs.

Object-oriented programming provides greater flexibility, modularity, and reusability. For years, object-oriented technology was perceived as elitist, requiring substantial investments in training and infrastructure. Java has helped object-oriented technology enter the mainstream of computing. Java has a simple and clean struc-ture to make programs easy to write and read. Java programs are extremely *expres-sive* in terms of the applications and designs.

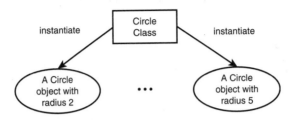

Figure 1.1   *Two* Circle *objects with radii 2 and 5 were created from the* Circle *class.*

Java Is Distributed

Distributed computing involves several computers on a network working together. Java is designed to make distributed computing easy. Networking capability is inherently integrated into Java. Writing network programs in Java is like sending and receiving data to and from a file. For example, Figure 1.2 shows three programs running on three different systems; the three programs communicate with each other to perform a joint task.

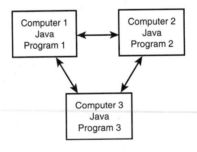

Figure 1.2   *Java programs can run on different systems that work together.*

Java Is Interpreted

You need an interpreter to run Java programs. The programs are compiled into Java Virtual Machine code called *bytecode*. The bytecode is machine independent and can run on any machine that has a Java interpreter.

Usually, a compiler translates a high-level language program to machine code. The code can only run on the native machine. If you run the program on other machines, the program has to be recompiled on the native machine. For instance, if you compile a C program in Windows, the executable code generated by the compiler can only run on the Windows platform. With Java, you compile the source code once, and the bytecode generated by a Java compiler can run on any platform. *The Java programs do not need to be recompiled on a target machine.*

Java Is Robust

Robust means *reliable*. No programming language can assure complete reliability. Java puts a lot of emphasis on early checking for possible errors, as Java compilers can detect many problems that would first show up at execution time in other languages. Java eliminated certain types of programming constructs in other languages that are prone to errors. It does not support pointers, for example, which eliminates the possibility of overwriting memory and corrupting data.

Java has a runtime exception-handling feature to provide programming support for robustness. Java can catch and respond to an exceptional situation so that the program can continue its normal execution and terminate gracefully when a runtime error occurs.

Java Is Secure

Java, being an Internet programming language, is used in a networked and distributed environment. You can download a Java applet (a special kind of program) and run it on your computer, and it will not cause damage to your system because Java implements several security mechanisms to protect your system from being damaged by a stray program. The security is based on the premise that *nothing should be trusted.*

There is no absolute security, however. Security bugs have been recently discovered in Java, but these bugs are subtle and few and have been addressed.

NOTE

A computer security team at Princeton University maintains a Web site devoted to Java security issues. You can find new security bugs and fixes at **www.cs.princeton.edu/sip/**.

Java Is Architecture Neutral

The most remarkable feature of Java is that it is *architecture neutral*, also known as platform independent. You can write one program that runs on any platform with a Java Virtual Machine. The major OS vendors have adopted the Java Virtual Machine, and soon Java will run on all machines.

Java's initial success lies in its Web programming capability. You can run Java applets from a Web browser, but Java is for more than just writing Web applets. You can also run stand-alone Java applications directly from operating systems by using a Java interpreter. Today, software vendors usually develop multiple versions of the same product to run on different platforms (Windows, OS/2, Macintosh, and various UNIX, VMS, Open/VMS, and IBM mainframes). Using Java, developers need to write only one version to run on all of the platforms.

Java Is Portable

Java programs can be run on any platform without being recompiled, making them very portable. Moreover, there are no platform-specific features in the Java language specification. In some languages, such as Ada, the largest integer varies on different platforms. But in Java, the size of the integer is the same on every platform, as is the behavior of arithmetic. This fixed size for numbers makes the program portable.

The Java environment itself is portable to new hardware and operating systems. In fact, the Java compiler itself is written in Java.

Java's Performance

The loudest criticism about Java is its poor performance. The execution of the byte-code is never as fast as a compiled language, such as C++. Because Java is interpreted, the bytecode is not directly executed by the system. The bytecode is run through the interpreter. However, the speed is more than adequate for most interactive applications, where the CPU is often idle, waiting for the input or waiting for data from other sources.

CPU speed has increased dramatically in the recent past, and it appears that this trend will continue. There are many ways to improve the performance. If you used the earlier Sun Java compiler, you will certainly notice that Java is slow. However, new compilers from Inprise, Microsoft, and Symantec are 10 or even 20 times faster than the Sun Java compiler. These new compilers are known as just-in-time compilers. They compile bytecodes "on-the-fly"; in other words, as they execute. Instead of interpreting bytecode one at a time, they compile each bytecode once, and then reinvoke the compiled code repeatedly when the bytecode is executed. Sun has recently unveiled a Java chip that comes with a hard-coded Java interpreter and part of the runtime environment. Therefore, the speed will continue to improve over time.

> **NOTE**
> Recently, IBM has formed a joint lab with Sun and Netscape to improve Java performance. IBM has been one of the strong and influential supporters of Java. IBM views Java as a glue to unify different platforms and various applications.

Java Is Multithreaded

Multithreading is the capability of a program to perform several tasks simultaneously within a program. For example, downloading a video file while playing the video would be considered multithreading. Multithread programming is smoothly integrated in Java. In other languages, you have to call operating system-specific procedures to enable multithreading.

Multithreading is particularly useful in graphical user interface (GUI) and network programming. In GUI programming, there are many things going on at the same time. A user can listen to an audio recording while surfing a Web page. In network programming, a server can serve multiple clients at the same time. Multithreading is a necessity in visual and network programming.

Java Is Dynamic

Java was designed to adapt to an evolving environment. You can freely add new methods and properties in a class without affecting their clients. For example, in the Circle class, you can add a new data property to indicate the color of the circle, and a new method to obtain the circumference of the circle. The original client program that uses the Circle class remains the same. Also at runtime, Java loads classes as they are needed.

Java and the World Wide Web

The World Wide Web (Web or WWW) is an electronic information repository that can be accessed on the Internet from anywhere in the world. You can book a hotel room, buy an airline ticket, register for a college course, download *The New York Times*, chat with friends, and listen to live radio using the Web. There are countless activities you can do on the Internet. Today, a lot of people spend a lot of their computer time surfing the Web for fun and profit.

The Internet is the infrastructure of the WWW. The Internet has been around for more than thirty years, but has only recently become popular. The colorful World Wide Web is the major reason for its popularity.

The primary authoring language for the Web is Hypertext Markup Language (HTML). HTML is a script language: a simple language for document layout, linking documents on the Internet, and bringing images, sound, and video alive on the Web. However, it cannot interact with the user except through simple forms. The Web pages in HTML essentially are static and flat.

Java programs can run from a Web browser. Because Java is a full-blown programming language, you can make the program responsive and interactive with the user. Java programs that run from a Web page are called *applets*. Applets use a modern graphical user interface, including buttons, text fields, text areas, option buttons, and so on. Applets can respond to user events, such as mouse movements and keystrokes.

Figure 1.3 shows an applet in an HTML page, and Figure 1.4 shows the HTML source. The source contains an applet tag, and the applet tag specifies the Java applet. The HTML source can be seen by choosing View, HTML Source from the HotJava Web Browser.

NOTE

For a demonstration of Java applets, visit **www.javasoft.com/applets/**. This site contains a rich Java resource.

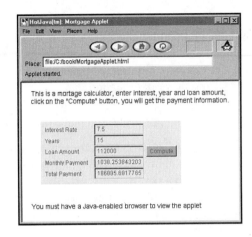

Figure 1.3 *A Java applet for computing a mortgage is embedded in an HTML page. The user can find the mortgage payment by using this applet.*

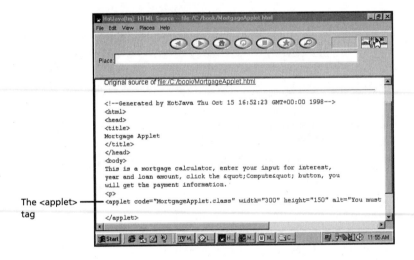

The <applet> tag

Figure 1.4 *The HTML source that contains the applet shows the tag specifying the Java applet.*

The Java Language Specification

Computer languages have strict rules of use. You must follow the rules when writing programs for them to be understood by the computer. Sun Microsystems, the originator of Java, intends to keep control of it for a good reason: to prevent the language from losing its unified standards. The complete reference of Java standards can be found in the book *Java Language Specification* by James Gosling, Bill Joy, and Guy Steele (Addison Wesley, 1996).

The specification is a technical definition of the language, including syntax, structures, and the *application programming interface* (API), which contains pre-defined classes. The language is still rapidly evolving. At the JavaSoft Web site (**www.javasoft.com**), you can view the latest version and updates of the language. Sun has maintained online documentation for the API and the language specification.

Sun releases each version of Java with a Java Development Toolkit (JDK), which is a primitive command-line tool set that includes a compiler, an interpreter, and the Applet Viewer, as well as other useful utilities. The current version of Java is JDK 1.2. This book's companion CD-ROM contains JDK 1.2 for Windows 95, Windows 98, and Window NT. JDK 1.2 is also available for Solaris. You can download the Solaris version of JDK 1.2 free from the JavaSoft site at **www.javasoft.com**.

Literally, JDK stands for Java Development Toolkit. However, JDK is not only a toolkit consisting of the compiler, the interpreter, and the Java running environment; it is also a Java language standard. This book is compliant with JDK 1.2, which is a substantial enhancement to JDK 1.1. JDK 1.1 benefits from significant improvements over the previous version, JDK 1.0. There are critical differences between JDK 1.0 and JDK 1.1. It is important to learn Java programming based on JDK 1.1 or above for the following reasons:

- The architecture has improved greatly in JDK 1.1, particularly regarding the event-handling model. The new architecture enables faster, more robust implementations of AWT and, therefore, makes your program work better.

- JDK 1.1 has many new features that you might want to use.

- JavaBeans and future additions to Java will be based on JDK 1.1.

- Certain old ways of programming, such as handling events using the `handleEvent()` method, are deprecated and will eventually be phased out.

The architecture of JDK 1.2 is the same as the one for JDK 1.1, but JDK 1.2 contains the following major enhancements:

- JFC Swing Set is a suite of GUI components with a "Pluggable Look and Feel" that are implemented in 100 percent Pure Java, and based on the JDK 1.1 Lightweight UI Framework.

- Java 2D API is a set of classes for advanced 2D graphics and imaging. It encompasses line art, text, and images in a single comprehensive model.

- Audio enhancements support the .wav and .aiff audio formats in addition to .au files. With the enhancements, audio clips can be created without an AppletContext, so that the audios can be played in an application as well as in applets.

- Enhancements of security, JavaBeans, RMI (Remote Method Invocation), serialization, JNI (Java Native Interface), and reflection.

- Performance enhancements, including a new fast Just In Time (JIT) compiler.

- Some methods, such as start() and stop() in the Thread class in JDK 1.1, are deprecated because of unsafe behavior.

The advanced components included in JDK 1.2, such as the Swing Set, are beyond the scope of this text.

NOTE
All the programs in this book can be compiled and run on either JDK 1.1 or JDK 1.2 and should also work with any Java development tools that support JDK 1.1 or above.

Java Development Tools

JDK consists of a set of separate programs, each of which is invoked from a command line. Besides JDK, there are more than a dozen Java development packages on the market today. The major development tools are

Visual J++ by Microsoft (**www.microsoft.com**)

JBuilder by Inprise (**www.inprise.com**)

Café by Symantec (**www.symantec.com**)

JFactory by Rouge Wave (**www.rougewave.com**)

Sun Java Workshop (**www.javasoft.com**)

Visual Age for Java by IBM (**www.ibm.com**)

These tools provide an *integrated development environment* (IDE) for rapidly developing Java programs. Development tools makes it easy and productive to develop dynamic Java programs.

You are encouraged to use an IDE tool for developing Java programs because such tools are very convenient. Editing, compiling, building, debugging, and online help are integrated in one graphical user interface. Just enter source code in one window, or open an existing file in a window, then click a button, menu item, or function key to compile the source code.

The compilation errors are shown in a second window. When you click the error message, the IDE tool directly points to the error in the source code. After fixing the errors, recompile the code. Click another button, menu, or function key to run your program. The program runs in a window, and error messages are shown in another window if the program encounters runtime errors. Figure 1.5 shows the Microsoft Visual J++ 6.0 IDE interface.

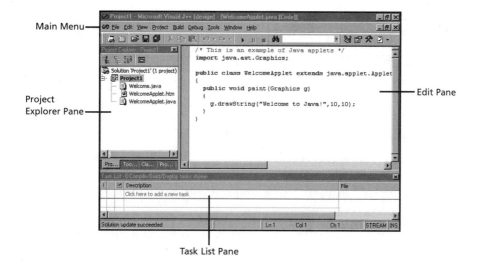

Main Menu

Project
Explorer Pane

Edit Pane

Task List Pane

Figure 1.5 *The Java integrated development environment provides editing, compiling, debugging, and running programs in one interface.*

NOTE

If you are learning Java using Microsoft Visual J++ 6.0 or Inprise JBuilder 2, I recommend two of my books, *Introduction to Java Programming with Visual J++ 6* or *Introduction to Java Programming with JBuilder 2,* published by Que Education and Training.

Java Applications

Java programs can be one of two types: *applications* or *applets*. Applications are standalone programs, such as any program written using high-level languages. Applications can be executed from any computer with a Java interpreter and are ideal for developing software. Applets are special kinds of Java programs that can run directly from a Java-compatible Web browser. Applets are suitable for deploying Web projects.

Let's begin with a simple Java application program that displays the message Welcome to Java! on the console.

Example 1.1 A Simple Application

This program shows how to write a simple Java application and demonstrates the compilation and execution of an application.

```
//This application program prints Welcome to Java!
public class Welcome
{
```

continues

Example 1.1   continued

```java
    public static void main(String[] args)
    {
      System.out.println("Welcome to Java!");
    }
  }
```

Example Review

In this program, `println("Welcome to Java!")` is actually the statement that prints the message. So why do you use the other statements in the program? Computer languages have rigid styles and strict syntax, and you need to write code that the Java compiler understands.

Every Java program must have at least one class. Each class begins with a class declaration that defines data and methods for the class. In this example, the class name is `Welcome`.

The class contains a method called `main()`. The `main()` method in this program contains the `println()` statement.

Compiling a Java Program

I use JDK commands to demonstrate compiling and running Java programs in this book. Even if you use a Java development tool, such as JBuilder, Café, or Visual J++, you can still use the command-line Java compiler and interpreter, which are included in these tools.

NOTE

The companion CD-ROM contains JDK 1.2. For installing JDK 1.2 on your system, please refer to Appendix F, "Using the Companion CD-ROM."

To execute the program, you have to compile it first. Assume that the source file for the program is named **Welcome.java**. By convention, Java program source files must end with the extension .java. The following command compiles **Welcome.java**.

```
javac Welcome.java
```

CAUTION

Java source programs are case sensitive. It would be wrong, for example, to replace `main()` in the program with `Main()`. The program filenames are case sensitive within UNIX and generally not case sensitive on PCs, but JDK treats filenames as case sensitive on any platform. If you try to compile the program using `javac welcome.java`, you will get a file-not-found error.

If there are no syntax errors, the *compiler* generates a file named **Welcome.class**. This file is not an object file as generated by other high-level language compilers. This file is called the *bytecode*, as shown in Figure 1.6. The bytecode is similar to machine instructions, but is architecture neutral and can run on any platform that has the Java interpreter and runtime environment. This is one of Java's primary advantages: Java bytecode can run on a variety of hardware platforms and operating systems.

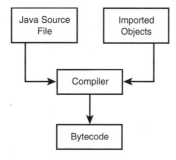

Figure 1.6 *The source code of a Java program is compiled into bytecode.*

Executing a Java Application

To execute a Java program is to run the program's bytecode. You can execute the bytecode on any platform that supports a Java interpreter.

The following command runs the bytecode:

```
java Welcome
```

The output of the run is shown in Figure 1.7.

Figure 1.7 *The output of Example 1.1 displays a message: Welcome to Java!*

■■■ CAUTION

Do not use the extension .class in the command line when executing the program. The Java interpreter assumes the first argument in the command is the filename and then fetches **filename.class** to execute. It would fetch **filename.class.class** if you used Java **filename.class** in the command line.

Anatomy of the Application Program

The application program in Example 1.1 has the following components:

Comments

Reserved words

Modifiers

Statements

Blocks

Classes

Methods

The `main()` method

To build a program, you need to understand these basic elements. The following sections explain each of them.

Comments

The first line in the program is a *comment*, which documents what the program is and how the program is constructed. Comments help the programmers or users communicate and understand the program. Comments are not programming statements and are ignored by the compiler. In Java, comments are preceded by two slashes (`//`) in a line, or enclosed between `/*` and `*/` in multiple lines. When the compiler sees `//`, it ignores all text after `//` in the same line. When it sees `/*`, it scans for the next `*/` and ignores any text between `/*` and `*/`.

For example, the following are the two types of comments:

```
// This application program prints Welcome to Java!

/* This application program prints Welcome to Java! */
```

Reserved Words

The *reserved words* or *keywords* are words that have specific meaning to the compiler and cannot be used for other purposes in the program. For example, when the compiler sees the word `class`, it understands the word after `class` is the name for the class. Other reserved words in Example 1.1 are `public`, `static`, and `void`.

TIP

Because Java is case sensitive, `class` is a reserved word, but `Class` is not. Nonetheless, for clarity and readability, it would be best to avoid using reserved words in other forms. (See Appendix A, "Java Keywords.")

Modifiers

Java uses certain reserved words called *modifiers* that specify the properties of the data, methods, and classes and how they can be used. Examples of modifiers are public and static. Other modifiers are private, final, abstract, and protected. A public data, method, and class can be accessed by other programs. A private data or method cannot be accessed by other programs. Modifiers are discussed further in Chapter 5, "Programming with Objects and Classes."

Statements

A *statement* represents an action or a sequence of actions. The statement println("Welcome to Java!") in the program in Example 1.1 is a statement to display the greeting Welcome to Java! Every statement in Java ends with a semicolon (;).

For example, the following lines of code are statements:

```
x = 5;

x = x + 5;
```

The first statement assigns 5 to the variable x, and the second adds 5 to the variable x.

Blocks

The braces in the program form the *block* structure that groups statements together. The use of blocks helps the compiler to identify components of the program. In Java, each block begins with an open brace ({) and ends with a closing brace (}). Blocks can be *nested*—that is, one block can be placed within another.

For example, the following code contains two blocks. The inner block is nested within the outer block.

```
{
  x = 5;
  x = x + 5;
  if (x > 6)
  {
    x = x - 1;
  }
}
```

Classes

The *class* is the essential Java construct. A class is a template or a blueprint for objects. To program in Java, you must understand classes and be able to write and use them. The mystery of the class will continue to be unveiled throughout this book. For now, though, understand that a program is defined by using one or more classes. Every Java program has at least one class, and programs are contained inside a class definition enclosed in blocks. The class can contain data declarations and method declarations.

NOTE

Each class in Java is compiled into a separate bytecode file with the extension .class.

Methods

What does `System.out.println()` mean? It is a *method*—a collection of statements that performs a sequence of operations to display a message on the console. `println()` is predefined as part of the standard Java language. It can be used even without fully understanding the details of how it works. It is used by invoking a calling statement with arguments. The arguments are enclosed within parentheses. In this case, the argument is `"Welcome to Java!"`. You can call the same `println()` method with a different argument to print a different message.

The *main()* Method

You can create your own method. Each Java application must have a user-declared `main()` method, which defines where the program begins. The `main()` method provides the control of program flow. The `main()` method will always look like this:

```
public static void main(String[] args)
{
// statements;
}
```

Java Applets

Applications and applets share many common programming features, although they differ slightly in some aspects. For example, every application must have a `main()` method, which contains the first sequence of instructions to be executed. The Java interpreter begins the execution of the application from the `main()` method.

Java applets, on the other hand, do not need a `main()` method. They run within the Web browser environment. Example 1.2 demonstrates the applet that displays the same message, Welcome to Java!

Example 1.2   A Simple Applet

This program shows how to write a simple Java applet and demonstrates compilation and execution of an applet.

```
/* This is an example of Java applets */
import java.awt.Graphics;

public class WelcomeApplet extends java.applet.Applet
{
  public void paint(Graphics g)
  {
    g.drawString("Welcome to Java!",10,10);
  }
}
```

Example Review

Applets run in a graphical environment. You need to display everything, including text, in graphical mode, and Java provides the `drawString()` method to display text in an applet.

The `drawString("Welcome to Java!",10,10)` method draws the string `"Welcome to Java!"` on the line. The baseline of the first character, W, in the string is displayed at the location `(10,10)`. The drawing area is measured in pixels, with `(0,0)` at the upper-left corner.

Compiling an Applet

You use the `javac` command to compile all Java programs, whether they are applications or applets, and the Java interpreter to run applications. However, applets are executed by a Web browser from an HTML file. You need to create an HTML file to tell the browser where to get the Java applet and how to run it.

Creating an HTML File

To run an applet, embed HTML tags that refer to the applet within a Web page. HTML is a script language that presents static documents on the Web. HTML uses tags to instruct the Web browser how to render a Web page. HTML contains a tag called `<applet>` that incorporates applets into a Web page.

The following HTML file contains a tag to invoke **WelcomeApplet.class**:

```
<html>
<head>
<title>Welcome Java Applet</title>
</head>
<body>
<applet
  code = "WelcomeApplet.class"
  width = 200
  height = 50>
</applet>
</body>
</html>
```

A tag is an instruction to the Web browser. The browser interprets the tags and decides how to display or otherwise treat the subsequent contents of the HTML document. Tags are enclosed inside brackets; the first word in a tag is called the *tag name*, which describes tag functions. Tags can have additional attributes, sometimes with values after an equal sign, which further define the tag's action. For example, in the following tag, `<applet>` is the tag name and `code`, `width`, and `height` are the attributes:

```
<applet code="WelcomeApplet.class" width = 100 height = 40>
```

The width and height attributes specify the rectangular viewing area of the applet.

Most tags have a *start tag* and a corresponding *end tag*. The tag has a specific effect on the region between the start tag and the end tag. For example, <applet...></applet> tells the browser to display an applet. An end tag is always the start tag's name preceded by a slash.

An HTML document begins with the <html> tag, which declares that the document is written with HTML. Each document has two parts, *head* and *body*, defined by <head> and <body> tags, respectively. The head part contains the document title using the <title> tag and other parameters the browser can use when rendering the document, and the body part contains the actual contents of the document. The header is optional.

HTML files can be created and saved as text files by using any word processing program. For more information, refer to Appendix E, "An HTML Tutorial."

Viewing Applets Using a Web Browser

Assume that the HTML file in Example 1.2 is named **WelcomeApplet.html**. You now can use a Web browser to view it. The result is displayed in Figure 1.8.

Figure 1.8 *The message Welcome to Java! is drawn on the browser.*

Applets can run from a Web browser on any platform. For example, the same applet can run on a Windows-based PC or on a UNIX workstation.

NOTE

Make sure that your Web browser supports JDK 1.1 or above. At the time of this writing, HotJava, Netscape Communicator 4.05, and Internet Explorer 4.0 support JDK 1.1. Other vendors will undoubtedly follow in the near future. HotJava, which can be downloaded from **www.javasoft.com**, is a thin client requiring only 8M to install. The HotJava Web browser is used to show the output of applets in this book.

Viewing Applets Using the Applet Viewer Utility

You can also view a Java applet using Java's Applet Viewer. Using this utility, you do not need to start a Web browser. Applet Viewer functions as a browser. It is a valuable utility to test an applet before deploying it on a Web site. The following command invokes **WelcomeApplet.html** (see Figure 1.9):

```
appletviewer WelcomeApplet.html
```

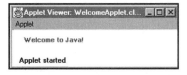

Figure 1.9 *The output of the* WelcomeApplet *program is running from the Applet Viewer utility, as if it were running in a Web browser.*

Anatomy of the Applet Program

Let's take a closer look at the program in Example 1.2 and examine its components: the import statement, the Graphics class, the extends keyword, the paint() method, the drawString() method, and the class instance. As you have seen, an application and an applet have much in common. Indeed, an applet is merely a special kind of Java program with certain characteristics that make it run from a Web browser. The components mentioned here are also used in other Java programs.

The *import* Statement

The first line after the comment is an import statement. The import statement tells the compiler to include existing Java programs in the current program. In this case, the existing program is java.awt.Graphics. You can use the operations in java.awt.Graphics in your program rather than rewriting the code. This is an example of software *reusability*, that is, the same program is written once and is used by many other people without rewriting it.

Java code is organized into packages and classes. Classes are inside packages, and packages are libraries of Java code that contain all kinds of operations ready for you to import and use. Java provides standard libraries, such as java.awt, that come with the compiler. Users can create their own libraries. Graphics is a class contained in the java.awt package. (See Chapter 5 for more information.)

Class Instance

The g in the paint() method is called an *instance* for the class Graphics. An instance is a concrete object of the class. g can access the methods defined in Graphics. drawString() is a method in Graphics, which now can be used in g by a call, such as g.drawString(). This is exactly the way object-oriented programming works. You can create an instance from a class and invoke the methods in the instance without knowing how the methods are implemented.

The *paint()* Method and the *Graphics* Class

Every applet that displays graphics must have a paint() method that looks like this:

```
public void paint(Graphics g) {...}
```

This method contains drawing methods to tell the Web browser what should be displayed.

Because the Web is a graphical environment, everything—including text—needs to be displayed as graphics. The Java Graphics class provides operations for drawing objects, such as text strings, lines, rectangles, ovals, arcs, and polygons. The drawing area is a rectangle measured in pixels with (0,0) at its upper-left corner. The following is an example:

```
public void paint(Graphics g)
{
  g.drawLine(10, 10, 50, 30);
  g.drawRect(10, 20, 20, 30);
  g.drawString("Welcome to Java", 30, 10);
}
```

The drawLine() method draws a line from (10, 10) to (50, 30). The drawRect() method draws a rectangle of width 20 and height 30; the upper-left corner of the rectangle is at (10, 20). The drawString() method draws the string "Welcome to Java" at (30, 10). See Figure 1.10 for the drawings.

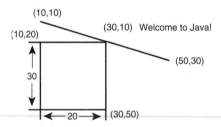

Figure 1.10 *The string* Welcome to Java! *is drawn at* (30, 10); *a line is drawn from* (10, 10) *to* (50, 30); *and a rectangle is drawn with its upper-left corner at* (10, 20) *with width of* 20 *and height of* 30.

The *extends* Keyword and Class Inheritance

The class definition in Example 1.2 is different from the class definition in Example 1.1; Example 1.2 has an extra keyword, extends, which tells the compiler that the class to be defined is an extension of an existing class. In this case, the class WelcomeApplet extends the existing class Applet. The extended class WelcomeApplet inherits all functionality and properties from class Applet. This is an example of *inheritance*, another software engineering concept. Inheritance complements and extends software reusability.

Applet is a class in the package java.applet. You could add the statement import java.applet.Applet at the beginning of the program and directly extend Applet, as follows:

```
import java.awt.Graphics;
import java.applet.Applet;

public class WelcomeApplet extends Applet
{
  public void paint (Graphics g)
  {
    g.drawString("Welcome to Java!",10,10);
  }
}
```

The import java.applet.Applet statement imports the Applet class so you can use it in the program without explicitly referencing Applet as java.applet.Applet.

Applications Versus Applets

You probably have many questions, such as "Do I need to write two programs—one for the application and one for the applet?" "When do I use applications and when do I use applets?" To answer these questions, it is important to understand the similarities and differences between applications and applets.

Much of the code for applications and applets is the same, but there are differences in the code dealing with their running environments. Applications run as stand-alone programs, as do programs written in any high-level language. Applets, however, must run from inside a Web browser. If your program is not required to run from a Web browser, choose applications. Developing Java applications is slightly quicker than developing applets because you do not need to create an HTML file and load it from a Web browser to view the results.

For security reasons, the following limitations are imposed on applets to prevent destructive programs from damaging the system on which the browser is running:

■ Applets are not allowed to read from, or write to, the file system of the computer. Otherwise, they could cause damage to files and spread viruses.

■ Applets are not allowed to run any programs on the browser's computer. Otherwise, applets might call destructive local programs and cause damage to the local system on the user's computer.

■ Applets are not allowed to establish connections between the user's computer and another computer except with the server where the applets are stored. This restriction prevents the applet from connecting the user's computer to another computer without the user's knowledge.

However, applications can directly interact with the computer on which they are running without these limitations. Applications can be used to develop fully functional software. In fact, applications can use the same graphical features used for applets, although applications would require slightly more effort in order to create the browser environment.

In general, you can convert a Java applet to run as an application without loss of functionality. However, an application cannot always be converted to run as an applet, due to security limitations imposed on the applets. In Chapter 10, "Applets and Advanced Graphics," you will learn how to convert between applications and applets.

Chapter Summary

In this chapter, you learned about Java and the relationship between Java and the World Wide Web. Java is an Internet programming language, and since its inception in 1995, it has quickly become a premier language for building fully portable Internet applets and applications.

Java is platform independent, meaning that you can write the program once and run it anywhere. Java is a simple, object-oriented programming language with built-in graphics programming, input and output, exception handling, networking, and multithreading support.

The Java source file ends with the .java extension. Every class is compiled into a separate file called a bytecode that has the same name as the class and ends with the .class extension.

Every Java program is a class definition. The keyword class introduces a class definition. The contents of the class are included in a block. A block begins with an open brace ({) and ends with a close brace (}). The class contains at least one method. A Java application must have a main() method. The main() method is the entry point where the application program starts when it is executed.

The Java applet always extends the Applet class. The keyword extends enables new classes to inherit from existing class definitions. The import statement loads classes required to compile a Java program.

Modifiers are the keywords that specify how the classes and methods can be accessed. A Java applet must be a public class so that a Web browser can access it.

The Web browsers control the execution of the Java applets. You must create an HTML file with an <applet> tag to specify the bytecode file (with the extension .class) for the applet, and the width and the height of the applet viewing area in pixels.

The Web browser calls the paint() method to display graphics in the applet's viewing area. The coordinates of the viewing area are measured in pixels with (0,0) at the upper-left corner. The drawString() method draws a string at a specified location in the viewing area.

Chapter Review

1. Briefly describe the history of Java.

2. Java is object oriented. What are the advantages of object-oriented programming?

3. Can Java run on any machine? What is needed to run Java on a computer?

4. What is the input and output of a Java compiler?

5. List some Java development tools. Are Visual J++ and JBuilder different languages from Java, or are they dialects or extensions of Java?

6. What is the relationship between Java and HTML?

7. Explain the concept of keywords. List some Java keywords you learned in this chapter.

8. Is Java case sensitive? What is the case for Java keywords?

9. What is the Java source filename extension, and what is the Java bytecode filename extension?

10. What is the command to compile a Java program?

11. What is the command to run a Java application?

12. What is a comment? What is the syntax for a comment in Java? Is the comment ignored by the compiler?

13. What is the statement to display a string on the console?

14. What is the `import` statement for?

15. What is `Graphics`, and what is the `paint()` method?

16. What are the differences between applications and applets? How do you run an application, and how do you run an applet? Is the compilation process different for applications and applets?

17. What is Applet Viewer?

18. Does it require a lot of work to convert between applications and applets?

19. List some security restrictions of applets.

Programming Exercises

1. Find the Java online JDK documentation at **www.javasoft.com**, and run samples of Java applets from that site.

2. Create a source file containing a Java program. Perform the following steps to compile the program and run it (see "Compiling a Java Program" earlier in this chapter):

   1. Create a file named Welcome.java for Example 1.1. You can use any editor that will save your file in ASCII format.

   2. Compile the source file.

   3. Run the bytecode.

   4. Replace "Welcome to Java" with "My first program" in the program; save, compile, and run the program. You will see the message My first program displayed.

   5. Replace main() with Main(), and recompile the source code. The compiler returns an error message because the Java program is case sensitive.

   6. Change it back, and compile the program again.

   7. Instead of the command javac Welcome.java, use javac welcome.java.

      What happens?

   8. Instead of the command java Welcome, use java Welcome.class.

      What happens? (The interpreter searches for `Welcome.class.class`.)

3. Create an HTML file that invokes a Java applet to display Welcome to Java! from a Web browser, as follows:

   1. Create a program named WelcomeApplet.java for Example 1.2.

   2. Create an HTML file named WelcomeApplet.html, as shown in Example 1.2.

   3. Compile `WelcomeApplet.java`.

   4. View **WelcomeApplet.html** from your Web browser.

   5. At your operating system command prompt, type the following to view the applet:

      appletviewer WelcomeApplet.html

   6. Replace the following `drawString()` statement:

      g.drawString("Welcome to Java!",10,10);

      with the following:

      g.drawString("Another Message!",10,10);

   Recompile, view, and find out what is new this time.

JAVA BUILDING ELEMENTS

Objectives

- Understand variables and constants.
- Write simple Java programs.
- Use assignment statements.
- Use Java primitive data types: `byte`, `short`, `int`, `long`, `float`, `double`, `char`, and `boolean`.
- Use Java operators and write Java expressions.
- Understand the classification of programming errors.
- Become familiar with the Java documentation, programming style, and naming conventions.

Introduction

In this chapter, you are introduced to basic programming elements, such as variables, constants, data types, operators, and expressions in Java.

To begin, let's look at a simple program that computes the area of a circle. The program reads in the radius of a circle and displays its area. The program will use variables to represent the circle and the area, will use a constant π, and will use an expression to compute the area.

Writing this program involves designing algorithms and data structures, as well as translating algorithms into programming codes. An algorithm describes how a problem is solved in terms of the actions to be executed, and it specifies the order in which these actions should be executed. Algorithms can help the programmer plan a program before writing it in a programming language. An algorithm is often described using a pseudocode.

The algorithm for this program can be described as follows:

1. Read in the radius.

2. Compute the area using the following formula:

   ```
   area = radius × radius × π
   ```

3. Display the area.

Many of the problems can be described by using simple, straightforward algorithms when you take an introduction to programming course using this text. As your education progresses, you will take courses on data structures, algorithm design, and analysis; you will encounter complex problems that have sophisticated solutions. You need to design correct, efficient algorithms with appropriate data structures in order to solve these problems.

Data structures involve data representation and manipulation. Java provides basic data types for representing integers, floats, characters, and Boolean types. Java also supports array and string types as objects. Some of the advanced data structures, such as stacks and hashing, are already supported by Java.

To novice programmers, coding is a daunting task. When you *code*, you translate the algorithm into a programming language that is understood by the computer. You already know that every Java program begins with a class declaration, in which the keyword class is followed by the class name. Assume that you have chosen TestComputeArea as the class name. The outline of the program would look like the following:

```
class TestComputeArea
{
  //data and methods to be given later
}
```

The program needs to read the radius entered by the user from the keyboard. You should consider two important issues next:

- Reading the radius

- Storing the radius in the program

Let's address the second issue first. How does a computer identify radius and area in the program? The program needs to declare a symbol called *variable*—which represents the radius in the program—in order to store the radius. Variables are used to store data and computational results in the program.

Choose the descriptive names `radius` for radius and `area` for area. To let the compiler know what `radius` and `area` are, specify their data types, indicating whether they are integer, float, or others. Declare `radius` and `area` as double-precision, floating-point numbers. The program can be expanded as follows.

```
class TestComputeArea
{
  static double radius, area;   //declare radius and area
  // method to be given later
}
```

The program declares `radius` and `area` as static variables. The reserved word `static` indicates that `radius` and `area` can be accessed by the `main()` method. Every application must have a `main()` method that controls the execution of the program. The first step is to read in `radius`. Use the method `readDouble()`, which will be defined in the class, to read a `double` value from the keyboard. When this method is executed, the computer waits for the input from the keyboard. You will learn the detail of the implementation of this method in Chapter 14, "Input and Output."

The second step is to compute area; assign the expression `radius` × `radius` × `PI` to `area`, where `PI` is a constant representing the number π.

In the final step, print area on the console by using method `System.out.println()`.

The program is completed in Example 2.1. The result is shown in Figure 2.1.

Example 2.1   Computing the Area of a Circle

This program lets the user enter the radius for a circle and then computes the area. Finally, it displays the area.

```
//Compute the area of a circle
import java.io.*;
import java.util.*;

public class TestComputeArea
{
  static double radius;
  static double area;
```

continues

Example 2.1   continued

```java
      static final double PI = 3.14159;

      static private StringTokenizer stok;
      static private BufferedReader br
        = new BufferedReader(new InputStreamReader(System.in), 1);

      public static void main(String[] args)
      {
        System.out.println("Enter radius");
        radius = readDouble();
        area = radius*radius*PI;
        System.out.println("The area for the circle of radius " +
          radius + " is " + area);
      }

      public static double readDouble()
      {
        double d = 0;
        try
        {
          String str = br.readLine();
          stok = new StringTokenizer(str);
          d = new Double(stok.nextToken()).doubleValue();
        }
        catch (IOException ex)
        {
          System.out.println(ex);
        }
        return d;
      }
    }
```

Example Review

`System.out.println()` is a system predefined method. It can print strings and numbers. The plus sign (+) in the `System.out.println("The area for the circle of radius " + radius + " is " + area)` statement means to concatenate strings and print all of the items together.

Create a source file for Example 2.1 and name the file **TestComputeArea.java**. Compile and run the program. Sample output is shown in Figure 2.1.

If you replaced

`static double radius;`

with

`double radius;`

you would get an error because `main()` is always a static method. The static method cannot reference non-static variables or methods. You would find the same type of error if you eliminated the word `static` from in front of the method `readDouble()`. You will learn more about the method and class modifiers in Chapter 5, "Programming with Objects and Classes."

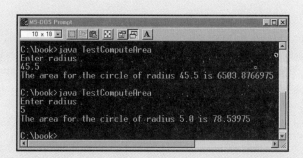

Figure 2.1 *The program receives the radius from the keyboard and displays the area of the circle.*

Identifiers

Just as every entity in the real world is identifiable with a name, you need to choose names for things you need to refer to in the programs. Programming languages use special symbols, called *identifiers*, for naming programming entities such as variables, constants, methods, classes, and packages. The rules for naming identifiers are the following:

- An identifier must start with a letter, an underscore, or a dollar sign.

- An identifier cannot contain operators, such as +, -, and so on.

- An identifier cannot be a reserved word. (See Appendix A, "Java Keywords," for a list of reserved words.)

- An identifier cannot be true, false, or null.

- An identifier can be of any length.

For example, $2, Area, Char, a, and α (the Greek alpha) are legal identifiers, while 2A and d+4 are illegal identifiers. Illegal identifiers are the ones that do not follow the rules. The Java compiler detects illegal identifiers and reports syntax errors.

NOTE

Java uses the Unicode specification for characters. A letter does not just mean an English letter. It can be any of the tens of thousands of Unicode letters representing international languages. Therefore, α is a legal identifier.

TIP

Identifiers are used for naming variables, constants, methods, classes, and packages. Descriptive identifiers make programs easy to read. Java is case sensitive; therefore, X and x are two different identifiers.

Variables

Variables are used to store data—input, output, or intermediate data. In the program in Example 2.1, radius and area were variables of double-precision, floating-point type. You can assign any float value to radius and area, and the value of radius and area can be reassigned. For example, you can write the following code to compute the area for different radii:

```
//Compute the first area
radius = 1.0;
area = radius*radius*3.14159;
System.out.println("The area is "+area+" for radius "+radius);

//Compute the second area
radius = 2.0;
area = radius*radius*3.14159;
System.out.println("The area is "+area+" for radius "+radius);
```

Declaring Variables

Variables are used to represent many different types of data. To use a variable, you need to declare it and tell the compiler the name of the variable as well as what type of data it represents. This is called a *variable declaration*. The syntax to declare a variable is as follows:

```
datatype variableName;
```

The following are examples of variable declarations:

```
int x;           //declares x to be an integer variable;
double radius;   //declares radius to be a double variable;
char a;          //declares a to be a character variable;
```

The examples use data types int, float, and char. You will be introduced to additional data types such as byte, short, long, float, char, and boolean in this chapter.

Assignment Statements

After a variable is declared, you can assign a value to that variable by using an *assignment statement*. The syntax for the assignment is one of the following formulations:

```
variable = value;
variable = expression;
```

For example, consider the following code:

```
x = 1;           // Assign 1 to x;
radius = 1.0;    // Assign 1.0 to radius;
a = 'A';         // Assign 'A' to a;
```

◾ CAUTION

In an assignment statement, the data type of the variable on the left must be compatible with the data type of the value on the right. For example, x = 1.0 would be illegal because the data type of x is int. You cannot assign a double value (1.0) to an int variable.

The variable name must be on the left. For example, 1 = x would be wrong.

An expression represents a computation involving values, variables, and operators. As an example, consider the following code:

```
area = radius*radius*3.14159;
```

The variable on the left can also be used in the expression on the right, as follows:

```
x = x + 1;
```

In this assignment statement, x + 1 is assigned to x. If x is 1 before the statement is executed, then x becomes 2 after the statement is executed.

CAUTION

The Java assignment statement uses the equal sign (=), not :=, which is often used in other languages.

Declaring and Initializing in One Step

Often, variables have initial values. You can declare a variable and initialize it in one step. For example, consider the following code:

```
int x = 1;
```

This is equivalent to the following two statements:

```
int x;
x = 1;
```

CAUTION

A variable must be declared before it can be assigned a value. A variable must be assigned a value before it can be read in a method.

TIP

Whenever possible, declare a variable and assign its initial value in one step. This makes the program easy to read.

Constants

The value of a variable may change during the execution of the program. A constant represents permanent data that never changes. In our TestComputeArea program, PI is a constant. If you use it frequently, you don't want to keep typing 3.14159; instead, you can define a constant for π. The following is the syntax for declaring a constant:

```
static final datatype CONSTANTNAME = VALUE;
```

The word final is a Java keyword. For example, in the TestComputeArea program, you might define

```
static final double PI = 3.14159;
```

and then use it in the following computation:

```
area = radius*radius*PI;
```

CAUTION

A constant must be declared before it can be used. You cannot change the constant value once it is declared.

Numerical Data Types

Each data type has a domain (range) of values. The compiler allocates memory space to store each variable or constant according to its data type. Java provides several primitive data types for numerical values, characters, and Boolean values. In this section, numeric data types are introduced.

Java has six numeric types: four for integers and two for floating-point numbers. Table 2.1 lists the six numeric data types, their domains, and their storage sizes.

TABLE 2.1   Numeric Data Types

Name	Domain	Storage Size
byte	-2^7 to 2^7-1	8-bit signed
short	-2^{15} to $2^{15}-1$	16-bit signed
int	-2^{31} to $2^{31}-1$	32-bit signed
long	-2^{63} to $2^{63}-1$	64-bit signed
float	$-3.4E38$ to $3.4E38$ (6 to 7 significant digits of accuracy)	32-bit IEEE 754
double	$-1.7E308$ to $1.7E308$ (14 to 15 significant digits of accuracy)	64-bit IEEE 754

Standard arithmetic operators for numerical data types include addition (+), subtraction (-), multiplication (*), division (/), and modulus (%). For examples, see the following code:

```
int i1 = 34 + 1;            //i1 becomes 35
float double d1 = 34.0 - 0.1;  //d1 becomes 33.9
long  i2 = 300*30;          //i2 becomes 90000
double d2 = 1.0/2.0;        //d2 becomes 0.5
int i3 = 1/2;               //i3 becomes 0; Note the result is
                            //the integer part of the division
byte i4 = 20%3;             //i4 becomes 2; Note the result is
                            //the remainder after the division
```

The result of integer division is an integer. For example, 5/2 = 2 instead of 2.5. The fraction part is truncated.

Numeric Literals

A *literal* is a primitive type value that directly appears in the program. For example, 34, 1,000,000, and 5.0 are literals in the following statements:

```
int i = 34;

long l = 1000000;

double d = 5.0;
```

Floating-point literals are written with a decimal point. By default, a floating-point literal is treated as a `double` type value. For example, 5.0 is considered a `double` value, not a `float` value. You can make a number a `float` or a `double` by appending the letters f, F, d, or D. For example, you can use `100.2f` or `100.2F` for floating-point numbers, and `100.2d` or `100.2D` for `double` numbers.

Shortcut Operators

It is common to use the current value of a variable, modify it, and reassign the results back to the same variable. For example, consider the following code:

```
i = i + 8;
```

This statement is equivalent to

```
i += 8;
```

The += is called a *shortcut operator*. The common shortcut operators are shown in Table 2.2.

TABLE 2.2   **Shortcut Operators**

Operator	Example	Equivalent
+=	i+=8	i = i+8
-=	f-=8.0	f = f-8.0
*=	i*=8	i = i*8
/=	i/=8	i = i/8
%=	i%=8	i = i%8

Two more shortcut operators are for incrementing and decrementing a variable by 1. This is handy because that's how much the value often needs to be changed. These two operators are ++ and - -. They can be used in prefix or suffix notation. For example:

```
x++ is equivalent to x = x+1;

++x is equivalent to x = x+1;
```

x-- is equivalent to x = x-1;

--x is equivalent to x = x-1;

Any numeric value can be applied to x. These operators are often used in loop statements. The loop statements are the structures that control how many times an operation or a sequence of operations is performed in succession. This structure as well as loop statements are introduced in Chapter 3, "Control Structures." If the operator is prefixed to the variable, the variable is incremented or decremented by 1 first, then used in the expression. If the operator is a suffix to the variable, the variable is used in the expression first, then incremented or decremented by 1. Therefore, the prefixes ++x and --x are referred to as the preincrement operator and the predecrement operator, respectively; and the suffixes x++ and x-- are referred to as the postincrement operator and the postdecrement operator, respectively. The following code illustrates this:

```
int i=10;
int newNum;
newNum = 10*i++;
```

In this case, i++ is evaluated after the entire expression (newNum = 10*i++) is evaluated. If i++ is replaced by ++i, ++i is evaluated before the entire expression is evaluated. So newNum is 100 for the first case and 110 for the second case. In both cases, i is incremented by 1.

Here is another example:

```
double x = 1.0;
double y = 5.0;
double z = x-- + ++y;
```

After all three lines are executed, y becomes 6.0, z becomes 7.0, and x becomes 0.0.

 TIP

Shortcut operators originally came from C. They were inherited by C++ and adopted by Java. Using shortcut operators makes expressions short; however, it also makes them complex and difficult to read. Avoid using shortcut operators in long expressions that involve many operators.

Numeric Type Conversion

Often, numerical values of different types need to be mixed in a computation. Consider the following statements:

```
byte i = 100;
long l = i*3+4;
double f = i*3.1+l/2;
```

Are these statements correct? Java allows binary operations on numerical variables and sometimes on values of different types. When performing the binary operation involving two operands of different types, Java automatically converts the operand with less accuracy to the type of the other operand with more accuracy. For example, if one operand is int and the other is float, the int operand is converted to float, since float is more accurate than int. If one of the operands is of the type double, the other is converted to double, since double has the best accuracy among all numerical types. So, the result of 1/2 is 0 and the result of 1.0/2 is 0.5.

You can always assign a value with less accuracy to a variable with more accuracy, such as assigning a long value to a float value. You cannot, however, assign a value with more accuracy to a variable with less accuracy without using *type casting*. Casting is an operation that converts a value of one data type into a value of another data type. The syntax for casting is to give the target type in parentheses, followed by the variable name. For example, see the following code:

```
float f = (float)10.1;
int i = (int)f;
```

In this case, i has a value of 10; the fractional part in f is truncated. Be careful when using casting. Lost information might lead to inaccurate results, as shown in the following example:

```
int i = 10000;
byte s = (short)i;
```

In this example, s becomes 16, which is totally distorted. To ensure correctness, you can test if the value is in the correct target type range (see Table 2.1) before performing casting.

■ CAUTION
Casting is necessary if assigning a value of more accuracy to a variable with less accuracy such as assigning a double value to an int variable. A compilation error would occur if casting were not used in these situations.

Character Data Type

The character data type, char, is used to represent a single character.

A character value is enclosed within single quotation marks. For example, consider the following code:

```
char letter = 'A';
char numChar = '4';
```

The first statement assigns character A to the char variable letter. The second statement assigns numerical character 4 to the char variable numChar. Note the following illegal statement:

```
char numChar = 4;
```

In this statement, 4, a numerical value, cannot be assigned to a character variable.

The char type only represents one character. To represent a string of characters, use a data structure called String. For example, the following line of code declares the message to be a string that has an initial value of Welcome to Java!

```
String message = "Welcome to Java!";
```

String is discussed in more detail in Chapter 6, "Arrays and Strings."

■■■ CAUTION

A string must be enclosed in quotation marks. A literal character is a single character enclosed in single quotation marks.

Java characters use *Unicode*, which is a 16-bit encoding scheme established by the Unicode Consortium to support the interchange, processing, and display of the written texts of the diverse languages of the world. (See the Unicode Web site at **www.unicode.org** for more information.) Unicode takes two bytes, expressed in four hexadecimal numbers that run from '\u0000' to '\uFFFF'. Most computers use ASCII code. Unicode includes ASCII code with '\u0000' to '\u00FF' corresponding to the 128 ASCII characters. (See Appendix B, "The ASCII Character Set," for a list of ASCII characters and their decimal and hexadecimal codes.)

You can use ASCII characters, such as 'X', '1', and '$', in a Java program, as well as Unicodes. Java also allows you to use the escape sequence for special characters, as shown in Table 2.3.

TABLE 2.3 Examples of Special Characters

Character Escape Sequence	ASCII	Unicode
Backspace	\b	\u0008
Tab	\t	\u0009
Linefeed	\n	\u000a
Carriage return	\r	\u000d

For example, the following statements are equivalent:

```
char letter = 'A';
char letter = '\u0041';
```

Both statements assign character A to char variable letter.

You can use casting to convert a character to a numerical code and vice versa. For example, to obtain the decimal code of a character, use a casting like this:

```
int decimalCode = (int)'0'
```

The variable decimalCode becomes 48.

boolean Data Type

The boolean data type comes from Boolean algebra. The domain of the boolean type consists of two values: true and false. For example, the following line of code assigns true to the boolean variable lightsOn.

```
boolean lightsOn = true;
```

The operators associated with Boolean values are comparison operators and Boolean operators. Comparison operators can be used in expressions that result in a Boolean value. Table 2.4 is a list of the comparison operators.

TABLE 2.4 Comparison Operators

Operator	Name	Example	Answer
<	less than	1 < 2	true
<=	less than or equal to	1 <= 2	true
>	greater than	1 > 2	false
>=	greater than or equal to	1 >= 2	false
==	equal to	1 == 2	false
!=	not equal to	1 != 2	true

■■■ CAUTION
The equality comparison operator is two equal signs (==), instead of a single equal sign (=). The latter symbol is for assignment.

Boolean operators operate on Boolean values to result in a new Boolean value. Table 2.5 contains a list of Boolean operators.

TABLE 2.5 Boolean Operators

Operator	Name	Description
!	not	logical negation
&&	and	logical conjunction
!!	or	logical disjunction
^	exclusive or	logical exclusion

These operators are demonstrated by using examples. In the examples, the variables width and height contain the values of 1 and 2, respectively.

Table 2.6 defines the not (!) operator. The not (!) operator negates true to false and false to true. For example, !(width == 3) is true since (width == 3) is false.

TABLE 2.6 Truth for Operator !

Operand	!Operand
true	false
false	true

Table 2.7 defines the and (&&) operator. The and (&&) of two Boolean operands is true if and only if both operands are true. For example, (width == 1) && (height > 1) is true since (width == 1) and (height > 1) are both true.

TABLE 2.7 **Truth for Operator &&**

Operand1	Operand2	Operand1 && Operand2
false	false	false
false	true	false
true	false	false
true	true	true

Table 2.8 defines the or (¦¦) operator. The or (¦¦) of two Boolean operands is `true` if at least one of the operands is `true`. For example, `(width > 1) ¦¦ (height > 2)` is `false` because `(width > 1)` and `(height > 2)` are both `false`.

TABLE 2.8 **Truth for Operator ¦¦**

Operand1	Operand2	Operand1 ¦¦ Operand2
false	false	false
false	true	true
true	false	true
true	true	true

Table 2.9 defines the exclusive or (^) operator. The exclusive or (^) of two Boolean operands is `true` if and only if two operands have different Boolean values. For example, `(width > 1) ^ (height == 2)` is `true` because `(width > 1)` is `false` and `(height == 2)` is `true`.

TABLE 2.9 **Truth for Operator ^**

Operand1	Operand2	Operand1 ^ Operand2
false	false	false
false	true	true
true	false	true
true	true	false

When evaluating `p1 && p2`, Java first evaluates `p1`, then evaluates `p2` if `p1` is `true`; if `p1` is `false`, `p2` is not evaluated. When evaluating `p1 ¦¦ p2`, Java first evaluates `p1`, then evaluates `p2` if `p1` is `false`; if `p1` is `true`, `p2` is not evaluated.

Java also provides the `&` and `¦` operators. The `&` operator works identically to the `&&` operator and the `¦` operator works identically to the `¦¦` operator with one exception—the `&` and `¦` operators always evaluate both operands. In some rare situations, you can use the `&` and `¦` operators to guarantee that the right operand is evaluated regardless of whether the left operand is `true` or `false`. For example, the expression `(width < 2) & (height- - < 2)` guarantees that `(height- - < 2)` is evaluated. Thus, the variable `height` will be decremented regardless of whether `width` is less than 2 or not.

TIP

Avoid using the & and ¦ operators. The benefits of the & and ¦ operators are marginal. Using the & and ¦ operators makes the program difficult to read and could cause errors. For example, the expression (x != 0) & (100/x) results in a runtime error if x is 0.

Operator Precedence

Operator precedence determines the order in which expressions are evaluated. Suppose that you have the following expression:

```
3 + 4*4 > 5*(4+3) - i++
```

What is its value? How does the compiler know the execution order of the operators? The expression inside the parentheses is evaluated first. (Parentheses can be nested, in which case the expression in the inner parentheses is executed first.) When evaluating an expression without parentheses, the operators are applied in the order shown in Table 2.10. Table 2.10 contains the operators you have learned in this section. (See Appendix C, "Operator Precedence Chart," for a complete list of the Java operators and their precedence.)

TABLE 2.10 **Operator Precedence Chart**

Precedence	*Operator*
Highest Order	++ and - -
	*, /, %
	+, -
	<, <=, >, =>
	==, !=
	&&
	¦¦
Lowest Order	=, +=, -=, *=, /=, %=

 TIP

You can use parentheses to force an evaluation order as well as to make a program easy to read.

Programming Errors

Programming errors are unavoidable, even for experienced programmers. The errors can be categorized into three types: *compilation errors,* *runtime errors,* and *logic errors.*

Compilation Errors

Errors that occur during compilation are called *compilation errors* or *syntax errors*. Compilation errors result from errors in code construction such as mistyping a keyword, omitting some necessary punctuation, or using an opening brace without a corresponding closing brace. These errors are usually easy to detect because the compiler tells you where they are and the reasons for them. For example, compiling the following program results in compilation errors, as shown in Figure 2.2.

```
//The program contains syntax errors
public class ShowErrors
{
  public static void main(String[] args)
  {
    i = 30;
    System.out.println(i+4);
  }
}
```

Figure 2.2 *The JDK compiler detects a syntax error: Undefined variable i.*

Both errors are a result of not declaring variable i. It is common for a single error to display multiple lines of compilation errors. Therefore, it is a good practice to start debugging from the top line and working downward. Fixing errors that occur earlier might fix cascading errors that occur later in the program.

In general, syntax errors are easy to find and easy to correct, because the compiler gives indications where the errors came from and why they are there. Finding runtime errors, on the other hand, can be very challenging.

An IDE tool can make debugging easy. Figure 2.3 shows the example of using Microsoft Visual J++ 6.0. The source code is in the Code Editor window. When you are compiling the source code, the compilation errors are displayed in the Task List window. Pointing the mouse and clicking on the line that shows the syntax error in the Task List window leads you to the line that causes the error in the source code.

NOTE

The JDK compiler showed two errors, while the Microsoft Visual J++ showed only one error and ignored the cascading error. Usually, Visual J++ ignores cascading errors.

Visual J++ points to the erroneous line

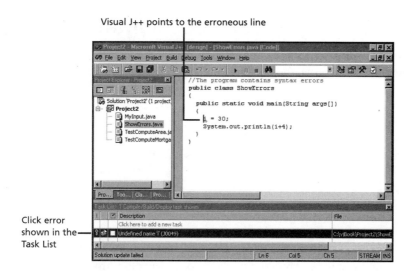

Click error
shown in the
Task List

Figure 2.3 *Clicking the error in the Task List window of Microsoft Visual J++ automatically
sets the arrow on the source code where the error occurs.*

Runtime Errors

Runtime errors are the errors that cause a program to terminate abnormally.
Runtime errors occur while the application is running and the environment detects
an operation that is impossible to carry out. A common example of runtime error
is input error.

An *input error* occurs when the user enters an unexpected input value that the program cannot handle. For instance, if the program expects to read in a number, but
instead the user enters a string, data-type errors occur in the program. To avoid the
input error, the program should prompt the user to enter the correct type of values. For instance, the program may display a message, such as "Please enter an integer," before reading an integer from the keyboard.

Another common source of runtime error is division by zero. It happens when the
divisor is zero or the divisor is too small, which causes overflow.

Logical Errors

Logical errors occur when a program doesn't perform the way it was intended to.
There are all kinds of reasons for logical errors. The errors are called *bugs;* the
process of finding errors is called *debugging.* A common approach to debugging is
to use a combination of methods to narrow down to the part of the program where
the bug is. Debugging a large program can be a daunting task. Debugging techniques are introduced in Chapter 4, "Methods."

Programming Style and Documentation

Programming style deals with the appearance of the program. You could write the entire program on one line, the program would compile and run fine. However, it is a bad programming style, because the program is hard to read. Programming documentation consists of the explanatory remarks and comments for the program. Programming style and documentation are as important as coding. Good programming style and appropriate documentation can reduce the chance for errors and make programs easy to read. Following are some guidelines for Java programming style and documentation.

Appropriate Comments

You should include a summary at the beginning of the program to explain what the program does, its key features, its supporting data structures, and unique techniques it uses. In addition, you should include comments to introduce each major step in a long program and to explain anything that is difficult to read. It is important to make your comments concise so that you do not crowd the program or make it difficult to read.

NOTE

In addition to the two comment styles, // and /*, Java supports a special type of comments, referred to as *javadoc comments*. Javadoc comments begin with /** and end with */. The javadoc comments are usually for documenting classes and data and methods. These comments can be extracted into an HTML file using the JDK's `javadoc` command. You can obtain an HTML file for describing the package and classes using the `javadoc` command. In Visual J++ 6.0, the javadoc comments are displayed in the Class Outline window.

Naming Conventions

You should choose descriptive names for variables, constants, classes, and methods so that their meanings are straightforward. Names are case sensitive. I recommend the following guidelines for naming variables, methods, and classes:

- For variables and methods, always use lowercase. If the name consists of several words, concatenate all into one, making the first word lowercase and capitalizing the first letter of each subsequent word in the name, for example, the variables `radius` and `area` and the method `readDouble`.

- For class names, capitalize the first letter of each word in the name; for example, the class name `TestComputeArea`.

- All letters in constants should be capitalized; for example, the constant `PI`.

TIP

It is important to become familiar with naming conventions. Understanding naming conventions helps you comprehend Java programs. Sticking with

---

those naming conventions makes programmers more willing to accept your program.

Proper Indentation

A consistent indentation style makes your programs clear and easy to read. Indentation can be used to illustrate structural relationships among the program's components or statements. Java can read the program even if all of the statements are in a straight line, but it is easier to read and maintain code that is aligned properly. You should indent each subcomponent or statement several spaces more than the structure within which it is nested. Many Java development tools indent components of the program automatically.

Separate Classes

You will frequently use readDouble() to get a double floating-point number from the keyboard. Do you have to code the method readDouble() in every program that invokes readDouble()? In Java, you can define a separate class for readDouble() so that all of the programs using readDouble() can use it without rewriting the code. You can place the separate class and the program that is using it in the same directory.

Now let's look at a new class called MyInput. This class contains the readDouble() and the readInt() methods for reading a double and an int literal, respectively, from the keyboard.

```java
import java.io.*;
import java.util.*;

public class MyInput
{
  static private StringTokenizer stok;
  static private BufferedReader br
    = new BufferedReader(new InputStreamReader(System.in),1);

  public static int readInt()
  {
    int i = 0;
    try
    {
      String str = br.readLine();
      StringTokenizer stok = new StringTokenizer(str);
      i = new Integer(stok.nextToken()).intValue();
    }
    catch (IOException ex)
    {
      System.out. println(ex);
    }
    return i;
  }

  public static double readDouble()
  {
    double d = 0;
    try
```

```
    {
      String str = br.readLine();
      stok = new StringTokenizer(str);
      d = new Double(stok.nextToken()).doubleValue();
    }
    catch (IOException ex)
    {
      System.out.println(ex);
    }
    return d;
  }
}
```

Example 2.2 shows how to use the MyInput class.

Example 2.2 Computing Mortgage

This example shows you how to write a program that computes mortgage payments. The program will let the user enter the interest rate, year, and loan amount, and then compute the monthly payment and the total payment. Finally, it will display the monthly and total final payments.

The formula to compute the monthly payment is as follows:

$$\frac{\text{principal} \times \text{monthly interest}}{(1-(1/(1+\text{monthly interest}))^{\text{years} \times 12})}$$

The mortgage calculation program follows, and the output is shown in Figure 2.4.

```
class TestComputeMortgage
{
  public static void main(String[] args)
  {
    double interestRate;
    int year;
    double loan;

    //enter input
    System.out.println(
      "Enter yearly interest rate, for example 8.25: ");
    //get monthly interest rate
    interestRate = MyInput.readDouble()/1200;
    System.out.println(
      "Enter number of years as an integer, for example 5: ");
    year = MyInput.readInt();
    System.out.println("Enter loan amount, for example 120000.95: ");
    loan = MyInput.readDouble();

    //calculate payment
    double monthlyPay =
      loan*interestRate/(1-(Math.pow(1/(1+interestRate),year*12)));
    double totalPay = monthlyPay*year*12;
```

```
        //display results
        System.out.println("The monthly pay is "+monthlyPay);
        System.out.println("The total pay is "+totalPay);
    }
}
```

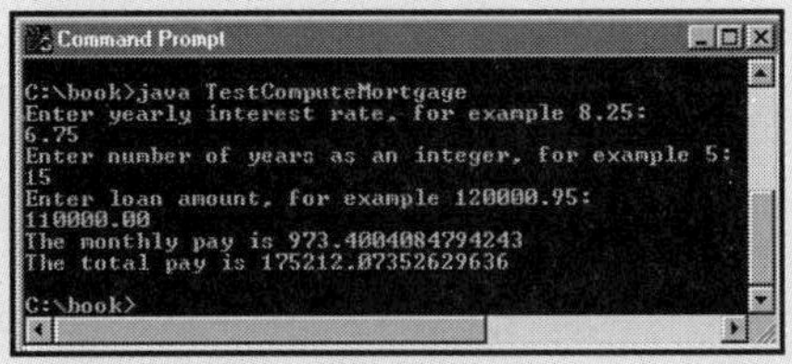

Figure 2.4 *The program receives interest rate, years, and loan amount, then displays the monthly payment and total payment.*

Example Review

The methods defined in the `MyInput` class are `readInt()` and `readDouble()`. They are available for use in this program because `MyInput` is compiled, and its bytecode is stored in the same directory as your test program. If you get a compilation error indicating that `MyInput` is not defined, make sure that `MyInput.class` is in the directory with `TestComputeMortgage.java`.

If you stored `MyInput.class` in a directory other than the directory that contains `TestComputeMortgage.java`, you need to include the directory in the `classpath` environment variable. See Chapter 5 for information about setting the `classpath` environment variable.

The method for computing b^p in the `Math` class is `pow(b, p)`. The `Math` class, which comes with the Java runtime system, is available to all Java programs. The `Math` class is introduced in Chapter 5.

NOTE

The `MyInput` class is used throughout the text. To run samples from the text, place the `MyInput` in the same directory as the sample source code. You only need to compile `MyInput` once to make it available for other programs.

Chapter Summary

In this chapter, you learned about data representation, operators, and expressions. These are the fundamental elements needed to construct Java programs. You also learned about programming errors, debugging, and programming styles. These are all important concepts and should be fully understood before you apply them in Java programming.

Identifiers are used for naming programming entities such as variables, constants, methods, classes, and packages. Variables are symbols that represent data. The value of a variable can be changed with an assignment statement. All variables must be declared with an identifier and a type before they can be used. An initial value must be assigned to the variable before the variable is read (or referenced).

The equal sign (=) is used to assign a value to a variable. The statement with the equal sign is called an assignment statement. When a value is assigned to a variable, it replaces the previous value in the variable, which is destroyed.

A constant is a symbol representing a value in the program that is never changed. Sometimes it is called a constant variable. You cannot assign a new value to a constant.

Java provides four integer types (`byte`, `short`, `int`, `long`) that represent integers of four different sizes. Two are floating-point types (`float`, `double`) that represent float numbers of two different sizes. Character type (`char`) represents a single character, and `boolean` type represents a `true` or `false` value. These are called primitive date types. Java's primitive types are portable across all computer platforms. When they are declared, the variables of these types are created and assigned with memory space.

Java provides operators for performing numerical operations such as + (addition), – (subtraction), * (multiplication), / (division), and % (modulus). The integer division (/) yields an integer result. The modulus operator (%) yields the remainder after integer division.

The increment operator (++) and the decrement operator (- -) increment or decrement a variable by 1. If the operator is prefixed to the variable, the variable is incremented or decremented by 1 first, then used in the expression. If the operator is a suffix to the variable, the variable is used in the expression first, then incremented or decremented by 1.

In a computation involving different types of numerical values, numbers are converted to a unifying type. The unifying type is chosen according to the data type of the operands in the following order: `double`, `float`, `long`, `int`, `short`, `byte`. You can assign a value that is in a lower order to a variable that is in a higher order. However, an explicit casting operator must be used if you assign a value of a higher order (for instance, `double`) to a variable of a lower order (for instance, `int`).

The operators in arithmetic expressions are evaluated in the order determined by the rules of operator precedence. Parentheses can be used to force the order of evaluation to occur in any sequence.

Chapter Review

1. Are the following identifiers valid?

   ```
   applet, Applet, a++, - -a, 4#R, $4, #44, apps
   ```

2. Declare the following:

   - An int variable with an initial value of 0.

   - A long variable with an initial value of 10000.

   - A float variable with an initial value of 3.4.

   - A double variable with an initial value of 34.45.

   - A char variable with an initial value of 4.

   - A boolean variable with an initial value of true.

3. Assume that a = 1 and d = 1.0 and that each expression is independent. What are the results of the following expressions?

   ```
   a = 46/9;

   a = 46%9+4*4-2;

   a = 45+43%5*(23*3%2);

   a = 45+45*50%a- -;

   a = 45+1+45*50%(- -a)

   d += 34.23*3+d++

   d -= 3.4*(a+5)*d++

   a %= 3/a+3;
   ```

4. Find the largest and smallest byte, short, int, long, float, and double.

5. Can different types of numeric values be used together in a computation?

6. Describe Unicode and ASCII code.

7. Can the following conversions involving casting be allowed? If so, find the converted result.

   ```
   char c = 'A';
   i = (int)c;

   boolean b = true;
   i = (int)b;

   float f = 1000.34f;
   int i = (int)f;

   double d = 1000.34;
   int i = (int)d;

   int i = 1000;
   char c = (char)i;

   int i = 1000;
   boolean b = (boolean)b;
   ```

8. What is the result of 25/4? How would you rewrite the expression if you wanted the quotient to be a floating-point number?

9. Are the following statements correct? If so, show the printout.

```
System.out.println("the output for 25/4 is "+ 25/4);

System.out.println("the output for 25/4.0 is "+ 25/4.0);
```

10. What does an explicit conversion from a double to an int do with the fractional part of the double value?

11. How would you write the following formula so that it produces a double value?

    4/3(r + 34)

12. List six comparison operators.

13. Show the result of the following Boolean expressions if the result can be determined.

```
(true) && (3 > 4)

!(x > 0) && (x > 0)

 (x > 0) ¦¦ (x < 0)

 (x != 0) ¦¦ (x == 0)

 (x >= 0) ¦¦ (x < 0)

 (x != 1) == !(x = 1)
```

14. Write a Boolean expression that evaluates to true if the number is between 1 and 100.

15. Write a Boolean expression that evaluates true if the number is between 1 and 100 or the number is negative.

16. Are the following expressions correct?

```
x > y > 0

x = y && y

x /= y

x or y

x and y
```

17. How do you denote a comment line? How do you denote a comment paragraph?

18. Describe compilation errors and runtime errors.

19. What are the conventional styles for class names, methods names, constants, and variables?

Programming Exercises

1. Write a program to convert Fahrenheit to Celsius. The formula for the conversion is as follows:

   ```
   celsius = (5/9)*(fahrenheit-32)
   ```

   Your program reads a Fahrenheit degree in double from the keyboard; it then converts it to Celsius and displays the result on the console.

2. Write a program to compute the volume of a cylinder. Your program reads in radius and length and computes volume using the following formulas:

   area = radius*radius*π;

   volume = area*length;

3. Write a program to display Welcome to Java in large block letters, each letter made up of the same character it represents. The letters should be six printed lines. For example, *W* is displayed as follows:

CONTROL STRUCTURES

Objectives

- Understand the concept of program control.
- Use various decision statements to control the execution of a program.
- Use various loop structures to control the repetition of statements.
- Understand and use the keywords break and continue.

Introduction

Program control can be defined as specifying the order in which statements are executed in a computer program. The programs that you have written so far execute the statements in sequence. However, you are often faced with situations in which you must provide alternative steps.

In Chapter 2, "Java Building Elements," if you entered a negative input for `radius` in Example 2.1, "Computing the Area of a Circle," for instance, the program would print an invalid result. If the radius is negative, you don't want the program to compute the area. Like all high-level programming languages, Java provides decision statements that let you choose actions with two or more alternative courses. You can use the decision statements in the following pseudocode to rewrite Example 2.1:

```
if the radius is negative
   the program displays a message indicating a wrong input;
else
   the program computes the area and displays the result;
```

Java supports several variations of decision statements. The three main forms are `if` statements, shortcut `if` statements, and `switch` statements.

Like other high-level programming languages, Java provides loop structures in order to control the repeated execution of statements. Suppose that you need to print the same message a hundred times. It would be tedious to write the same statement repeatedly. Java provides a powerful control structure called a *loop*, which controls how many times an operation or a sequence of operations is performed in succession. Using a loop construct, you can simply tell the computer to print the message a hundred times without actually coding the print statement a hundred times. Java has three basic loop constructs: `for` loops, `while` loops, and `do` loops.

In this chapter, you will learn various decision and loop control structures.

Using *if* Statements

Java has two types of `if` statements: the simple `if` statement and the `if...else` statement. The simple `if` statement executes an action only if the condition is `true`. The actions that the `if...else` statement specify differ based on whether the condition is `true` or `false`.

The Simple *if* Statement

The syntax for the simple `if` statement is as follows:

```
if (booleanExpression)
{
   statement(s);
}
```

The execution flow chart is shown in Figure 3.1.

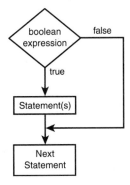

Figure 3.1 *The* if *statement executes the statements if the* boolean *expression evaluates as* true.

If booleanExpression evaluates as true, the statements inside the block are executed. For example, see the following code:

```
if (radius >= 0)
{
  area = radius*radius*PI;
  System.out.println("The area for the circle of radius " +
    radius + " is " + area);
}
```

If the value of radius is greater than or equal to 0, then the area is computed and the result is displayed; otherwise, the two statements inside the block will not be executed.

▉▉ CAUTION

The booleanExpression is always enclosed inside the parentheses for all forms of the if statement.

The curly braces can be omitted if they enclose a single statement. For example:

```
if ((i >= 0) && (i <= 10))
  system.out.println("i is an integer between 0 and 10");
```

The *if...else* Statement

The simple if statement takes an action if the specified condition is true. If the condition is false, nothing is done. But what can you do if you want to take alternative actions when the condition is false? You can use the if...else statement. The syntax for that statement is as follows:

```
if (booleanExpression)
{
  statement(s)-for-the-true-case;
}
else
{
  statement(s)-for-the-false-case;
}
```

The flow chart of the if...else statement is shown in Figure 3.2.

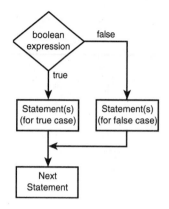

Figure 3.2 *The* if...else *statement executes the statements for the* true *case if the* boolean *expression evaluates as* true; *otherwise, the statements for the* false *case are executed.*

If the booleanExpression evaluates as true, the statement(s) for the true case is executed; otherwise, the statement(s) for the false case is executed. For example, consider the following code:

```
if (radius >= 0)
{
  area = radius*radius*PI;
  System.out.println("The area for the circle of radius " +
    radius + " is " + area);
}
else
{
  System.out.println("Negative input");
}
```

If radius >= 0 is true, area is computed and displayed; if it is false, the message "Negative input" is printed.

As usual, the curly braces can be omitted if there is only one statement inside. The curly braces enclosing the System.out.println() statement can therefore be omitted in the previous example.

Nested *if* Statements

The statements inside the if or the if...else statements can be any legal Java statement—including another if or if...else statement. The inner if statement is said to be *nested* inside the outer if statement. The inner if statement can contain another if statement; in fact, there is no limit to the depth of the nesting. For example, the following is a nested if statement:

```
if (i > k)
{
  if (j > k)
    System.out.print("i and j are greater than k");
}
else
  System.out.println("i is less than or equal to k");
```

The if (j > k) statement is nested inside the if (i > k) statement.

The nested if statement can be used to implement multiple alternatives. For example, the following statement assigns a letter grade to the variable grade according to the score with multiple alternatives:

```
if (score >= 90.0)
  grade = 'A';
else
  if (score >= 80.0)
    grade = 'B';
  else
    if (score >= 70.0)
      grade = 'C';
    else
      if (score >= 60.0)
        grade = 'D';
      else
        grade = 'F';
```

The execution of this if statement proceeds as follows. The first condition (score >= 90.0) is tested. If it is true, the grade becomes 'A'. If it is false, the second condition (score >= 80.0) is tested. If the second condition is true, the grade becomes 'B'. If that condition is false, the third condition and the rest of the conditions (if necessary) continue to be tested until a condition is met or all of the conditions have proven to be false. If all the conditions are false, the grade becomes 'F'. It is important to know that a condition is tested only when all of its previous conditions are false.

The preceding if statement is equivalent to the following:

```
if (score >= 90.0)
  grade = 'A';
else if (score >= 80.0)
  grade = 'B';
else if (score >= 70.0)
  grade = 'C';
else if (score >= 60.0)
  grade = 'D';
else
  grade = 'F';
```

In fact, this is the preferred writing style for multiple alternative if statements. This style avoids deep indentation and makes the program easy to read.

Example 3.1   Using Nested *if* Statements

In Example 2.2, "Computing Mortgage," you built a program that reads interest rate, year, and loan amount and computes mortgage payments. In this example, assume the interest rate depends on the year.

Suppose that you have three different interest rates: 7.25 percent for 7 years, 8.5 percent for 15 years, and 9 percent for 30 years. The program prompts the user

continues

Example 3.1   continued

to enter a loan amount and the number of years of the loan, then finds the interest rate according to year. The program finally displays the monthly payment amount and the total amount paid. Figure 3.3 shows a sample run of the program.

```java
class TestIfElse
{
  public static void main(String[] args)
  {
    double interestRate = 0;
    int year;
    double loan;

    //enter number of years and find interestRate rate
    System.out.println("Enter number of years: 7, 15 and 30 only :");
    year = MyInput.readInt();
    if (year == 7)
      interestRate = 7.25/1200;
    else if (year == 15)
      interestRate = 8.50/1200;
    else if (year == 30)
      interestRate = 9.0/1200;
    else
    {
      System.out.println("Wrong year");
      System.exit(0);
    }

    //enter loan amount
    System.out.println("Enter loan amount, for example 120000.95: ");
    loan = MyInput.readDouble();

    //compute mortgage
    double monthlyPay =
      loan*interestRate/(1-(Math.pow(1/(1+interestRate),year*12)));
    double totalPay = monthlyPay*year*12;

    //display results
    System.out.println("The monthly pay is "+monthlyPay);
    System.out.println("The total pay is "+totalPay);
  }
}
```

Example Review

The program receives the year and assigns the interest rate: 7.25 percent for 7 years, 8.5 percent for 15 years, and 9 percent for 30 years. If the year value is not 7, 15, or 30, the program displays Wrong Year.

Note that an initial value of 0 is assigned to interestRate. A syntax error would occur if it had no initial value because all of the other statements that assign values to interestRate are within the if statement. The compiler thinks that these statements might not be executed and therefore reports a syntax error.

Figure 3.3 *The program in Example 3.1 validates the input year, obtains the interest rate according to the year, receives the loan amount, and displays the monthly payment and the total payment.*

Shortcut *if* Statements

You might want to assign a value to a variable that is restricted by certain conditions. For example, the following statement assigns 1 to y if x is greater than 0 and −1 to y if x is less than or equal to 0.

```
if (x > 0) y = 1
else y = -1;
```

Alternatively, you can use a shortcut `if` statement to achieve the same result:

```
y = (x > 0) ? 1 : -1;
```

The shortcut form of the `if` statement is in a completely different style. There is no explicit `if` in the statement. The syntax is as follows:

```
variable = booleanExpression ? true-result-expression : false-result
  expression;
```

This is equivalent to the following:

```
if (booleanExpression)
  variable = true-result-expression;
else
  variable = false-result-expression;
```

TIP

The shortcut `if` statement originally comes from C. It is unfamiliar to many programmers who do not have a C background. Because the statement is not descriptive, you should avoid using it.

Using *switch* Statements

The `if` statement in Example 3.1 makes decisions based on a single `true` or `false` condition. There are three cases for assigning interest rates, which depend on the year value. To fully account for all cases, nested `if` statements were used. Clearly, the overuse of the nested `if` statement makes the program difficult to read. Java provides a `switch` statement to handle multiple conditions efficiently. You could write the following `switch` statement to replace the nested `if` statement in Example 3.1:

```
switch (year)
{
  case 7:  interestRate = 7.25;
           break;
  case 15: interestRate = 8.50;
           break;
  case 30: interestRate = 9.0;
           break;
  default: System.out.println("Wrong Year");
}
```

The flow chart of the preceding `switch` statement is shown in Figure 3.4.

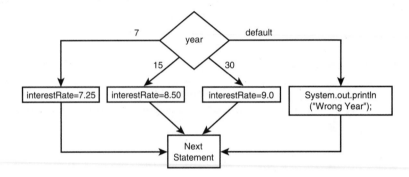

Figure 3.4 *The* `switch` *statement obtains the interest rate according to the year.*

This statement checks to see if the year matches the value 7, 15, or 30, in that order. If matched, the corresponding statement is executed; if not matched, a message is displayed. The full syntax for the `switch` statement is as follows:

```
switch (switch-expression)
{
  case value1: statement(s)1;
               break;
  case value2: statement(s)2;
               break;
  ...
  case valueN: statement(s)N;
               break;
  default:     statement(s)-for-default;
}
```

The `switch` statement observes the following rules:

- The `switch-expression` must yield a value of `char`, `byte`, `short`, or `int` type and must always be enclosed in parentheses.

- The `value1...valueN` must have the same data type as the value of the `switch-expression`. The resulting statements in the `case` statement are executed when the value in the `case` statement matches the value of the `switch-expression`. (Each `case` statement is executed in sequential order.)

- The keyword break is optional. The break statement terminates the entire switch statement. If the break statement is not present, the next case statement will be executed.

- The default case, which is optional, can be used to perform actions when none of the specified cases is true. The default case always appears last in the switch block.

▬▬▬ CAUTION

Do not forget to use the break statement when one is needed. For example, the following code always displays Wrong Year, regardless of what year is. Suppose the year is 15. The statement interestRate = 8.50 is executed, then the statement interestRate = 9.0 is executed and finally the statement System.out.println("Wrong Year") is executed.

```
switch (year)
{
  case 7:  interestRate = 7.25;
  case 15: interestRate = 8.50;
  case 30: interestRate = 9.0;
  default: System.out.println("Wrong Year");
}
```

Using Loop Structures

Loops are structures that control repeated execution of a block of statements. The part of the loop that contains the statements to be repeated is called the *loop body*. The one-time execution of the loop body is referred to as an *iteration of the loop*. Each loop contains a loop continue-condition, a Boolean expression, which controls the execution of the body. After each iteration, the continue-condition is re-evaluated. If the condition is true, the body is repeated. If the condition is false, the loop terminates.

The concept of looping is fundamental to programming. Java provides three types of loop structures: the for loop, the while loop, and the do loop.

The *for* Loop

A common type of program loop is the for loop. The for loop is a construct that causes the loop body to be repeated for a fixed number of times. The syntax of the for loop is as follows:

```
for (control-variable-initializer; continue-condition;
     adjustment-statement)
{
  //loop-body;
}
```

The flow chart of the loop is shown in Figure 3.5.

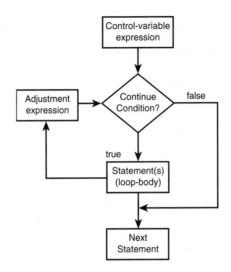

Figure 3.5 *The* for *loop initializes the control variable, executes the statements in the loop body, and then evaluates the adjustment expression repeatedly when the* continue-condition *evaluates as* true.

The loop construct starts with the keyword for, followed by the three control elements, which are enclosed by the parentheses, and the loop body, which is inside the curly braces. The control elements, which are separated by semicolons, control how many times the loop body is executed and when the loop terminates. For example, the following for loop prints Welcome to Java! 100 times:

```java
int i;
for (i = 0; i<100; i++)
{
  System.out.println("Welcome to Java!");
}
```

The flow chart of the statement is shown in Figure 3.6.

The first element, i = 0, initializes the control variable, i. The control variable tracks how many times the loop body has been executed. The adjustment statement changes the value of the variable.

The next element, i < 100, which is the continue-condition, is a Boolean expression. The expression is evaluated at the beginning of each iteration. If the continue-condition is true, execute the loop body. If it is false, the loop terminates and the program control turns to the line following the loop.

The adjustment statement, i++, is a statement that adjusts the control variable. This statement is executed after each iteration. Usually, an adjustment statement either increments or decrements the control variable. Eventually, the value of the control variable forces the continue-condition to become false.

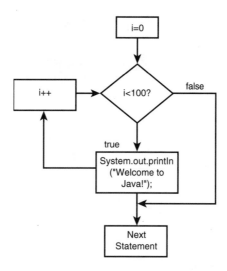

Figure 3.6 *The* for *loop initializes* i *to* 0*, executes the* println() *statement, and then repeatedly evaluates* i++ *when* i *is less than* 100*.*

The loop control variable can be declared and initialized in the for loop. An equivalent statement for the previous example is as follows:

```
for (int i = 0; i<100; i++)
{
   System.out.println("Welcome to Java!");
}
```

If there is only one statement in the loop body, as in this example, the curly braces can be omitted.

Example 3.2 Using *for* Loops

This example computes the summation of a series, starting with 0.01 and ending with 1.0. The numbers in the series will increment by 0.01, as follows: 0.01+0.02+0.03 and so on. The output of this program appears in Figure 3.7.

```
//Compute sum = 0.01 + 0.02 + ... + 1;
class TestSum
{
  public static void main(String[] args)
  {
    float sum = 0;
    for (float i=0.01f; i <= 1.0f ; i = i+0.01f)
      sum += i;
    System.out.println("The summation is " + sum);
  }
}
```

continues

Example 3.2 continued

Figure 3.7 *Example 3.2 uses a* for *loop to sum a series from 0.01 to 1 in increments of 0.01.*

Example Review

The for loop repeatedly adds the control variable i to the sum. This variable, which begins with 0.01, is incremented by 0.01 after each iteration. The loop terminates when i exceeds 1.0.

From this example, you can see that a control variable can be a float type. In fact, it can be any numeric data type.

If you run the program and get a result close to, but not exactly, 50.499985, you probably are using an earlier version of JDK.

You may have already noticed that the answer is not precise. This is because the computers have to use a fixed number of bits to represent the floating-point numbers; some floating-point numbers cannot be represented exactly. If you change float in the program to double, you will see slight improvements on precision because a double variable takes 64 bits while a float variable takes 32 bits.

CAUTION

Always use semicolons instead of commas in the for loop header to separate the control elements. A common mistake is to use commas in the for loop header.

TIP

Do not change the value of the control variable inside the for loop, even though it is perfectly legal to do so. Changing the value makes the program difficult to understand and could lead to subtle errors.

Example 3.3 Using Nested *for* Loops

The following program uses nested for loops to print a multiplication table. Nested loops are composed of an outer loop and one or more inner loops. Each time the outer loop is repeated, the inner loops are reentered, their loop control parameters are reevaluated, and all required iterations are performed. The output of the program is shown in Figure 3.8.

```
class TestMulTable
{
  public static void main(String[] args)
  {
    //display the title
    System.out.println("        Multiplication Table");
    System.out.println("----------------------------------");

    //display the number title
    System.out.print(" | ");
    for (int j=1; j<=9; j++)
      System.out.print(" "+j);
    System.out.println(" ");

    //print table body
    for (int i=1; i<=9; i++)
    {
      System.out.print(i+" | ");
      for (int j=1; j<=9; j++)
      {
        // display the product and align properly
        if (i*j < 10)
          System.out.print(" "+i*j);
        else
          System.out.print(" "+i*j);
      }
      System.out.println(" ");
    }
  }
}
```

Figure 3.8 *Example 3.3 uses nested* for *loops to print a multiplication table.*

Example Review

The first for loop displays a title on the first line, dashes (-) on the second line, and the numbers 1 through 9 on the third line.

The next loop is a nested for loop with the control variable i on the outer loop and j on the inner loop. For each i, the product i*j is displayed on a line in the inner loop, with j being 1, 2, 3, ..., 9. The if statement in the inner loop is used so that the product is aligned properly. If the product is a single digit, it is displayed with a space before it.

continues

Example 3.3   continued

 CAUTION
The control variable must always be declared inside the control structure of the loop or before the loop. If the variable is declared inside the loop control structure, it cannot be referenced outside of the loop.

The *while* Loop

If you know the number of times you need to repeat an operation, you can use a `for` loop to control the repetition of the statements. If the number of repeats is unknown, the `for` loop cannot help you. Suppose that you need to find the sum of all numbers entered from the keyboard. If you know that the total number is 100, it is easy to use a `for` loop like the following:

```java
int sum = 0;
for (int i = 1; i < 100; i++)
  sum += readInt();
```

Assume that the total number is not specified. However, you do know that you will have all of the numbers when the input is 0—that is, the input 0 signifies the end of the input. You need to use a `while` loop for this problem. The `while` loop handles an unspecified number of repetitions. The syntax for the `while` loop is as follows:

```java
while (continue-condition)
{
  //loop-body;
}
```

The `while` loop flow chart is shown in Figure 3.9.

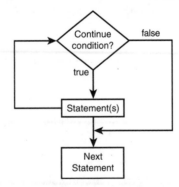

Figure 3.9 *The* `while` *loop repeatedly executes the statements in the loop body when* `continue-condition` *evaluates as* `true`.

The `continue-condition`, a Boolean expression, must appear inside the parentheses. It is always evaluated before the loop body is executed. If its evaluation is `true`, the loop body is executed; if its evaluation is `false`, the entire loop terminates and the program control turns to the statement that follows the `while` loop.

Example 3.4   Using a *while* Loop

This example reads and calculates an unspecified number of integers. The input 0 signifies the end of the input.

The program's sample run is shown in Figure 3.10.

```
class TestWhile
{
  public static void main(String[] args)
  {
    int data;
    int sum = 0;

    data = MyInput.readInt();
    while (data != 0)
    {
      sum += data;
      data = MyInput.readInt();
    }

    System.out.println("The sum is "+sum);
  }
}
```

Figure 3.10   *Example 3.4 uses a* `while` *loop to add an unspecified number of integers.*

Example Review

If `data` is not 0, it is added to the sum and the next input data is read. If `data` is 0, the loop body is not executed and the `while` loop terminates.

Note that if the first input read is 0, the loop body never executes, and the resulting `sum` is 0.

NOTE

The `while` loop is more powerful than the `for` loop. You can use a `while` loop to rewrite every `for` loop. Nevertheless, the `for` loop has clear advantages: It is easy to read and takes little time to write.

---

continues

Example 3.4   continued

> **CAUTION**
> Ensure that the `continue-condition` eventually becomes `false` so that the program will terminate.

> **TIP**
> You should avoid using floating-point values for equality checking in a loop control. Using them could result in imprecise counter values and inaccurate results because floating-point values are approximations.

The *do* Loop

The do loop is a variation of the `while` loop. Its syntax is the following:

```
do
{
  //loop body;
} while (continue-condition)
```

Its execution flow chart is shown in Figure 3.11.

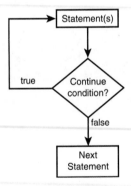

Figure 3.11 *The do loop body executes once when* `continue-condition` *evaluates as* `false`, *and it executes repeatedly when* `continue-condition` *evaluates as* `true`.

The loop body is executed first. Then the `continue-condition` is evaluated. If the evaluation is `true`, the loop body is executed again; if it is `false`, the do loop terminates. The major difference between a `while` loop and a `do` loop is the order in which the `continue-condition` is evaluated and the loop body is executed. The `while` loop and the `do` loop have equal expressive power. Sometimes it is more convenient to choose one over the other. For example, you can rewrite Example 3.4 as follows:

```
class TestDo
{
  public static void main(String[] args)
  {
    int data;
    int sum = 0;
```

```
      do
      {
        data = MyInput.readInt();
        sum += data;
      } while (data != 0);

      System.out.println("The sum is " + sum);
    }
  }
```

■■■ TIP

The do loop body is always executed at least once. I recommend the do loop if you have statements inside the loop that must be executed at least once, as in the case of the do loop in the preceding TestDo program. These statements must appear before the loop as well as inside the loop if you are using a while loop.

Using the Keywords *break* and *continue*

Two statements, break and continue, can be used in the loop constructs to provide the loop with additional control:

- **break**—This keyword immediately ends the innermost loop that contains it.

- **continue**—This keyword only ends the current iteration. Program control goes to the next iteration of the loop.

You have already used the keyword break in a switch statement. You can also use break and continue in any of the three kinds of loop constructs.

The diagrams in Figure 3.12 and Figure 3.13 help illustrate the work of break and continue in a loop statement.

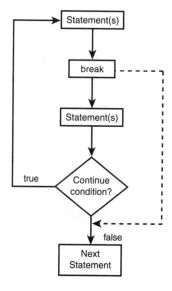

Figure 3.12 *The break statement forces its containing loop to exit.*

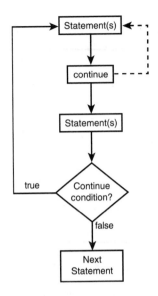

Figure 3.13 *The* `continue` *statement forces the current iteration of the loop to end.*

Example 3.5   Testing the *break* Statement

In this example, you will see how the `break` statement affects the results of the following program.

```java
class TestBreak
{
  public static void main(String[] args)
  {
    int sum = 0;
    int item = 0;

    do
    {
      item ++;
      sum += item;
      if (sum >= 6) break;
    } while (item < 5);

    System.out.println("The sum is " + sum);
  }
}
```

Example Review

Without the `if` statement, this program calculates the sum of the numbers from 1 to 5. But with the `if` statement, the loop terminates when the sum becomes greater than or equal to 6. The output of the program is shown in Figure 3.14.

Figure 3.14 *The* break *statement in the TestBreak program forces the* do *loop to exit when* sum *is greater than 6.*

If you changed the if statement to the following, the output would resemble that in Figure 3.15:

```
if (sum == 5) break;
```

Figure 3.15 *The* break *statement is not executed in the modified TestBreak program because* sum == 5 *cannot be* true.

In this case, the if condition would never be true. Therefore, the break statement would never be executed.

Example 3.6   Using the *continue* Statement

In this example, you will see the effect of the continue statement on a particular program.

```
class TestContinue
{
  public static void main(String[] args)
  {
    int sum = 0;
    int item = 0;

    do
    {
      item++;
      if (item == 2) continue;
      sum += item;
    } while (item < 5);

    System.out.println("The sum is " + sum);
  }
}
```

continues

Example 3.6   continued

Example Review

With the `if` statement in the program, the `continue` statement is executed when `item` becomes 2. The `continue` statement ends the current iteration so that the rest of the statement in the loop body is not executed; therefore, `item` is not added to `sum` when it is 2. The output of the program is shown in Figure 3.16.

Figure 3.16   *The* `continue` *statement in the* `TestContinue` *program forces the current iteration to end when* `item` *equals 2.*

Without the `if` statement in the program, the output would look like Figure 3.17.

Figure 3.17   *The modified* `TestContinue` *program has no* `continue` *statement; therefore, every item is added to* `sum`.

Without the `if` statement, all of the items are added to `sum`, including when `item` is 2. Therefore, the result is 15, which is two more than it was with the `if` statement.

 NOTE

You can always write a program without using `break` or `continue` in a loop. See the last item in the "Chapter Review" section at the end of this chapter.

Chapter Summary

You can use program control to specify the order in which statements should be executed in a program. In this chapter, you learned about two types of control structures: the decision control and the loop control.

The decision statements are for building decision steps into programs. You learned several forms of decision structures: `if` statements, `if...else` statements, nested `if` statements, `switch` statements, and shortcut `if` statements.

The various `if` statements all make control decisions based on a Boolean expression. Based on the `true` or `false` evaluation of that expression, these statements take one or two possible courses. The switch statements make control decisions based on a switch variable that can be of type char, byte, short, or int. The short-cut if statement is rarely used.

You learned three types of repetition statements: the for loop, the while loop, and the do loop. In designing loops, you need to consider both the loop control structure and the loop body.

The for loop is usually used to execute a loop body for a predictable number of times; this number is not determined by the loop body. The loop control has three parts. The first part is a control variable, which has an initial value. The second part is the continue-condition, which determines whether the loop body is to be executed. The third part is the adjustment statement, which changes the control variable. Usually, the loop control variables are initialized and changed in the control structure.

The while loop control structure contains the continue-condition, which is dependent on the loop body. Therefore, the number of repetitions is determined by the loop body. The while loop is often used for an unspecified number of repetitions.

The while loop checks the continue-condition first. If the condition is true, the loop body is executed; if it is false, the loop terminates. The do loop is similar to the while loop, except that the do loop executes the loop body first and then checks the continue-condition to decide whether to continue or to terminate.

You also learned the break and continue keywords. The break keyword immediately ends the innermost loop, which contains the break. The continue keyword only ends the current iteration.

Chapter Review

1. Show the output of the following code, if any:

```
x = 2;
y = 3;
if (x > 2)
  if (y > 2)
  {
    int z = x + y;
    System.out.println("z is " + z);
  }
else
  System.out.println("x is " + x);
```

2. Show the output of the following code, if any:

```
x = 3;
y = 2;
if (x > 2)
{
  if (y > 2)
  {
    int z = x + y;
    System.out.println("z is " + z);
```

```
      }
   }
   else
      System.out.println("x is " + x);
```

3. Can you convert a `switch` statement to an equivalent `if` statement, or vice versa?

4. What are the advantages of using the `switch` statement?

5. What data types are required for a switch variable? If the keyword `break` is not used after a case is processed, what is the next statement to be executed?

6. Use a `switch` statement to rewrite the following `if` statement:

```
if (a == 1)
   x += 5;
else if (a == 2)
   x += 10;
else if (a == 3)
   x += 16;
else if (a == 4)
   x += 34;
```

7. What are the three parts in a `for` loop control? Write a `for` loop that will print numbers from 1 to 100.

8. What does the following statement do?

```
for (;;)
{
   do something;
}
```

9. If a variable is declared in the `for` loop control, can the variable be used after the loop exits?

10. Can you convert a `for` loop to a `while` loop? List the advantages of using `for` loops.

11. Convert the following `for` loop statement to a `while` loop and to a `do` loop:

```
long sum = 0;
for (int i=0; i<= 1000; i++)
   sum = sum + i;
```

12. How many times is the following loop body repeated? What is the printout of the loop?

```
int i = 1;
while (i < 10)
   if ((i++)%2==0)
      System.out.println(i);
```

13. What are the differences between a `while` loop and a `do` loop?

14. What is the keyword `break` for? Will the following program terminate? If so, give the output.

```
int balance = 1000;
while (true)
{
   if (balance < 9)
```

```
      break;
    balance = balance - 9;
  }

  System.out.println("balance is " +balance);
```

15. What is the keyword `continue` for? Will the following program terminate? If so, give the output.

```
int balance = 1000;
while (true)
{
  if (balance < 9)
    continue;
  balance = balance - 9;
}

System.out.println("balance is " + balance);
```

16. Can you always convert a `while` loop into a `for` loop? Convert the following `while` loop into a `for` loop.

```
int i = 1;
int sum = 0;
while (sum < 10000)
{
  sum = sum + i;
  i++;
}
```

17. Rewrite the programs `TestBreak` and `TestContinue` without using `break` and `continue` (see Example 3.5 and Example 3.6).

Programming Exercises

1. Write a program that will read an integer and find out whether the integer is even or odd.

2. Write a program that will determine which of three integers is the largest. The integers are entered from the keyboard and stored in variables i1, i2, and i3, respectively. The program sorts the numbers so that i1 ≤ i2 ≤ i3.

3. Write a program that will compute sales commissions. The following scheme is used to determine the commission rate:

Sales Amount	Commission Rate
$1–$5,000	8 percent
$5,001–10,000	10 percent
10,001 and above	12 percent

Your program reads the sales amount from the keyboard and displays the result on the console.

4. Write a nested `for` loop that will print the following output:

```
1
1 2
1 2 3
1 2 3 4
1 2 3 4 5
```

5. Write a nested `for` loop that will print the following output:

```
                                1
                            1   2   1
                        1   2   4   2   1
                    1   2   4   8   4   2   1
                1   2   4   8  16   8   4   2   1
            1   2   4   8  16  32  16   8   4   2   1
        1   2   4   8  16  32  64  32  16   8   4   2   1
    1   2   4   8  16  32  64 128  64  32  16   8   4   2   1
```

6. Write a program that will check whether an input integer is a prime number. (An integer is a prime number if its only divisor is 1 or itself.)

7. Write a program that will read an unspecified number of integers and will determine how many positive and negative values have been read. Your program ends when the input is 0.

8. Write a program that will read doubles and will find the total and average of the input values. Your program ends with the input 0.

9. Use a `while` loop to find the smallest n such that n^2 is greater than 10,000.

10. Suppose that the sales commission rate is given, as in Exercise 3 earlier in this section. To get $30,000 in sales commissions, how much do you need to sell?

11. You can approximate π by using the following series:

$\pi = 4*(1-1/3+1/5-1/7+1/9-1/11+1/13+...)$

Write a program that will find out how many terms of this series you need to use before you get 3.14159.

METHODS

Objectives

- ⊚ Understand and use methods.
- ⊚ Create and invoke methods.
- ⊚ Understand the role of arguments in a method.
- ⊚ Use pass by value for primitive type parameters.
- ⊚ Understand method overloading.
- ⊚ Understand method abstraction and its use in developing software.
- ⊚ Become familiar with recursion.

Introduction

In Chapter 2, "Java Building Elements," and Chapter 3, "Control Structures," you learned about methods, such as `println()`, which is used to print messages, and `readDouble()` and `readInt()`, which are used to read `double` and `int` numbers, respectively. A method is a collection of statements that are grouped together to perform an operation. When you call the method `println()`, for example, the system actually executes several statements in order to display a message on the console.

This chapter introduces many topics that involve, or are related to, methods. You will learn how to create your own methods with or without return values, invoke a method with or without parameters, overload methods using the same names, write a recursive method that invokes itself, and apply method abstraction in the program design.

Creating a Method

In general, a method has the following structure:

```
modifier returnvaluetype methodName(list of parameters)
{
  //method body;
}
```

The method `readDouble()` was created in Chapter 2 to read an integer from the keyboard. Figure 4.1 illustrates the components of this method.

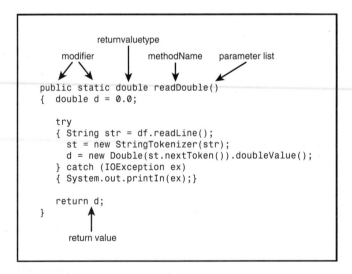

Figure 4.1 *The method* `readDouble()` *has a signature that consists of modifiers, return type, and the method name, which is followed by the method body block.*

The method heading specifies the *modifiers, returning value type, method name,* and the *parameters* of the method. The modifier, which can be optional, specifies the *property* of the method and tells the compiler how the method can be called.

Modifiers are discussed in more depth in Chapter 5, "Programming with Objects and Classes."

A method may return a value. The `returnvaluetype` is the data type of the value the method returns. If the method does not return a value, the `returnvaluetype` is the keyword `void`. For example, the `returnvaluetype` in the `main()` method is `void`. All methods except constructors require `returnvaluetype`. For a detailed discussion of constructors, see Chapter 5.

A method can have a list of parameters—*formal parameters*—in the method specification. When a method is called, these formal parameters are replaced by variables or data, which are referred to as *actual parameters*. Parameters are optional. The `readDouble()` method does not have any parameters, for example.

The method body contains a collection of statements that define what the method does. Let's take a look at a method created to find which of two integers is the largest. This method, named `max`, has two `int` parameters, `num1` and `num2`, the larger of which is returned by the method.

```
int max(int num1, int num2)
{
  if (num1 > num2)
    return num1;
  else
    return num2;
}
```

This method body simply uses an `if` statement to determine which number is larger and to return the value of that number. The keyword `return` is required for non-void methods. The return statement can also be used in a void method for simply terminating the method and returning to the method's caller. The method terminates when a `return` statement is executed.

NOTE
In some other languages, methods are referred to as *procedures* and *functions*. A method with a return value type is called a *function*; a method with a `void` return value type is called a *procedure*.

CAUTION
You need to declare a data type for each parameter separately. For instance, `int i, j` should be replaced by `int i, int j`.

Calling a Method

How do you know if a method works? You need to test it by calling it in a test program. There are two ways to call a method; the choice is based on whether the method returns a value or not.

If the method returns a value, a call to the method is usually treated as a value. For example,

```
int larger = max(3, 4);
```

calls `max(3, 4)` and assigns the result of the method to the variable `larger`. Another example of a call that is treated as a value is

```
System.out.println(max(3, 4));
```

which prints the return value of the method call `max(3, 4)`.

If the method returns `void`, a call to the method must be a statement. For example, the method `println()` returns `void`. The following call is a statement:

```
System.out.println("Welcome to Java!");
```

NOTE

A method with return value also can be invoked as a statement in Java. In this case, the return value is simply ignored by the caller. In the majority of the cases, a call to a method with return value is treated as a value. In some cases, however, the caller is not interested in the return value. For example, many methods in database applications return a Boolean value to indicate whether the operation is successful. You can choose to ignore the return value if you know the operation will always succeed. I, however, recommend that you always treat the call to a method with return value as a value to avoid programming errors.

When a program calls a method, program control is transferred to the called method. A called method returns control to the caller when its return statement is executed, or when its method-ending right brace is reached.

The following example gives the complete program that is used to test the `max()` method.

Example 4.1   Testing the *max()* Method

This example demonstrates how to create a test program for the `max()` method. The output of the program is shown in Figure 4.2.

```
class TestMax
{
  public static void main(String[] args)
  {
    int num1 = 5;
    int num2 = 2;
    int num3 = max(num1, num2);
    System.out.println("The maximum between " + num1 +
      " and " + num2 + " is " + num3);
  }

  static int max(int num1, int num2)
  {
    if (num1 > num2)
      return num1;
```

```
        else
            return num2;
    }
}
```

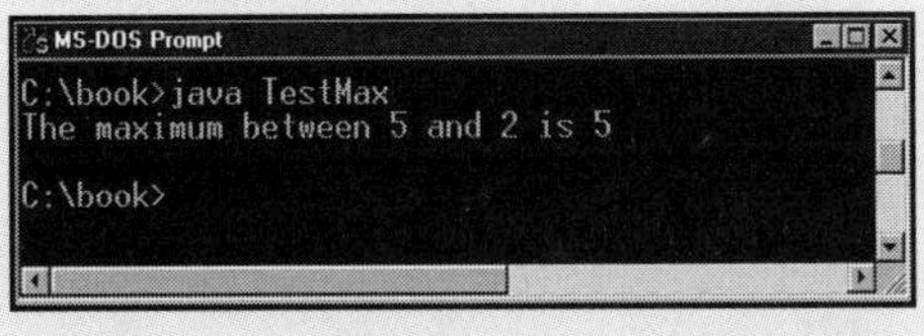

```
MS-DOS Prompt
C:\book>java TestMax
The maximum between 5 and 2 is 5

C:\book>
```

Figure 4.2 *The program invokes* max(5, 2) *in order to discover whether 5 or 2 is the maximum value.*

Example Review

This program contains the main() method and the max() method. The main() method is just like any other method, with one exception: It is invoked by the Java interpreter.

The main() method's heading is always the same, like the one in this example, with modifiers public and static, return type value void, method name main, and parameters String[] args. String[] indicates that args is an array of String, which is addressed in Chapter 6, "Arrays and Strings."

The statements in main() may invoke other methods that are defined in the class that contains the main() method or in other classes. In this example, the main() method invokes max(num1, num2), which is defined in the same class with main().

Passing Parameters

The power of a method is its ability to work with parameters. You can use println() to print any message and max() to find the maximum between any two numbers. When calling a method, you need to provide actual parameters, which must be given in the same order as their respective formal parameters in the method specification. This is known as *the parameter order association*. For example, the following method prints a message n times:

```
void nPrintln(String message, int n)
{
  for (int i=0; i<n;  i++)
    System.out.println(message);
}
```

You can use nPrintln("Hello", 3) to print Hello three times. The nPrintln ("Hello", 3) statement passes the actual string parameter, "Hello", to the formal parameter, message; passes 3 to n; and prints Hello three times. However, the statement nPrintln(3,"Hello") would be wrong. The data type of 3 does not match the data type for the first formal parameter, message, nor does the second parameter, "Hello", match the second formal parameter, n.

CAUTION
The actual parameters must match the formal parameters in type, order, and number.

Pass by Value

When invoking a method with a parameter of primitive data type, such as int, the copy of the value of the actual parameter is passed to the method. This is referred to as *pass by value*. The actual variable outside the method is not affected, regardless of the changes made to the formal parameter inside the method. Let's examine an interesting scenario in the following example, in which the formal parameter is changed inside the method, but the actual parameter is not affected.

Example 4.2   Testing Pass by Value

The following program shows the effect of passing by value. The output of the program is shown in Figure 4.3.

```java
class TestPassByValue
{
  public static void main(String[] args)
  {
    int times = 3;
    System.out.println("Before the call, variable times is "+times);
    nPrintln("Welcome to Java!", times);
    System.out.println("After the call, variable times is "+times);
  }

  static void nPrintln(String message, int n)
  {
    while (n > 0)
    {
      System.out.println("n = "+n);
      System.out.println(message);
      n--;
    }
  }
}
```

Example Review

A while loop with a changing formal parameter of n was used to rewrite the nPrintln() method in the previous section. The method nPrintln("Welcome to Java!", times) was then invoked. Before the call, the times variable was 3. Interestingly, after the call, the times variable is still 3. This is because n is a parameter of primitive data type. Java passes the value of times to n. The times variable itself is not affected, regardless of the changes made to n inside the method.

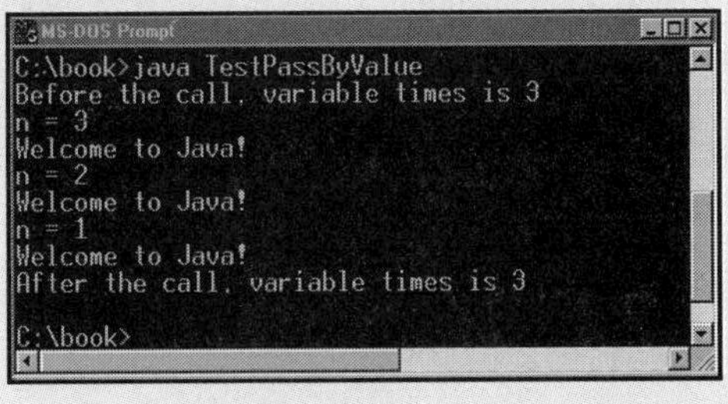

Figure 4.3 *The* times *variable is passed by value to the method* nPrintln(); *therefore,* times *is not changed by the method.*

Another twist is to change the formal parameter name n in nPrintln() to times. What is the consequence? No change occurs because it does not matter whether the formal parameter and the actual parameter have the same name. The formal parameter represents imaginary data, which does not exist until it is associated with an actual parameter.

See Chapter 5 to learn about another mechanism for passing objects: *pass by reference.*

Overloading Methods

The max() method that was used earlier works only with the int data type. But what if you need to find which of two floating-point numbers has the maximum value? The solution is to create another method with the same name but with different parameters, as shown in the following code:

```
double max(double num1, double num2)
{
  if (num1 > num2)
    return num1;
  else
    return num2;
}
```

If you call max() with int parameters, the max() method that expects int parameters will be invoked; if you call max() with double parameters, the max() method that expects double parameters will be invoked. This is referred to as *method overloading*; that is, two methods have the same name, but have different parameter profiles. Java compiler is able to determine which method to invoke based on the number and types of parameters passed to that method.

Example 4.3   Overloading the *max()* Method

In the following program, two methods are created. One method finds the maximum integer; the other finds the maximum double. Both methods are named max(). The output of the program is shown in Figure 4.4.

```java
class TestMethodOverloading
{
  public static void main(String[] args)
  {
    System.out.println("The maximum between 3 and 4 is "
      + max(3, 4));
    System.out.println("The maximum between 3.0 and 5.4 is "
      + max(3.0, 5.4));
  }

  static double max(double num1, double num2)
  {
    if (num1 > num2)
      return num1;
    else
      return num2;
  }

  static int max(int num1, int num2)
  {
    if (num1 > num2)
      return num1;
    else
      return num2;
  }
}
```

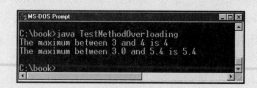

Figure 4.4. *The program invokes two different* max() *methods—*max(3, 4) *and* max(3.0, 5.4)*—even though both have the same name.*

Example Review

Two max() methods were created in the same class with different types of parameters—one for finding maximum integers and the other for finding maximum doubles.

When calling max(3.0, 5.4), the max() method for finding maximum doubles is invoked. When calling max(3, 4), the max() method for finding maximum integers is invoked.

TIP

Overloading methods can make programs clear and more readable. Methods that perform closely related tasks should be given the same name.

Creating Methods in Separate Classes

Thus far in this chapter, methods in the examples have been placed in the same class as that in which they were invoked. You can create methods in separate classes so that they can be used by other classes.

Example 4.4   Computing a Square Root

In this example, you can see how a program that computes a square root is written. The square root of a number, num, can be approximated by repeatedly performing a calculation using the following formula:

```
nextGuess = (lastGuess + (num / lastGuess))/2
```

When nextGuess and lastGuess are almost identical, nextGuess is the approximated square root.

The initial guess will be the starting value of lastGuess. If the difference between nextGuess and lastGuess is less than a very small number, such as 0.001, you can claim that nextGuess is the approximated square root of num. The sample output of the following program is shown in Figure 4.5.

```
class TestSquareRoot
{
  public static void main(String[] args)
  {
    System.out.println(
      "The square root for 9 is "+SquareRoot.sqrt(9.0));
    System.out.println(
      "The square root for 2000 is "+SquareRoot.sqrt(2000.0));
  }
}

//This class contains sqrt() method
class SquareRoot
{
  public static double sqrt(double num)
  {
    double nextGuess;
    double lastGuess = 1.0;
    double difference;
    do
    {
      nextGuess = (lastGuess + (num/lastGuess))*0.5;
      difference = nextGuess - lastGuess;
```

continues

85

Example 4.4   continued

```
        lastGuess = nextGuess;
        if (difference < 0)
          difference = -difference;
      } while (difference >= 0.001);

      return nextGuess;
    }
  }
```

Figure 4.5 *The program invokes the* `sqrt()` *method in order to compute the square root.*

Example Review

The `sqrt()` method is defined in the `SquareRoot` class. To invoke `sqrt()`, put the class name `SquareRoot` in front of the `sqrt()`.

The `sqrt()` method implements the approximation algorithm for finding the square root. In this case, the constant 0.001 is often referred to as error tolerance. The smaller the difference, the better the approximation.

Method Abstraction

The key to developing software is to apply the concept of abstraction. *Method abstraction* is defined as separating the use of a method from the implementation of that method. This is referred to as *information hiding*. The client can use a method without knowing how that method is implemented. If you decide to change the implementation, the client program will not be affected.

When writing a large program, you should use the "divide and conquer" strategy to decompose a problem into more manageable sub-programs. You can apply method abstraction to make programs easy to manage. See the following example, which demonstrates method abstraction in software development.

Example 4.5   Illustrating Method Abstraction in Developing a Large Project

In this example, a program is created that displays the calendar for a given month of the year. The program prompts the user to enter the year and the month and then displays the entire calendar for the month, as shown in Figure 4.6.

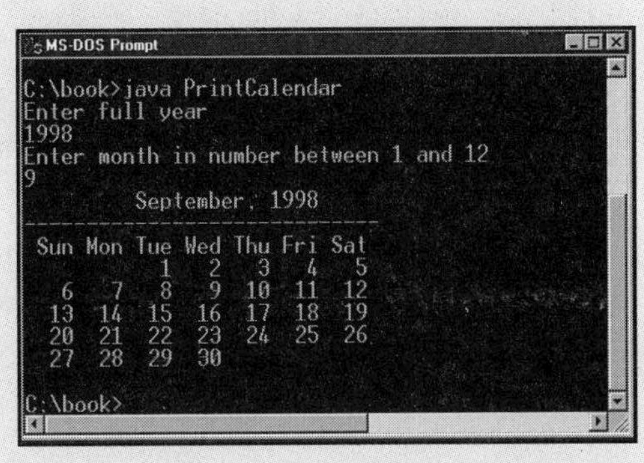

MS-DOS Prompt
C:\book>java PrintCalendar
Enter full year
1998
Enter month in number between 1 and 12
9
September, 1998
Sun Mon Tue Wed Thu Fri Sat
1 2 3 4 5
6 7 8 9 10 11 12
13 14 15 16 17 18 19
20 21 22 23 24 25 26
27 28 29 30
C:\book>

Figure 4.6. *After prompting the user to enter the year and the month, the program displays the calendar for that month.*

How would you get started on such a program? Would you start coding immediately? Beginning programmers often start by trying to work out the solution to every detail. Although details are important in the final program, concern for detail at the early stages could block the problem-solving process. To make problem solving flow as smoothly as possible, this example uses method abstraction to isolate details from design first and implements details later.

For this example, the problem is first broken into two sub-problems: get input from the user and print the monthly calendar. At this stage, the creator of such a program should be concerned with what the sub-problems will achieve but not with the ways in which the sub-problems would get input and print the calendar for the month. Notice the structure chart, which is used to help you visualize those sub-problems (see Figure 4.7).

printCalendar
(main)
readInput
printMonth

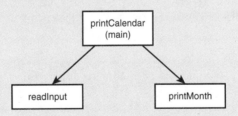

Figure 4.7 *The structure chart shows that the* `printCalendar` *problem is divided into two sub-problems:* `readInput` *and* `printMonth`.

You may use `System.out.println()` to display a message to prompt the user for the year and the month. Then, `MyInput.readInt()` can be used to get the input.

In order to print the calendar for a month, you would need to know the day for the first date in the month and the number of days in that month. With that information, you could print the title and the body of the calendar. Therefore, the print

continues

Example 4.5 continued

month problem would be further decomposed into four sub-problems: get the start day, get the number of days in a month, print title, and print month body.

How would you get the start day for the first date in a month? There are several ways to find the start day. The simplest approach is to use the `Date` and `Calendar` classes in Chapter 7, "Class Inheritance." For now, an alternative approach is used. Assume that you know that the start day (`startDay1800 = 3`) for Jan 1, 1800 is Wednesday. You could compute the total number of days (`totalNumOfDays`) between Jan 1, 1800, and the first date of the calendar month. The start day for the calendar month is (`totalNumOfDays + startDay1800) % 7`.

To compute the total days (`totalNumOfDays`) between Jan 1, 1800, and the first date of the calendar month, you could find the total number of days between the year 1800 and the calendar year and then figure out the total number of days prior to the calendar in the calendar year. The sum of these two totals is `totalNumOfDays`.

You would also need to know the number of days in a month and in a year. Remember the following:

- January, March, May, July, August, October, and December have 31 days.

- April, June, September, and November have 30 days.

- February has 28 days during a regular year and 29 days during a leap year. A regular year, therefore, contains 365 days, while a leap year contains 366 days.

To determine whether a year is a leap year, you could use the following condition:

```
if ((year % 400 == 0) || ((year % 4 == 0) && (year % 100 != 0)))
   return true;
else
   return false;
```

To print a title, you could use `println()` to display three lines, as shown in Figure 4.8.

Figure 4.8 *The calendar title consists of three lines: month and year, a dash line, and the names of the seven days of the week.*

To print a body, you would first pad some space before the start day and then print the lines for every week, as shown for September 1998 (refer to Figure 4.6).

In general, a sub-problem corresponds to a method in the implementation, although some are so simple that this is unnecessary. You would need to decide which modules should be implemented as methods and which could be combined in other methods. You should base these kinds of decisions on whether the overall program would be easier to read as a result of your choice. In this example, the sub-problem `readInput` was implemented in the `main()` method (see Figure 4.9).

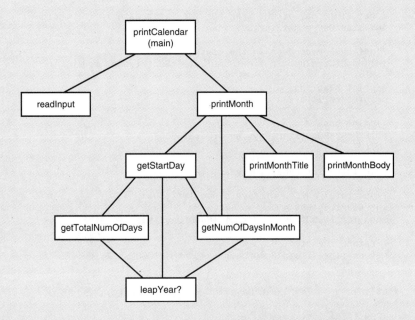

Figure 4.9 *The structure chart shows the hierarchical relationship of the sub-problems in the program.*

When implementing the program, you should use the "top-down" approach. In other words, you can implement one method in the structure chart at a time—from the top to the bottom. You could use stubs for the methods waiting to be implemented. You would implement the `main()` method first and then use a stub for the `printMonth()` method. For example, you could simply let `printMonth()` display the year and the month in the stub.

The sample run of the following program is shown in Figure 4.6.

```
class PrintCalendar
{
  public static void main(String[] args)
  {
    //the user enters year and month
    System.out.println("Enter full year");
    int year = MyInput.readInt();
    System.out.println("Enter month in number between 1 and 12");
    int month = MyInput.readInt();
```

continues

Example 4.5   continued

```java
      //print calendar for the month of the year
      printMonth(year, month);
    }

    static void printMonth(int year, int month)
    {
      //get start day of the week for the first date in the month
      int startDay = getStartDay(year, month);

      //get number of days in the month
      int numOfDaysInMonth = getNumOfDaysInMonth(year, month);

      //print headings
      printMonthTitle(year, month);

      //print body
      printMonthBody(startDay, numOfDaysInMonth);
    }

    static int getStartDay(int year, int month)
    {
      //get total number of days since 1/1/1800
      int startDay1800 = 3;
      long totalNumOfDays = getTotalNumOfDays(year, month);

      //return the start day
      return (int)((totalNumOfDays + startDay1800) % 7);
    }

    static long getTotalNumOfDays(int year, int month)
    {
      long total = 0;

      //get the total days from 1800 to year -1
      for (int i = 1800; i < year; i++)
      if (leapYear(i))
        total = total + 366;
      else
        total = total + 365;

      //add days from Jan to the month prior to the calendar month
      for (int i = 1; i < month; i++)
        total = total + getNumOfDaysInMonth(year, i);

      return total;
    }

    static int getNumOfDaysInMonth(int year, int month)
    {
      if (month == 1 || month==3 || month == 5 || month == 7 ||
        month == 8 || month == 10 || month == 12)
        return 31;

      if (month == 4 || month == 6 || month == 9 || month == 11)
        return 30;

      if (month == 2)
        if (leapYear(year))
          return 29;
        else
          return 28;
```

```java
      return 0; //if month is incorrect.
  }

  static boolean leapYear(int year)
  {
    if ((year % 400 == 0) || ((year % 4 == 0) && (year % 100 != 0)))
      return true;

    return false;
  }

  static void printMonthBody(int startDay, int numOfDaysInMonth)
  {
    //print padding space before the first day of the month
    int i = 0;
    for (i = 0; i < startDay; i++)
      System.out.print("    ");

    for (i = 1; i <= numOfDaysInMonth; i++)
    {
      if (i < 10)
        System.out.print("  "+i);
      else
        System.out.print("  "+i);

      if ((i + startDay) % 7 == 0)
        System.out.println();
    }

    System.out.println();
  }

  static void printMonthTitle(int year, int month)
  {
    System.out.println("          "+getMonthName(month)+", "+year);
    System.out.println("---------------------------");
    System.out.println(" Sun Mon Tue Wed Thu Fri Sat");
  }

  static String getMonthName(int month)
  {
    String monthName = null;
    switch (month)
    {
      case 1: monthName = "January"; break;
      case 2: monthName = "February"; break;
      case 3: monthName = "March"; break;
      case 4: monthName = "April"; break;
      case 5: monthName = "May"; break;
      case 6: monthName = "June"; break;
      case 7: monthName = "July"; break;
      case 8: monthName = "August"; break;
      case 9: monthName = "September"; break;
      case 10: monthName = "October"; break;
      case 11: monthName = "November"; break;
      case 12: monthName = "December";
    }

    return monthName;
  }
}
```

continues

Example 4.5   continued

Example Review

The program does not validate user input. For instance, if the user entered a month not in the range between 1 and 12, or a year before 1800, the program would display an erroneous calendar. To avoid this error, you can simply add an `if` statement to check the input before printing the calendar.

This program can print calendars for a month. It could be easily modified to print calendars for a whole year. This program can only print months after January 1800. You could modify the program so that it could trace the day of a month before 1800.

See Chapter 7 to find out how to simplify the program using the `Date` and `Calendar` classes.

NOTE

Method abstraction helps modularize programs in a neat, hierarchical manner. Programs should be written as collections of concise methods so that they are easier to write, debug, maintain, and modify than they would otherwise be. This writing style also promotes method reusability.

TIP

When implementing a large program, use the top-down coding approach. Start with the main method and code and test one method at a time. Do not write the entire program at once. This approach seems to take more time in coding (because you are compiling and running a program repeatedly), but it actually saves time and makes debugging easier.

Debugging

Now turn your attention to *debugging*. Debugging is finding errors—*bugs*—in a program and correcting them. You have learned that programming errors can be separated into syntax errors, runtime errors, and logical errors. Syntax errors are detected and reported by the compiler. Runtime errors that cause the program to abort are reported by the Java runtime system. In general, they are easy to locate and to fix. Therefore, this section focuses on the more difficult problem, the runtime error.

Logical errors can result in incorrect output or cause a program to terminate unexpectedly. To find logical errors, you can *hand trace* the program (that is, catch errors by reading the program), or insert print statements in order to show the values of the variables or the execution flow of the program. This approach might work for a short, simple program. But for a large, complex program—such as the print calendar program in the previous section—the most effective approach for debugging is using a debugger utility.

JDK includes a command-line debugger (jdb), which is invoked with a class name. Jdb is itself a Java program, running its own copy of Java interpreter. All the Java IDE tools include integrated debuggers. The debugger utilities let you follow the execution of a program. They vary from one system to another, but they all support most of the following helpful features:

- **Executing a single statement at a time**—The debugger allows you to execute one statement at a time so that you can see the effect of each statement.

- **Tracing into or stepping over a method**—If a method is being executed, you can ask the debugger to enter the method and execute one statement at a time in the method, or you can ask it to step over the entire method. You should step over the entire method if you know the method works. For example, you should always step over the system-supplied methods, such as `System.out.println()`.

- **Setting breakpoints**—You can also set a breakpoint at a specific statement. Your program pauses when it reaches a breakpoint, and the line with the breakpoint is displayed. You can set as many breakpoints as you want. Breakpoints are particularly useful when you know where your programming error starts. You can set a breakpoint at that line and have the program execute until it reaches the breakpoint.

- **Displaying variables**—The debugger lets you select several variables and display their values. As you trace through a program, the content of a variable is continuously updated.

- **Using call stacks**—The debugger lets you trace all of the method calls, and it lists all pending methods. This feature is helpful when you need to see a large picture of the program execution flow.

- **Modifying variables**—Some debuggers enable you to modify the value of a variable when debugging. This is convenient when you want to test a program with different samples but do not want to leave the debugger.

TIP

The debugger is an indispensable, powerful tool that boosts your programming productivity. It could take some time to become familiar with it, but your investment will pay off in the long run.

Recursion

You have seen a method calling another method—that is, a statement contained in the method body calling another method. Can a method call itself? And what happens if it does? This section examines these questions and uses two classic examples to demonstrate recursive programming.

Recursion—a powerful mathematical concept—is the process of a method calling itself, directly or indirectly. In some cases, using it enables you to give a natural, straightforward, simple solution to a program that would otherwise be difficult to solve. Consider the well-known Fibonacci series problem. The Fibonacci series begins with two 1s in succession (1, 1, 2, 3, 5, 8, 13, 21, 34, and so on); each subsequent number is the sum of the previous two numbers in the series. The series can be recursively defined as follows:

```
fib(1) = 1;
fib(2) = 1;
fib(n) = fib(n-2) + fib(n-1); n > 2
```

The Fibonacci series was originally introduced by Leonardo Fibonacci, a medieval mathematician, to model the growth of the rabbit population. It can be applied in numeric optimization and in various other areas.

How do you find fib(n) for a given n? It is easy to find fib(3) because you know fib(1) and fib(2). Assuming that you know fib(n-2) and fib(n-1), fib(n) can be obtained immediately. Thus, the problem of computing fib(n) is reduced to computing fib(n-2) and fib(n-1). When computing fib(n-2) and fib(n-1), you can apply the idea recursively until n is reduced to 1 or 2.

If you call the method with n=1 or n=2, the method immediately returns the result. The method knows how to solve the simplest case, which is referred to as the *base case* or the *stopping condition*. If you call the method with n>2, the method divides the problem into two sub-problems of the same nature. The sub-problem is essentially the same as the original problem, but is slightly simpler or smaller than the original. Because the sub-problem has the same property as the original, you can call the method with a different actual parameter, which is referred to as a *recursive call*.

The recursive algorithm for computing fib(n) can be simply described as follows:

```
if ((n==1) || (n==2))
   return 1;
else
   return fib(n-1)+fib(n-2);
```

The recursive call can result in many more recursive calls as the method is dividing a sub-problem into new sub-problems. For a recursive method to terminate, the problem eventually must be reduced to a stopping case. When it reaches a stopping case, the method returns a result to its caller. The caller then performs some computation and returns the result to its own caller. This process continues until the result is passed back to the original caller. The original problem can now be solved immediately by adding the results of the two sub-problems.

Example 4.6   Computing Fibonacci Numbers

In this example, a recursive method is written for computing a Fibonacci number fib(n), given index n. The test program prompts the user to enter the index n, then calls the method and displays the result.

A sample run of the following program is shown in Figure 4.10.

```java
public class TestFibonacci
{
  public static void main(String args[])
  {
    //read index n
    System.out.println("Enter an index for the Fibonacci number");
    int n = MyInput.readInt();
    System.out.println("Fibonacci number at index "+n+" is
"+fib(n));
  }

  public static long fib(long n)
  {
    if ((n==0)||(n==1))  //stopping condition
      return 1;
    else  //reduction and recursive calls
      return fib(n-1) + fib(n-2);
  }
}
```

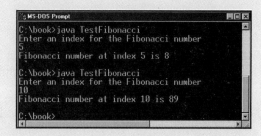

Figure 4.10 *The program prompts the user to enter an index for the Fibonacci number and then displays the number at that index.*

Example Review

The implementation of the method is, in fact, very simple and straightforward. The solution is slightly more difficult if you do not use recursion. For a hint on computing Fibonacci numbers using iterations, see Exercise 8 of the "Programming Exercises" section at the end of this chapter.

Much work is done behind the scenes by the computer, which is not shown in the program. Figure 4.11 shows successive recursive calls for evaluating fib(5). The original method, fib(5), makes two recursive calls—fib(4) and fib(3)—and then returns fib(4)+fib(3). But in which order are these methods called? In Java, the operands are simply evaluated from left to right. In Figure 4.11, the upper-left corner labels show the order in which methods are called.

As shown in Figure 4.11, there are many duplicated recursive calls. For instance, fib(3) is called two times, fib(2) is called three times, and fib(1) is called two

continues

Example 4.6   continued

times. In general, computing `fib(n)` requires twice as many recursive calls as you need for computing `fib(n-1)`. As you try larger index values, the number of calls substantially increases.

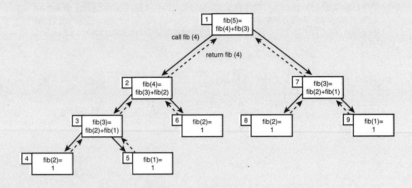

Figure 4.11 *Invoking* `fib(5)` *spawns recursive calls to* `fib()`.

Besides the large number of recursive calls, the computer requires more time and space to run recursive methods. See Exercise 8 in the "Programming Exercises" section at the end of this chapter for a more efficient method.

Each time a method is invoked, the system stores parameters, local variables, and system registers into a certain kind of space—a *stack*. When a method calls another method, the caller's stack space is kept intact, and new space is created for handling the new method call. When a method finishes its work and returns to its caller, its associated space is released. The use of stack space for recursive calls is shown in Figure 4.12.

NOTE

All of the recursive methods have the following common characteristics:

- One or more base cases (the simplest case) are used to stop recursion.

- Every recursive call reduces the original problem, bringing it increasingly close to a base case until it becomes that case.

CAUTION

Infinite recursion can occur if recursion does not reduce the problem in a manner that allows that problem to eventually converge into the base case.

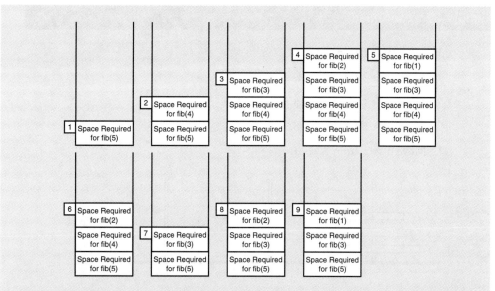

Figure 4.12 *When* `fib(5)` *is being executed,* `fib()` *is called recursively, causing memory space to dynamically change.*

You have seen a recursive method with a return value. Following is an example of a recursive method with a return type of `void`.

Example 4.7   Solving the Towers of Hanoi Problem

This example finds a solution for the Towers of Hanoi problem. This problem involves moving a specified number of disks of a distinct size from one tower to another while observing the following rules:

- There are *n* disks labeled 1, 2, 3, ...,*n*, and three towers labeled A, B, and C.

- No disk can be on top of a smaller disk at any time.

- Initially, all disks are placed on tower A.

- Only one disk can be moved at a time, and this disk must be the top disk of a tower.

The objective of this problem is to move all disks from A to B with the assistance of C. For example, if you have three disks, as shown in Figure 4.13, the following steps will move all of the disks from A to B:

1. Move disk 1 from A to B.

2. Move disk 2 from A to C.

continues

Example 4.7   continued

3. Move disk 1 from B to C.

4. Move disk 3 from A to B.

5. Move disk 1 from C to A.

6. Move disk 2 from C to B.

7. Move disk 1 from A to B.

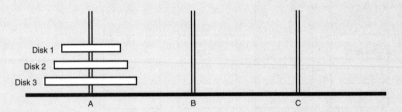

Figure 4.13 *The goal of the Towers of Hanoi problem is to move disks from tower A to tower B without breaking the rules.*

In the case of three disks, you could find the previous solution manually. However, the problem is quite complex for a large number of disks—even for four. Fortunately, the problem has an inherently recursive nature, which leads to a straightforward recursive solution.

The base case for the problem is n=1. If n=1, you could simply move the disk from A to B. When n>1, you could split the original problem into the following three sub-problems and solve them sequentially:

1. Move the first n-1 disks from A to C with the assistance of tower B.

2. Move disk n from A to B.

3. Move n-1 disks from C to B with the assistance of tower A.

The following method moves *n* disks from the fromTower to the toTower with the assistance of the auxTower:

```
void moveDisks(int n, char fromTower, char toTower, char auxTower)
```

The algorithm for the method can be described as follows:

```
if (n==1) //stopping condition
  Move disk 1 from the fromTower to the toTower;
else
{
  moveDisks(n-1, fromTower, auxTower, toTower);
```

```
        Move disk n from the fromTower to the toTower;
        moveDisks(n-1, auxTower, toTower, fromTower);
    }
```

The sample run of the following program appears in Figure 4.14.

```
public class TowersOfHanoi
{
    public static void main(String[] args)
    {
        //read number of disks, n
        System.out.println("Enter number of disks");
        int n = MyInput.readInt();
        System.out.println("The moves are:");
        moveDisks(n, 'A', 'B', 'C');
    }

    public static void moveDisks(int n, char fromTower,
        char toTower, char auxTower)
    {
        if (n==1) //stopping condition
          System.out.println("Move disk "+n+" from "+
            fromTower+" to "+toTower);
        else
        {
          moveDisks(n-1, fromTower, auxTower, toTower);
          System.out.println("Move disk "+n+" from "+
            fromTower+" to "+toTower);
          moveDisks(n-1, auxTower, toTower, fromTower);
        }
    }
}
```

Example Review

This problem is inherently recursive. Using recursion enables a natural, simple solution to be found for this problem. It would be difficult to solve this problem without using recursion.

Consider tracing the program for n=3. The successive recursive calls are shown in Figure 4.15. As you can see, writing the program is easier than tracing the recursive calls. The system uses stacks to trace the calls behind the scenes. To some extent, recursion provides a level of abstraction that hides iterations and other details from the user.

The fib() method in the previous example returns a value to its caller, but the moveDisks() method in this example does not return any value to its caller.

continues

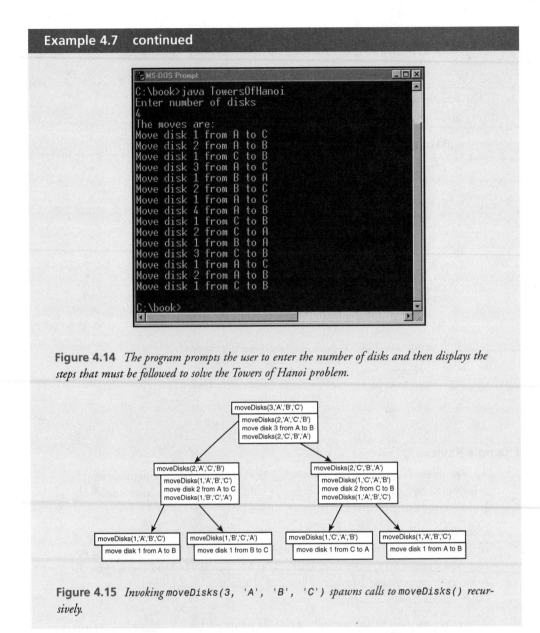

Figure 4.14 *The program prompts the user to enter the number of disks and then displays the steps that must be followed to solve the Towers of Hanoi problem.*

Figure 4.15 *Invoking* moveDisks(3, 'A', 'B', 'C') *spawns calls to* moveDisks() *recursively.*

Recursion Versus Iteration

Recursion is an alternative form of program control. It is essentially repetition without a loop control. When you use loops, you specify a loop body. The repetition of the loop body is controlled by the loop control structure. In recursion, the method itself is called repeatedly. The successive recursive calls are handled behind the scenes by the system. There is always a decision structure to control the repetition.

Recursion bears substantial overhead. Each time the program calls a method, the system must assign space for all of the local variables and parameters of the method. This can consume considerable memory, and it requires extra time to manage the additional space.

Any problem that can be solved recursively can be solved non-recursively with iterations. Recursion has many negative aspects—it uses up too much time and too much memory. Why should you ever use it? In some cases, using recursion enables you to specify a clear, simple solution that is otherwise difficult to obtain.

You should decide whether to use recursion or iteration based on the nature of the problem you are trying to solve and your understanding of that problem. The rule of thumb is to use recursion or iteration to develop an intuitive solution that naturally mirrors the problem. If an iterative solution is obvious, use it. It will generally be more efficient than the recursive option.

TIP

If you are concerned about the performance of your program, avoid using recursion because it takes more time and consumes more memory than iteration.

CAUTION

Your recursive program could run out of memory, causing a runtime error. In Chapter 11, "Exception Handling," you learn how to handle errors so the program terminates gracefully when there is a stack overflow.

Chapter Summary

One of the central goals in software engineering is to make programs modular and reusable. Java provides many constructs to achieve this goal. The method is one such powerful construct.

In this chapter, you have learned to write reusable methods. You now know how to create a method with a method specification, the interface that specifies how the method can be used; and a method body, which defines what the method does.

You have also learned how to call a method by passing actual parameters that replace the formal parameters in the method specification. The arguments that are passed to a method should have the same number, type, and order as the parameters in the method definition. Outside of the method, the actual values of the primitive parameters—which are passed by the value—are not affected by the method call.

In addition, you learned that a method can be overloaded. For example, two methods can have the same name as long as their method parameter profiles differ.

You are now familiar with the "divide and conquer" strategy. The best way to develop and maintain a large program is to divide it into several sub-problems, each of which is more manageable than the original problem. Sub-problems are written in Java as classes and methods.

You learned the techniques needed to write recursive methods. Recursion is an alternative form of program control. Recursion can be used to specify simple and clear solutions for some inherently recursive problems that would otherwise be difficult to solve.

Chapter Review

1. What is the purpose of using a method? How do you declare a method? How do you invoke a method?

2. What is a return value of a main() method?

3. What would be wrong if you did not write a return statement in a non-void method? Can you have a return statement in a void method, such as the following?

```java
public static void main(String[] args)
{
  int i;
  while (true)
  {
    i - MyInput.readInt();
    if (i == 0) return;
    System.out.println("i = "+i);1
  }
}
```

4. What is method overloading? Can you define two methods that have the same name but different parameter types? Can you define two methods in a class that have identical method names and parameter profiles with different return value types or different modifiers?

5. How do you pass actual parameters to a method? Can the actual parameter have the same name as its formal parameter?

6. What is "pass by value"? Show the result of the following method call:

```java
class Test
{
  public static void main(String[] args)
  {
    int max = 0;
    max(1, 2, max);
    System.out.println(max);
  }

  public static void max(int value1, int value2, int max)
  {
    if (value1 > value2)
      max = value1;
    else
      max = value2;
  }
}
```

7. A call for the method with a void return type is always a statement itself, but a call for the method with a non-void return type is always a component of an expression. Is the statement true or false?

8. In many other languages, you can define methods inside a method. Can you define a method inside a method in Java?

9. For each of the following, decide whether a void method or a non-void method is the most appropriate implementation:

   ■ Computing a sales commission given the sales amount and the commission rate.

   ■ Printing a calendar for a month.

   ■ Computing a square root.

   ■ Testing whether a number is even and returning true if it is.

   ■ Printing a message for a specified number of times.

10. Describe common debugging commands—executing a single statement, stepping over a method, setting breakpoints, displaying variables, displaying call stacks, and modifying variables.

11. What is a recursive method?

12. Describe the characteristics of recursive methods.

13. Show the printout of the following program:

```java
class Test
{
  public static void main(String[] args)
  {
    int sum = xMethod(5);
    System.out.println("Sum is "+sum);
  }

  public static int xMethod(int n)
  {
    if (n==1)
      return 1;
    else
      return n + xMethod(n-1);
  }
}
```

Programming Exercises

1. Write a method to find the ceiling of a double value, and write a method to find its floor. The ceiling of a number *d* is the smallest integer greater than or equal to *d*. The floor of a number *d* is the largest integer less than or equal to *d*. For example, the ceiling of 5.4 is 6 and the floor of 5.4 is 5.

2. Write a method to compute the sum of the digits in an integer. Use the following method declaration:

   ```java
   public static int sumDigits(long n)
   ```

   For example, sumDigits(234) returns 2+3+4=9.

3. Write a method to compute future investment value at a given interest rate for a specified number of years. The future investment is determined using the following formula:

```
futureInvestmentValue = investmentAmount x (1 + interestRate)^years
```

Use the flowing method declaration:

```
public static double futureInvestmentValue(double
    investmentAmount, double interestRate, int years)
```

For example, `futureInvestmentValue(10000, 0.05, 5)` returns 12762.82.

4. Write a method to convert Celsius to Fahrenheit using the following declaration:

```
public static double celsToFahr(double cels)
```

Write a program that uses a `for` loop and calls the `celsToFahr` method in order to result in the following output:

```
Cels. Temp.      Fahr. Temp.
.............................
40.00            104.00
39.00            102.20
38.00            100.40
37.00            98.60
36.00            96.80
35.00            95.00
34.00            93.20
33.00            91.40
32.00            89.60
31.00            87.80
```

5. Write a program to print the following table using the `sqrt()` method from Example 4.4.

```
RealNumber        SquareRoot
.............................
0                 0.0000
2                 1.4142
4                 2.0000
6                 2.4495
8                 2.8284
10                3.1623
12                3.4641
14                3.7417
16                4.0000
18                4.2426
20                4.4721
```

6. Modify Example 4.5 with the following additional requirements:

- Enable the program to print a calendar for any year before or after 1800.

- Print a calendar for the whole year instead of just the month.

7. Write a recursive method that will compute factorials. The factorial of a natural number is defined as follows:

```
factorial(0) = 1;
factorial(n) = factorial(n-1)xn; for n>0
```

8. Write a nonrecursive method to compute Fibonacci numbers.

   Hint: To compute `fib(n)` without recursion, you need to obtain `fib(n-2)` and `fib(n-1)` first. Let `f1` and `f2` denote the two previous Fibonacci numbers. The current Fibonacci number would then be `f1+f2`. The algorithm can be described as follows:

   ```
   f1 = 0; //for fib(0)
   f2 = 1; //for fib(1)
   for (int i=1; i<=n; i++)
   {
     currentFib = f1+f2;
     f1 = f2;
     f2 = currentFib;
   }

   //after the loop, currentFib is fib(n)
   ```

9. Modify Example 4.7 so that the program finds the number of moves needed to move n disks from tower A to tower B.

10. Write a recursive method for the greatest common divisor (GCD). Given two positive integers, the GCD is the largest integer that divides them both. `GCD(m, n)` can be defined as follows:

    `GCD(m, n)` is n if n is less than or equal to m and n divides m.

    `GCD(m, n)` is `GCD(n, m)` if m is less than n.

    `GCD(m, n)` is `GCD(n, m%n)`, otherwise.

PART II

OBJECT-ORIENTED PROGRAMMING

You learned to write simple Java applications using primitive data types, control structures, and methods in Part I, "Fundamentals of Java Programming." These are the common features available in the conventional programming languages. Java is a class-centric, object-oriented programming language that uses abstraction, encapsulation, inheritance, and polymorphism to provide great flexibility, modularity, and reusability for developing software. You will learn how to define, extend, and work with classes in this Part.

CHAPTER 5

PROGRAMMING WITH OBJECTS AND CLASSES

Objectives

- Understand objects and classes and the relationship between them.
- Learn how to define a class and how to create an object of the class.
- Understand the roles of constructors and modifiers.
- Learn how to pass objects to methods.
- Understand instance and class variables.
- Understand instance and class methods.
- Understand the scope of variables.
- Learn how to use packages.
- Understand the organization of the Java API.
- Become familiar with the Math class.

Introduction

Programming in procedural languages—such as C, Pascal, BASIC, Ada, and COBOL—involves choosing data structures, designing algorithms, and translating algorithms into code.

Object-oriented languages, such as Java, combine the power of conventional languages with an added dimension, which provides such benefits as abstraction, encapsulation, reusability, and inheritance. The object-oriented programming (OOP) approach organizes programs in a way that models real-life objects. Programming in Java involves thinking in terms of objects; a Java program can be viewed as a collection of cooperating objects.

This chapter introduces the fundamentals of object-oriented programming: declaring classes, creating objects, manipulating objects, and making objects work together.

Objects and Classes

Object-oriented programming (OOP) involves programming using objects. *Object* is a broad term that stands for many things. For example, a student, a desk, a circle, and even a mortgage loan can all be viewed as objects. Certain properties define an object, and certain behaviors define what it does. Those properties are known as *data fields*, and the objects' behaviors are defined by *methods*. Figure 5.1 shows a diagram of an object with its data fields and methods.

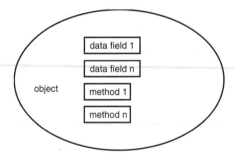

Figure 5.1 *An object contains data and methods.*

For example, a `Circle` object has a data field `radius`, which is the property that characterizes a circle. One behavior of a circle is that its area can be computed. A `Circle` object is shown in Figure 5.2.

Classes are structures that define objects. In a Java class, you can use data to describe properties and methods to define behaviors. A class for an object contains a collection of method and data definitions. The following is an example of the class for a circle:

```
class Circle
{
```

```
double radius = 1.0;

double findArea()
{
  return  radius*radius*3.14159;
}
}
```

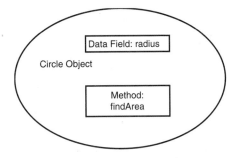

Figure 5.2 *A* Circle *object contains the* radius *data field and the* findArea *method.*

This class is different from all of the other classes you have seen thus far. The Circle class does not have a main() method, nor does it extend java.applet.Applet. Therefore, you cannot run this class; it is merely a definition that is used to declare and create Circle objects. For convenience, the class that contains the main() method will be referred to as the *main class* in this book.

Declaring and Creating Objects

A class is a blueprint that defines what an object's data and methods will be. An object is an instance of a class. You can create many instances of a class (see Figure 5.3). Creating an instance is referred to as *instantiation*. In order to declare an object, you must use a variable to represent that object (which is similar to declaring a variable for a primitive data type). The syntax for declaring an object is as follows:

```
ClassName objectName;
```

For example, the following statement declares the variable myCircle to be an instance of the Circle class:

```
Circle myCircle;
```

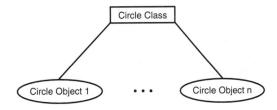

Figure 5.3 *A class can have many different objects.*

Creating an object of a class is called *creating an instance of the class*. An object is similar to a variable that has a class type. To create variables of a primitive data type, you would simply declare them, as is done in the following line:

```
int i;
```

This statement creates a variable and allocates memory space for i.

However, for object variables, declaring and creating are two separate steps. The declaration of an object simply associates the object with a class, making the object an instance of that class. The declaration does not create the object. To actually create myCircle, you would need to use the operator new in order to tell the computer to create an object for myCircle and to allocate memory space for it. The syntax for creating an object is as follows:

```
objectName = new ClassName();
```

For example, the following statement creates an object, myCircle, and allocates memory for it:

```
myCircle = new Circle();
```

You can combine the declaration and instantiation together in one statement by using the following syntax:

```
ClassName objectName = new ClassName();
```

The following is an example of creating and instantiating myCircle in one step:

```
Circle myCircle = new Circle();
```

After an object is created, it can access its data and methods by using the following dot notation:

objectName.data—References an object's data

objectName.method—References an object's method

For example, myCircle.radius indicates what the radius of myCircle is, and myCircle.findArea() returns the area of myCircle.

Example 5.1   Using Objects

The program in this example creates a Circle object from the Circle class and uses the data and method in the object. The output of the program is shown in Figure 5.4.

```
class TestCircle
{
  public static void main(String[] args)
  {
    Circle myCircle = new Circle();
```

```
        System.out.println("The area of the circle of radius "
          + myCircle.radius + " is " + myCircle.findArea());
    }
  }

  class Circle
  {
    double radius = 1.0;
    double findArea()
    {
      return radius*radius*3.14159;
    }
  }
```

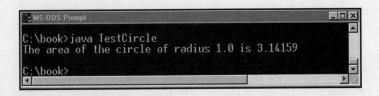

```
MS-DOS Prompt                                    _ □ X
C:\book>java TestCircle
The area of the circle of radius 1.0 is 3.14159

C:\book>
```

Figure 5.4 *This program creates a* Circle *object and displays its* radius *and* area.

Example Review

The program contains two classes. The first class, TestCircle, is the main class. Its sole purpose is to test the second class, Circle. Every time you run the program, the Java runtime system invokes its main() method in the main class.

The main class contains the main() method that creates an object of the Circle class and prints the circle's radius and area. The Circle object class contains the findArea() method and the radius data field.

NOTE

The creation of variables of primitive type is implied when those variables are declared. However, declaration and the creation of objects are separate tasks. The compiler allocates memory space for the variables of primitive type when they are declared, but does not allocate space for objects when those objects are declared.

CAUTION

You must always use the new operator to create an object before manipulating that object. Manipulating an object that has not been created would cause a runtime error.

NOTE

The default value of a data field is null for object type, 0 for numerical type, false for boolean type, and '\u0000' for char type. For example, if

continues

Example 5.1   continued

radius is not initialized in the `Circle` class, Java assigns a default value of `0` to radius. However, Java assigns no default value to a local variable inside a method. For example, the following code is erroneous because `x` is not defined:

```
class Test
{
  public static void main(String[] args)
  {
    int x;
    System.out.println("x is " + x);
  }
}
```

Constructors

One problem with the `Circle` class that was just discussed is that all of the objects created from it have the same radius (1.0). Wouldn't it be more useful to create circles with radii of various lengths? Java enables you to define a special method in the class—known as the *constructor*—that will initialize an object's data. You can use a constructor to assign an initial radius when you are creating an object.

The constructor has exactly the same name as the class it comes from. Constructors can be overloaded, making it easier to construct objects with different kinds of initial data values. Let's see what happens when the following constructors are added to the `Circle` class:

```
Circle(double r)
{
  radius = r;
}

Circle()
{
  radius = 1.0;
}
```

When creating a new `Circle` object that has a radius of 5.0, you can use the following, which assigns 5.0 to `myCircle.radius`:

```
myCircle = new Circle(5.0);
```

If you create a circle using the following statement, the second constructor is used, which assigns the default radius 1.0 to `myCircle.radius`:

```
myCircle = new Circle();
```

NOTE

Constructors are special methods that do not require a return type—not even void.

Now you know why the object is created using the syntax `ClassName()`. This syntax is used to call a constructor. If the class has no constructors, a default constructor is used, which will not initialize your object's data. If you don't use constructors, all of your objects will be the same.

Example 5.2   Using Constructors

In this example, a program is written that will use constructors in the `Circle` class to create two different objects. The output of the program is shown in Figure 5.5.

```java
class TestCircleWithConstructors
{
  public static void main(String[] args)
  {
    //Test Circle with radius 5.0
    Circle myCircle = new Circle(5.0);
    System.out.println("The area of the circle of radius "
      + myCircle.radius + " is " + myCircle.findArea());

    //Test Circle with default radius
    Circle yourCircle = new Circle();
    System.out.println("The area of the circle of radius "
      + yourCircle.radius + " is " + yourCircle.findArea());
  }
}

class Circle
{
  double radius;

  Circle(double r)
  {
    radius = r;
  }

  Circle()
  {
    radius = 1.0;
  }

  double findArea()
  {
    return radius*radius*3.14159;
  }
}
```

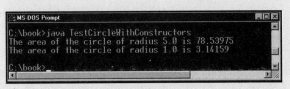

Figure 5.5 *The program constructs* `circle` *objects of radii 5 and 1 and displays their radii and areas.*

continues

Example 5.2   continued

Example Review

The Circle class has two constructors. You can specify a radius or use the default radius to create a Circle object. In this example, two objects were created. The constructor Circle(5.0) was used to create myCircle with a radius of 5.0. And the constructor Circle() was used to create yourCircle with a default radius of 1.0.

These two objects (myCircle and yourCircle) have different data but share the same methods. Therefore, you can compute their respective areas by using the findArea() method.

Modifiers

Java provides modifiers to control access to data, methods, and classes. The following are frequently used modifiers:

- **static**—Defines data and methods. It represents class-wide information that is shared by all instances of the class. It is discussed in more detail in the sections "Instance Variables and Class Variables" and "Instance Methods and Class Methods," later in this chapter.

- **public**—Defines classes, methods, and data in such a way that all programs can access them.

- **private**—Defines methods and data in such a way that they can be accessed by the declaring class, but not by the subclasses.

NOTE

The modifiers static and private apply solely to variables or to methods. If public or private is not used, by default, the classes, methods, and data are accessible by any class in the same package.

CAUTION

The variables associated with modifiers are the members of the class, not local variables inside the methods. Using modifiers inside a method body would cause a compilation error.

More modifiers are described in Chapter 7, "Class Inheritance." Appendix D, "Java Modifiers," contains a table that summarizes all Java modifiers.

Example 5.3   Using the *private* Modifier

In this example, private data is used for the radius to prevent clients from modifying the radius of a `Circle` object. A method, `getRadius()`, is added so that clients can retrieve the radius. Such a method is sometimes referred to as a *getter* for obtaining private data value. The output is the same as in the previous example. (Refer to Figure 5.5.)

```
public class TestCircleWithPrivateModifier
{
  public static void main(String[] args)
  {
    //Test Circle with radius 5.0
    Circle myCircle = new Circle(5.0);
    System.out.println("The area of the circle of radius "
      + myCircle.getRadius() + " is " + myCircle.findArea());

    // Test Circle with default radius
    Circle yourCircle = new Circle();
    System.out.println("The area of the circle of radius "
      + yourCircle.getRadius() + " is " + yourCircle.findArea());
  }
}

//Declare class Circle with constructors and private data
class Circle
{
  private double radius;

  public Circle(double r)
  {
    radius = r;
  }

  public Circle()
  {
    radius = 1.0;
  }

  public double getRadius()
  {
    return radius;
  }

  public double findArea()
  {
    return radius*radius*3.14159;
  }
}
```

Example Review

If a client program were allowed to change the radius in a `Circle` object, programming errors might occur that would make bugs difficult to detect. In this example, the `private` modifier in the data declaration is used to prevent the client program from changing the circle's properties. Therefore, the data in the object can never be changed after its creation.

continues

Example 5.3   continued

If you want to access private data from the object, you can provide a getter method to retrieve the data, such as `getRadius()`.

The private data can only be accessed within its defining class. You cannot use `myCircle.radius` in the client program. A compilation error would occur if you attempted to access private data from a client.

▉▉ TIP

You cannot have two `public` classes in one file because Java requires the `public` class to be stored in a source file with the same name as the class. For example, if you add the modifier `public` in front of the `Circle` class in this example, you will get the following compilation error message:

Public class `Circle` must be defined in a file called **Circle.java**.

Passing Objects to Methods

Just as you can pass the value of variables to methods, you can also pass objects to methods as actual parameters. The following example passes the `myCircle` object as an argument to the method `printCircle()`:

```java
class TestPassingObject
{
  public static void main(String[] args)
  {
    Circle myCircle = new Circle(5.0);
    printCircle(myCircle);
  }

  public static void printCircle(Circle c)
  {
    System.out.println("The area of the circle of radius "
      + c.getRadius() + " is " + c.findArea());
  }
}
```

There are important differences between passing a value of variables of primitive data types and passing objects.

Passing a variable of a primitive type means that the value of the variable is passed to a formal parameter. Changing the value of the local parameter inside the method does not affect the value of the variable that is outside of the method.

Passing an object means that the reference of the object is passed to the formal parameter. Any changes to the local object that occur inside the method body will affect the original object that was passed as the argument. In programming terminology, this is referred to as *passing by reference*.

You will see the difference in the following example.

Example 5.4   Passing Objects as Arguments

In this example, a program is written to pass a `Circle` object to the method `colorCircle`, which changes the color of the `Circle` object. The output of the program is shown in Figure 5.6.

```java
//This example shows that passing by reference may change the
//value inside the object.
public class TestPassingObjectCircle
{
  public static void main(String[] args)
  {
    Circle myCircle = new Circle(5.0,"white");
    printCircle(myCircle);
    colorCircle(myCircle,"black");
    printCircle(myCircle);
  }

  public static void colorCircle(Circle c, String color)
  {
    c.color = color;
  }

  public static void printCircle(Circle c)
  {
    System.out.println("The area of the circle of radius "
      + c.getRadius() + " is " + c.findArea());
    System.out.println("The color of the circle is "
      + c.color);
  }
}

class Circle
{
  private double radius;
  String color;

  public Circle(double r, String c)
  {
    radius = r;
    color = c;
  }

  public Circle()
  {
    radius = 1.0;
    color = "white";
  }

  public double getRadius()
  {
    return radius;
  }

  public double findArea()
  {
    return radius*radius*3.14159;
  }
}
```

continues

Example 5.4   continued

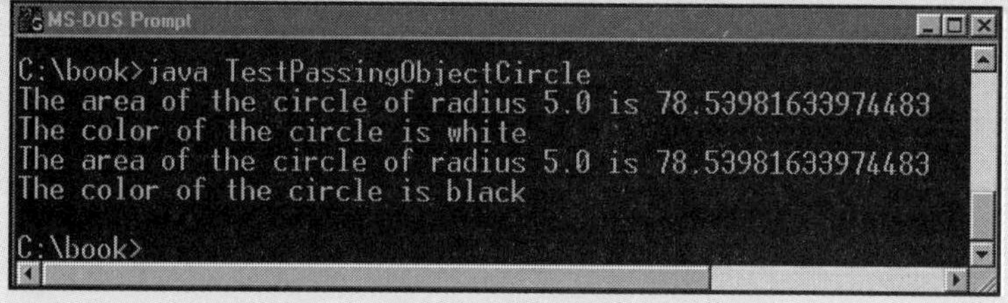

Figure 5.6 *The program passes* Circle *objects as parameters to the method* printCircle, *which displays the radius and the area.*

Example Review

The data field radius is private, so it cannot be changed by an assignment such as the following:

```
myCircle.radius = newRadius;
```

However, the data field color can be changed by the following assignment statement:

```
myCircle.color = newColor;
```

In the main() method, a "white" object, myCircle, is created with a radius of 5.0. The method colorCircle is then called with the argument myCircle and a new color, "black". This call changes the color field in the myCircle object to "black" because the object's reference (and not a copy of it) was passed to the method and that made it possible for the method to change the color value in the object myCircle.

You should use the private modifier for color to prevent the user from accidentally changing the color field. If the color field is private, can it be changed safely? Yes, you can declare a method in the Circle class to set a new color. Such a method is referred to as a setter. See the following example.

Example 5.5   Changing Data in a Private Field Using a Setter

In this example, a program is written to demonstrate a safe way to change the data in an object. The output of the program is shown in Figure 5.7.

```
public class TestChangingObjectPrivateData
{
  public static void main(String[] args)
  {
    Circle myCircle = new Circle(5.0,"white");
    printCircle(myCircle);
    myCircle.setColor(myCircle,"black");
```

120

```java
      printCircle(myCircle);
  }

  public static void printCircle(Circle c)
  {
    System.out.println("The area of the circle of radius "
      + c.getRadius() + " is " + c.findArea());
    System.out.println("The color of the circle is "
      + c.getColor());
  }
}

class Circle
{
  private double radius;
  private String color;

  public Circle(double r, String c)
  {
    radius = r;
    color = c;
  }

  public Circle()
  {
    radius = 1.0;
    color = "white";
  }

  public double getRadius()
  {
    return radius;
  }

  public String getColor()
  {
    return color;
  }

  public void setColor(Circle c, String color)
  {
    c.color = color;
  }

  public double findArea()
  {
    return radius*radius*3.14159;
  }
}
```

Example Review

The setColor method in the Circle class allows you to change the color of the object. Such a method is sometimes referred to as a *setter*. A setter is always a void type method, while a getter has a return type.

This example demonstrates that you can protect the data from mistakes by using the private modifier and providing a setter to change the data safely.

continues

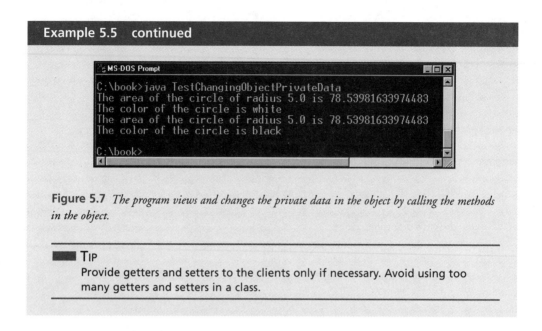

Example 5.5 continued

```
C:\book>java TestChangingObjectPrivateData
The area of the circle of radius 5.0 is 78.53981633974483
The color of the circle is white
The area of the circle of radius 5.0 is 78.53981633974483
The color of the circle is black

C:\book>
```

Figure 5.7 *The program views and changes the private data in the object by calling the methods in the object.*

▬ TIP
Provide getters and setters to the clients only if necessary. Avoid using too many getters and setters in a class.

Instance Variables and Class Variables

The variables radius and color in the Circle class in Example 5.5 are known as *instance variables*. Instance variables belong to each instance of the class; they are not shared among objects of the same class. For example, suppose that you create the following objects:

```
Circle myCircle = new Circle();
Circle yourCircle = new Circle();
```

The data in myCircle is independent of the data in yourCircle, and is in different memory locations (see Figure 5.8). Changes made to myCircle's data do not affect yourCircle's data, and vice versa.

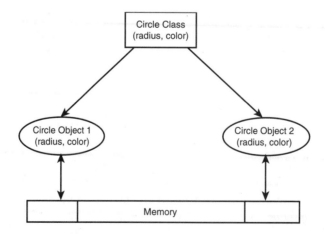

Figure 5.8 *The instance variables, which belong to the instances, have memory storage independent of each other.*

If you want the instances of a class to share data, you can use *class variables*. Class variables store values for the variables in a common memory location (see Figure 5.9). Because of this common location, all objects of the same class are affected if one object changes the value of a class variable.

To declare a class variable, put the modifier static in the variable declaration. Suppose that you want to add weight to circles. Assuming that all circles have the same weight, you can define the class variable as follows:

```
static double weight;
```

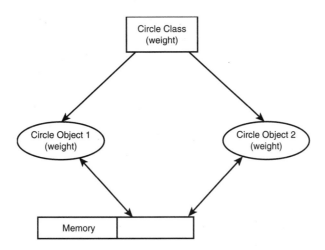

Figure 5.9 *The class variables are shared by all of the instances of the same class.*

Following is an example that shows you the effect of using instance variables and class variables.

Example 5.6   Testing Instance and Class Variables

The program in this example shows you how to use instance and class variables and illustrates the effects of using them. For this program, assume that all of the Circle objects are of the same weight. So, weight is defined as a class variable. By default, the weight is 1.0.

This program creates two circles (myCircle and yourCircle). You will see the effect of using instance and class variables after changing data in the circles. The output of the program is shown in Figure 5.10.

```
public class TestInstanceAndClassVariable
{
  public static void main(String[] args)
  {
    //create and display myCircle
    Circle myCircle = new Circle(4.0, "white", 5.0);
```

continues

Example 5.6   continued

```
            System.out.print("myCircle:");
            printCircle(myCircle);

            //create and display yourCircle
            Circle yourCircle = new Circle(5.0, "black", 3.0);
            System.out.print("yourCircle:");
            printCircle(yourCircle);

            //change the weight in myCircle
            myCircle.weight = 15.5;

            //display myCircle and yourCircle
            System.out.print("myCircle:");
            printCircle(myCircle);
            System.out.print(" yourCircle:");
            printCircle(yourCircle);
        }

        public static void printCircle(Circle c)
        {
            System.out.println("radius ("+c.getRadius() +
                "), color (" + c.color +") and weight (" + c.weight + ")");
        }
    }

    //declare class Circle with static field color
    class Circle
    {
        private double radius;
        String color;
        static double weight;

        public Circle(double r, String c, double w)
        {
            radius = r;
            color = c;
            weight = w;
        }

        public Circle()
        {
            radius = 1.0;
            color = "white";
            weight = 1.0;
        }

        public double getRadius()
        {
            return radius;
        }

        public double findArea()
        {
            return radius*radius*Math.PI;
        }
    }
```

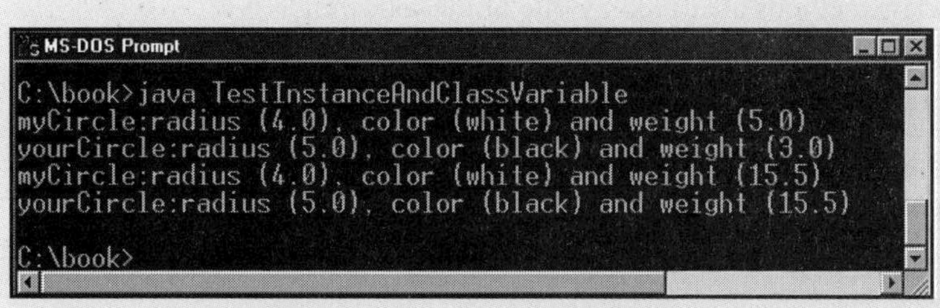

```
MS-DOS Prompt                                                    _ □ ×
C:\book>java TestInstanceAndClassVariable
myCircle:radius (4.0), color (white) and weight (5.0)
yourCircle:radius (5.0), color (black) and weight (3.0)
myCircle:radius (4.0), color (white) and weight (15.5)
yourCircle:radius (5.0), color (black) and weight (15.5)

C:\book>
```

Figure 5.10 *The program uses the instance variables* radius *and* color *as well as the class variable* weight. *All of the objects have the same* weight.

Example Review

What is Math.PI, used in the findArea() method? If you had followed the Java naming conventions introduced in the "Programming Style and Documentation" section of Chapter 2, "Java Building Elements," you would immediately recognize that PI is a constant and Math is a class name. The Math class comes with the Java system. PI is a constant for π that is defined in the Math class. The Math class is introduced in the section "The Math Class" later in this chapter.

Notice that Math.PI was used to access PI and myCircle.radius in Example 5.1 was used to access radius. Math is the class name and myCircle is an object of the Circle class. To access a constant, such as PI, you can use either the ClassName.CONSTANTNAME or the objectName.CONSTANTNAME. To access an instance variable, such as radius, you need to use objectName.variableName.

TIP

You should define a constant as static data that can be shared by all class objects. Do not change the value of a constant.

Variables that describe common properties of objects should be declared as class variables.

Instance Methods and Class Methods

Instance methods belong to instances. These methods can only be applied after the instances are created. They are called by the following:

```
objectName.methodName();
```

The methods defined in the Circle class are instance methods. Java supports class methods as well as class variables. Class methods can be called without creating an instance of the class. To define class methods, put the modifier static in the method declaration as follows:

```
static returnValueType staticMethod();
```

Examples of class methods are the readDouble() and the readInt() in the class MyInput.

The class methods are called by one of the following:

```
ClassName.methodName();
objectName.methodName();
```

For example, `MyInput.readInt()` is a call that reads an integer from the keyboard. `MyInput` is a class, not an object.

 TIP

A method that does not use instance variables can be defined as a class method. This method can be invoked without creating an object of the class.

The Scope of Variables

The *scope of a variable* determines where the variable can be referenced in a program. In general, the scope of a variable is within the block where that variable is declared. You can declare a variable only once in a block. But you can declare the same variable multiple times in different blocks. For example, x is defined twice in the following program:

```
class Foo
{
  int x = 0;
  int y = 0;

  Foo()
  {
  }

  void p()
  {
    int x = 1;
    System.out.println("x = " + x);
    System.out.println("y = " + y);
  }
}
```

What is the printout for `f.p()`, in which f is an instance of Foo? To answer this question, you need to understand the scope rules that determine how a variable is accessed. The following Java scope rules are based on blocks:

- The scope of a variable is the block in which it is declared. Therefore, a variable declared in block B can be accessed in block B or in the inner block that is nested inside block B.

- If a variable x that was originally declared in block B is declared again in a block that is nested inside block B—block C—the scope of x that is declared in block B excludes that inner block .

Therefore, the printout for `f.p()` is 1 (for x) and 0 (for y), based on the following reasons:

- x is declared again in the method p() with an initial value of 1.

- y is declared outside the method p(), but is accessible inside it.

▬▬ TIP

As demonstrated in the example, it is easy to make mistakes. Therefore, you should avoid declaring the same variable names, as that might confuse you.

▬▬ CAUTION

Do not declare a variable inside a block and then use it outside the block. An example of a common mistake is as follows:

```
for (int i=0; i<10; i++)
{
}

int j = i;
```

The last statement would cause an error because variable `i` is not defined outside of the `for` loop.

▬▬ NOTE

A variable declared in a method is referred to as a *local variable*. You cannot declare a local variable twice in a method even though the variable is declared in different blocks and nested blocks. For example, the following code would cause a compilation error because x is declared in the `for` loop body block, which is nested inside the method body block where another x is declared.

```
public void xMethod()
{
  int x = 1;
  int y = 1;

  for (int i = 1; i<10; i++)
  {
    int x = 0;
    x += i;
  }
}
```

Case Studies

By now, you have formed some ideas about objects and classes and their programming features. Object-oriented programming is centered on objects; it is particularly involved with getting objects to work together. OOP provides abstraction and encapsulation. You can create the `Circle` object and find the area of the circle without knowing how the area is computed. The object might have many other data and methods.

The detail of the implementation is encapsulated and hidden from the client. This is referred to as *class abstraction*. You can draw upon many real-life examples to illustrate the OOP concept.

Consider building a computer system, for example. Your personal computer consists of many components, such as a CPU, CD-ROM, floppy disk, motherboard, fan, and so on. Each component can be viewed as an object that has properties and methods. To get them to work together, all you need to know is how a component is used and how it interacts with others. You don't need to know how it works internally. The internal implementation is encapsulated and hidden from you. You can build a computer without knowing how a component is implemented.

This precisely mirrors the object-oriented approach. Each component can be viewed as an object of the class for the component. For example, you might have a class that models all kinds of fans for use on a computer with properties like fan size, speed, and so on; and methods such as start, stop, and so on. A specific fan is an instance of this class with specific property values.

Consider paying a mortgage, for another example. A specific mortgage can be viewed as an object of a mortgage class. Interest rate, loan amount, and loan period are its data properties, and computing monthly payment and total payment are its methods. When you buy a house, a mortgage object is created by instantiating the class with your mortgage interest rate, loan amount, and loan period. You can then easily find the monthly payment and total payment of your loan using the mortgage methods.

Examples 5.7 and 5.8 are case studies of designing classes.

Example 5.7   Using the *Mortgage* Class

In this example, a mortgage class with properties—interest rate, loan amount, loan period, and total payment—and methods—`monthlyPayment()` and `totalPayment()`—is created.

Following is the test program. Figure 5.11 shows the output of a sample run of the program.

```
public class TestMortgageClass
{
  public static void main(String[] args)
  {
    double interestRate;
    int year;
    double loan;

    //enter input
    System.out.println(
      "Enter yearly interest rate, for example 8.25: ");
    interestRate = MyInput.readDouble();
    System.out.println(
      "Enter number of years as an integer, for example 5: ");
    year = MyInput.readInt();
    System.out.println(
      "Enter loan amount, for example 120000.95: ");
    loan = MyInput.readDouble();

    //creating Mortgage object
    Mortgage m = new Mortgage(interestRate, year, loan);

    //display results
    System.out.println("The monthly pay is "+m.monthlyPay());
    System.out.println("The total paid is "+m.totalPay());
```

```
    }
  }

  class Mortgage
  {
    private double interest;
    private int year;
    private double loan;

    public Mortgage(double i, int y, double l)
    {
      interest = i/1200.0;
      year = y;
      loan = l;
    }

    public double getInterest()
    {
      return interest;
    }

    public double getYear()
    {
      return year;
    }

    public double getLoan()
    {
      return loan;
    }

    public double monthlyPay()
    {
      return loan*interest/(1-(Math.pow(1/(1+interest),year*12)));
    }

    public double totalPay()
    {
      return monthlyPay()*year*12;
    }
  }
```

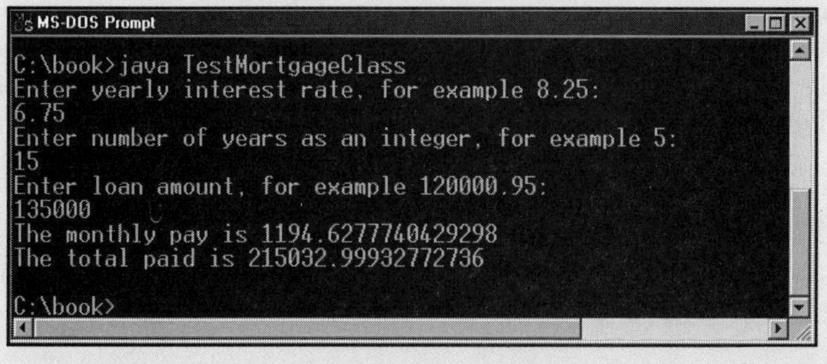

```
MS-DOS Prompt

C:\book>java TestMortgageClass
Enter yearly interest rate, for example 8.25:
6.75
Enter number of years as an integer, for example 5:
15
Enter loan amount, for example 120000.95:
135000
The monthly pay is 1194.6277740429298
The total paid is 215032.99932772736

C:\book>
```

Figure 5.11 *The program creates a* Mortgage *instance with the interest rate, year, and loan amount, and displays monthly payment and total payment by invoking the methods of the instance.*

continues

Example 5.7   continued

Example Review

The Mortgage class contains a constructor, three getters, and the methods for finding monthly payment and total payment. You can construct a Mortgage object by using three parameters: interest rate, payment years, and loan amount. The three getters getInterest(), getYear(), and getLoan() return interest rate, payment years, and loan amount, respectively.

The main class reads interest rate, payment period (in years), and loan amount; creates a Mortgage object; and then obtains the monthly payment and total payment using the instance methods in the Mortgage class.

Example 5.8   Using the *Rational* Class

In this example, a class for rational numbers is defined. The class provides constructors and addition, subtraction, multiplication, and division methods.

A rational number is a number with a numerator and a denominator in the form a/b, where a is a numerator and b is a denominator—for example, 1/3, 3/4, and 10/4.

A rational number cannot have a denominator of 0, but a numerator of 0 is fine. Every integer a is equivalent to a rational number a/1. Rational numbers are used in exact computations involving fractions; for example, 1/3 = 0.33333.... This number cannot be precisely represented in floating-point format using data type double or float. To obtain the exact result, you should use rational numbers.

There are many equivalent rational numbers; for example, 1/3 = 2/6 = 3/9 = 4/12. For convenience, 1/3 is used in this example to represent all rational numbers that are equivalent to 1/3. The numerator and the denominator of 1/3 have no common divisors except 1, so 1/3 is said to be in lowest terms.

To reduce a rational to its lowest terms, you need to find the greatest common divisor, or GCD, of the absolute values of its numerator and denominator, then divide both numerator and denominator by this value. Here is the classic Euclid's algorithm for finding the GCD of two int values n and d.

```
t1 <- abs(n); t2 <- abs; //get absolute value of n and d;
r = t1 % t2; //r is the remainder of t1 divided by t2;
while (r!= 0)
{
  t1 = t2;
  t2 = r;
  r = t1 % t2;
}

//when r is 0, t2 is the common divisor between t1 and t2
return t2;
```

The program follows. Its output is shown in Figure 5.12.

```java
public class TestRationalClass
{
  public static void main(String[] args)
  {
    //create and initialize two rational numbers r1 and r2.
    Rational r1 = new Rational(4,2);
    Rational r2 = new Rational(2,3);

    //display results
    System.out.println(r1.toString() + " + " + r2.toString() +
      " = " + (r1.add(r2)).toString());
    System.out.println(r1.toString() + " - " + r2.toString() +
      " = " + (r1.subtract(r2)).toString());
    System.out.println(r1.toString() + " * " + r2.toString() +
      " = " + (r1.multiply(r2)).toString());
    System.out.println(r1.toString() + " / " + r2.toString() +
      " = " + (r1.divide(r2)).toString());
  }
}

class Rational
{
  private long numer, denom;

  Rational(long n, long d)
  {
    long k = gcd(n,d);
    numer = n/k;
    denom = d/k;
  }

  Rational()
  {
    this(0, 1);
  }

  private long gcd(long n, long d)
  {
    long t1 = Math.abs(n);
    long t2 = Math.abs;
    long remainder = t1%t2;

    while (remainder != 0)
    {
      t1 = t2;
      t2 = remainder;
      remainder = t1%t2;
    }

    return t2;
  }

  public long getNumer()
  {
    return numer;
  }
```

continues

131

Example 5.8   continued

```java
    public long getDenom()
    {
      return denom;
    }

    public Rational add(Rational r)
    {
      long n = numer*r.denom + denom*r.numer;
      long d = denom*r.denom;
      return new Rational(n,d);
    }

    public Rational subtract(Rational r)
    {
      long n = numer*r.denom - denom*r.numer;
      long d = denom*r.denom;
      return new Rational(n,d);
    }

    public Rational multiply(Rational r)
    {
      long n = numer*r.numer;
      long d = denom*r.denom;
      return new Rational(n,d);
    }

    public Rational divide(Rational r)
    {
      long n = numer*r.denom;
      long d = denom*r.numer;
      return new Rational(n,d);
    }

    public String toString()
    {
      return numer + "/" + denom;
    }
}
```

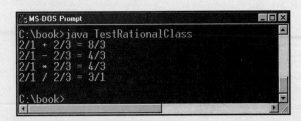

Figure 5.12 *The program creates two instances of the* Rational *class and displays their addition, subtraction, multiplication, and division by invoking the instance methods.*

Example Review

The main class creates two rational numbers, r1 and r2, and displays the results of r1+r2, r1-r2, r1xr2, and r1/r2.

The rational number is encapsulated in a `Rational` object. Internally, a rational number is represented in its lowest terms; in other words, the greatest common divisor between the numerator and the denominator is 1.

The `gcd()` method is private; it is not intended for a client to use. The `gcd()` method is only for internal use by the `Rational` class.

The `abs(x)` method is defined in the `Math` class that returns the absolute value of `x`.

The equation `r1 + r2` is called in the form of `r1.add(r2)`, in which `add` (which is a method in the object `r1`) returns the following:

```
(r1.numer*r2.denom+r1.denom*r1.numer)/(r1.denom*r2.denom).
```

The `numer` data field of the object `r1` is `r1.numer` and the `denom` data field of object `r1` is `r1.denom`.

The return value of `r1 + r2` is a new `Rational` object.

The `r.toString()` method returns the rational number `r` in the form numerator/denominator.

When you are dividing rational numbers, what happens if the divisor is zero? In this example, the program would terminate with a runtime error. You need to make sure this does not occur when you are using the division method. In Chapter 11, "Exception Handling," you will learn to deal with the zero divisor case for a `Rational` object.

Packages

A *package* is a collection of classes. It provides a convenient way to organize those classes. You can put the classes that you developed in packages, and distribute the packages to other people. You can think of packages as libraries to be shared by many users.

The Java language itself comes with a rich set of packages that you can use to build applications. You learned the `java.awt` package in Chapter 1, "Introduction to Java," and you will learn more about Java system predefined packages in the section "Java Application Programming Interface," later in this chapter.

In this section, you will learn about Java package-naming conventions, creating packages, and using packages.

Package-Naming Conventions

Packages are hierarchical, and you can have packages within packages. For example, `java.awt.Button` indicates that `Button` is a class in the package awt and that awt is a package within the package `java`. You can use levels of nesting to ensure the uniqueness of package names.

Choosing unique names is important because your package might be used on the Internet by other programs. Java designers recommend that you use your Internet domain name in reverse order as a package prefix. This avoids naming conflicts because Internet domain names are unique. Suppose you want to create a package named `mypackage.io` on the host machine with the Internet domain name `liangy.ipfw.indiana.edu`. To follow the naming convention, you would name the entire package as `edu.indiana.ipfw.liangy.mypackage.io`.

Java expects one-to-one mapping of the package name and the file system directory structure. For the package named `edu.indiana.ipfw.liangy.mypackage.io`, you must create a directory as shown in Figure 5.13. In other words, a package is actually a directory that contains the bytecode of the classes.

Figure 5.13 *The package* `edu.indiana.ipfw.liangy.mypackge.io` *is mapped to a directory structure in the file system.*

The *CLASSPATH* Environment Variable

The `edu` directory does not have to be the root directory. In order for Java to know where your package is in the file system, you must modify the environment variable `CLASSPATH` so that it points to the directory in which your package resides. For example, the following line defines three directories in `CLASSPATH`.

```
CLASSPATH=.;c:\jdk1.2beta4\lib;c:\edu\ipfw\indiana\liangy;
```

The period (.) indicating the current directory is always in `CLASSPATH`. The directory `c:\jdk1.2beta4\lib` is where the standard Java package resides and is always in `CLASSPATH`. The directory `c:\edu\ipfw\indiana\liangy` is in `CLASSPATH` so that you can use the package `mypackage.io` in the program.

You can add as many directories as necessary in `CLASSPATH`. The order in which the directories are specified is the order in which the classes are searched. If you have two classes of the same name in different directories, Java uses the first one it finds.

The `CLASSPATH` variable is set differently in Windows 95, Windows NT, and UNIX, as follows:

- **Windows 95**—Edit **autoexec.bat** using a text editor, such as Microsoft Notepad.

- **Windows NT**—Go to the Start button and choose Control Panel, select the System icon, and then modify `CLASSPATH` in the environment.

■ **UNIX**—Use the `setenv` command to set CLASSPATH, such as

```
setenv CLASSPATH .:/home/edu/indiana/ipfw/liangy
```

You can insert this line into the **.cshrc** file, so the CLASSPATH variable is automatically set when you log on.

TIP

You must restart the system for the CLASSPATH variable to take effect on Windows 95. On Windows NT, however, the settings are stored permanently, and affect any new command line windows, but not any existing command line windows.

NOTE

If you use an IDE tool, such as Visual Café, MS VJ++, and JBuilder, please consult the user's manual for setting the CLASSPATH environment variable.

Putting Classes into Packages

Every class in Java belongs to a package. The class is added to the package when it is compiled. All the classes that you have used so far in this book were placed in the current directory (a default package) when the Java source programs were compiled. To put a class in a specific package, you need to add the following line as the first non-comment and non-blank statement in the program:

```
package packagename;
```

Example 5.9   Putting Classes into Packages

This example creates the class `MyInput` and stores it in the package `mypackage.io`.

```
//class with methods to read integers and doubles
package mypackage.io;

import java.io.*;
import java.util.*;

public class MyInput
{
  static private StringTokenizer stok;
  static private BufferedReader br
            = new BufferedReader(new InputStreamReader(System.in), 1);

  public static int readInt()
  {
    int i = 0;
    try
    {
      String str = br.readLine();
      StringTokenizer stok = new StringTokenizer(str);
      i = new Integer(stok.nextToken()).intValue();
```

continues

Example 5.9   continued

```
        }
        catch (IOException ex)
        {
          System.out.println(ex);
        }
        return i;
      }

      public static double readDouble()
      {
        double d = 0;
        try
        {
          String str = br.readLine();
          stok = new StringTokenizer(str);
          d = new Double(stok.nextToken()).doubleValue();
        }
        catch (IOException ex)
        {
          System.out.println(ex);
        }
        return d;
      }
    }
```

Example Review

The class must be defined as public for it to be accessed by other programs. The directory for the package is not automatically created using the `javac` compiler in JDK. So, you have to manually create it before compiling it.

If you use the `javac` compiler in JDK to compile this program, you must use the following command with the `-d` option to specify the destination of the bytecode file in order for the bytecode file to be placed in the `\edu\indiana\ipfw\liangy\mypackage\io` directory:

```
javac MyInput.java -d c:\edu\indiana\ipfw\liangy\mypackage\io
```

If you use JBuilder, it automatically creates a directory `mypackage\io` under CLASSPATH for the package if the directory does not exist. The JBuilder compiler then places the bytecode of the program into this directory.

TIP
If you want to put several classes into the package, you have to create separate source files for them because one file can have only one public class.

NOTE
The class files can be archived into a single file for convenience. All the Java packages, for example, come with a single compressed file, **classes.zip**, under `\jdk1.2beta4\lib`.

Using Packages

To use a class from a package in your program, you should add an import statement to the top of the program, for example:

```
import mypackage.io.MyInput;
```

If you have many classes to use from the same package, you can use the asterisk (*) to indicate use of all classes in the package, for example:

```
import mypackage.io.*;
```

This statement imports all classes in the `mypackage.io` package.

Example 5.10   Using Your Own Packages

This example shows a program that uses the `MyInput` class in the `mypackage.io` package. The program reads data and echo prints it. The output of the program is shown in Figure 5.14.

```
import mypackage.io.MyInput;
public class TestMyInput
{
  public static void main(String[] args)
  {
    System.out.println("Enter an integer");
    int i = MyInput.readInt();
    System.out.println("You entered " + i);

    System.out.println("Enter a double");
    double d = MyInput.readDouble();
    System.out.println("You entered "+d);
  }
}
```

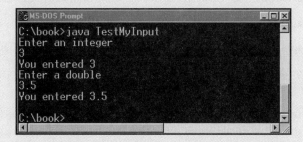

Figure 5.14 *The program uses the* `MyInput` *class to read an* int *value and* double *value, and echo prints the values onscreen.*

Example Review

Before compiling this program, make sure that `MyInput` is stored in the package `mypackage.io` and that the environment variable `CLASSPATH` is properly set. Also

continues

Example 5.10 continued

please note that MyInput is defined as public so it can be used by classes in other packages.

The program uses the import statement to get the class `MyInput`. You have used this class in previous examples in this book (such as Example 3.1, "Using Nested `if` Statements"). You did not use the `import` statement, however, because it was included in the same directory with these examples.

You cannot import entire packages such as `mypackage.*.*`. Only one asterisk (*) can be used in the `import` statement.

Java Application Programming Interface

The Java Application Programming Interface—JDK 1.2 API—consists of numerous classes and interfaces that are grouped into 15 core packages, such as `java.lang`, `java.awt`, `java.awt.event`, `java.applet`, `java.util`, `java.text`, `java.io`, and `java.net`. These classes provide an interface that allows Java programs to interact with the system:

- **java.lang**—Contains core Java classes (such as `Object`, `String`, `System`, `Math`, `Number`, `Character`, `Boolean`, `Byte`, `Short`, `Integer`, `Long`, `Float`, and `Double`). This package is implicitly imported to every Java program.

- **java.awt**—Contains classes for drawing geometrical objects and for creating and managing the graphical user interface components, such as windows, frames, panels, menus, buttons, fonts, lists, and many others.

- **java.awt.event**—Contains classes for handling events in graphics programming.

- **java.applet**—Contains classes for supporting applets.

- **java.io**—Contains classes for input and output streams and files.

- **java.util**—Contains many utilities, such as date, system properties, vectors, hashing, and stacks.

- **java.text**—Contains classes for formatting information, such as date and time, in a number of formatting styles that are based on a language, country, and culture.

- **java.net**—Contains classes for supporting network communications.

The `java.lang` is the most fundamental package supporting the basic operations. Many of the popular classes in `java.lang` are introduced later in the book. See the following chapters for information on these classes:

- Chapter 6, "Arrays and Strings," introduces classes `java.lang.String`, `java.lang.StringBuffer`, and `java.util.StringTokenizer` for storing and processing strings.

- Chapter 7, "Class Inheritance," covers the numeric wrapper classes such as `Integer` and `Double` in the `java.lang` package. This chapter also introduces `java.util.Date`, `java.util.Calendar`, and `java.text.DateFormat` for processing and formatting date and time.

- Chapter 8, "Getting Started with Graphics Programming," and Chapter 9, "Creating User Interfaces," introduce `java.awt` and `java.awt.event`, which are used for drawing geometrical objects, responding to mouse movements and keyboard entries, and designing graphical user interfaces.

- Chapter 10, "Applets and Advanced Graphics," introduces `java.applet`, which is used to program Java applets.

- Chapter 11, "Exception Handling," discusses using the `java.lang.Throwable` class and its subclasses for exception handling.

- Chapter 12, "Multithreading," focuses on the `java.lang.Thread` class and the `java.lang.Runnable` interface, which are used for multithreading.

- Chapter 13, "Multimedia," addresses the use of multimedia by several classes from `java.awt` and `java.applet`.

- Chapter 14, "Input and Output," discusses the use of `java.io` by input and output streams.

- Chapter 15, "Networking," discusses using `java.net` for network programming.

NOTE

After you understand the concept of programming, the most important lesson in Java is learning how to use the API to develop useful programs. The core Java API is introduced in the coming chapters.

The *Math* Class

The `Math` class contains the methods needed to perform basic mathematical functions. Two useful constants, `PI` and `E` (the base of the natural logarithms), are provided in the `Math` class. You have already used `Math.PI` to obtain the PI value instead of again declaring that value in the program. The constants are `double` values. Most methods operate on `double` parameters and return `double` values. The methods in the `Math` class can be categorized as trigonometric methods, exponent methods, and miscellaneous methods.

NOTE

I strongly recommend that you browse through the class definitions for each new class you learn. If you use an IDE tool, this information is available from the Help menu. You can always obtain the online documentation from the JavaSoft Web site at **www.javasoft.com**.

Trigonometric Methods

The Math class contains the following trigonometric methods, among many others:

```
public static double sin(double a)

public static double cos(double a)

public static double tan(double a)

public static double asin(double a)

public static double acos(double a)

public static double atan(double a)
```

Each method has a single `double` parameter, and its return type is `double`. For example, `Math.sin(Math.PI)` returns the trigonometric sine of π.

Exponent Methods

There are four methods related to exponents in the Math class:

```
public static double exp(double a)
//returns e raised to the power of a

public static double log(double a)
//returns the natural logarithm of a

public static double pow(double a, double b)
//returns a raised to the power of b

public static double sqrt(double a)
//returns the square root of a
```

You have used the `Math.pow()` method in the mortgage calculation program. Note that the parameter in the `Math.sqrt()` method must not be negative.

The *min()*, *max()*, *abs()*, and *random()* Methods

Other useful methods in the Math class are the `min()` and `max()` methods, the `abs()` method, and the random generator `random()`.

The `min()` and `max()` functions return the minimum and the maximum numbers between two numbers (`int`, `long`, `float`, or `double`). For example, `max(3.4, 5.0)` returns `5.0`, and `min(3, 2)` returns `2`.

The `abs()` function returns the absolute value of the number (`int`, `long`, `float` and `double`). For example, `abs(-3.03)` returns `3.03`.

The Math class also has a powerful method, `random()`, which generates a random double floating-point number between 0 and 1.

NOTE

All methods and data in the `Math` class are `static`. They are class methods and class variables. Most methods operate on `double` parameters and return a `double` value.

TIP

Occasionally, you want to prohibit the user from creating an instance for a class. For example, there is no reason to create an instance from the `Math` class because all of the data and methods are of class-wide information. One solution is to define a dummy private constructor in the class. The `Math` class has a private constructor, as follows:

```
private Math() { };
```

Therefore, the `Math` class cannot be instantiated.

Chapter Summary

In this chapter, you learned how to program using objects and classes. You learned how to define classes, create objects, and use objects. You also learned about modifiers, instance variables, class variables, instance methods, and class methods.

A class is a template for objects. It defines the generic properties of objects and provides methods to manipulate them.

An object is an instance of a class. It is declared in the same way as a primitive type variable. You use the new operator to create an object, and you use the dot (.) operator to access members of that object.

A constructor is a special method that is called when an object is created. Constructors can be overloaded. I recommend that you provide a constructor for each class so that an instance of the class is properly initialized (although it is legal to write a class without constructors).

Modifiers specify how the class, method, and data are accessed. You learned about the public, private, and static modifiers. A public class, method, or piece of data is accessible to all clients. A private method or piece of data is only visible inside the class. You should make instance data private. You can provide a getter method to enable clients to see the data. A class variable or a class method is defined using the keyword static.

The objects are passed to methods using pass by reference. Any changes to the object inside the method affect the object that is passed as the argument.

An instance variable is a variable that belongs to the instance of a class. Its use is associated with individual objects. A class variable is a variable shared by all objects of the same class.

An instance method is a method that belongs to the instance of a class. Its use is associated with individual objects. A class method is a method that is called without using instances.

A *package* is a structure for organizing classes. JDK 1.2 API has numerous classes and interfaces that are organized into 15 core packages. Programming in Java is essentially using these classes to build your projects.

The Math class contains methods that perform trigonometric functions (sin, cos, tag, acos, asin, atan), exponent functions (exp, log, pow, sqrt), and some miscellaneous functions (min, max, abs, random). All of these methods operate on double values; min, max, and abs can also operate on int, long, float and double.

Chapter Review

1. Describe the relationship between an object and its defining class. How do you declare a class? How do you declare an object? How do you create an object? How do you declare and create an object in one statement?

2. What are the differences between constructors and methods?

3. List the modifiers that you learned in this chapter and describe their purposes.

4. Describe pass by reference and pass by value. Show the output of the following program:

```java
public class Test
{
  public static void main(String[] args)
  {
    Count myCount = new Count();
    int times = 0;

    for (int i=0; i<100; i++)
      increment(myCount, times);

    System.out.println("count is " + myCount.count);
    System.out.println("times is " + times);
  }

  public static void increment(Count c, int times)
  {
    c.count++;
    times++;
  }
}

class Count
{
  public int count;

  Count(int c)
  {
    count = c;
  }

  Count()
  {
    count = 1;
  }
}
```

5. Suppose that the class Foo is defined as follows:

```java
public class Foo
{
  int i;
  static String s;

  void imethod()
  {
  }

  static void smethod()
  {
  }
}
```

Let f be an instance of Foo. Are the following statements correct?

```java
System.out.println(f.i);

System.out.println(f.s);

f.imethod();

f.smethod();

System.out.println(Foo.i);

System.out.println(Foo.s);

Foo.imethod();

Foo.smethod();
```

6. What is the output of the following program?

```java
public class Foo
{
  static int i = 0;
  static int j = 0;

  public static void main(String[] args)
  {
    int i = 2;
    int k = 3;

    {
      int j = 3;
      System.out.println("i + j is " + i+j);
    }

    k = i + j;
    System.out.println("k is "+k);
    System.out.println("j is "+j);
  }
}
```

7. What is wrong with the following program?

```java
public class ShowErrors
{
  public static void main(String[] args)
  {
    int i;
    int j;
```

```
        j = MyInput.readInt();
        if (j > 3)
          System.out.println(i+4);
    }
  }
```

8. What is wrong with the following program?

```
public class ShowErrors
{
  public static void main(String[] args)
  {
    for (int i=0; i<10; i++);
      System.out.println(i+4);
  }
}
```

9. Describe a package and its relationship with classes.

10. What is the recommended naming convention for creating your own packages?

11. Your packages can be stored in any directory or subdirectory. How does the compiler know where to find the packages? Describe the role of the CLASS-PATH environment variable.

Programming Exercises

1. Rewrite the Rational class with the following additional methods:

```
public boolean lessThan(Rational r)
//returns true if this Rational is < r

public boolean greaterThan(Rational r)
//returns true if this Rational is > r

public boolean equal(Rational r)
//returns true if this Rational is = r

public boolean lessThanOrEqual(Rational r)
//returns true if this Rational is <= r

public boolean greaterThanOrEqual(Rational r)
//returns true if this Rational is >= r

static Rational max(Rational r1, Rational r2)
//returns the larger one
```

   Write a client program to test the new Rational class.

2. Write a program that will compute the following summation series using the Rational class from Example 5.8.

   $1/1 + 1/2 + 1/3 +...+ 1/n$

   $1/1 + 1/2 + 1/2^2 +...+ 1/2^n$

3. Write a class named Rectangle to encapsulate rectangles. The private data fields are width, length, area, and color. Use double for width and length and String for color. The methods are getWidth(), getLength(), getColor(),

and findArea(). Suppose that all rectangles have the same color. Use a class variable for color.

```
public class Rectangle
{
  private double width, length;
  static String color;

  public Rectangle(double w, double l, String c)
  {
  }

  public double getWidth()
  {
  }

  public double getLength()
  {
  }

  public String getColor()
  {
  }

  public double findArea()
  {
  }
}
```

Write a client program to test the class Rectangle. In the client program, create two Rectangle objects. Assign any widths and lengths to the two objects. Assign the first object the color red and the second yellow. Display both objects' properties and find their areas.

4. The cancellation error occurs when you are manipulating a very large number with a very small number. The large number may cancel out the smaller number. For example, the result of 10000.0 + 0.000001 is equal to 10000.0 on some computers. To avoid cancellation errors and obtain more accurate results, select the order of computations carefully. For example, in computing the following series, you should compute from left to right to obtain more accurate results:

```
1 + 1/2 + 1/3 + ... + 1/n
```

Write a program to compare the results of the summation of the preceding series, computing from left to right and from right to left with n = 50000.

6

ARRAYS AND STRINGS

Objectives

- Understand the concept of arrays.

- Learn the steps involved in using arrays—declaring, creating, initializing, and processing arrays.

- Become familiar with sorting and search algorithms.

- Use objects as array elements.

- Become familiar with the copy array utility.

- Learn how to use multidimensional arrays.

- Recognize the difference between arrays and strings.

- Become familiar with the String class, the StringBuffer class, and the StringTokenizer class.

- Know how to use command-line arguments.

Introduction

In earlier chapters, you studied examples in which values were overwritten during the execution of a program. In those examples, such as Example 3.4 in Chapter 3, "Control Structures," you did not need to worry about storing former values. However, in some cases, you will have to store a large number of values in memory during the execution of a program. For example, suppose that you want to sort a group of numbers. These numbers must all be stored in memory because later you have to compare each number with all of the other numbers.

To store the numbers requires declaring variables in the program. It is practically impossible to declare variables for individual numbers. You need an efficient, organized approach. All of the high-level languages—including Java—provide you with a data structure, *array*, which stores a collection of the same types of data. Java treats these arrays as objects.

Strings and arrays are based on similar concepts. A string is a sequence of characters. In many languages, strings are treated as arrays of characters. But in Java, a *string* is used very differently from an array object.

Declaring and Creating Arrays

To use arrays in the program, you need to declare arrays and the type of elements that could be stored in arrays. The syntax to declare an array is as follows:

```
datatype[] arrayName;
```

or

```
datatype arrayName[];
```

The following code is an example of this syntax:

```
double[] myList;
```

or

```
double myList[];
```

NOTE

The style `datatype[] arrayName` is preferred. The style `datatype arrayName[]` comes from the C language and was adopted in Java to accommodate C programmers.

A Java array is an object, so the declaration does not allocate any space in memory for the array. You cannot assign elements to the array unless the array is already created.

After an array is declared, you can use the `new` operator to create the array with the following syntax:

```
arrayName = new datatype[arraySize];
```

You can combine declaration and creation in one statement, as follows:

```
datatype[] arrayName = new datatype[arraySize];
```

or

```
datatype arrayName[] = new datatype[arraySize];
```

The following is an example of such a statement:

```
double[] myList = new double[10];
```

This statement creates an array of 10 elements of `double` type, as shown in Figure 6.1. The array size must be given to specify the number of elements that could be stored in the array when allocating space for the array. After the array is created, its size cannot be changed.

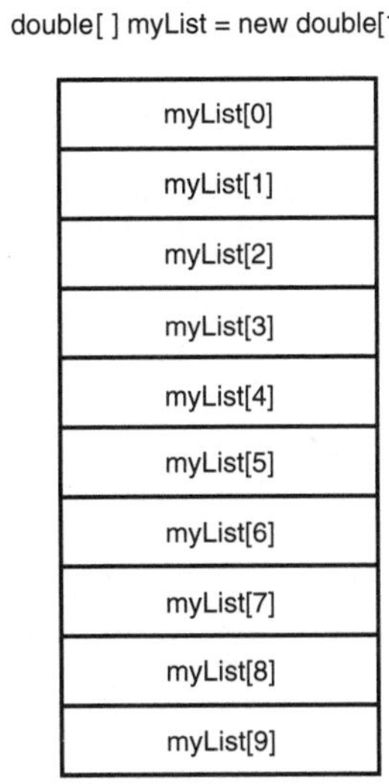

double[ ] myList = new double[10]

| myList[0] |
| myList[1] |
| myList[2] |
| myList[3] |
| myList[4] |
| myList[5] |
| myList[6] |
| myList[7] |
| myList[8] |
| myList[9] |

Figure 6.1 *The array* `myList` *has 10 elements of* `double` *type and integer indices from 0 to 9.*

Initializing and Processing Arrays

When arrays are created, the elements are assigned the default value of `0` for the numeric primitive data type variables, `'\u0000'` for `char` variables, `false` for `boolean` variables, and `null` for object variables. The array elements are accessed through the index. The array indices are from `0` to `arraySize-1`. In the example in Figure 6.1, `myList` holds 10 `double` values and the indices are from `0` to `9`.

Each element in the array is represented using the following syntax:

```
arrayName[index];
```

For example, `myList[9]` represents the last element in the array.

▰ NOTE

In Java, an array index is always an integer that starts with 0. In many other languages, such as Ada and Pascal, the index can be an integer or another type of value.

▰ CAUTION

Some languages use parentheses to reference an array element, as in `myList(9)`. But Java uses brackets, as in `myList[9]`.

After an array is created, you can enter values into array elements. For example, see the following loop:

```
for (int i = 0; i < myList.length; i++)
  myList[i] = (double)i;
```

In this example, `myList.length` returns the array size (10) for `myList`.

▰ NOTE

The size of an array is denoted by `arrayObject.length`. After an array is created, the `length` data field is assigned a value that denotes the number of elements in the array.

▰ CAUTION

The word `length` is a data field belonging to an array object, not to a method. Therefore, using `length()` would result in an error.

Java has a shorthand notation that creates an array object and initializes it at the same time. The following is an example of its syntax at work:

```
double[] myList = {1.9, 2.9, 3.4, 3.5};
```

This statement creates the array `myList`, which consists of four elements. Therefore, `myList.length` is 4 and `myList[0]` is 1.9. Note that the `new` operator was not used in the syntax.

When processing array elements, you will often use a `for` loop for the following reasons:

- All of the elements in the array are of the same type and have the same properties. They are even processed in the same fashion—by repeatedly using a loop.

- The size of the array is known; therefore, it is natural to use a `for` loop.

Example 6.1   Assigning Grades

In this example, a program is written that will read student scores (`int`) from the keyboard, get the best score, and then assign grades based on the following scheme:

Grade is A if score is >= best − 10;

Grade is B if score is >= best−20;

Grade is C if score is >= best−30;

Grade is D if score is >= best−40;

Grade is F otherwise.

The program prompts the user to enter the total number of students. It then prompts the user to enter all of the scores. Finally, it displays grades.

The output of a sample run of the program is shown in Figure 6.2.

```
public class AssigningGrade
{
  public static void main(String[] args)
  {
    int numOfStudents;
    int[] scores; //declare array scores
    int best = 0;
    char grade;

    //get number of students
    System.out.println("Please enter number of students");
    numOfStudents = MyInput.readInt();

    //create array scores
    scores = new int[numOfStudents];

    //read scores and find the best score
    System.out.println("Please enter scores");
    for (int i=0; i<scores.length; i++)
    {
      scores[i] = MyInput.readInt();
      if (scores[i] > best)
        best = scores[i];
    }

    //assign and display grades
    for (int i=0; i<scores.length; i++)
    {
      if (scores[i] >= best - 10)
        grade = 'A';
      else if (scores[i] >= best - 20)
        grade = 'B';
      else if (scores[i] >= best - 30)
        grade = 'C';
      else if (scores[i] >= best - 40)
        grade = 'D';
      else
        grade = 'F';

      System.out.println("Student "+i+" score is "+scores[i]+
        " and grade is " + grade);
    }
  }
}
```

continues

Example 6.1   continued

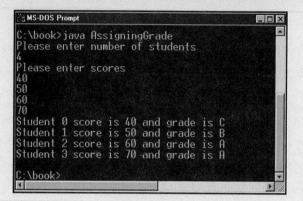

```
MS-DOS Prompt

C:\book>java AssigningGrade
Please enter number of students
4
Please enter scores
40
50
60
70
Student 0 score is 40 and grade is C
Student 1 score is 50 and grade is B
Student 2 score is 60 and grade is A
Student 3 score is 70 and grade is A

C:\book>
```

Figure 6.2 *The program receives the number of students and their scores and then assigns grades.*

Example Review

Array scores[] is declared in order to store scores. At the time this array is declared, the size of the array is undetermined. After the user enters the number of students into numOfStudents, an array with a size of numOfStudents is created.

The array is not needed to find the best score. However, the array is needed to keep all of the scores so that grades can be assigned later on, and it is needed when scores are printed along with the students' grades.

■■■ CAUTION

A common programming error is accessing an array out of bounds. To avoid this error, make sure that you do not use an index beyond arrayObject.length-1.

Programmers often mistakenly reference the first element in an array with index 1, so the index of the tenth element becomes 10. This is called the *off-by-one* error.

Sorting Arrays

Sorting is a common task in computer programming. For example, it would be used if you wanted to display the grades from the previous example in alphabetical order. There are many algorithms used for sorting. In this section, a simple, intuitive sorting algorithm, *selection sort*, is introduced.

Suppose that you want to sort a list in non-descending order. Selection sort finds the largest number in the list and places it last. It then finds the largest number remaining and places it last, and so on, until the remaining list contains a single number.

Consider the following list, for example:

2 9 5 4 8 1 **6**

If you had selected 9 (the largest number) and swapped it with 6 (the last in the list), the new list would be the following:

2 **6** 5 4 8 1 **9**

The number 9 would then be placed in the correct position in the list; therefore, it would not need to be considered any longer. You could apply selection sort to the remaining numbers in the list as follows:

2 6 5 4 **8** 1

From the remaining list, you would select 8 and swap it with 1. The new list would be the following:

2 6 5 4 **1 8**

The number 8 would then be placed in the correct position in the list; therefore, it would not need to be considered any longer. If you would continue in the same process, eventually the entire list would be sorted.

The algorithm could be described as follows:

```
for (int i=list.length-1; i>=1; i--)
{
  select the largest element in list[1..i];
  swap the largest with list[i], if necessary;
  //list[i] is in place. The next iteration apply on list[1..i-1]
}
```

The code is given in the following example. The selectionSort() method in this program works only for a list of double values. In Chapter 7, "Class Inheritance," you will learn the techniques for writing a generic method that will sort any type of elements in a list.

Example 6.2   Using Arrays in Sorting

In this example, the selectionSort() method is used to write a program that will sort a list of double floating-point numbers. The output of the program is shown in Figure 6.3.

```
public class TestSelectionSort
{
  public static void main(String[] args)
  {
    double[] myList = {5.0, 4.4, 1.9, 2.9, 3.4, 3.5};
    System.out.println("My list before sort is: ");
```

continues

Example 6.2   continued

```
        //print the original list
        printList(myList);
        selectionSort(myList);

        //print the sorted list
        System.out.println("My list after sort is: ");
        printList(myList);
    }

    static void printList(double[] list)
    {
      for (int i=0; i<list.length; i++)
        System.out.println(list[i]);
    }

    static void selectionSort(double[] list)
    {
      double currentMax;
      int currentMaxIndex;

      for (int i=list.length-1; i>=1; i--)
      {
        //find the maximum in the list[0..i]
        currentMax = list[i];
        currentMaxIndex = i;

        for (int j=i-1; j>=0; j--)
        {
          if (currentMax < list[j])
          {
            currentMax = list[j];
            currentMaxIndex = j;
          }
        }

        //swap list[i] with list[currentMaxIndex] if necessary;
        if (currentMaxIndex != i)
        {
          list[currentMaxIndex] = list[i];
          list[i] = currentMax;
        }
      }
    }
  }
```

Example Review

An array myList of length 6 was created. Its initial values are listed in the following single statement:

```
    double[] myList = {5.0, 4.4, 1.9, 2.9, 3.4, 3.5};
```

The selectionSort(double[] list) method sorts any array of double elements. The method is implemented with a nested for loop. The outer loop (with the loop control variable i) is iterated in order to find the largest element in the list—which ranges from list[0] to list[i]—and to exchange it with the current last element, list[i].

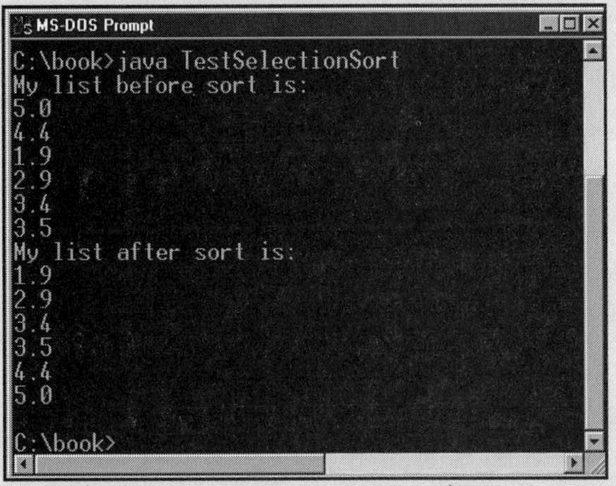

Figure 6.3 *The program invokes* `selectionSort` *in order to sort a list of* `double` *values.*

The variable `i` is initially `list.length-1`. After each iteration of the outer loop, `list[i]` is in the right place. Eventually, all the elements are put in the right place; therefore, the whole list is sorted.

Searching Arrays

Searching is the process of looking for a particular element in the array—for example, discovering whether a particular score is included in a list of scores. Searching, like sorting, is a common task in computer programming. There are many algorithms and data structures devoted to searching. In this section, two commonly used approaches are discussed, *linear search* and *binary search*.

The Linear Search Approach

The linear search approach compares the key element, `key`, with each element in the array `list[]`. The method continues to do so until the key matches an element in the list or the list is exhausted without a match being found. If a match is made, the linear search returns the index of the element in the array that matches the key. If no match is found, the search returns -1. The algorithm can be simply described as follows:

```
for (int i=0; i<list.length; i++)
{
  if (key == list[i])
    return i;
}

return -1;
```

The following example demonstrates a linear search.

Example 6.3   Testing Linear Search

In this example, a program is written that will implement and test the linear search method. This program creates an array of 10 elements of int type randomly and then displays this array. The program prompts the user to enter a key for testing linear search. The output of a sample run of the program is shown in Figure 6.4.

```java
public class TestLinearSearch
{
  public static void main(String[] args)
  {
    int[] list = new int[10];

    //create the list randomly and display it
    System.out.print("The list is  ");
    for (int i=0; i<list.length; i++)
    {
      list[i] = (int)(Math.random()*10);
      System.out.print(list[i]+"  ");
    }
    System.out.println(" ");

    //prompt the user to enter a key
    System.out.print("Enter a key  ");
    int key = MyInput.readInt();
    int index = linearSearch(key, list);
    if (index != -1)
      System.out.println("The key is found in index "+index);
    else
      System.out.println("The key is not found in the list");
  }

  public static int linearSearch(int key, int[] list)
  {
    for (int i=0; i<list.length; i++)
      if (key == list[i])
        return i;
    return -1;
  }
}
```

Figure 6.4 *The program uses linear search to find a key in a list of int elements.*

Example Review

`Math.random()` generates a random `double` value between 0 and 1. Therefore, `(int)(Math.random()*10)` is a random integer value between 0 and 10.

In case of a match, the algorithm returns the index of the first element in the array that matches the key. In case of no match, the algorithm returns `-1`.

The linear search method compares the key with each element in the array. The elements in the array can be in any order. On average, the algorithm will have to compare half of the elements in an array. The execution time of the linear search increases linearly as the number of array elements increases. Therefore, the linear search is inefficient for a large array.

The Binary Search Approach

Binary search is the other common search approach. For binary search to work, the array must already be in the right order. Without loss of generality, assume that the array is in non-descending order. The binary search first compares the key with the element in the middle of the array. Consider the following three cases:

- If the key is less than the middle element, you only need to search the key in the first half of the array.

- If the key is equal to the middle element, the search ends with a match.

- If the key is greater than the middle element, you only need to search the key in the second half of the array.

Clearly, the binary search method eliminates half of the array after each comparison. Suppose that the array has n elements. For convenience, let n be a power of 2. After the first comparison, there are $n/2$ elements left for further search; after the second comparison, there are $(n/2)/2$ elements left for further search. After the kth comparison, there are $n/2^k$ elements left for further search. When $k = \log_2 n$, only one element is left in the array, and you only need one more comparison. Therefore, in the worst case, you need $\log_2 n + 1$ comparisons for finding an element in the sorted array when using the binary search approach. For a list of 1,024 (2^{10}) elements, the binary search requires only 11 comparisons in the worst case.

The array being searched shrinks after each comparison. Let `low` and `up` denote the first index and the last index, respectively, of the array that is currently being searched. Initially, `low` is `0` and `up` is `list.length-1`. Let `binarySearch(int key, int[] list, int low, int up)` denote the method that finds the key in the list that has the specified `low` index and `up` index. The algorithm can be described recursively as follows:

```
public static int binarySearch(int key, int[] list, int low, int up)
{
```

```
      if (low > up)
        the list has been searched without a match, return -1;

      //find mid, the index of the middle element in list[low..up]
      int mid = (low+up)/2;
      if (key < list[mid])
        //Search in list[low..mid-1] recursively.
        return binarySearch(key, list, low, mid-1);
      else if (key == list[mid])
        //A match is found
        return mid;
      else if (key > list[mid])
        //Search in list[mid+1..up] recursively.
        return binarySearch(key, list, mid+1, up);
    }
```

The following example demonstrates the binary search approach.

Example 6.4   Testing Binary Search

In this example, a program is written that will implement and test the binary search method. The program first creates an array of 10 elements of int type. It displays that array and then prompts the user to enter a key for testing binary search. The output of sample runs of the program is shown in Figure 6.5.

```
public class TestBinarySearch
{
  public static void main(String[] args)
  {
    int[] list = new int[10];

    //create a sorted list and display it
    System.out.print("The list is  ");
    for (int i=0; i<list.length; i++)
    {
      list[i] = 2*i+1;
      System.out.print(list[i]+"  ");
    }
    System.out.println(" ");

    //prompt the user to enter a key
    System.out.print("Enter a key  ");
    int key = MyInput.readInt();
    int index = binarySearch(key, list);
    if (index != -1)
      System.out.println("The key is found in index "+index);
    else
      System.out.println("The key is not found in the list");
  }

  public static int binarySearch(int key, int[] list)
  {
    int low = 0;
    int up = list.length-1;
    return binarySearch(key, list, low, up);
  }
```

```
public static int binarySearch(int key, int[] list, int low, int up)
{
  if (low > up)  //the list has been exhausted without a match
    return -1;

  int mid = (low+up)/2;
  if (key < list[mid])
    return binarySearch(key, list, low, mid-1);
  else if (key == list[mid])
    return mid;
  else if (key > list[mid])
    return binarySearch(key, list, mid+1, up);

  return -1;
}
}
```

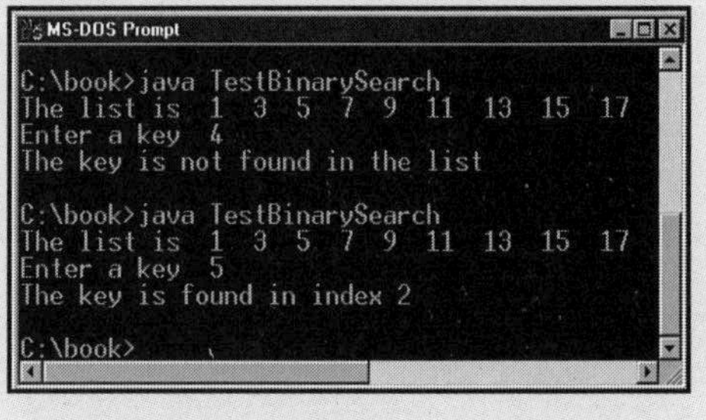

Figure 6.5 *The program uses binary search to find a key in a list of* int *elements.*

Example Review

There are two methods named binarySearch in the program: binarySearch(int key, int[] list) and binarySearch(int key, int[] list, int low, int up). The first method finds a key in the whole list. The second method finds a key in the list with index from low to up.

The first binarySearch method passes the initial array with low = 0 and up = list.length-1 to the second method. The second method is invoked recursively to find the key in an ever-shrinking subarray. It is a common design technique in recursive programming to choose a second method that can be called recursively.

The return statement in the last line of the second binarySearch is never executed. Its sole purpose is to fool the Java compiler. The Java compiler requires a return statement that is inside the method body but is not embedded in an inner block. All of the other return statements in the second method are embedded in the if statements, which are inner blocks in the method.

> **NOTE**
> Linear search is useful for finding an element in small arrays or unsorted arrays; however, it is inefficient for large arrays. If the array is sorted, binary search can be used more efficiently.

Array of Objects

In the previous examples, arrays of primitive type elements were created. It is also possible to create arrays of objects. For example, the following statement declares and creates an array of 10 `Circle` objects:

```
Circle[] circleArray = new Circle[10];
```

To initialize the `circleArray`, you can use a `for` loop such as the following:

```
for (int i=0; i<circleArray.length; i++)
{
  circleArray[i] = new Circle();
}
```

The following example demonstrates how to use an array of objects.

Example 6.5   Adding an Array of Rationals

In this example, a program is written that will summarize an array of rational numbers. The program creates an array, `rationalArray`—which is composed of 10 `Rational` objects—and initializes it with random values, then invokes the `sum()` method to add all rational numbers in the list. The output of a sample run of the program is shown in Figure 6.6.

```
public class TestArrayOfObjects
{
  public static void main(String[] args)
  {
    //create and initialize rationalArray
    Rational[] rationalArray = new Rational[10];

    //initialize rationalArray
    System.out.println("The Rational numbers are ");
    for (int i=0; i<rationalArray.length; i++)
    {
      rationalArray[i] = new Rational(
        (int)(Math.random()*10), 1+(int)(Math.random()*10));
      System.out.print(rationalArray[i] + " ");
    }

    System.out.println(" ");

    //compute and display the result
    System.out.println("the sum of the rational numbers is " +
    sum(rationalArray));
  }
```

```
        public static Rational sum(Rational[] rationalArray)
        {
          Rational sum = new Rational(0, 1);

          for (int i = 0; i < rationalArray.length; i++)
            sum = sum.add(rationalArray[i]);

          return sum;
        }
      }
```

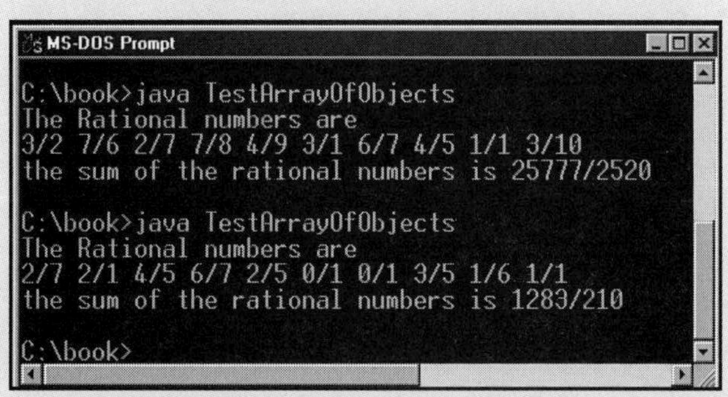

```
MS-DOS Prompt                                    _ □ ×

C:\book>java TestArrayOfObjects
The Rational numbers are
3/2 7/6 2/7 7/8 4/9 3/1 6/7 4/5 1/1 3/10
the sum of the rational numbers is 25777/2520

C:\book>java TestArrayOfObjects
The Rational numbers are
2/7 2/1 4/5 6/7 2/5 0/1 0/1 3/5 1/6 1/1
the sum of the rational numbers is 1283/210

C:\book>
```

Figure 6.6 *The program passes an array of* Rational *objects to the method* sum(), *which returns the sum of all the numbers in the array.*

Example Review

The program creates an array of 10 Rational objects and passes the array to the sum() method that adds all rational numbers in the array Rational[] and returns the sum. The Rational class was introduced in the "Case Studies" section of Chapter 5, "Programming with Objects and Classes."

The rational numbers were randomly generated using the Math.random() method. To avoid having a denominator of 0, 1 is added to the denominator purposely.

Copying Arrays

Often in a program, you need to duplicate an array or a part of an array. You could attempt to use the assignment statement (=), as follows:

```
newList = list;
```

It seems to work fine. But if you ran the following program, you would discover that it does not work. The following example explains the reason.

Example 6.6   Copying Arrays

In this example, you will see that the simple assignment cannot copy arrays in the following program. The program simply creates two arrays and attempts to copy one to the other using an assignment statement. The output of the program shown in Figure 6.7 demonstrates that the two arrays reference the same object after the attempted copy.

```java
public class TestCopyArray
{
  public static void main(String[] args)
  {
    int[] list = {0, 1, 2, 3, 4, 5};
    int[] newList = new int[list.length];

    newList = list;
    System.out.println("Before modifying list");
    printList("list is ", list);
    printList("newList is", newList);

    //modifying list
    for (int i=0; i<list.length; i++)
      list[i] = 0;

    System.out.println("After modifying list");
    printList("list is ", list);
    printList("newList is", newList);
  }

  public static void printList(String s, int[] list)
  {
    System.out.print(s+" ");
    for (int i=0; i<list.length; i++)
      System.out.print(list[i]+" ");

    System.out.print('\n');
  }
}
```

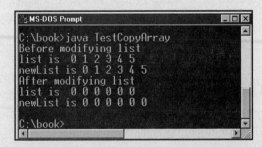

Figure 6.7 *When you are using the assignment statement to copy a source array to a target array, both arrays refer to the same memory location, just as objects do when they are copied using assignment statements.*

Example Review

The program creates two arrays, list and newList; assigns list to newList; and displays both list and newList. The program then changes the value in list and redisplays list and newList. You may have noticed that the newList's value was also changed. This occurs because the assignment statement newList = list makes newList point to list's memory location. Conversely, if you change the value in newList, list will see the same change.

The print('\n') method in the printList() method prints the new line character ('\n'), which causes the next print statement to print from a new line.

NOTE

In Java, you can copy primitive data type variables using assignment statements, but not objects, such as arrays. Assigning one object to another object makes both objects point to the same memory location.

There are two ways to copy arrays: copying individual elements using a loop and using the arraycopy() method.

One way to copy arrays is to write a loop that will copy every element, from the source array to the corresponding element in the target array. For example, the following code copies the sourceArray to the targetArray:

```
for (int i = 0; i < sourceArrays.length; i++)
   targetArray[i] = sourceArray[i];
```

This approach is problematic if the elements of the array are objects. To remedy this problem, Java offers an efficient way to copy arrays. You can use the System.arraycopy() method to copy arrays instead of using a loop. The syntax for arraycopy() is as follows:

```
arraycopy(sourceArray, src_pos, targetArray, tar_pos, length);
```

The parameters src_pos and tar_pos indicate the starting position in sourceArray and in targetArray, respectively. The number of elements copied from sourceArray to targetArray is indicated by length. For example, you can rewrite the loop using the following statement:

```
int[] sourceArray = {2, 3, 1, 5, 10};
int[] targetArray = new int[sourceArray.length];
System.arraycopy(sourceArray, 0, targetArray, 0, sourceArray.length);
```

The arraycopy() method does not allocate memory space for the target array. The target array must already be created with its memory space allocated. After the copying takes place, targetArray and sourceArray have independent memory locations. The arraycopy() method can copy any type (primitive type or object type) of array elements.

Multidimensional Arrays

Thus far, you have used one-dimensional arrays to model a linear collection of elements. To represent a matrix or a table, you can use a two-dimensional array. A two-dimensional array in Java is declared as an array of array objects. For example, you can use the following code to declare and create a 5-by-5 matrix:

```
int[][] matrix = new int[5][5];
```

or

```
int matrix[][] = new int[5][5];
```

You can also use a shorthand notation to declare and initialize a two-dimensional array. For example,

```
int[][] matrix =
{
  {1, 2, 3, 4, 5},
  {2, 3, 4, 5, 6),
  {3, 4, 5, 6, 7),
  {4, 5, 6, 7, 8},
  {5, 6, 7, 8, 9}
};
```

Two subscripts are used in a two-dimensional array, one for the main array and the other for the array contained within the main array. For convenience, these are referred to as the *main subscript* and the *secondary subscript*. To assign a value 7 to a specific element at main subscript 2 and secondary subscript 0, you can use the following:

```
matrix[2][0] = 7;
```

Occasionally, you will need to represent multidimensional data structures. In Java, you can create *n* dimensional arrays for any integer *n*, as long as your computer has sufficient memory to store the array.

Example 6.7   Testing Multidimensional Arrays

In this example, a program is written that uses two-dimensional arrays to create two matrices. The program then adds the two matrices. The output of this program is shown in Figure 6.8.

```java
public class TestMatrixAddition
{
  public static void main(String[] args)
  {
    int[][] matrix1 = new int[5][5];
    int[][] matrix2 = new int[5][5];

    //assign random values to matrix1 and matrix2
    for (int i=0; i<matrix1.length; i++)
      for (int j=0; j<matrix1[i].length; j++)
      {
        matrix1[i][j] = (int)(Math.random()*1000);
```

```
            matrix2[i][j] = (int)(Math.random()*1000);
        }

      printMatrix(matrix1);
      System.out.println();
      printMatrix(matrix2);
      System.out.println();
      System.out.println();

      int[][] resultMatrix = new int[5][5];
      resultMatrix = addMatrix(matrix1, matrix2);
      printMatrix(resultMatrix);
    }

    public static int[][] addMatrix(int[][] m1, int[][] m2)
    {
      int[][] temp = new int[m1.length][m1[0].length];

      for (int i=0; i<m1.length; i++)
        for (int j=0; j<m1[i].length; j++)
          temp[i][j] = m1[i][j] + m2[i][j];

      return temp;
    }

    public static void printMatrix(int[][] m)
    {
      for (int i=0; i<m.length; i++)
      {
        for (int j=0; j<m[0].length; j++)
          System.out.print(" "+m[i][j]);
        System.out.println();
      }
    }
}
```

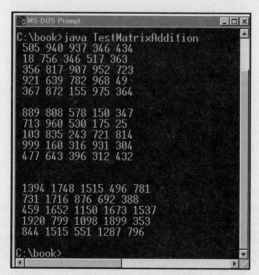

Figure 6.8 *The program adds two matrices that are represented in two-dimensional arrays.*

continues

Example 6.7   continued

Example Review

The statement `int[ ][ ] matrix1 = new int[5][5]` declares and creates a 5-by-5 matrix.

Nested `for` loops are often used to process multidimensional array elements. The matrices `matrix1` and `matrix2` are initialized by using a nested `for` loop with random values.

The `addMatrix(int[ ][ ] m1, int[ ][ ] m2)` method adds `m1` and `m2` and returns the result matrix.

The *String* Class

The `java.lang.String` class represents character strings. You have used string literals, such as the parameters in the `println()` method. The Java compiler actually converts the string literal into a string object and passes it to `println()`.

To create a string explicitly, use the syntax like this:

```
String newString = new String(s);
```

The component `s` is a sequence of characters enclosed inside double quotes. For example, the following statement creates a `String` object `message` for the string literal `"Welcome to Java!"`:

```
String message = new String("Welcome to Java!");
```

Alternatively, you can declare and create a string like this:

```
String message = "Welcome to Java!";
```

String Comparisons

Often in a program, you need to compare the contents of two strings. You could attempt to use the `==` operator as follows:

```
if (string1 == string2)
   System.out.println("string1 and string2 are the same object");
else
   System.out.println("string1 and string2 are different objects");
```

However, the `==` operator only checks whether `string1` and `string2` refer to the same object; it does not tell you whether `string1` and `string2` contain the same contents when they are different objects. Therefore, you cannot use the `==` operator to find whether two string variables have the same contents. You should instead use the `equals()` method for the equality comparison of the contents of objects. For example, you can use the following code to compare two strings:

```
if (string1.equals(string2))
```

```
        System.out.println("string1 and string2 have the same contents");
    else
        System.out.println("string1 and string2 are not equal");
```

To compare two strings, you can also use the `compareTo()` method. For example, see the following code:

```
    s1.compareTo(s2)
```

The method returns the value 0 if s1 is equal to s2, a value less than 0 if s1 is lexicographically less than s2, and a value greater than 0 if s1 is lexicographically greater than s2.

The actual value returned depends on the offset of the first two distinct characters in s1 and s2 from left to right. For example, suppose s1 is "abc" and s2 is "abe", and s1.compareTo(s2) returns -2. The first two characters (a versus a) from s1 and s2 are compared. Because they are equal, the second two characters (b versus b) are compared. Because they are also equal, the third characters (c versus e) are compared. Because the character c is 2 less than e, the comparison returns -2.

▬▬ CAUTION

It would cause syntax errors to compare strings by using comparison operators, such as >, >=, <, <=, or !=. Instead, you have to use s1.compareTo(s2).

The `equals()` method returns `true` if two strings are equal and `false` if they are not equal. The `compareTo()` method returns 0, a positive integer, or a negative integer, depending on whether a string is equal to, greater than, or less than the other string.

The `String` class also provides `equalsIgnoreCase()` and `regionMatches()` methods for comparing strings. The `equalsIgnoreCase()` method ignores the case of the letters when determining if two strings are equal. The `regionMatches()` method compares portions of two strings for equality. For more information, please refer to the JDK documentation.

String Concatenation

You can concatenate two or more strings using the plus sign (+). For example, the following code combines the three strings `message`, `" and "`, and `"HTML!"` into one string.

```
    String myString = message + " and " + "HTML!";
```

Recall that you have used the + sign to concatenate numbers with strings in the `println()` method. The numbers are converted into strings and then concatenated.

Substrings

After a string is created, its value cannot be changed individually. For example, you cannot change `"Java"` in `message` to `"HTML"`. The JDK documentation refers to `String` as an immutable class. So what can you do if you need to change the message string? You can assign a new string to message. For example, see the following code:

```
message = "Welcome to HTML!";
```

Alternatively, you can use the substring() method. You can extract a substring from a string using the substring() method in the String class as follows:

```
String message = message.substring(0,10) + "HTML!";
```

The string message now becomes "Welcome to HTML!". The first character in a Java string has a position of 0.

String Length and Retrieving Individual Characters in a String

You can get the length of a string by invoking its length() method. For example, message.length() returns the length of the string message.

CAUTION
To get the length of an array, you use the array's property length. To get the length of a string, you use the string's length() method. For example a.length indicates the number of elements in array a, while s.length() returns the number of characters in string s.

You can use the s.charAt(index) method to retrieve a specific character in a string s, where the index is between 0 and s.length-1. For example, message.charAt(0) returns the character W.

CAUTION
It is incorrect to use s[0] to access the first character in string s. Instead, you must use s.charAt(0).

The *StringBuffer* Class

The StringBuffer class is an alternative to the String class. In general, a string buffer can be used wherever a string is used. StringBuffer is more flexible than String. You can add, insert, or append new contents into a string buffer. However, the value of a string is fixed once the string is created.

Many of the methods in the StringBuffer class are synchronized to ensure that the contents in StringBuffer are not corrupted when running with multiple threads (which is introduced in Chapter 12, "Multithreading"). The StringBuffer class provides three constructors:

- **public StringBuffer()**—Constructs a string buffer with no characters in it and with an initial capacity of 16 characters.

- **public StringBuffer(int length)**—Constructs a string buffer with no characters in it and an initial capacity specified by the length argument.

■ **public StringBuffer(String str)**—Constructs a string buffer so that it represents the same sequence of characters as the `string` argument. The initial capacity of the string buffer is 16 plus the length of the `string` argument.

Appending and Inserting New Contents into a *StringBuffer*

You can append new contents at the end of the string buffer or insert new contents at a specified position in the string buffer.

The `StringBuffer` class provides 10 overloaded methods to append `boolean`, `char`, `char array`, `double`, `float`, `int`, `long`, `String`, and so on into a string buffer. For example, the following code appends strings and characters into `strBuf` to form a new string, `"Welcome to Java"`.

```
StringBuffer strBuf = new StringBuffer();
strBuf.append("Welcome");
strBuf.append(' ');
strBuf.append("to");
strBuf.append(' ');
strBuf.append("Java");
```

The `StringBuffer` class also contains 9 overloaded methods to insert `boolean`, `char`, `char array`, `double`, `float`, `int`, `long`, `String`, and so on into a string buffer. For example, consider the following code:

```
strBuf.insert(11, "HTML and ");
```

Suppose `strBuf` contains `"Welcome to Java"` before the `insert` method is applied. This code inserts `"HTML and "` at position 11 in `strBuf` (just before `J`). The new `strBuf` is `"Welcome to HTML and Java"`.

NOTE
Every string buffer has a capacity. If the capacity of a string buffer is exceeded, the buffer is automatically made larger to accommodate the additional characters.

The *capacity()*, *reverse()*, *length()*, *setLength()*, *charAt()*, and *setCharAt()* Methods

The `StringBuffer` class provides many other methods for manipulating string buffers. Here are some examples.

The following method returns the current capacity of the string buffer:

```
public int capacity()
```

The `capacity` is the number of new characters that can be stored in the string buffer.

The following method reverses the sequence of the string contained in this string buffer:

```
public synchronized StringBuffer reverse()
```

The following method returns the number of characters in this string buffer:

```
public int length()
```

The following method sets the length of this string buffer:

```
public synchronized setLength(int newLength)
```

If the newLength argument is less than the current length of the string buffer, then the string buffer is truncated to contain exactly the number of characters given by the newLength argument. If the newLength argument is greater than, or equal to, the current length, sufficient null characters ('\u0000') are appended to the string buffer so that length becomes the newLength argument. The newLength argument must be greater than or equal to 0.

The following method returns the character at a specific index in the string buffer:

```
public synchronized charAt(int index)
```

The first character of a string buffer is at index 0, the next at index 1, and so on, for array indexing. The index argument must be greater than or equal to 0, and less than the length of this string buffer.

The following method sets the character at the specified index of this string buffer to ch:

```
public synchronized void setCharAt(int index, char ch)
```

Example 6.8   Testing *StringBuffer*

This example gives a program to print the multiplication table created in Example 3.3, "Using Nested for Loops," from Chapter 3. Rather than printing one number at a time in the table, the program appends all the elements of the table into a string buffer. After the table is completely constructed in the string buffer, the program prints the entire string buffer on the console once. The output of the program is the same as shown in Figure 3.8.

```
public class TestMulTableUsingStringBuffer
{
  public static void main(String[] args)
  {
    StringBuffer strBuf = new StringBuffer();

    //display the title
    strBuf.append("      Multiplication Table" + '\n');
    strBuf.append("----------------" + '\n');

    //display the number title
    strBuf.append("   ¦ ");

    for (int j=1; j<=9; j++)
      strBuf.append("  "+j);

    strBuf.append('\n');
```

```
        for (int i=1; i<=9; i++)
        {
          strBuf.append(i+" ¦ ");
          for (int j=1; j<=9; j++)
          {
            //display the product and align properly
            if (i*j < 10)
              strBuf.append("  "+i*j);
            else
              strBuf.append(" "+i*j);
          }

          strBuf.append(" " + '\n');
        }

        System.out.println(strBuf);
      }
    }
```

Example Review

The program builds the multiplication table and stores it in the string buffer strBuf using the append() method. The program is the same as that used in Example 3.3 except that all the print statements in Example 3.3 are replaced by the strBuf.append() statements.

The System.out.println(strBuf) displays the string stored in strBuf to the console.

This program should run faster than that in Example 3.3 because the print() method is called only once to display the entire table onscreen. You can measure the runtime to confirm the performance improvements after you learn to use the Date class in Chapter 7.

TIP

You can use StringBuffer to construct an output string and display the whole string once to reduce I/O time and improve performance.

If the string does not require any change, you should use String rather than StringBuffer. Java can perform some optimizations for String, such as sharing one string among multiple references, because strings do not change after they are created.

The *StringTokenizer* Class

The java.util.StringTokenizer class is used to break a string into pieces so that information contained in the string can be retrieved and processed. For example, to get all of the words in a string such as "I am learning Java now", you can create an instance of the StringTokenizer class for the string and then retrieve individual words in the string by using the methods in the StringTokenizer class.

How does the `StringTokenizer` class recognize individual words? You can specify a set of characters as delimiters when constructing a `StringTokenizer` object. The delimiters break a string into pieces, which are known as *tokens*.

The following code constructs a `StringTokenizer` for string s with specified delimiters:

```
public StringTokenizer(String s, String delim, boolean returnTokens)
```

If `returnTokens` is `true`, the delimiter is returned as a token.

The following constructor constructs a `StringTokenizer` for string s with specified delimiters `delim`, and the delimiter is not considered a token:

```
public StringTokenizer(String s, String delim)
```

The following constructor constructs a `StringTokenizer` for string s with default delimiters `" \t\n\r"` (space, tab, new line, and carriage return), and the delimiter is not considered a token:

```
public StringTokenizer(String s)
```

You can use the following instance methods in the `StringTokenizer` class. The following method returns `true` if there is any token left in the string:

```
public boolean hasMoreTokens()
```

The following method returns the next token in the string:

```
public String nextToken()
```

The following method returns the next token in the string after resetting the delimiter to `delim`:

```
public String nextToken(String delim)
```

Example 6.9   Testing *StringTokenizer*

In this example, a program is written that will retrieve words from a string `"I am learning Java. Show me how to use StringTokenizer."` using a string tokenizer and display them on the console. The output of the program is shown in Figure 6.9.

```
import java.util.StringTokenizer;

public class TestStringTokenizer
{
  public static void main(String[] args)
  {
    //create a string and string tokenizer
    String s =
      "I am learning Java. Show me how to use StringTokenizer.";
    StringTokenizer st = new StringTokenizer(s);

    //retrieve and display tokens
    System.out.println("The total number of words is "+
      st.countTokens());
```

```
        while (st.hasMoreTokens())
          System.out.println(st.nextToken());
     }
   }
```

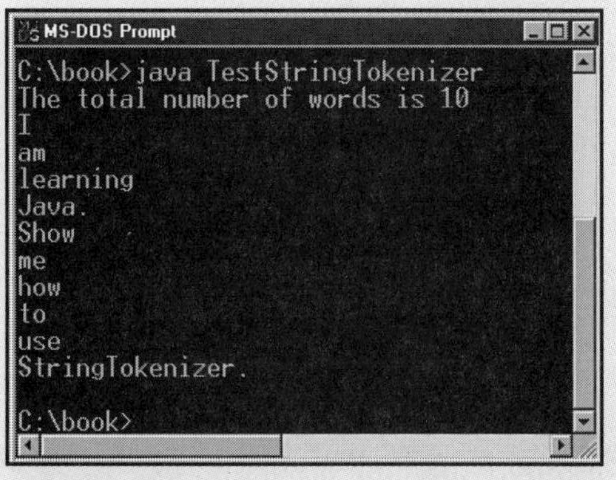

Figure 6.9 *The program uses the* `StringTokenizer` *class to extract tokens from a string.*

Example Review

The `String` class is in the `java.lang` package, so it is automatically imported. But the `StringTokenizer` class is in the `java.util` package. You need to import the `StringTokenizer` class from the `java.util` package. After all tokens are read, `st.countTokens()` is 0.

If you redefine `StringTokenizer` as follows, the same words will be displayed in the program, but the dot will not be shown:

```
StringTokenizer st = new StringTokenizer(s, ". \n\t\r");
```

Command-Line Arguments

Perhaps you have already noticed the unusual declarations for the `main()` method, which has parameter `args` of `String[]` type. It is clear that `args` is an array of strings. The `main()` method is just like a regular method with parameters. You can call a regular method by passing actual parameters. Can you pass parameters to `main()`? This section will discuss how to pass and process arguments from the command line.

Passing Arguments to Java Programs

You can pass arguments to a Java program from the command line when you run the program. For example, the following command line starts the program TestMain with three arguments: arg0, arg1, and arg2:

```
java TestMain arg0 arg1 arg2
```

173

These arguments are strings, but they do not have to appear in double quotes on the command line. The arguments are separated by a space. If an argument itself contains a space, you must use double quotes to group all of the items in the argument. For example, consider the following command line:

```
java TestMain "First num" alpha 53
```

It starts the program with three arguments: `"First num"` and `alpha`, which are strings, and `53`, a numeric string. Note that `53` is actually treated as a string. You can use `"53"` instead of `53` in the command line.

Processing Command-Line Parameters

The arguments passed to the main program are stored in `args`, which is an array of strings. The first parameter is represented by `args[0]`, and `args.length` is the number of arguments passed.

Example 6.10   Using Command-Line Parameters

In this example, a program is written that will perform binary operations on integers. The program receives three parameters: an operator and two integers. For example, to add two integers, the following command could be used:

```
java TestCommandParameters + 2 3
```

The program will display the following output:

```
2 + 3 = 5
```

The output of sample runs of the program is shown in Figure 6.10.

```java
public class TestCommandParameters
{
    public static void main(String[] args)
    {
      int result = 0;

      if (args.length != 3)
      {
        System.out.println(
          "please use java TestCommandParameters " +
          "operator operand1 operand2");
        System.exit(0);
      }

      switch (args[0].charAt(0))
      {
        case '+': result = Integer.parseInt(args[1]) +
                           Integer.parseInt(args[2]);
                  break;
        case '-': result = Integer.parseInt(args[1]) -
                           Integer.parseInt(args[2]);
                  break;
        case '*': result = Integer.parseInt(args[1]) *
                           Integer.parseInt(args[2]);
```

```
                        break;
          case '/': result = Integer.parseInt(args[1]) /
                             Integer.parseInt(args[2]);
        }

        System.out.println(args[1]+args[0]+args[2]+"="+result);
      }
    }
```

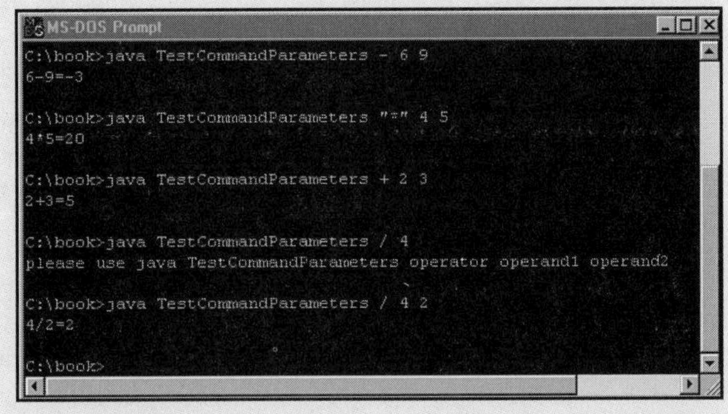

Figure 6.10 *The program takes three parameters (an operator and two operands) from the command line and displays the expression and the result of the arithmetic operation.*

Example Review

The program first tests whether three command-line arguments have been provided. If not, System.exit(0) terminates the program.

The arithmetic operations are performed according to args[0], the operator.

Integer.parseInt(args[1]) converts a digital string into an integer. The string must consist of digits. If not, the program will terminate abnormally. Integer, a class in java.lang, is introduced in Chapter 7.

In the sample run, "*" is used instead of * for the command java TestCommandParameters "*" 4 5. In JDK 1.1 or above, the * symbol refers to all the files in the current directory when it is used on a command line. For example, the following program displays all the files in the current directory when issuing the command java Test *.

```
public class Test
{
  public static void main(String[] args)
  {
    for (int i=0; i<args.length; i++)
      System.out.println(args[i]);
  }
}
```

Chapter Summary

In this chapter, you learned about using array objects to store a collection of data of the same type and using `String` objects for processing character strings. You also learned about passing and processing command-line arguments.

You learned how to declare and create arrays and how to access individual elements in an array. Java stores lists of values in arrays, which are contiguous groups of adjacent memory locations. To refer to a particular location or element of an array, you should specify the name of the array and then give the index, which should be placed in brackets. An index must be an integer or an integer expression.

A Java array is an object. After an array is created, its size becomes permanent and can be obtained using `arrayObject.length`. The index of an array always begins with 0. Therefore, the last index is always `arrayObject.length-1`. An out-of-bounds error would occur if you attempted to reference elements beyond the bounds of an array.

The `for` loop is often used to process all of the elements in an array. You can use `for` loops to initialize arrays, to display arrays, and to control and manipulate array elements.

Arrays can be passed to a method as actual parameters. An array is an object, so arrays are passed by reference; that is, the called method can modify the elements in the caller's original arrays.

You can use arrays of array objects to form multidimensional arrays. You learned a convenient syntax that can be used to declare multidimensional arrays, and you saw an example of using a multidimensional array.

Strings are objects, encapsulated in the `String` class. You learned how to create and initialize a string, compare strings, concatenate strings, use substrings, and access individual characters in strings.

The `StringBuffer` class can be used to replace the `String` class. The `String` object is immutable, but you can add, insert, or append new contents into a `StringBuffer` object. Use `String` if the string contents do not require any change, and use `StringBuffer` if the string contents change.

The `StringTokenizer` class is used to retrieve and process tokens in a string. You learned the role of delimiters, how to create a string tokenizer from a string, and how to use the `countTokens()`, `hasMoreTokens()`, and `nextToken()` methods to process a string tokenizer.

Chapter Review

1. How do you declare and create an array?

2. Is an array an object or a primitive type value?

3. Is memory allocated when an array is declared? When is the memory allocated for an array?

4. Indicate true or false for the following statements:

    a. Every element in an array has the same type.

    b. The array size is fixed after it is declared.

    c. The array size is fixed after it is created.

    d. The element in the array must be of primitive data type.

5. Which of the following statements are valid array declarations?

```
int i = new int(30);

double d[] = new double[30];

Rational[] r = new Rational(1..30);

int i[] = (3, 4, 3, 2);

float f[] = {2.3, 4.5, 5.6};

char[] c = new char();

Rational[][] r = new Rational[2];
```

6. What is the array index type? What is the lowest index?

7. What is the representation of the third element in an array named a? Write a method to discover whether array a has an element that has a value of 2. If it does, find the index of that element.

8. What happens when your program attempts to access an array element with an invalid index?

9. What does the following program do?

```
public class Test
{
  public static void main(String[] args)
  {
    Rational[] r = {new Rational(2,3), new Rational(-1, 3),
                    new Rational(3,5)};
    double[] d = new double[r.length];

    for (int i=0; i<r.length; i++)
      d[i] = r[i].getNumer() / r[i].getDenom();
  }
}
```

10. Use `arraycopy()` to copy r to d in the previous problem.

11. Declare and create a 4×5 int matrix.

12. Suppose that s1 and s2 are two strings. Which of the following statements or expressions are incorrect?

```
String s = new String("new string");

String s3 = s1 + s2;
```

```
String s3 = s1 - s2;
s1 == s2;
s1 >= s2;
s1.compareTo(s2);
int i = s1.length();
char c = s1(0);
char c = s1.charAt(s1.length());
```

13. Declare a `StringTokenizer` for a string s with slash (/) and backslash (\) as delimiters.

Programming Exercises

1. Write a program that will read 100 integers and display the numbers in reverse order.

2. Use recursion to rewrite the selection sort that is used in Example 6.2.

3. Use iterations to rewrite the binary search that is used in Example 6.4.

4. Write a program that meets the following requirements:

   a. Create a class for students. The class must contain the student's name (`String`), ID (`int`), and status (`int`). The status indicates the student's class standing: 1 for freshman, 2 for sophomore, 3 for junior, and 4 for senior.

   b. Create 20 students whose names are Name1, Name2, and so on to Name20, and whose IDs and status are assigned randomly.

   c. Find all juniors and print their names and IDs.

5. Write a program that meets the following requirements:

   a. Write a method that will multiply two `int` square matrices. The method is declared as follows:

      ```
      public static int[][] multiply(int[][] m1, int[][] m2)
      ```

      The algorithm for matrix multiplication can be described as follows:

      ```
      for (int i=0; i<m.length; i++)
        for (int j=0; j<m.length; j++)
        {
          c[i][j] = 0;
          for (int k=0; k<m.length; k++)
            c[i][j] = c[i][j] + m1[i][k]*m2[k][j];
        }
      ```

   b. Write a `main()` method in the same class to test the method.

6. Write a sort method using the bubble sort algorithm. The bubble sort algorithm makes several passes through the array. On each pass, neighboring pairs

are compared successively. If a pair is in decreasing order, its values are swapped; otherwise, the values remain unchanged. The technique is called *bubble sort* or *sinking sort* because the smaller values gradually "bubble" their way to the top and the larger values sink to the bottom.

The algorithm can be described as follows:

```
boolean changed = true;
do
{
  changed = false;
  for (int j=0; j<list.length-1; j++)
    if (list[j] > list[j+1])
    {
      swap list[j] with list[j+1];
      changed = true;
    }
}
while (changed);
```

Clearly, the list is in increasing order when the loop terminates. It is easy to show that the do loop executes at most list.length −1 times.

7. Write a program that meets the following requirements:

   a. Write a method that will check whether a string is a palindrome: a string that reads the same forward and backward.

   b. Write a program that will take a string from a command-line argument in order to check whether it is a palindrome.

8. Write a program similar to the one in Example 6.10. Instead of using integers, use rationals. You will need to use the StringTokenizer class to retrieve numerators and denominators.

CHAPTER 7

CLASS INHERITANCE

Objectives

- Understand the concept of class inheritance and the relationship between superclasses and subclasses.

- Create new classes from existing classes.

- Learn to use two keywords: super and this.

- Learn to use three modifiers: protected, final, and abstract.

- Become familiar with casting objects.

- Become familiar with the Number class and its subclasses.

- Design abstract classes in generic programming.

- Learn to use the Java date- and time-processing capabilities.

- Understand the concept of interfaces.

- Know inner classes.

- Become familiar with class design guidelines.

Introduction

With object-oriented programming, you can derive new classes from existing classes. This is called *inheritance*. In Chapter 1, "Introduction to Java," you created the WelcomeApplet applet by deriving it from the Applet class. Inheritance is an important and powerful concept in Java. In fact, every class you define in Java is inherited from an existing class, either explicitly or implicitly. The Circle class is actually derived implicitly from the class Object.

This chapter introduces the concept of inheritance. Specifically, it discusses superclasses and subclasses, the use of keywords super and this, the protected modifier, the final modifier, the abstract modifier, casting objects, several useful Java classes (such as Object, Number, Date, and Calendar), the interface, and class design guidelines.

Superclasses and Subclasses

In Java terminology, the existing class is called the *superclass*. The class derived from the superclass is called the *subclass*. Sometimes a superclass is referred to as a *parent class* or a *base class*, and a subclass is referred to as a *child class*, an *extended class*, or a *derived class*. You can reuse or change the methods of superclasses, and you can add new data and new methods in the subclasses. Subclasses usually have more functionality than their superclasses.

NOTE

Contrary to conventional interpretation, a subclass is not a subset of its superclass. In fact, a subclass usually contains more functions and more detailed information than its superclass.

Example 7.1   Demonstrating Inheritance

To demonstrate inheritance, this example creates a new class for Cylinder from Circle. The Cylinder class inherits all the data and methods from the Circle class. In addition, the Cylinder class has a new data field length and a new method findVolume().

The relationship of these two classes is shown in Figure 7.1.

The Cylinder class can be declared as follows:

```
public class Cylinder extends Circle
{
  private double length;

  //default constructor
  public Cylinder()
  {
    super();
```

```
        length = 1.0;
    }

    //constructor
    public Cylinder(double r, double l)
    {
        super(r);
        length = l;
    }

    //getter method
    public double getLength()
    {
        return length;
    }

    //find cylinder volume
    public double findVolume()
    {
        return findArea()*length;
    }
}
```

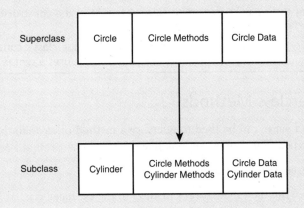

Figure 7.1   *The* Cylinder *class inherits data and methods from the* Circle *class and extends the* Circle *class with its own data and methods.*

Example Review

Before compiling this program, make sure you have already compiled the Circle class defined in Example 5.3, "Using the private Modifier," in Chapter 5, "Programming with Objects and Classes."

The reserved word extends tells the compiler that the Cylinder class is derived from the Circle class, thus inheriting data and methods from Circle.

The keyword super is used in the constructors. This keyword is discussed in the following section.

Using the Keyword *super*

The keyword super refers to the superclass of the class in which super appears. This keyword can be used in two ways:

- To call a superclass constructor
- To call a superclass method

Calling Superclass Constructors

The syntax to call a superclass constructor is

```
super(parameters);
```

In the Cylinder class, for example, super() and super(r) are used to call the constructors from the Circle class to initialize the radius. The component super() must appear in the first line of the constructor and is the only way to invoke a superclass's constructor.

> ### CAUTION
> Java requires the super() statement to appear first in the constructor, even before data fields.
>
> It also requires using the keyword super to call the superclass's constructor. Invoking a superclass constructor's name in a subclass causes a syntax error.

Calling Superclass Methods

The keyword super can be used to reference a method other than the constructor in the superclass. The syntax can look like this:

```
super.method(parameters);
```

You could rewrite the findVolume() method in the Cylinder class as follows:

```
double findVolume()
{
  return super.findArea()*length;
}
```

It is not necessary to put super before findArea() in this case, however, because findArea() is a method in the Circle class and can be accessed in the Cylinder class. Nevertheless, in some cases the keyword super is needed.

The following two examples demonstrate the use of inheritance and the super keyword.

Example 7.2 Testing Inheritance

This example shows a program that creates a Cylinder object and explores the relationship between the Cylinder and Circle classes by accessing the data and methods (radius, findArea()) defined in the Circle class and the data and methods (length, findVolume()) defined in the Cylinder class. The output of the program is shown in Figure 7.2.

```
public class TestCylinder
{
  public static void main(String[] args)
  {
    //create a Cylinder object and display its properties
    Cylinder myCylinder = new Cylinder(5.0, 2.0);
    System.out.println("The length is " + myCylinder.getLength());
    System.out.println("The radius is " + myCylinder.getRadius());
    System.out.println("The volume of the cylinder is " +
      myCylinder.findVolume());
    System.out.println("The area of the circle is " +
      myCylinder.findArea());
  }
}
```

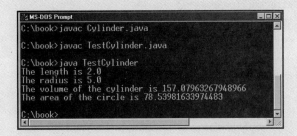

Figure 7.2 *The program creates a* Cylinder *object and accesses the data and methods defined in the* Circle *class and in the* Cylinder *class.*

Example Review

Because this program uses the Cylinder class, you should have compiled the program in Example 7.1 before compiling this program. The Cylinder class extends all functionality of the Circle class. The myCylinder object inherits all the data and methods in Circle. Therefore, it can access data (radius) and methods (findArea()) defined in the Circle class.

A subclass cannot call a superclass's constructor without using the super keyword. If you replace super() with Circle() in the Cylinder class, you will get a compilation error.

Overriding Methods

The subclass inherits methods from the superclass. Sometimes, it is necessary for the subclass to modify the methods defined in the superclass. This is referred to as *method overriding*.

Example 7.3   Overriding the Methods in the Superclass

In this example, the Cylinder class defined in Example 7.1 is modified to override the findArea() method in the Circle class. The findArea() method in the Circle class is to compute the area of a circle, while the findArea() method in the Cylinder class computes the surface area of a cylinder. The output of the program is shown in Figure 7.3.

```
public class TestModifyingMethods
{
  public static void main(String[] args)
  {
    Cylinder myCylinder = new Cylinder(5.0, 2.0);
    System.out.println("The surface area of the cylinder is "+
      myCylinder.findArea());
    System.out.println("The volume of the cylinder is "+
      myCylinder.findVolume());
  }
}

class Cylinder extends Circle
{
  private double length;

  //default constructor
  public Cylinder()
  {
    super();
    length = 1.0;
  }

  //constructor
  public Cylinder(double r, double l)
  {
    super(r);
    length = l;
  }

  public double getLength()
  {
    return length;
  }

  public double findArea()
  {
    return 2*super.findArea()+2*getRadius()*Math.PI*length;
  }

  public double findVolume()
  {
    return super.findArea()*length;
  }
}
```

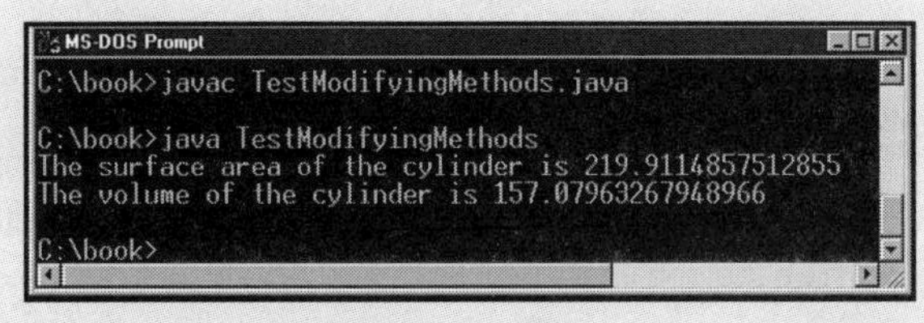

Figure 7.3 *The* Cylinder *class overrides the* findArea() *method defined in the* Circle *class.*

Example Review

The example demonstrates that you can modify the method in the superclass (Circle) and can use super to invoke a method in the superclass. The findArea() method is defined in the Circle class and modifies the Cylinder class. A Cylinder object can use both methods. To use the findArea() method in the Circle class, a Cylinder object must invoke super.findArea().

A subclass of the Cylinder class can no longer access the findArea() method defined in the Circle class because the findArea() method is redefined in the Cylinder class.

The Keyword *this*

The keyword super is used to reference superclasses. Occasionally, you need to reference the current class. Java provides another keyword, this, for referencing the current object. Use of the this keyword is analogous to use of super.

You can use this in the constructor. For example, you can redefine the Circle class as follows:

```
public class Circle
{
  private double radius;

  public Circle(double radius)
  {
    this.radius = radius;
  }

  public Circle()
  {
    this(1.0);
  }

  public double findArea()
  {
    return radius*radius*Math.PI;
  }
}
```

The line this.radius = radius means "assign argument radius to the object's data field radius." Here, this means "this object." The line this(1.0) invokes the constructor with a double value argument in the class.

NOTE

Java requires the this() statement to appear first in the constructor, even before data fields.

You don't need to use the this keyword in the Circle class declaration. However, the this keyword can be useful in some cases, which are discussed later in this book; for instance, you can use new Thread(this) to create a thread for this object, as described in Chapter 12, "Multithreading."

The *Object* Class

Every class in Java is descended from the java.lang.Object class. If no inheritance is specified when a class is defined, the superclass of the class is Object. Classes such as Rational, Mortgage, and Circle are implicitly the child classes of Object (as are all the main classes you have seen in this book so far). It is important to be familiar with the methods provided by the Object class so that you can use them in your classes. Two useful instance methods in the Object class are

- public boolean equals()

- public String toString()

The *equals()* Method

The equals() method tests whether two objects are equal. Two objects of the same class are identical if—and only if—they have the same data value. The equals() method returns a Boolean value. The syntax to use equals() is as follows:

```
object1.equals(object2);
```

The components object1 and object2 are of the same class.

You have already used the equals() method to compare two strings in Chapter 6, "Arrays and Strings." The equals() method in the String class is inherited from the Object class and is modified in the String class to test whether two strings are identical.

TIP

You must use the equals() method instead of the == comparison operator to test whether two objects have the same contents. The == comparison operator is used for comparing two primitive data type values, or for determining whether two objects have the same references.

The *toString()* Method

The object.toString() method returns a string that represents the value of this object. By default, it returns a string consisting of a class name of which the object is an instance, the at sign (@), and a number representing the object. For example, consider the following code:

```
Cylinder myCylinder = new MyCylinder(5.0, 2.0);
System.out.println(myCylinder.toString());
```

This code displays something like `Cylinder@15037e5`. This message is not very helpful and not informative. Usually, you should overwrite the `toString()` method so that it returns a digestible string representation of the object. For example, you can override the `toString()` method in the `Cylinder` class:

```
public String toString()
{
  return "Cylinder length = " + length;
}
```

Then, `System.out.println(myCylinder.toString())` displays something like the following:

```
Cylinder length = 2
```

 TIP

Alternatively, you could write `System.out.println(myCylinder)` instead of `System.out.println(myCylinder.toString())`. The Java compiler automatically translates `myCylinder` into a string by invoking its `toString()` method when it is used in the `print` method.

The *protected, final,* and *abstract* Modifiers

You have already used the modifiers `static`, `private`, and `public`. Three new modifiers will now be introduced: `protected`, `final`, and `abstract`. These three modifiers are used with respect to class inheritance.

The *protected* Modifier

The `protected` modifier can be applied on data and methods in a class. A protected data or a protected method in a public class can be accessed by any class in the same package or its subclasses, even if the subclasses are in a different package.

Suppose class `C1` contains a protected data named x in package `P1`. Consider the following scenarios:

1. If class `C2` in package `P2` is a subclass of `C1`, then x is accessible in `C2`, since x can be accessed by any subclasses of `C1`.

2. If class `C3` in package `P1` contains an instance of `C1`, named `c1`, then x is visible in `c1`, since `C3` and `C1` are in the same package.

3. If class `C4` in package `P2` contains an instance of `C1`, named `c1`, then x is not visible in `c1`, because `C4` and `C1` are in different packages.

The *final* Modifier

You have already seen the `final` modifier used in declaring constants. Occasionally, you want to prevent classes from being extended. You can use the `final` modifier to indicate that a class is final and cannot be a parent class. The `Math` class introduced in Chapter 5 is a final class.

You also can define a method to be final; the final method can no longer be modified by its subclasses.

NOTE

The modifiers are used on classes and class members (data and methods), except that the `final` modifier can also be used on local variables in a method. A final local variable is a constant inside the method.

The *abstract* Modifier

In the inheritance hierarchy, classes *become* more specific and concrete *with each new subclass*. If you move from a subclass back up to a superclass, the classes become more general and less specific. When designing classes, a superclass should have common features that are shared by subclasses. Sometimes the superclass is so abstract that it cannot have any specific instances. These classes are called *abstract classes* and are declared using the `abstract` modifier.

Abstract classes are like regular classes with data and methods, but you cannot create instances of abstract classes using the `new` operator. Abstract classes usually contain abstract methods. An *abstract method* is a method signature without implementation. Its implementation is provided by its subclasses. For example, you can design an abstract class for all geometric objects as follows:

```
public abstract class GeometricObject
{
  private String color;
  private double weight;

  public GeometricObject(String c, double w)
  {
    color = c;
    weight = w;
  }

  public GeometricObject()
  {
    color = "white";
    weight = 1.0;
  }

  public String getColor()
  {
    return color;
  }

  public double getWeight()
  {
    return weight;
  }
```

```
   public abstract double findArea();

   public abstract double findCircumference();
}
```

This abstract class provides the common features (data and methods) for geometric objects. Because you don't know how to compute areas and volumes of geometric objects, findArea() and findCircumference() are defined as abstract methods. These methods are to be implemented in the subclasses. For example, you can make Circle a subclass of GeometricObject. The possible implementation of the Circle class is as follows:

```
public class Circle extends GeometricObject
{
  private double radius;

  public Circle(double r, double w, String c)
  {
    super(c, w);
    radius = r;
  }

  public Circle()
  {
    this(1.0, 1.0, "white");
  }

  public Circle(double r)
  {
    super("White", 1.0);
    radius = r;
  }

  public double getRadius()
  {
    return radius;
  }

  public double findArea()
  {
    return radius*radius*Math.PI;
  }

  public double findCircumference()
  {
    return 2*radius*Math.PI;
  }

  public String toString()
  {
    return "Circle radius = " + radius;
  }
}
```

TIP

Use abstract classes to generalize common properties and methods of subclasses. Use abstract methods to define the common methods that must be implemented in subclasses.

■■■ CAUTION

An abstract method cannot be contained in a non-abstract class. In a non-abstract subclass extended from an abstract class, all abstract methods must be implemented, even if they are not used in the subclass.

Casting Objects

You have already used the casting operator to convert variables of one primitive type to another. Similarly, casting also can be used to convert an object of one class type to another within an inheritance hierarchy. To perform this type of casting, use a syntax similar to the one used for casting among primitive data types. Enclose the target object type in parentheses and place it before the object to be cast. For example:

```
Circle myCircle = (Circle)myCylinder;
Cylinder myCylinder = (Cylinder)myCircle;
```

The first statement converts myCylinder to its superclass variable myCircle; the second converts myCircle to its subclass variable myCylinder.

It is always possible to convert a subclass to a superclass. For this reason, explicit casting can be omitted. For example:

```
Circle myCircle = myCylinder;
```

is equivalent to

```
Circle myCircle = (Circle)myCylinder;
```

When converting a superclass to its subclass object, explicit casting must be used to confirm your intention to the compiler with the (SubclassName) cast notation. For the casting to be successful, you must make sure the object to be cast is an instance of the subclass. If the superclass object is not an instance of the subclass, a runtime error occurs. It is good practice, therefore, to ensure that the object is an instance of another object before attempting a casting. This can be accomplished using the instanceof operator. For example, consider the following code:

```
Circle myCircle = new Circle();
if (myCircle instanceof Cylinder)
{
  //performing casting if myCircle is an instance of Cylinder
  Cylinder myCylinder = (Cylinder)myCircle;
  ...
}
```

You might wonder how myCircle could become an instance of the Cylinder class and why it is necessary to perform casting. There are some cases in which a superclass becomes an instance of a subclass. To fully explore the properties and functions, you need to cast the object to its subclass. This is shown in the following example.

Example 7.4   Casting Objects

Suppose you have an array of geometric objects; some are circles and some are cylinders. This example shows a program that uses implicit casting to assign circles and cylinders to the array; it then uses explicit casting to access data and methods in the objects when processing the array. The output of a sample run of the program is shown in Figure 7.4.

```java
public class TestCasting
{
  public static void main(String[] args)
  {
    //create geoObject array with two objects and initialize it
    GeometricObject geoObject[] = new GeometricObject[2];
    geoObject[0] = new Circle(5.0, 2.0, "white");
    geoObject[1] = new Cylinder(5.0, 2.0, "black", 4.0);

    //display properties of the objects
    for (int i=0; i<2; i++)
    {
      if (geoObject[i] instanceof Cylinder)
      {
        System.out.println("Object is cylinder");
        System.out.println("Cylinder volume is "+
          ((Cylinder)geoObject[i]).findVolume());
      }
      else if (geoObject[i] instanceof Circle)
      {
        System.out.println("Object is circle");
        System.out.println("Circle area is "+
          ((Circle)geoObject[i]).findArea());
      }
    }
  }
}

class Cylinder extends Circle
{
  private double length;

  //default constructor
  public Cylinder()
  {
    super();
    length = 1.0;
  }

  //constructor
  public Cylinder(double r, double w, String c, double l)
  {
    super(r, w, c);
    length = l;
  }

  public Cylinder(double r, double l)
  {
    this(r, 1.0, "white", l);
  }
```

continues

Example 7.4   continued

```
    public double getLength()
      {
        return length;
      }

    public double findVolume()
      {
        return findArea()*length;
      }
}
```

Figure 7.4   *The program creates an array of objects of* GeometricObject *type and casts the objects to subclasses of* GeometricObject *in order to use the data and methods defined in the subclasses* Circle *and* Cylinder.

Example Review

The program concerns three classes: GeometricObject, Circle, and Cylinder. Their inheritance hierarchy is shown in Figure 7.5. You should have compiled the GeometricObject class and the Circle class defined in the previous section before compiling this program.

Casting can be done only when the source object is an instance of the target class. The program uses the instanceof operator to ensure that the source object is an instance of the target class before performing a casting.

The program uses implicit casting to assign a Circle object to geoObject[0] and a Cylinder object to geoObject[1]. The reason for this casting is to store the Circle object and the Cylinder object in the geoObject array.

Explicit casting was needed to cast geoObject[i] to Cylinder or to Circle. The reason for casting to Cylinder and Circle is to explore the properties and functions available only in the subclasses.

In the for loop, the surface area of the geometric object is displayed if the object is a cylinder; the circle area of the object is displayed if the object is a circle.

Note that the order in the if statement is significant. If the order is reversed (for example, testing whether the object is an instance of Circle first), then the cylinder will never be cast into Cylinder because Cylinder is an instance of Circle. Try to run the program with the following if statement and observe the effect.

194

```
if (geoObject[i] instanceof Circle)
{
  System.out.println("Object is circle");
  System.out.println("Circle area is " +
    ((Circle)geoObject[i]).findArea());
}
else if (geoObject[i] instanceof Cylinder)
{
  System.out.println("Object is cylinder");
  System.out.println("Cylinder volume is  " +
    ((Cylinder)geoObject[i]).findVolume());
}
```

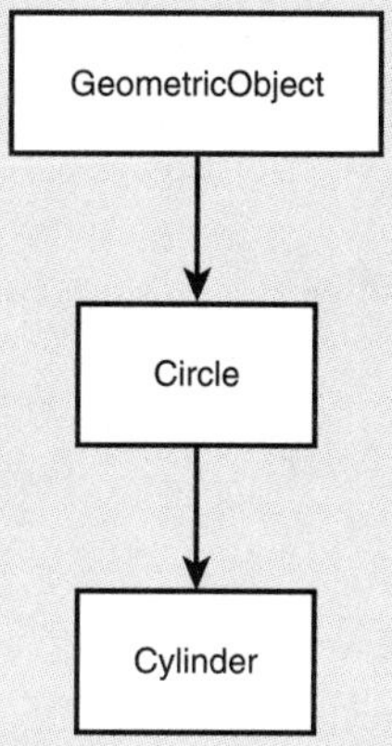

Figure 7.5 *Cylinder is a subclass of* Circle, *and* Circle *is a subclass of* GeometricObject.

■■■ TIP

I recommend that you use the instanceof operator to ensure that the source object is an instance of the target class before performing a casting.

Processing Numeric Values as Objects

Most Java methods require using objects as arguments. Java offers a convenient way to wrap a primitive data type into an object (for example, wrapping int into the class Integer). The corresponding class is called a wrapper class in Java terminology.

By using wrapper objects instead of a primitive data type variable, you can take advantage of generic programming. The wrapper classes provide constructors, constants, and conversion methods for manipulating various data types. Java provides Boolean, Character, Double, Float, Byte, Short, Integer, and Long wrappers for primitive data types. All the wrapper classes are grouped in the java.lang package.

■■■ NOTE

The wrapper class name for a primitive type is the same as the primitive data type name, except the first letter is capitalized. The exception is Integer.

195

The following section discusses numeric wrapper classes, specifically the `Integer` and `Double` classes. For more detailed information about all the wrapper classes, refer to the Java API documentation in the companion CD.

The *Number* Class

Because numeric wrapper classes are very similar, their common methods are generalized in an abstract superclass named `Number`. The `Number` class defines abstract methods to convert the represented numeric value to `byte`, `double`, `float`, `int`, `long`, and `short`. These methods are implemented in the subclasses of `Number`:

```
public byte byteValue()
```

This returns the number as a `byte`.

```
public double doubleValue()
```

This returns the number as a `double`.

```
public float floatValue()
```

This returns the number as a `float`.

```
public int intValue()
```

This returns the number as an `int`.

```
public long longValue()
```

This returns the number as a `long`.

```
public short shortValue()
```

This returns the number as a `short`.

Numeric Wrapper Class Constructors

You can construct a numeric wrapper object either from a primitive data type value or from a string representing the numeric value. The constructors are

```
public Integer(int value);

public Integer(String s);

public Double(double value);

public Double(String s);
```

For example:

```
Double doubleObject = new Double(5.0);
```

or

```
Double doubleObject = new Double("5.0");
```

This constructs a wrapper object for `Double` value 5.0.

```
Integer integerObject = new Integer(5);
```

or equivalently

```
Integer integerObject = new Integer("5");
```

This constructs a wrapper object for `Integer` value 5.

Numeric Class Constants

Each numerical wrapper class has constants: `MAX_VALUE` and `MIN_VALUE`. `MAX_VALUE` represents the maximum value of the corresponding primitive data type. For `Byte`, `Short`, `Integer`, and `Long`, `MIN_VALUE` represents the minimum byte, short, int and long value. For `Float` and `Double`, `MIN_VALUE` represents the minimum *positive* float and double value. The following statements, for example, display the maximum integer (2,147,483,647), minimum positive float (1.4E−45), and the maximum double floating-point number (1.79769313486231570e+308d).

```
System.out.println("The maximum integer is " + Integer.MAX_VALUE);
System.out.println("The minimum positive float is " +
  Float.MIN_VALUE);
System.out.println
  ("The maximum double precision floating-point number is " +
  Double.MAX_VALUE);
```

Conversion Methods

Each numeric wrapper class implements the abstract methods `doubleValue()`, `floatValue()`, `intValue()`, `longValue()`, and `shortValue()`, which are defined in the `Number` class. It also overrides the `toString()` method defined in the `Object` class.

For example:

```
long l = doubleObject.longValue();
```

This converts `doubleObject`'s double value to a long variable `l`.

```
int i = integerObject.intValue();
```

This assigns the `int` value of `integerObject` to `i`.

```
double d = 5.9;
Double doubleObject = new Double(d);
String s = doubleObject.toString();
```

This converts double `d` to a string `s`.

The *valueOf()* and *parseInt()* Methods

The numeric wrapper classes have a useful class method `valueOf(String s)`. This method creates a new object, initialized to the value represented by the specified string. For example:

```
Double doubleObject = Double.valueOf("12.4");
Integer integerObject = Integer.valueOf("12");
```

The Integer wrapper class has some methods that are not available in Double. The parseInt() method, for example, is only available in integer wrappers Integer and Long, but not in Double or Float.

```
static int parseInt(String s, int radix)
```

This returns the integer value represented in the string s with the specified radix. If radix is omitted, base 10 is assumed.

Example 7.5   Designing Abstract Classes

This example gives a generic class for matrix arithmetic. This class implements matrix addition and multiplication common for all types of matrices. (You will use the Integer matrix and the Rational matrix to test this generic class in Example 7.6.)

The generic matrix class is given as follows:

```
public abstract class GenericMatrix
{
  private Object[][] matrix;

  public GenericMatrix(Object[][] matrix)
  {
    this.matrix = matrix;
  }

  public Object[][] addMatrix(Object[][] matrix)
  {
    Object[][] result =
      new Object[matrix.length][matrix[0].length];

    //check bounds
    if ((this.matrix.length != matrix.length) ||
        (this.matrix[0].length != matrix.length))
    {
      System.out.println(
        "The matrices do not have the same size");
      System.exit(0);
    }

    //perform addition
    for (int i=0; i<result.length; i++)
      for (int j=0; j<result[i].length; j++)
        result[i][j] = add(this.matrix[i][j],matrix[i][j]);

    return result;
  }

  public Object[][] multiplyMatrix(Object[][] matrix)
  {
    Object[][] result =
      new Object[this.matrix.length][matrix[0].length];

    //check bounds
    if (this.matrix[0].length != matrix.length)
    {
      System.out.println("Bounds error");
      System.exit(0);
    }
```

```
      for (int i=0; i<result.length; i++)
        for (int j=0; j<result[0].length; j++)
      {
        result[i][j] = zero();
        for (int k=0; k<this.matrix[0].length; k++)
        {
          result[i][j] = add(result[i][j],
            multiply(this.matrix[i][k],matrix[k][j]));
        }
      }

      return result;
    }

  public abstract Object add(Object o1, Object o2);

  public abstract Object multiply(Object o1, Object o2);

  public abstract Object zero();

  public static void displayMatrix(Object[][] m)
  {
    for (int i=0; i<m.length; i++)
    {
      for (int j=0; j<m[0].length; j++)
        System.out.print(m[i][j].toString()+"  ");
      System.out.print('\n');
    }
  }
}
```

Example Review

Because the element type in the matrix is not specified, the program doesn't know how to add or multiply two matrix elements and doesn't know what the zero value is for the element (for example, 0 for int or 0/1 for Rational). Therefore, add(), multiply(), and zero() are defined as abstract methods. These methods are implemented in the subclasses in which the matrix element type is specified.

The matrix element type is Object. This enables you to use any data type in subclasses, as long as you can implement the add(), multiply(), and zero() methods.

The addMatrix() and multiplyMatrix() methods are concrete methods, defined and implemented in this generic class. They are ready to use as long as the add(), multiply(), and zero() methods are implemented.

The displayMatrix() method displays the matrix on the console. The toString() method is used to display the element.

The addMatrix() and multiplyMatrix() methods check bounds of the matrices before performing operations. If the two matrices have incompatible bounds, the program terminates.

Example 7.6   Extending Abstract Classes

This example gives two programs that utilize the GenericMatrix class for integer matrix arithmetic and rational matrix arithmetic.

The following program creates two integer matrices and performs addition and multiplication operations. The output of the program is shown in Figure 7.6.

```java
public class TestIntegerMatrix
{
  public static void main(String[] args)
  {
    //create integer arrays m1, m2
    Integer[][] m1 = new Integer[4][4];
    Integer[][] m2 = new Integer[4][4];

    //initialize Integer arrays m1 and m2
    for (int i=0; i<m1.length; i++)
      for (int j=0; j<m1[0].length; j++)
      {
        m1[i][j] = new Integer(i);
      }

    for (int i=0; i<m2.length; i++)
      for (int j=0; j<m2[0].length; j++)
      {
        m2[i][j] = new Integer(i+j);
      }

    //create an instance of IntegerMatrix
    IntegerMatrix im1 = new IntegerMatrix(m1);

    //perform integer matrix addition, and multiplication
    Object[][] m3 = im1.addMatrix((Object[][])m2);
    Object[][] m4 = im1.multiplyMatrix(m2);

    //display m1, m2, m3, m4
    System.out.println("m1 is ...");
    IntegerMatrix.displayMatrix(m1);
    System.out.println("m2 is ...");
    IntegerMatrix.displayMatrix(m2);
    System.out.println("m1+m2 is ...");
    IntegerMatrix.displayMatrix(m3);
    System.out.println("m1*m2 is ...");
    IntegerMatrix.displayMatrix(m4);
  }
}

class IntegerMatrix extends GenericMatrix
{
  public IntegerMatrix(Integer[][] m)
  {
    super(m);
  }

  public Object add(Object o1, Object o2)
  {
    Integer i1 = (Integer)o1;
    Integer i2 = (Integer)o2;
    return new Integer(i1.intValue() + i2.intValue());
  }
```

```
      public Object multiply(Object o1, Object o2)
      {
        Integer i1 = (Integer)o1;
        Integer i2 = (Integer)o2;
        return new Integer(i1.intValue() * i2.intValue());
      }

      public Object zero()
      {
        return new Integer(0);
      }
    }
```

The following program creates two rational matrices and performs addition and multiplication operations. The output of the program is shown in Figure 7.7.

```
  public class TestRationalMatrix
  {
    public static void main(String[] args)
    {
      //declare rational arrays m1, m2
      Rational[][] m1 = new Rational[4][4];
      Rational[][] m2 = new Rational[4][4];

      //initialize Rational arrays m1 and m2
      for (int i=0; i<m1.length; i++)
        for (int j=0; j<m1[0].length; j++)
        {
          m1[i][j] = new Rational(i,i+1);
          m2[i][j] = new Rational(i,i+1);
        }

      //create RationalMatrix instance rm1
      RationalMatrix rm1 = new RationalMatrix(m1);

      //perform Rational matrix addition, and multiplication
      Object[][] m3 = rm1.addMatrix(m2);
      Object[][] m4 = rm1.multiplyMatrix(m2);

      //display m1, m2, m3, m4
      System.out.println("m1 is ...");
      RationalMatrix.displayMatrix(m1);
      System.out.println("m2 is ...");
      RationalMatrix.displayMatrix(m2);
      System.out.println("m1+m2 is ...");
      RationalMatrix.displayMatrix(m3);
      System.out.println("m1*m2 is ...");
      RationalMatrix.displayMatrix(m4);
    }
  }

  class RationalMatrix extends GenericMatrix
  {
    public RationalMatrix(Rational[][] m1)
    {
      super(m1);
    }

    public Object add(Object o1, Object o2)
    {
      Rational r1 = (Rational)o1;
```

continues

Example 7.6   continued

```
        Rational r2 = (Rational)o2;
        return r1.add(r2);
    }

    public Object multiply(Object o1, Object o2)
    {
        Rational r1 = (Rational)o1;
        Rational r2 = (Rational)o2;
        return r1.multiply(r2);
    }

    public Object zero()
    {
        return new Rational(0,1);
    }
}
```

Figure 7.6   *The program creates two* int *matrices and performs addition and multiplication on them.*

Figure 7.7   *The program creates two matrices of rational numbers and performs addition and multiplication on them.*

Example Review

IntegerMatrix and RationalMatrix are concrete subclasses of GenericMatrix for integer matrix arithmetic. These classes extend the GenericMatrix class and implement the add(), multiply(), and zero() methods.

Casting the object from type Object to type Integer in the IntegerMatrix class is needed because the program needs to use the intValue() method for integer addition and multiplication, which is not available in Object. The similar casting is needed from type Object to type Rational in the RationalMatrix class for the same reason.

The TestIntegerMatrix program creates and initializes two matrices: m1 and m2. The result of adding them is stored in m3, and the result of multiplying them is stored in m4. The TestRationalMatrix program performs similar operations.

The statement IntegerMatrix im1 = new IntegerMatrix(m1) in IntegerMatrix creates im1 as an instance of IntegerMatrix for matrix m1, so you can use im1.addMatrix(m2) and im1.multiplyMatrix(m2) to perform matrix addition and multiplication for m1 and m2. The variable rm1 was created for the same reason in RationalMatrix.

■■■ NOTE

Generic programming also is known as polymorphism. Generic programming enables a method to operate on arguments of multiple types, making the method reusable with multiple types.

Processing Date and Time

Your applications often need to access system date and time. Java provides a system-independent encapsulation of date and time in the java.util.Date class; it also provides java.util.Calendar and java.util.GregorianCalendar for extracting detailed information from Date. You can also use java.text.DateFormat, java.text.SimpleDateFormat, java.util.Locale, and java.util.TimeZone to format Date based on the default or a given locale and a number of formatting styles.

The *Date* Class

The Date class represents a specific instant in time, with millisecond precision. You can construct a Date object using one of the following two constructors in this class:

```
public Date()
```

This creates a new Date object with the current computer time.

```
public Date(long time)
```

This allocates a Date object and initializes it to represent the specified number of milliseconds since January 1, 1970, 00:00:00 GMT.

For example:

```
Date currentTime = new Date();
```

This creates a new `Date` object called `currentTime` and initializes it to the current time.

The following instance methods are useful for a `Date` object:

```
public long getTime();
```

This returns the number of milliseconds since January 1, 1970, 00:00:00 GMT, represented by a `Date` object.

```
public setTime(long time);
```

This sets the `Date` object to represent the specified number of milliseconds since January 1, 1970, 00:00:00 GMT.

```
public boolean after(Date d);
```

This tests whether the `Date` object is after the specified date.

```
public boolean before(Date d);
```

This tests whether the `Date` object is before the specified date.

You also can use `toString()` to display a canonical string representation of a `Date` object in a form like the following:

```
"Fri Aug 1 02:30:00 CST 1997".
```

Example 7.7   Estimating Program Running Time

Occasionally, you need to estimate program running time. This example shows a program that uses the `Date` class to estimate the execution time of a loop running 100,000 times, 1,000,000 times, 10,000,000 times, and 100,000,000 times. The output of the program is shown in Figure 7.8.

```java
import java.util.*;

public class EstimatingRunningTime
{
  public static void main(String[] args)
  {
    /*estimating execution time for a loop,
      repeating 100,000 times.
    */
    Date start1 = new Date();
    long sum = 0;

    for (int i=0; i<100000; i++)
      sum = sum + i;

    Date end1 = new Date();
    System.out.println(
      "The elapsed time for the loop (100,000 repetitions) is "+
      (end1.getTime()-start1.getTime()) + " milliseconds");
```

```
/*estimating execution time for a loop,
  repeating 1,000,000 times.
*/
Date start2 = new Date();
sum = 0;
for (int i=0; i<1000000; i++)
  sum = sum + i;

Date end2 = new Date();
System.out.println(
  "The elapsed time for the loop (1,000,000 repetitions) is "+
  (end2.getTime()-start2.getTime()) + " milliseconds");

/*estimating execution time for a loop,
  repeating 10,000,000 times.
*/
Date start3 = new Date();
sum = 0;
for (int i=0; i<10000000; i++)
  sum = sum + i;

Date end3 = new Date();
System.out.println(
  "The elapsed time for the loop (10,000,000 repetitions) is "+
  (end3.getTime()-start3.getTime()) + " milliseconds");

/*estimating execution time for a loop,
  repeating 100,000,000 times.*/
Date start4 = new Date();
sum = 0;
for (int i=0; i<100000000; i++)
  sum = sum + i;

Date end4 = new Date();
System.out.println(
  "The elapsed time for the loop (100,000,000 repetitions) is "+
  (end4.getTime()-start4.getTime()) + " milliseconds");
  }
}
```

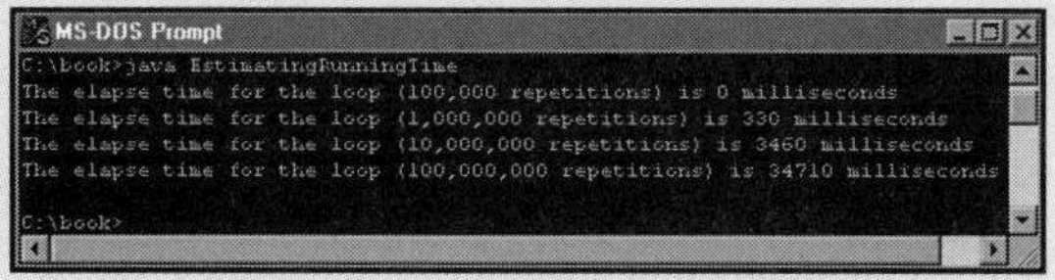

Figure 7.8 *The program estimates the time for running a loop 100,000 times, 1,000,000 times, 10,000,000 times, and 100,000,000 times.*

Example Review

The Date class belongs to the java.util package. Unlike the java.lang package, this package must be explicitly imported.

The getTime() method extracts time in Date in milliseconds. Note that (end1.getTime()-start1.getTime()) must be enclosed in parentheses when used in the println() method.

The *TimeZone* Class and the *Locale* Class

The class TimeZone represents a time zone offset; it also figures out daylight-saving time. Typically, you can get a TimeZone object using its class method getDefault(), which creates a TimeZone object based on the time zone in which the program is running. For a program running in Japan, for example, getDefault() creates a TimeZone object based on Japanese Standard Time.

You also can get a TimeZone object by using the class method getTimeZone(), along with a time zone ID. For example, the time zone ID for central standard time is CST. Therefore, you can get a CST TimeZone object with the following:

```
TimeZone tz = TimeZone.getTimeZone("CST");
```

You can use the getAvailableIDs method to see all the supported time zone IDs. You then can choose a supported ID to get a desired TimeZone.

A Locale object represents a specific geographical or cultural region. An operation that requires a Locale to perform its task is called locale-sensitive. You can use Locale to tailor information to the user. To display a number as date and time, for example, is a locale-sensitive operation; the number should be formatted according to the customs and conventions of the user's native country, region, or culture.

To create a Locale object, you can use the following constructor in the Locale class:

```
Locale(String language, String country)
```

The first argument should be a valid ISO language code. These codes are the lowercase, two-letter codes defined by ISO-639 (for example, da for Danish and en for English). You can find a full list of these codes at a number of sites, such as the following:

www.ics.uci.edu/pub/ietf/http/related/iso639.txt

The second argument should be a valid ISO country code. These codes are the uppercase, two-letter codes defined by ISO-3166 (for example, JP for Japan and FR for France). You can find a full list of these codes at a number of sites, such as the following:

www.chemie.fu-berlin.de/diverse/doc/ISO_3166.html

The Locale class also contains many predefined locale constants. For example, Locale.CANADA is a useful locale constant for Canada, and Locale.ENGLISH can be used for all English-language-sensitive locales.

The *Calendar* Class and Its Subclass *GregorianCalendar*

A Date object represents a specific instant in time with millisecond precision. Calendar is an abstract base class for converting between a Date object and a set of integer fields, such as year, month, day, hour, minute, and second.

Subclasses of Calendar interpret a Date according to the rules of a specific calendar system. The Java API provides one concrete subclass of Calendar— GregorianCalendar. Future subclasses could represent various types of lunar calendars in use in many parts of the world.

You can create an instance of a GregorianCalendar using one of its six constructors with a specified or default time, time zone, and locale.

For example:

```
GregorianCalendar(TimeZone tz, Locale locale)
```

This constructs a GregorianCalendar object based on the current time in the given time zone with the given locale.

```
GregorianCalendar(int year, int month, int day)
```

This constructs a GregorianCalendar object with the given date set in the default time zone with the default locale.

The get() method is useful to extract year, month, day, hour, minute, second, and so on from a GregorianCalendar object.

```
public final int get(int field)
```

This retrieves the value for a given time field from a GregorianCalendar object. The parameter field is a constant, such as YEAR, MONTH, DAY, HOUR, MINUTE, SECOND, DAY_OF_WEEK, DAY_OF_MONTH, DAY_OF_YEAR, WEEK_OF_MONTH, and WEEK_OF_YEAR.

For example:

```
GregorianCalendar rightNow = new GregorianCalendar();
System.out.println("week of the year is " +
  rightNow.get(GregorianCalendar, WEEK_OF_YEAR));
```

This displays the week of the year for the current time.

The *DateFormat* Class and Its Subclass *SimpleDateFormat*

A Calendar object can produce all the time field values needed to implement the date and time formatting for a particular language and calendar style. The date and time format strings, however, are not part of the definition of a calendar. You need to use java.text.DateFormat and its subclass java.text.SimpleDateFormat to format date and time.

The DateFormat class is an abstract class that provides many class methods for obtaining default date and time formatters based on the default or a given locale and a number of formatting styles. The formatting styles include standard FULL, LONG, MEDIUM, and SHORT. The exact result depends on the locale, but generally,

- SHORT is completely numeric, such as 7/24/98 (for date) and 4:49 PM (for time);

- MEDIUM is longer, such as 24-Jul-98 (for date) and 4:52:09 PM (for time);

- LONG is even longer, such as July 24, 1998 (for date) and 4:53:16 PM EST (for time);

- FULL is completely specified, such as Friday, July 24, 1998 (for date) and 4:54:13 o'clock PM EST (for time).

You can use the `getDateTimeInstance()` method to obtain a `DateFormat` object.

```
public static final DateFormat getDateTimeInstance (int dateStyle,
    int timeStyle, Locale aLocale)
```

This gets the date and time formatter with the given formatting styles for the given locale.

You can set a time zone using the instance method `setTimeZone()` in the `DateFormat` class. You can use the `format()` method to format a date to a string.

The following statements, for example, display current time with a specified time zone (CST), formatting style (full date and full time), and locale (France).

```
GregorianCalendar myCal = new GregorianCalendar();
DateFormat myFormat = DateFormat.getDateTimeInstance(
  DateFormat.FULL, DateFormat.FULL, Locale.FRANCE);
tz = TimeZone.getTimeZone("CST");
myFormat.setTimeZone(tz);
System.out.println("The local time is "+
  myFormat.format(myCal.getTime()));
```

The date and time formatting subclass, such as `SimpleDateFormat`, enables you to choose any user-defined patterns for date and time formatting. You can use the following constructor to create a `SimpleDateFormat` object and use the object to convert a `Date` object into a string with the desired format:

```
public SimpleDateFormat(String pattern)
```

The parameter pattern is a string consisting of characters with special meanings. For example, y means year, M means month, d means day in month, G is for era designator, h means hours, m means minute in hour, s means second in minute, and z means time zone. Therefore, the following code will display a string like "Current time is 1997.11.12 AD at 04:10:18 PST" because the pattern is "yyyy.MM.dd G 'at' hh:mm:ss z".

```
SimpleDateFormat formatter
  = new SimpleDateFormat ("yyyy.MM.dd G 'at' hh:mm:ss z");
date currentTime = new Date();
String dateString = formatter.format(currentTime);
System.out.println("Current time is " + dateString);
```

Example 7.8   Displaying Time

This example shows a program that displays current time based on the specified locale and time zone. The language, country, and time zone are passed to the program as command-line arguments like this:

```
java DisplayTime en US CST
```

The following is the program, and its output is shown in Figure 7.9.

```
import java.util.*;
import java.text.*;
```

```java
public class DisplayTime
{
  public static void main(String[] args)
  {
    Locale locale = Locale.getDefault();
    TimeZone tz = TimeZone.getDefault();

    //check usage and get language, country and time zone
    if (args.length > 3)
    {
      System.out.println(
        "Usage: java DisplayTime language country timezone");
      System.exit(0);
    }
    else if (args.length == 3)
    {
      locale = new Locale(args[0], args[1]);
      tz = TimeZone.getTimeZone(args[2]);
    }
    else if (args.length == 2)
    {
      locale = new Locale(args[0], args[1]);
      tz = TimeZone.getDefault();
    }
    else if (args.length == 1)
    {
      System.out.println(
        "Usage: java DisplayTime language country timezone");
      System.exit(0);
    }
    else
    {
      locale = Locale.getDefault();
      tz = TimeZone.getDefault();
    }

    //get current time using GregorianCalendar
    GregorianCalendar cal = new GregorianCalendar();
    DateFormat myFormat = DateFormat.getDateTimeInstance(
    DateFormat.FULL, DateFormat.FULL, locale);
    myFormat.setTimeZone(tz);
    System.out.println("The local time is "+
    myFormat.format(cal.getTime()));
  }
}
```

Example Review

This program creates a Locale object and a TimeZone object with default values or command-line parameters. It displays date and time in the default or specified locale and time zone.

The GregorianCalendar() constructor creates a GregorianCalendar object representing the current time. The getDateTimeInstance() creates a DateFormat object with the specified style and locale. setTimeZone(tz) sets the time zone for the DateFormat object. format(cal.getTime()) formats the Calendar object into a string with the desired format.

continues

Example 7.8   continued

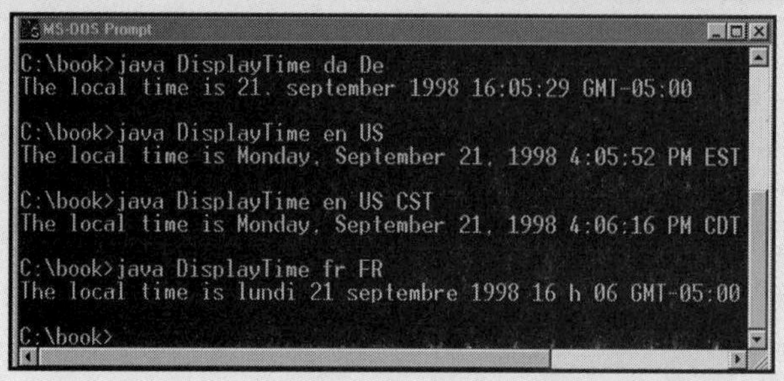

```
C:\book>java DisplayTime da De
The local time is 21. september 1998 16:05:29 GMT-05:00

C:\book>java DisplayTime en US
The local time is Monday, September 21, 1998 4:05:52 PM EST

C:\book>java DisplayTime en US CST
The local time is Monday, September 21, 1998 4:06:16 PM CDT

C:\book>java DisplayTime fr FR
The local time is lundi 21 septembre 1998 16 h 06 GMT-05:00

C:\book>
```

Figure 7.9   *The program displays the current time with specified language, country locale, and time zone.*

NOTE

The Date class represents a specific instant in time with millisecond precision. The Calendar class and its subclasses are used to produce date fields, such as year, month, day, hour, minute, and second. The DateFormat class and its sub-class SimpleDateFormat are used for formatting date and time into a string in specified style, locale, and time zone.

Interfaces

Occasionally, it is necessary to derive a subclass from several classes, thus inheriting the data and methods from those classes. If you use the extends keyword to define a subclass, the subclass can have only one parent class. With interfaces, you can obtain the effect of multiple inheritance.

An interface is treated like a special class in Java. Each interface is compiled into a separate bytecode file, just like a regular class. You cannot create an instance for the interface. In most cases, however, you can use an interface in a similar way as you use an abstract class. For example, you can use an interface as a data type for a variable, as the result of casting, and so on.

The structure of a Java interface is similar to that of an abstract class in that you can have data and methods. The data, however, must be constants, and the methods can have only declarations without implementation. The syntax to declare an interface is as follows:

```
modifier interface InterfaceName
{
  //constants declarations;
  //methods signatures;
}
```

Suppose you want to design a generic sort method to sort elements. The elements can be an array of objects such as students, circles, and cylinders. Because compare methods are different for different types of objects, you need to define a generic compare method to determine the order of two objects. Then you can tailor the method to comparing students, circles, and cylinders. For example, you can use student ID as the key for comparing students, radius as the key for comparing circles, and volume as the key for comparing cylinders. You can use an interface to define a generic compare() method as follows:

```java
public interface CompareObject
{
  public static final int LESS = -1;
  public static final int EQUAL = 0;
  public static final int GREATER = 1;

  public int compare(CompareObject otherObject);
}
```

The compare() method determines the order of objects a and b of the CompareObject type. The method a.compare(b) returns a value of -1 if a is less than b; a value of 0 if a is equal to b; or a value of 1 if a is greater than b.

A generic sort method for an array of CompareObject objects can be declared in a class named Sort as follows:

```java
class Sort
{
  public static void sort (CompareObject[] o)
  {
    CompareObject currentMax;
    int currentMaxIndex;

    for (int i=o.length-1; i>=1; i--)
    {
      //find the maximum in the o[0..i]
      currentMax = o[i];
      currentMaxIndex = i;

      for (int j=i-1; j>=0; j--)
      {
        if (currentMax.compare(o[j]) == -1)
        {
          currentMax = o[j];
          currentMaxIndex = j;
        }
      }

      //swap list[i] with o[currentMaxIndex] if necessary;
      if (currentMaxIndex != i)
      {
        o[currentMaxIndex] = o[i];
        o[i] = currentMax;
      }
    }
  }
}
```

The Sort class contains the method named sort. This method is based on the same algorithm as Example 6.2, "Using Arrays in Sorting" (see Chapter 6), except that the order of two elements is determined by the compare() method here.

To use the sort() method for an array of objects of a specific type, you need to implement the CompareObject interface for that type. The following example demonstrates using the interface.

Example 7.9   Using Interfaces

In this example, a program is written to use the generic sorting method to sort an array of circles in increasing order of their radii and an array of cylinders in increasing order of their volumes. The output of the program is shown in Figure 7.10.

```java
public class TestSortCircleCylinder
{
  public static void main (String[] args)
  {
    CompareCircle[] c = new CompareCircle[10];

    for (int i=0; i<c.length; i++)
      c[i] = new CompareCircle(100*Math.random(),1.0,"white");

    Sort.sort(c); //sort an array of circles

    System.out.println("Sorted circles");
    printObject(c);

    CompareCylinder[] cyl = new CompareCylinder[10];
    for (int i=0; i<cyl.length; i++)
      cyl[i] = new CompareCylinder(
        100*Math.random(),1.0,"white",100*Math.random());

    Sort.sort(cyl); //sort an array of cylinders

    System.out.println("Sorted cylinders");
    printObject(cyl);
  }

  public static void printObject(Object[] c)
  {
    for (int i=0; i<c.length; i++)
      System.out.println(""+c[i]);
  }
}

class CompareCircle extends Circle implements CompareObject
{
  public CompareCircle(double r, double w, String c)
  {
    super(r, w, c);
  }

  public int compare(CompareObject otherObject)
  {
    Circle c = (Circle) otherObject;
    if (getRadius() < c.getRadius())
      return LESS;
    else if (getRadius() == c.getRadius())
      return EQUAL;
    else return GREATER;
  }
}
```

```
class CompareCylinder extends Cylinder implements CompareObject
{
  CompareCylinder(double r, double w, String c, double l)
  {
    super(r, w, c, l);
  }

  public int compare(CompareObject otherObject)
  {
    Cylinder c = (Cylinder) otherObject;
    if (findVolume() < c.findVolume())
      return LESS;
    else if (findVolume() ==  c.findVolume())
      return EQUAL;
    else return GREATER;
  }

  public String toString()
  {
    return "Cylinder volume = "+findVolume();
  }
}
```

Figure 7.10 *The program sorts a list of* Circle *objects by their radii and sorts a list of* Cylinder *objects by their volumes.*

Example Review

The example creates the classes CompareCircle and CompareCylinder in order to utilize the generic sorting method. The relationship of the class hierarchy is shown in Figure 7.11.

▬ NOTE

A rectangular box is used to denote a class and a parallelogram box to denote an interface in the class hierarchy diagram, such as in Figure 7.11.

---

continues

213

Example 7.9 continued

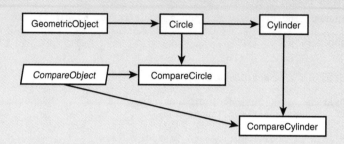

Figure 7.11 *The* `CompareCircle` *class extends* `Circle` *and implements* `CompareObject`, *and* `CompareCylinder` *extends* `Cylinder` *and implements* `CompareObject`.

The common functionality is to compare objects in this example, but the `compare()` methods are different for different types of objects. Therefore, the interface `CompareObject` is used to generalize common functionality and to leave the detail for the subclasses to implement.

The keyword `implements` in the `CompareCircle` class indicates that `CompareCircle` inherits all data from the interface `CompareObject` and implements the methods in the interface.

The `CompareCircle` class implements the `compare()` method for comparing the radii of two circles, and the `CompareCylinder` class implements the `compare()` method for comparing the cylinders based on their volumes.

Before you compile this program, you should have already compiled the `CompareObject` interface and the `Sort` class.

An interface provides another form of generic programming. It would be difficult to use a generic sort method for sorting all types of objects without using an interface in this example, because multiple inheritance is necessary to inherit the `CompareObject` class and an object's class such as `Circle` or `Cylinder`.

CAUTION

Defining an interface is similar to defining an abstract class. There are, however, a few differences:

- In an interface, the data must be constants; an abstract class can have all types of data.
- Each method in an interface has only signature without implementation; an abstract class can have concrete methods.
- No abstract modifier appears in an interface; you must put the abstract modifier before an abstract method in an abstract class.

TIP

Abstract classes and interfaces both can be used to achieve generic programming. You should use interfaces if multiple inheritance is needed. You should use abstract classes if single inheritance is sufficient. Generally, using an abstract class is simpler than using an interface.

Inner Classes

An *inner class,* or *nested class,* is a class defined within the scope of another class. Here is an example of rewriting TestCasting.java in Example 7.4 using inner classes:

```java
public class TestCastingInnerClass
{
  public static void main(String[] args)
  {
    TestCastingInnerClass instance = new
    TestCastingInnerClass();
  }

  public TestCastingInnerClass()
  {
    //create geoObject array with two objects and initialize it
    GeometricObject geoObject[] = new GeometricObject[2];
    geoObject[0] = new Circle(5.0, 2.0, "white");
    geoObject[1] = new Cylinder(5.0, 2.0, "black", 4.0);

    //display properties of the objects
    for (int i=0; i<2; i++)
    {
      if (geoObject[i] instanceof Cylinder)
      {
        System.out.println("Object is cylinder");
        System.out.println("Cylinder volume is "+
          ((Cylinder)geoObject[i]).findVolume());
      }
      else if (geoObject[i] instanceof Circle)
      {
        System.out.println("Object is circle");
        System.out.println("Circle area is "+
          ((Circle)geoObject[i]).findArea());
      }
    }
  }

  class Cylinder extends Circle
  {
    private double length;
    //default constructor

    public Cylinder()
    {
      super();
      length = 1.0;
    }

    //constructor
    public Cylinder(double r, double w, String c, double l)
```

```
      {
        super(r, w, c);
        length = l;
      }

      public Cylinder(double r, double l)
      {
        this(r, 1.0, "white", l);
      }

      public double getLength()
      {
        return length;
      }

      public double findVolume()
      {
        return findArea()*length;
      }
    }
  }
```

The class `Cylinder` is defined inside `TestCastingInnerClass`. This inner class is just like any regular class with the following features:

- An inner class can reference the data and methods defined in the outer class in which it nests, so you do not need to pass the reference of the outer class to the constructor of the inner class.

- Inner classes can make programs simple and concise. As you see, the new class is shorter and leaner. Many Java development tools use inner classes to generate adapters for handling events. Event-driven programming is introduced in Chapter 8, "Getting Started with Graphics Programming."

- An inner class is only for supporting the work of its containing outer class, and it is compiled into a class named *OutClassName*$*InnerClassName*.class. For example, the inner class `Cylinder` in `TestCastingInnerClass` is compiled into `TestCastingInnerClass$Cylinder.class`.

Class Design Guidelines

The key to object-oriented programming is to model the application in terms of cooperative objects. Carefully designed classes are critical when developing projects. There are many levels of abstractions in system design. You have learned method abstraction and have applied it to developing large programs. Methods are means to group statements. Classes extend abstraction to a higher level and provide a means of grouping methods. Classes do more than just group methods, however; they also contain data fields. Methods and data fields together describe the properties and behaviors of classes.

The power of classes is further extended by inheritance. Inheritance enables a class to extend existing classes without knowing the details of the existing classes.

Developing a Java program is applying class abstraction to decompose the problem into a set of related classes and applying method abstraction to design classes.

The following are some guidelines for designing classes:

■ A class should use the `private` modifier to hide its data from direct access by clients. This prevents the clients from damaging the data. A class also should hide methods not intended for client use. The `gcd()` method in the `Rational` class is private, for example, because it is only for internal use within the class. You can use getter methods and setter methods to provide users with access to the hidden data, but only to hidden data you might want the user to see or to modify.

■ It is recommended that you follow standard Java programming style. You should choose informative names for classes, data fields, and methods. Always place data declaration before methods. You also should always provide a constructor and initialize variables to avoid programming errors.

■ A class should describe a single entity or a set of similar operations. You can use a class for students, for example, but do not combine students and staff in the same class. The `Math` class provides mathematical operations; therefore, it is natural to group the mathematical methods in one class. Even for a single entity with too many responsibilities, you can break it into several classes to separate responsibilities. The `String` class and `StringTokenizer` class both deal with strings, for example, but they have different responsibilities.

■ Group common data fields and operations shared by other classes. You should use inheritance to model the is-a relationship. A student or faculty member is a person, for example, so `student` can be designed as a subclass of `person`.

Chapter Summary

In this chapter, you learned about inheritance, an important and powerful concept in object-oriented programming. You can immediately see the benefits of inheritance in Java graphics programming, exception handling, multithreading, multimedia, I/O, network programming, and every Java program that inherits and extends existing classes.

You learned how to create a subclass from a superclass by adding new fields and methods. You also can override the methods in the superclass. The keywords `super` and `this` are used to reference the superclass and the subclass, respectively.

You learned to use the `protected` modifier to allow data and methods to be accessed by its subclasses, even if the subclasses are in different packages.

You learned to use the `final` modifier to prevent changes to a class, method, or variable. A final class cannot be extended. A final method cannot be overridden. A final variable is a constant.

You learned to use the abstract modifier to design generic superclasses. An abstract class cannot be instantiated. An abstract method contains only the method description without implementation. Its implementation is provided by subclasses.

You learned how to process numeric values as objects. Because most Java methods require the use of objects as arguments, Java provides wrapper classes for modeling primitive data types as objects. You can take advantage of generic programming by using wrapper objects instead of a primitive data type variable.

You learned how to process date and time using the classes Date, TimeZone, Locale, Calendar, GregorianCalendar, DateFormat, and SimpleDateFormat. The Date class provides a system-independent encapsulation of date and time in the Date class. The Calendar class and its subclass GregorianCalendar are used for extracting detailed information from Date. You can use the classes DateFormat, SimpleDateFormat, Locale, and TimeZone to format date based on the default, a given locale, or a number of formatting styles.

You learned to use an interface to enable multiple inheritance. An interface cannot be instantiated. A subclass can only extend one superclass, but it can implement many interfaces to achieve multiple inheritance.

Chapter Review

1. Describe the following terms: inheritance, superclass, subclass, the keywords super and this, the modifiers protected, final, and abstract, casting objects, and interface.

2. Suppose you create a new Cylinder class by extending the Circle class as follows. Identify the problems in the following classes:

```
class Circle
{
  private double radius;

  public Circle(double radius)
  {
    radius = radius;
  }

  public double getRadius()
  {
    return radius;
  }

  public double findArea()
  {
    return radius*radius*Math.PI;
  }
}

class Cylinder
{
  private double length;
```

```
        Cylinder(double radius, double length)
        {
          Circle(radius);
          length = length;
        }

        //find the surface area for the cylinder
        public double findArea()
        {
          return findArea()*length;
        }
      }
```

3. Indicate true or false for the following statements:

   1. A final class can have instances.

   2. An abstract class can have instances.

   3. A final class can be extended.

   4. An abstract class can be extended.

   5. A final method can be overridden.

   6. You can always successfully cast a subclass to a superclass.

   7. You can always successfully cast a superclass to a subclass.

   8. An interface can be a separate unit and can be compiled into a bytecode file.

   9. The order in which modifiers appear before a class or a method is important.

4. Given the assumption

   ```
   Circle c = new Circle(1);
   Cylinder cy = new Cylinder(1,1);
   ```

   are the following Boolean expressions true or false?

   ```
   (c instanceof Cylinder)
   ```

   ```
   (cy instanceof Circle)
   ```

5. Are the following statements correct?

   ```
   Cylinder cy = new Cylinder(1,1);
   Circle cy = cy;
   ```

6. Are the following statements correct?

   ```
   Cylinder cy = new Cylinder(1,1);
   Circle c = (Circle)cy;
   ```

7. Describe the difference between method overloading and method overriding.

8. Does every class have a toString() method and an equals() method? Where do they come from? How are they used?

9. Describe primitive-type wrapper classes. Why do you need these wrapper classes?

10. Are the following statements correct?

```
Integer i = new Integer("23");

Integer i = new Integer(23);

Integer i = Integer.valueOf("23");

Integer i = Integer.parseInt("23",8);

Double d = new Double();

Double d = Double.valueOf("23.45");

int i = (Integer.valueOf("23")).intValue();

double d = (Double.valueOf("23.4")).doubleValue();

int i = (Double.valueOf("23.4")).intValue();

String s = (Double.valueOf("23.4")).toString();
```

11. Can an inner class be used in a class other than the class in which the inner class nests?

Programming Exercises

1. Write a subclass for `Triangle` that extends `GeometricObject`. The class `Triangle` is defined as follows:

```
public class Triangle extends GeometricObject
{
  private double side1, side2, side3;

  //constructor
  public Triangle(double side1, double side2, double side3);

  //implement the abstract method findArea in GeometricObject
  public double findArea();

  //implement the abstract method findCircumference in
  //GeometricObject
  public double findCircumference();
}
```

2. Write a program to display a calendar for a specified month using the `Date`, `Calendar`, and `GregorianCalendar` classes. Your program receives the month and year from the command line. For example:

```
java DisplayCalendar 5 1997
```

This displays the calendar shown in Figure 7.12.

You also can run the program without the year. In this case, the year is the current year. If you run the program without specifying a month and a year, the month is the current month.

3. Modify Example 7.5 to add the following two methods for performing scalar arithmetic with matrix:

```
//add k with each element in this.matrix
public Object[][] addScalar(Object k);
```

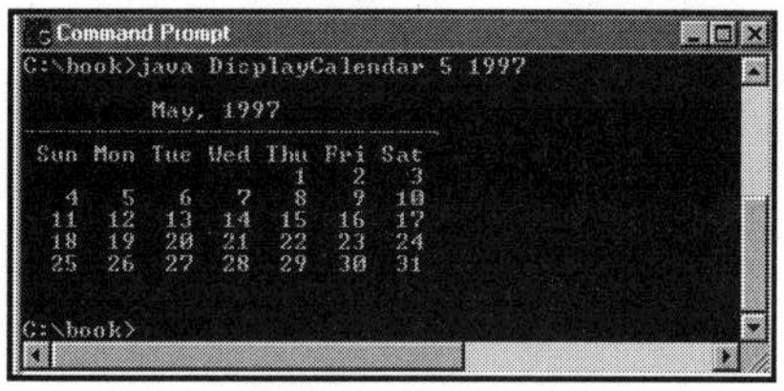

Figure 7.12 *The program displays a calendar for May, 1997.*

```
//multiply k with each element in this.matrix
public Object[][] multiplyScalar(Object k);
```

Write a client program to test the new methods with `double` type.

4. Write a project to meet the following requirements:

   ■ Write a generic class for vector arithmetic. The following is the outline of the class structure:

```
abstract class GenericVector
{
  Object[] vector;

  //constructor
  public GenericVector(Object[] vector);

  /*vector addition, return is a new vector. For example,
    (1, 2, 3) + (1, 2, 3) = (2, 4, 6)
  */
  public Object[] addVector(Object[] vector);

  /*vector multiplication, return is a scalar value. For example,
    (1, 2, 3) * (1, 2, 3) = 1*1 + 2*2 + 3*3 = 11
  */
  public Object multiplyVector(Object[] vector);

  public abstract Object add(Object o1, Object o2);

  public abstract Object multiply(Object o1, Object o2);

  public abstract Object zero();

  public static void displayVector(Object[] m);
}
```

   ■ Write a class for Double vectors and Rational vectors, extending the abstract vector class.

   ■ Write a client program to test the Double and Rational vector classes.

5. Use inner class to rewrite Example 5.5, "Changing Data in a Private Field Using a Setter." Make the `Circle` class an inner class.

PART III

GRAPHICS PROGRAMMING

You learned the basics of object-oriented programming in Part II, "Object-Oriented Programming." The design of the API for Java graphics programming is an excellent example of applying object-oriented principles. You will learn the architecture of Java graphics programming API and use the user interface components to develop graphics applications and applets in this Part.

CHAPTER 8

GETTING STARTED WITH GRAPHICS PROGRAMMING

Objectives

- Describe the AWT class hierarchy.

- Understand the concept of event-driven programming.

- Become familiar with the Java event delegation model: event registration, listening, and handling.

- Use frames, panels, and simple UI components.

- Understand the role of layout managers.

- Use `FlowLayout`, `GridLayout`, and `BorderLayout` managers.

- Become familiar with the `Graphics` class and its methods: `repaint()`, `update()`, and `paint()`.

- Become familiar with the classes `Color`, `Font`, and `FontMetrics`.

- Be able to use the drawing methods in the `Graphics` class.

Introduction

Until now, you have used only text-based input and output. You used `MyInput.readInt()` and `MyInput.readDouble()` to read numbers from the keyboard and `System.out.println()` to display results on the console. This is the old-fashioned way to program. Today's client/server and Web-based applications use a graphical user interface, known as a GUI (pronounced gooee).

Java has a rich set of classes to help you build graphical user interfaces. You can use various GUI-building classes—such as frames, panels, labels, buttons, text fields, text areas, list boxes, choice boxes, choice box groups, and menus—to construct user interfaces. These classes are grouped in the packages `java.awt`, `java.awt.event`, `java.awt.image`, `java.awt.datatransfer`, and `java.applet`, called the *Abstract Window Toolkit* (AWT).

The AWT classes provide a platform-independent interface to develop visual programs and graphical user interfaces. For each platform on which Java runs, the AWT components are automatically mapped to the platform-specific components. This mapping enables the user applications to be consistent with other applications running on the specific platform. Therefore, a Java user interface on Windows 95 looks the same as other Windows 95 applications. For the same reason, a GUI might look slightly different when it is running on different platforms.

This chapter introduces the AWT concepts. Specifically, it discusses AWT components and their relationships, event-driven programming, and the classes `Frame` and `Panel`. This chapter gives examples of using layout managers to place user interface components (`Buttons`, `TextField`, and so on) in `Frame` and `Panel`. Finally, it introduces the `Canvas` and `Graphics` classes for drawing geometric figures, such as lines, rectangles, ovals, arcs, and polygons.

The Abstract Window Toolkit Class Hierarchy

The design of the AWT is an excellent example of using classes, inheritances, and interfaces. The AWT contains the following essential classes. The classes' hierarchical relationship is shown in Figure 8.1.

- **`Component`**—This is a superclass of all AWT user interface classes.

- **`Container`**—This is used to group components. A container can be embedded in another container. A layout manager is used to position and place the components in the desired location and style in a container. Examples of containers are frames and panels.

- **`Window`**—The `Window` class can be used to create a top-level window; however, often `Window`'s subclasses—`Frame` and `Dialog`—are used instead.

- **Frame**—This is a window that is not contained inside another window. Frame is the basis to contain other user interface components in Java graphical applications.

- **Dialog**—This is a pop-up window that is usually used as a temporary window to receive additional information from the user or to provide notification that an event has occurred.

- **Panel**—This is an invisible container that holds user interface components. You can place panels in a frame in Java applications or in an applet in Java applets.

- **Applet**—This is a subclass of Panel. Anything you place in a panel can also be placed in an applet. You use Frame when writing applications and Applet when writing applets.

- **Graphics**—This is an abstract class that provides a graphical context for drawing strings, lines, and shapes.

- **Color**—This deals with colors of graphics components. For example, you can specify background or foreground colors in a component, such as Frame and Panel, or you can specify colors of lines, shapes, and strings in drawings.

- **Font**—This is used to draw strings in Graphics. For example, you can specify the font type (Times New Roman), style (bold), and size (24 points) for a string.

- **FontMetrics**—This is an abstract class that is used to get properties of the fonts used in drawings.

Finally, the classes Button, Canvas, Checkbox, Menu, Choice, Label, List, Scrollbar, TextField, and TextArea are for constructing the GUI.

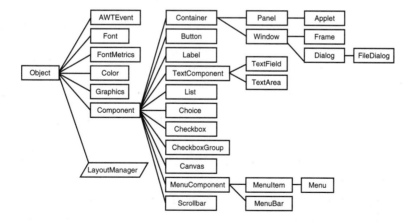

Figure 8.1   *Java graphics programming utilizes the classes shown in this hierarchical diagram.*

Figure 8.2 and Figure 8.3 provide examples of possible user interface layout in applications and in applets, respectively.

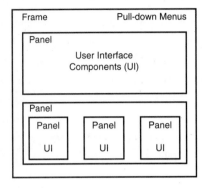

Figure 8.2   *A frame can contain menus, panels, and user interface components. Panels are used to group user interface components. Panels can contain other panels.*

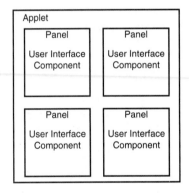

Figure 8.3   *An applet can contain the same components in the frame except that it has no menus or titles.*

Frames

A *frame* is a top-level window with a title. All the graphical elements in Java applications must be placed in a frame.

A frame is a Java object, created from the Frame class in AWT. The following program creates a frame:

```
import java.awt.*;

public class MyFrame
{
  public static void main(String[] args)
  {
    Frame f = new Frame("Test Frame");
    f.setSize(400,300);
```

```
        f.setVisible(true);
    }
}
```

Because `Frame` is in the package `java.awt`, the statement `import java.awt.*` makes all classes from the `java.awt` package—including `Frame`—available so that they can be used in the `MyFrame` class.

You can use the following two constructors to create a `Frame` object.

```
Frame f = new Frame(String title);
```

This declares and creates a `Frame` object `f` with a specified title.

```
Frame f = new Frame();
```

This declares and creates a `Frame` object `f` that is untitled.

The frame is not displayed until `f.setVisible(true)` method is applied. `f.setSize(400,300)` specifies that the frame is 400 pixels wide and 300 pixels high. If the `setSize()` method is not used, the frame will be sized at 0×0 pixels, and nothing will be seen except the title bar. The `setSize()` and `setVisible()` methods are both defined in the `Component` class; therefore, they are inherited by the `Frame` class. Later you will see that these methods are also useful in many other subclasses of `Component`.

When you run the program `MyFrame`, the following window will be displayed onscreen (see Figure 8.4).

Figure 8.4   *The program creates and displays a frame with the title Test Frame.*

Suppose that you want to close the window. Customarily, you would click the window close button on the upper-right corner or click the upper-left corner to reveal a menu and select Close from the menu. But the window is not closed by either method because you did not tell the program how to close the window. The following section introduces event handling so that you can tell the program how to close the window.

■ **NOTE**

In Windows 95 and Windows NT, you can stop the program by pressing Ctrl+C at the DOS prompt window. With UNIX, you need to use the `kill` command to kill the process for the program.

Event-Driven Programming

Until this chapter, the programs were object oriented, but executed in a procedural order. You used decision and loop statements to control the flow of execution, but the program dictated the flow of execution. Java graphics programming is event driven. In event-driven programming, the codes are executed upon activation of events. This section introduces the Java event model.

Event and Event Source

When you are writing programs using the AWT, the program interacts with the user and the events drive the execution of the program. An *event* can be defined as a type of signal to the program that something has happened. The event is generated by external user actions, such as mouse movements, mouse button clicks, and keystrokes, or by the operating system, such as a timer. The program can choose to respond or ignore the event.

The GUI component on which the event is generated is called a *source object*. For example, clicking a button triggers an event. The button is the source object. The source object can be obtained by using the getSource() method on the event. Every event is a subclass of the AWTEvent class. Various types of AWT events deal with user component actions, mouse movement, and keystrokes. For convenience, all the AWT event classes are included in the java.awt.event package. The hierarchy relationship of the AWT events is shown in Figure 8.5.

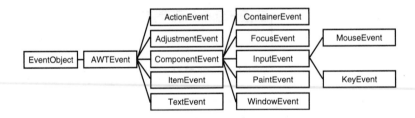

Figure 8.5   *An event is an object of one of the classes in the diagram.*

Event classes contain whatever data values are pertinent to the particular event type. For example, the KeyEvent class defines all key constants such as VK_DOWN (for the down-arrow key) and methods such as getKeyChar() (returns the character associated with the event).

Table 8.1 lists external user action, source object, and event type generated.

TABLE 8.1   User Action, Source Object, and Event Type

User Action	Source Object	Event Type Generated
Clicked on a button	Button	ActionEvent
Changed text	TextComponent	TextEvent
Pressed return on a text field	TextField	ActionEvent

User Action	Source Object	Event Type Generated
Double-clicked on a list item	List	ActionEvent
Selected or deselected an item with a single click	List	ItemEvent
Selected or deselected an item	Choice	ItemEvent
Selected or deselected an item	Checkbox	ItemEvent
Selected a menu item	MenuItem	ActionEvent
Moved the scroll bar	Scrollbar	AdjustmentEvent
Window opened, closed, iconified, deiconified, or closing	Window	WindowEvent
Component added or removed from the container	Container	ContainerEvent
Component moved, resized, hidden, or shown	Component	ComponentEvent
Component gained or lost focus	Component	FocusEvent
Key released or pressed	Component	KeyEvent
Mouse movement	Component	MouseEvent

Event Registration, Listening, and Handling

JDK event handling is a delegation-based model: An external user action on a source object triggers an event. An object interested in the event receives the event. Such an object is called a *listener*. Not all objects can receive events. To become a listener, the object must be registered as a listener by the source object. The source object maintains a list of listeners and notifies all the registered listeners when the event occurs. Upon receiving the notification, the Java runtime system invokes the event-handling method on the listener object to respond to the event, as shown in Figure 8.6.

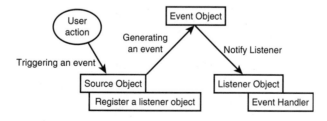

Figure 8.6   *An event is triggered by user actions on the source object, and the source object generates the event object and invokes the handler of the listener object to process the event.*

For example, if a Frame object is interested in the external events on a Button source object, the Frame object must register with the Button object. The registration is done by invoking a method from the Button object to declare that the Frame object is a listener for the Button object. When you click the button, the system generates an ActionEvent event and notifies the listener by automatically invoking a standard method to handle the event.

> **NOTE**
>
> A source object and a listener object might be the same. A source object might have many listeners. The AWT runtime system maintains a queue for all the listeners on a source object.

The registration methods are dependent on the event type. For ActionEvent, the method is addActionListener(). In general, the method is named addXListener() for XEvent.

For the system to invoke the handler on a listener, the listener must implement the standard handler. The handler is defined in the corresponding event listener interface. Java provides a listener interface for each type of AWT event. For example, the corresponding listener interface for ActionEvent is ActionListener; each listener for ActionEvent should implement the ActionListener interface.

Table 8.2 lists event types, the corresponding listener interface, and the methods defined in the listener interface.

TABLE 8.2   Events, Event Listeners, and Listener Methods

Event Class	Listener Interface	Listener Methods (Handlers)
ActionEvent	ActionListener	actionPerformed(ActionEvent e)
ItemEvent	ItemListener	itemStateChanged(ItemEvent e)
WindowEvent	WindowListener	windowClosing(WindowEvent e)
		windowOpened(WindowEvent e)
		windowIconified(WindowEvent e)
		windowDeiconified(WindowEvent e)
		windowClosed(WindowEvent e)
		windowActivated(WindowEvent e)
		windowDeactivated(WindowEvent e)
ContainerEvent	ContainerListener	componentAdded(ContainerEvent e)
		componentRemoved(ContainerEvent e)
ComponentEvent	ComponentListener	componentMoved(ComponentEvent e)
		componentHidden(ComponentEvent e)
		componentResized(ComponentEvent e)
		componentShown(ComponentEvent e)
FocusEvent	FocusListener	focusGained(FocusEvent e)
		focusLost(FocusEvent e)

Event Class	Listener Interface	Listener Methods (Handlers)
TextEvent	TextListener	textValueChanged(TextEvent e)
KeyEvent	KeyListener	keyPressed(KeyEvent e)
		keyReleased(KeyEvent e)
		keyTyped(KeyEvent e)
MouseEvent	MouseListener	mousePressed(MouseEvent e)
		mouseReleased(MouseEvent e)
		mouseEntered(MouseEvent e)
		mouseExited(MouseEvent e)
		mouseClicked(MouseEvent e)
	MouseMotionListener	mouseDragged(MouseEvent e)
		mouseMoved(MouseEvent e)
AdjustmentEvent	AdjustmentListener	adjustmentValueChanged
		(AdjustmentEvent e)

NOTE

In general, the listener interface is named *X*Listener for *X*Event, except for MouseMotionListener.

Handling Events

A listener object must implement the corresponding listener interface. For example, a listener for a Button source object must implement the ActionListener interface. The ActionListener interface contains the actionPerformed(ActionEvent e) method. This method must be implemented in the listener class. Upon receiving the notification, the Java runtime system invokes this method to handle the event; therefore, the method is also referred to as a *handler*.

An event object is passed to the handling method. The event object contains information pertinent to the event type. You can get useful data values from the event object for processing the event. For example, for an event object e of the MouseEvent type, you can use e.getX() and e.getY() to obtain the mouse pointer location; in the ActionEvent, you can use e.getSource() to obtain the source object in order to determine whether it is a button, a list, or a menu item.

Example 8.1   Closing Windows

This example creates a new frame class that extends the Frame class with window closing capability. The closing window event is the WindowEvent type, and its corresponding listener interface is WindowListener; therefore, our program must implement the WindowListener interface.

continues

Example 8.1   continued

The new program MyFrameWithExitHandling is given as follows:

```java
import java.awt.*;
import java.awt.event.*;

public class MyFrameWithExitHandling extends Frame
  implements WindowListener
{
  public static void main(String[] args)
  {
    Frame f = new MyFrameWithExitHandling("Test Frame");
    f.setSize(200,150);
    f.setVisible(true);
  }

  public MyFrameWithExitHandling(String str)
  {
    super(str);
    addWindowListener(this);
  }

  public MyFrameWithExitHandling()
  {
    super();
    addWindowListener(this);
  }

  public void windowClosed(WindowEvent event)
  {
  }

  public void windowDeiconified(WindowEvent event)
  {
  }

  public void windowIconified(WindowEvent event)
  {
  }

  public void windowActivated(WindowEvent event)
  {
  }

  public void windowDeactivated(WindowEvent event)
  {
  }

  public void windowOpened(WindowEvent event)
  {
  }

  public void windowClosing(WindowEvent event)
  {
    dispose();
    System.exit(0);
  }
}
```

Example Review

The main method creates a Frame instance, sets the window size for the frame using setSize(), and makes it visible using setVisible(true). The frame will not be shown without setVisible(true).

MyFrameWithExitHandling extends Frame and implements WindowListener. The WindowListener interface defines several abstract methods (windowActivated(), windowClosed(), windowClosing(), windowDeactivated(), windowDeiconified(), windowIconified(), windowOpened()) for handling the window events when the window is activated, closed, closing, deactivated, deiconified, iconified, or opened.

When a window event such as activation occurs, the windowActivated() method is triggered. You should implement the windowActivated() method with a concrete response if you want this event to be processed.

Because all these methods in the WindowListener interface are abstract, you must implement them all even if your program does not care about some of the events. In MyFrameWithExitHandling, all the window event handlers are implemented, although only the windowClosing() handler is needed. When the window is in the process of closing, the event triggers the windowClosing() method to execute. System.exit(0) terminates the program.

For the object to receive event notification, the object must register as an event listener. addWindowListener(this) registers the object of MyFrameWithExitHandling as a window event listener so that the object can receive notification about the window event. MyFrameWithExitHandling is both a listener and a source object.

The dispose() method disposes the frame object when the object is no longer needed.

TIP

For all Java AWT applications, you can simply extend the MyFrameWithExitHandling class to inherit Frame with closing capability.

Following are two more examples that use event handling—one for the MouseEvent and the other for the ButtonEvent.

Example 8.2   Handling Simple Mouse Events

This example gives a program to create a frame and display a solid square at the mouse pointer when the mouse is pressed. The output of the program is shown in Figure 8.7.

continues

Example 8.2   continued

```java
import java.awt.*;
import java.awt.event.*;

public class TestMouseEvent extends MyFrameWithExitHandling
  implements MouseListener
{
  private int x, y = 0; //x, y coordinates

  public TestMouseEvent()
  {
    setTitle("TestMouseEvent");
    addMouseListener(this);
  }

  public static void main(String[] args)
  {
    Frame f = new TestMouseEvent();
    f.setSize(200,200);
    f.setVisible(true);
  }

  /*when the mouse is pressed, the mouse pointer location
    will be stored in (x, y).
  */
  public void mousePressed(MouseEvent e)
  {
    //get (x, y) coordinates using getX() and getY() methods
    x = e.getX();
    y = e.getY();
    repaint();
  }

  public void mouseClicked(MouseEvent e)
  {
  }

  public void mouseEntered(MouseEvent e)
  {
  }

  public void mouseExited(MouseEvent e)
  {
  }

  public void mouseReleased(MouseEvent e)
  {
  }

  //draw a small solid square around the point (x,y)
  public void paint(Graphics g)
  {
    g.fillRect(x-5,y-5, 10, 10);
  }
}
```

Figure 8.7 *When the mouse button is pressed, a solid square appears that surrounds the area where the mouse pointed.*

Example Review

This program extends MyFrameWithExitHandling. For all Java AWT applications throughout the book, you can extend the MyFrameWithExitHandling class to inherit Frame with closing capability without rewriting the same code.

The setTitle() method is defined in the Frame class to set the title for a window.

Pressing a mouse button triggers a mouse event (MouseEvent) and causes the system to invoke the mousePressed() method. This method obtains the mouse pointer location by using the e.getX() and e.getY() method.

The repaint() method is invoked in the mousePressed() method. The repaint() method is defined in the Component class, and invoking repaint() causes the paint() method to be called.

The paint() method displays graphics on the frame. The paint() method is defined in the Component class. You should always override it to tell the system what you want to paint. The paint() and repaint() methods will be further discussed in the section "The repaint(), update(), and paint() Methods."

The g.fillRect() method is in the Graphics class to display a filled rectangle. The parameters in fillRect() specify where the rectangle is drawn. Drawing various geometric shapes is introduced in the section "Drawing Geometric Figures," later in this chapter.

Example 8.3 Handling Simple Action Events

This example presents a program to display a Close button in the window. You can terminate the program by clicking the Close button in the window or on the title bar. Figure 8.8 shows the output of the program.

```
import java.awt.*;
import java.awt.event.*;

public class TestActionEvent extends MyFrameWithExitHandling
  implements ActionListener
{
  private Button btClose; //object for "Close" button
```

continues

Example 8.3   continued

```java
    public TestActionEvent()
    {
      //set window title
      setTitle("TestActionEvent");

      /*set FlowLayoutManager to arrange the components
        inside the frame
      */
      setLayout(new FlowLayout());

      //create a button object "Close" and add it to the window
      btClose = new Button("Close");
      add(btClose);

      //register listener
      btClose.addActionListener(this);
    }

    public static void main(String[] args)
    {
      TestActionEvent f = new TestActionEvent();
      f.setSize(100,80);
      f.setVisible(true);
    }

    //This method will be invoked when a button is clicked.
    public void actionPerformed(ActionEvent e)
    {
      String actionCommand = e.getActionCommand();
      if (e.getSource() instanceof Button)
        if (actionCommand.equals("Close"))
          System.exit(0);
    }
  }
```

Figure 8.8 *You can close the program by clicking the Close button inside the frame or by clicking the Close button on the title bar.*

Example Review

FlowLayout is one of the layout management styles discussed in the next section, "Layout Managers." The layout manager tells the system how to lay out the components in the container. The FlowLayout manager places the components in the container from left to right and row by row.

The statement btClose = new Button("Close") creates a Button object btClose. The add(btClose) method adds the button closeBT in the frame. Button is a user interface component whose use is further discussed in Chapter 9, "Creating User Interfaces."

The statement `btClose.addActionListener(this)` registers this (referring to `TestActionEvent`) to listen to actionEvent on `btClose`.

Clicking the Close button triggers the `actionPerformed()`. The `e.getSource()` method returns the source object and `e.getActionCommand()` returns a string representation of the source object. In this case, the string is `"Close"`.

NOTE

Java provides an adapter class for each listener interface. The adapter is a simple implementation of the interface, containing empty methods for each method defined in the interface. If you create a class to specifically implement a listener interface, you can create the class that extends the corresponding adapter. The adapters are named *X*Adapter for *X*Listener. For example, `ActionListener`'s corresponding adapter is `ActionAdapter`.

CAUTION

A common mistake with event handling is missing listener registration. Because the system doesn't notify the listener, the listener cannot act on the events.

Layout Managers

In many other windowing systems, the user interface components are often arranged by using hard-coded pixel measurements. For example, put a button at location (`10,10`) in the window. In the AWT, the window might be displayed on many windowing systems on many screens. Using hard-coded pixel measurements, the user interface might look fine on one system, but become unusable on another. Java's layout managers provide a level of abstraction to automatically map your user interface on all windowing systems.

The AWT components are placed in containers. Each container has a layout manager to arrange the AWT components within the container. Notice that in Example 8.3, you did not specify where to place the Close button in the frame. Java knows where to place this button because the layout manager works behind the scenes to place the components in the correct locations. The AWT provides five layout managers: `FlowLayout`, `GridLayout`, `GridBagLayout`, `BorderLayout`, and `CardLayout`. These classes implement the `LayoutManager` interface.

The layout managers are defined by implementing the `LayoutManager` interface. The `LayoutManager` interface defines the common methods that each layout manager uses to arrange components. The common methods are `add()` and `remove()`.

Use the add() method to add a component to the container and the remove() method to remove a component from the container.

The syntax to set the layout manager is as follows:

```
c.setLayout(new specificLayout());
```

The component c is a container, such as a frame, a panel, or an applet, and specificLayout() is one of the five Java AWT layout managers.

The following sections introduce the FlowLayout, GridLayout, and BorderLayout managers. The CardLayout and GridBagLayout managers are introduced in Chapter 10, "Applets and Advanced Graphics."

FlowLayout

FlowLayout is the simplest layout manager. The components are arranged in the container from left to right in the order in which they were added. When one row becomes filled, a new row is started. You can specify the way the components are aligned by using one of three constants: FlowLayout.RIGHT, FlowLayout.CENTER, and FlowLayout.LEFT. You can also specify the gap between components in pixels. FlowLayout has the following three constructors:

```
public FlowLayout(int align, int hGap, int vGap)
```

This constructs a new FlowLayout with a specified alignment, horizontal gap, and vertical gap. The gaps are the distances in pixels between components.

```
public FlowLayout(int alignment)
```

This constructs a new FlowLayout with a specified alignment and a default gap of five pixels for both horizontal and vertical.

```
public FlowLayout()
```

This constructs a new FlowLayout with a default center alignment and a default gap of five pixels for both horizontal and vertical.

Example 8.4 Testing the *FlowLayout* Manager

This example enables a program to arrange components in a frame by using the FlowLayout manager with a specified alignment and horizontal and vertical gaps. The program uses the following simple code to arrange 10 buttons in a frame. The output is shown in Figure 8.9.

```
import java.awt.*;
import java.awt.event.*;

public class ShowFlowLayout extends MyFrameWithExitHandling
{
  public ShowFlowLayout()
  {
    setTitle("Show FlowLayout");
```

```
      /*Set FlowLayout, aligned left with horizontal gap 10
        and vertical gap 20 between components
      */
      setLayout(new FlowLayout(FlowLayout.LEFT, 10, 20));
      for (int i=1; i<=10; i++)
        add(new Button("Component "+i)); //add buttons to the frame
    }

    public static void main(String[] args)
    {
      Frame f = new ShowFlowLayout();
      f.setSize(200,200);
      f.setVisible(true);
    }
  }
```

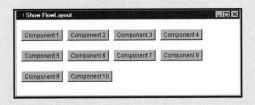

Figure 8.9   *The components are added to fill in the rows one after another in the container with the* FlowLayout *manager.*

Example Review

If you resize the frame, the components are automatically rearranged to fit in the new window.

If you replace the setLayout statement with setLayout(new FlowLayout (FlowLayout.LEFT, 0, 0)), you will see all the buttons left-aligned with no gaps.

The setLayout(new FlowLayout()) is equivalent to the following code:

```
      FlowLayout layout = new FlowLayout();
      setLayout(layout);
```

■■ CAUTION

Do not forget to put the new operator before LayoutManager when setting a layout style, for example, setLayout(new FlowLayout()).

GridLayout

The GridLayout manager arranges components in a grid (matrix) formation with the number of rows and columns defined by the constructor. The components are placed in the grid from left to right starting with the first row, then the second, and so on, in the order in which they are added. The GridLayout manager has two constructors:

```
public GridLayout(int rows, int columns)
```

This constructs a new GridLayout with the specified number of rows and columns.

```
public GridLayout(int rows, int columns, int hGap, int vGap)
```

This constructs a new GridLayout with the specified number of rows and columns, along with specified horizontal and vertical gaps between components.

Example 8.5   Testing the *GridLayout* Manager

This example presents a program to arrange components on a frame with GridLayout. The program gives the following code to arrange 10 buttons in a grid of four rows and three columns. Its output is shown in Figure 8.10.

```
import java.awt.*;
import java.awt.event.*;

public class ShowGridLayout extends MyFrameWithExitHandling
{
  public ShowGridLayout()
  {
    setTitle("Show GridLayout");

    /*Set GridLayout, 4 rows, 3 columns, and gaps 5 between
      components horizontally and vertically
    */
    setLayout(new GridLayout(4, 3, 5, 5));

    for (int i=1; i<=10; i++)
      add(new Button("Component "+i));  //add buttons to the frame
  }

  public static void main(String[] args)
  {
    Frame f = new ShowGridLayout();
    f.setSize(200,200);
    f.setVisible(true);
  }
}
```

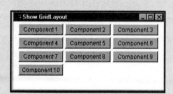

Figure 8.10   *The* GridLayout *manager divides the container into grids, then the components are added to fill in the cells, row by row.*

Example Review

If you resize the frame, the layout of the buttons remains unchanged (that is, the number of rows and columns does not change, and the gaps don't change either).

All components in the layout are given equal size in GridLayout.

Replacing the setLayout statement with setLayout(new GridLayout(4,4) would yield four rows and four columns. You would see only three rows, however, because no buttons were placed in the fourth row.

NOTE

In FlowLayout and GridLayout, the order in which the components are added into the container is important. This order determines the order of the components in the container.

BorderLayout

The BorderLayout manager divides the window into five areas: East, South, West, North, and Center. Components are added to a BorderLayout by using add(String, Component), where String is "East", "South", "West", "North", or "Center". You can use one of the following two constructors to create a new BorderLayout:

```
public BorderLayout(int hGap, int vGap)
```

This constructs a new BorderLayout with the specified horizontal and vertical gaps between the components.

```
public BorderLayout()
```

This constructs a new BorderLayout without horizontal or vertical gaps.

The components are laid out according to their preferred sizes and the constraints of the container's size. The North and South components can be stretched horizontally; the East and West components can be stretched vertically; the Center component can stretch both horizontally and vertically to fill any empty space.

Example 8.6   Testing the *BorderLayout* Manager

This example enables a program to place five buttons in the window by using the BorderLayout manager. The program presents the following code to place East, South, West, North, and Center buttons in the frame by using BorderLayout. The output of the program is shown in Figure 8.11.

continues

Example 8.6   continued

```java
import java.awt.*;
import java.awt.event.*;

public class ShowBorderLayout extends MyFrameWithExitHandling
{
  public ShowBorderLayout()
  {
    setTitle("Show BorderLayout");

    //set BorderLayout with horizontal gap 5 and vertical gap 10
    setLayout(new BorderLayout(5, 10));

    //add buttons to the frame
    add("East", new Button("East"));
    add("South", new Button("South"));
    add("West", new Button("West"));
    add("North", new Button("North"));
    add("Center", new Button("Center"));
  }

  public static void main(String[] args)
  {
    Frame f = new ShowBorderLayout();
    f.setSize(200,200);
    f.setVisible(true);
  }
}
```

Figure 8.11   *The* BorderLayout *divides the container into five areas, each of which can hold a component.*

Example Review

The buttons are added to the frame. Note that the add() method for BorderLayout is different from FlowLayout and GridLayout. You specify where to put the components using BorderLayout.

It is unnecessary to place components to occupy all the areas. If you remove the East button from the program and rerun it, you will see that the center stretches rightward to occupy the East area.

■■■ NOTE

For convenience, BorderLayout interprets the absence of a string specification as "Center". For example, add(component) is the same as add("Center", Component).

■■■ TIP

Always explicitly set a layout style for a container, even though BorderLayout is used by default for frames.

■■■ CAUTION

The first letters of the strings Center, East, South, West, and North are capitalized.

Panels

Suppose that you want to place 10 buttons and a text field on a frame. The buttons are placed in grid formation, but the text field is placed on a separate row. It is difficult to achieve the desired look by placing all the components using a single container. With AWT programming, you can divide a window into panels. Panels act as smaller containers for grouping user interface components. You can add the buttons in one panel and the text fields in another and then add the panels into the frame.

The constructor in the Panel class is simply Panel(). For example, to add a button to the panel p, you can use

```
Panel p = new Panel();
p.add(new Button("ButtonName"));
```

By default, panels use FlowLayout. Panels can be placed inside a frame or inside another panel. For example, the following statement places panel p into frame f:

```
f.add(p);
```

Example 8.7   Testing Panels

This example uses panels to organize components. The program creates a panel for ten buttons labeled 0, 1, 2, and so on to 9, using the GridLayout manager. The panel is placed in the frame by using the BorderLayout manager. The number is displayed in the text field when a number button is clicked. The output is shown in Figure 8.12.

```
import java.awt.*;
import java.awt.event.*;
```

continues

Example 8.7   continued

```java
public class TestPanels extends MyFrameWithExitHandling
  implements ActionListener
{
  private TextField tfNum; //declare a text field
  //create an array of buttons
  private Button btNum[] = new Button[10];

  public TestPanels()
  {
    setTitle("TestPanels");

    //set BorderLayout for the frame
    setLayout(new BorderLayout());

    //create panel p1 for the buttons and set GridLayout
    Panel p1 = new Panel();
    p1.setLayout(new GridLayout(3,4));

    //add buttons to p1
    for (int i=0; i<=9; i++)
    {
      p1.add(btNum[i] = new Button(" "+i));
      btNum[i].addActionListener(this);
    }

    //create a new text field
    tfNum = new TextField();

    //add the panels to the frame
    add("Center", p1);
    add("South", tfNum);
  }

  public static void main(String[] args)
  {
    Frame f = new TestPanels();
    f.setSize(200,250);
    f.setVisible(true);
  }

  public void actionPerformed(ActionEvent e)
  {
    String actionCommand = e.getActionCommand();
    if (e.getSource() instanceof Button)
      tfNum.setText(actionCommand);
  }
}
```

Example Review

Panel p1 is used to group the number buttons by using the GridLayout manager. The program places panel p1 in the center of the frame and a text field below the panel.

Clicking a number button triggers the actionPerformed() method to display the number in the text field. If you resize the window, you will see that the button size changes, but all the components remain in the same relative position.

Figure 8.12   *The program uses a panel to group the buttons labeled 0 through 9.*

> ■ **NOTE**
> Panels are invisible and are used as small containers to group components
> for achieving a desired layout look.

The *repaint()*, *update()*, and *paint()* Methods

In Java graphics programming, drawings are painted in graphics mode. The
repaint(), update(), and paint() methods in the Component class cause strings,
lines, figures, and images to be displayed in graphics mode.

```
public void repaint()
```

The Java system or your program might call this method to request that the window be refreshed. Typically, you call it if you have new things to display. Never
override this method. It calls the update() method to clear and repaint the screen.

```
public void update(Graphics g)
```

If you don't override this method, it clears the area and then calls the paint(g)
method. You should not directly invoke this method. The method is called by the
repaint() method. You may override this method to perform additional functions.
In Chapter 13, "Multimedia," you will override the update() method to reduce
animation flickering.

```
public void paint(Graphics g)
```

This method is always called by the Java system when the component needs to be
displayed or redisplayed, or called by update(g) as a result of calling repaint(). You
should never invoke it directly. You should override this method to paint the things
you want to see on the screen, for example, using drawing methods to draw lines
and shapes.

The Java system automatically creates a default graphics context, an object of the
Graphics class, and passes it as a parameter to the update() and paint() methods. This
object is local to those methods, and it cannot be used outside of those methods.

247

■■■ NOTE

The `repaint()` method lodges a request to update the viewing area and returns immediately. Its effect is asynchronous, and if several requests are outstanding, it is likely that only the last `paint()` will be done.

■■■ CAUTION

The `paint()` methods are for drawing strings, geometric figures, and images. They are not for displaying user interface components. The UI components are displayed in the container using the `setVisible()` method.

An example using these three methods is provided in the following section.

Canvases

`Canvas` is a UI component that can be used to draw graphics and enable user interaction. When you create and display a `Canvas` object, it appears as a blank space inside the container. Only a few functions enable you to manipulate a `Canvas`, such as setting the color and size and getting events. If you extend this class, however, you can customize your own `Canvas` and use it as a backdrop for your GUI.

The following is an example of creating a `Canvas`:

```
Canvas c = new Canvas();
c.setSize(50, 50);
c.setBackground(Color.blue);
add(c);
```

This code adds a new `Canvas` object and sets its size to 50×50 pixels with a blue background. Onscreen, this `Canvas` will look like a blue square.

You can create a user canvas to extend functions of the `Canvas` class. You can then display strings, draw geometric shapes, and view images on the canvas. Although you can display strings in a frame or directly in an applet, it is recommended that you use `Canvas` to draw messages and shapes and to show images; this way your drawing does not interfere with other components.

Example 8.8   Using Canvases

This example presents a program to create a `Canvas` that will display a message. You can use the mouse to move the message. The message is displayed at the mouse point as the mouse drags. The output of the program is shown in Figure 8.13.

```
import java.awt.*;
import java.awt.event.*;

public class CanvasDemo extends MyFrameWithExitHandling
{
    private MyCanvas c; //declare a Canvas
```

```java
public static void main(String[] args)
{
  CanvasDemo f = new CanvasDemo();
  f.setSize(300,200);
  f.setVisible(true);
}

public CanvasDemo()
{
  setTitle("Canvas Demo");

  //create a MyCanvas instance
  c = new MyCanvas("Welcome to Java");
  c.setBackground(Color.yellow);
  c.setForeground(Color.black);
  c.setSize(300,50);

  //place canvas in the frame
  setLayout(new FlowLayout());
  add(c);
}

//MyCanvas draws a message. This class is defined as inner class
class MyCanvas extends Canvas implements MouseMotionListener
{
  private String message;
  private int x = 10;
  private int y = 10;

  public MyCanvas(String s)
  {
    message = s;
    this.addMouseMotionListener(this);
    repaint();
  }

  public void paint(Graphics g)
  {
    g.drawString(message, x, y);
  }

  public void mouseMoved(MouseEvent e)
  {
  }

  public void mouseDragged(MouseEvent e)
  {
    x = e.getX();
    y = e.getY();
    repaint();
  }
}
}
```

Example Review

The class `MyCanvas` extends `Canvas` and implements `MouseMotionListener`. The `MyCanvas` class is used to display a message. The message is passed to `MyCanvas` through the constructor when creating an object of `MyCanvas`.

continues

249

Example 8.8 continued

Figure 8.13 *The program displays* Welcome to Java *on a canvas placed in a frame.*

The MouseMotionListener interface contains two handlers, mouseMoved() and mousePressed(), for handling the mouse motion events. When you move the mouse with the button pressed, the mousePressed() method is invoked to repaint the viewing area and display the message at the mouse point.

You have used the drawString() method to display a string on an applet in Example 1.2, "Writing a Simple Applet." The drawing method draws on the canvas in this example. The drawString(s, x, y) method draws a string s whose left end of the baseline starts at (x, y).

The repaint(), update() and paint() methods are defined in the Component class. The paint() method is overridden in the MyCanvas class. By default, the update() method clears the viewing area and invokes the paint() method. If you want to draw the new message while keeping the old drawings, you could override the update() method as follows:

```
public void update(Graphics g)
{
  paint(g);
}
```

The program creates an instance of MyCanvas and places it in the frame. The methods c.setBackground(Color.yellow) and c.setForeground(Color.black) set the background and foreground colors for the canvas instance c. The c.setSize(300,50) method sets the canvas size to 300 pixels wide and 50 pixels tall.

If you modify the program by using BorderLayout and place the canvas in the center, you will see that the canvas fills out the entire frame and its size is unimportant. In that case, you can omit the setSize() method for the canvas.

TIP

You must specify the size of the canvas if the container for the canvas uses a layout manager other than BorderLayout, or if the canvas is not placed in the center with BorderLayout. Otherwise, the canvas might not be displayed. Try to run the program without specifying the canvas size and observe the effect.

The *Color* Class

You can set colors for AWT components by using the `java.awt.Color` class. Colors are made of a red, a green, and a blue component, each of which is represented by a byte value to describe the color's intensity, ranging from 0 (darkest shade) to 255 (lightest shade). This is commonly known as the RGB model.

The syntax to create a `color` object is

```
Color color = new Color(r, g, b);
```

in which r, g, and b specify a color by its red, green, and blue components; for example:

```
Color color = new Color(128, 100, 100);
```

You can use the `setBackground(Color c)` and `setForeground(Color c)` methods to set a component's background and foreground colors.

Following is an example of setting the background by using `Color c`:

```
Canvas myCanvas = new Canvas();
myCanvas.setBackground(c);
```

Alternatively, you can use one of the 13 standard colors (`black`, `blue`, `cyan`, `darkGray`, `gray`, `green`, `lightGray`, `magenta`, `orange`, `pink`, `red`, `white`, `yellow`) defined as constants in `java.awt.Color`. For example, you can use the following code to display a message that uses yellow:

```
Canvas myCanvas = new Canvas();
myCanvas.setBackground(Color.yellow);
```

NOTE

The standard color names are constants, but they are named as variables with lowercase first for the first word and uppercase for the first letters of subsequent words. The color names violate the Java naming convention.

Drawing Geometric Figures

This section introduces you to drawing objects in the `Graphics` context. Java provides a set of methods in the `Graphics` class that makes it easy to draw geometric figures. These methods are contained in the `Graphics` class.

All the drawing methods have arguments that specify the locations of the subjects to be drawn. The Java coordinate system has x in the horizontal axis and y in the vertical axis, with the origin (`0,0`) at the upper-left corner of the screen. The x coordinate increases to the right and the y coordinate increases downward. All measurements in Java are made in pixels, as shown in Figure 8.14.

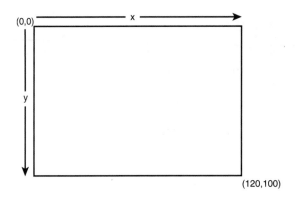

Figure 8.14   *The Java graphics coordinate system is measured in pixels, with (**0**,**0**) at its upper-left corner.*

To draw geometric figures, you must either override the paint() method or create a Graphics object and draw graphics there. In many cases, it is easier to draw graphics by overriding paint(). In some cases, however, you must create your own Graphics object to draw graphics by using the getGraphics() method. You will learn when and how to use the getGraphics() method in Example 10.6, "Handling a Complex Mouse Event" in Chapter 10.

The paint() method takes a Graphics object as an argument. The Graphics object contains a collection of settings, such as fonts and colors. You can set fonts and colors for drawing text, shapes, and images.

The *Font* and *FontMetrics* Classes

You can set the font for the subjects you draw and use font metrics to obtain font size. Fonts and font metrics are encapsulated in two AWT classes: Font and FontMetrics.

Whatever font is current will be used in the subsequent drawing. To set a font, you need to create a Font object from the Font class. The syntax is

```
Font myFont = new Font(name, style, size);
```

You can choose a font name from TimesRoman, Courier, Helvetica, Symbol, or Dialog, and choose a style from Font.PLAIN, Font.BOLD, and Font.ITALIC. The styles can be combined. For example, consider the following code:

```
Font myFont = new Font("TimesRoman", Font.BOLD, 16);
Font myFont = new Font("Courier", Font.BOLD+Font.ITALIC, 12);
```

You can use FontMetrics to compute the exact length and width of a string, which is helpful for measuring string size in order to display it in the right position. For example, you can center strings in the viewing area with the help of the FontMetrics class. A FontMetrics is measured by the following attributes (see Figure 8.15):

- **Leading**—Pronounced *ledding*, this is the amount of space between lines of text.

- **Ascent**—This is the height of a character, from the baseline to the top.

- **Descent**—This is the distance from the baseline to the bottom of a descending character, such as *j*, *y*, and *g*.

- **Height**—This is the sum of leading, ascent, and descent.

Figure 8.15   *The* FontMetrics *class can be used to determine the font properties of characters.*

To get a FontMetrics object for a specific font, use

```
g.getFontMetrics(Font f); or
g.getFontMetrics(); //get FontMetrics for current font
```

You can use the following instance methods to obtain font information:

```
public int getAscent()

public int getDescent()

public int getLeading()

public int getHeight()

public int stringWidth(String str)
```

Example 8.9   Using *FontMetrics*

This example presents a program to display Welcome to Java in Helvetica 20-point bold, centered in the frame. The output of the program is shown in Figure 8.16.

```
import java.awt.*;
import java.awt.event.*;

public class TestFontMetrics extends MyFrameWithExitHandling
{
  public static void main(String[] args)
  {
    TestFontMetrics f = new TestFontMetrics();
    f.setSize(300,200);
    f.setVisible(true);
  }

  public TestFontMetrics()
  {
```

continues

Example 8.9   continued

```
        setTitle("TestFontMetrics");
    }

    public void paint(Graphics g)
    {
        String message = "Welcome to Java";  //string to draw

        //create and set font
        Font f = new Font("Helvetica", Font.BOLD, 20);
        g.setFont(f);

        //get font metrics for the font
        FontMetrics fm = g.getFontMetrics(f);

        //find the center location to display
        int w = fm.stringWidth(message);  //get the string width
        int h = fm.getAscent();
        int x = (getSize().width-w)/2;
        int y = (getSize().height+h)/2;
        g.drawString(message, x, y);
    }
}
```

Figure 8.16   *The program uses the* FontMetrics *class to measure the string width and height and displays it at the center of the frame.*

Example Review

The statement Font f = new Font("Helvetica", Font.BOLD, 20) creates a new font with the specified style and size. g.setFont(f) sets font for g. The statement FontMetrics fm = g.getFontMetrics(f) obtains a FontMetrics instance for font f.

The getSize() method defined in the Component class returns the size of this component in the form of a Dimension object. The height field of the Dimension object contains the component's height, and the width field of the Dimension object contains the component's width.

Resizing the frame results in the message always being displayed in the center of the frame.

TIP

The coordinates at the upper-left corner of a frame are (0,0). The frame title bar is inside the frame in JDK 1.1 or above. If you attempt to draw in the title bar area, nothing will be shown. The height of the title bar is about 25 pixels. For example, the statement g.drawString("Something", 20, 20) will display nothing on a frame.

Drawing Lines

You can draw a straight line by using the following method:

```
drawLine(x1, y1, x2, y2);
```

The components (x1, y1) and (x2, y2) are the starting and ending points of the line, as shown in Figure 8.17.

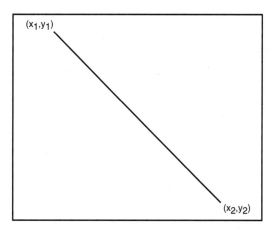

Figure 8.17   *The drawLine() method draws a line between two specified points.*

Drawing Rectangles

Java provides six methods for drawing rectangles in outline or filled with color. You can draw plain rectangles, rounded rectangles, or 3D rectangles.

To draw a plain rectangle, use

```
drawRect(x, y, w, h);
```

To draw a rectangle filled with color, use the following code:

```
fillRect(x, y, w, h);
```

The component x, y is the upper-left corner of the rectangle, and w and h are the width and height of the rectangle (see Figure 8.18).

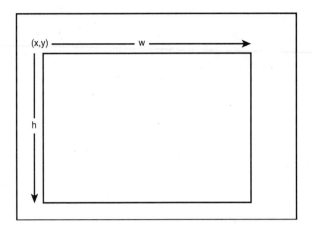

Figure 8.18   *The* drawRect() *method draws a rectangle with specified upper-left corner* (x, y), *width, and height.*

To draw a rounded rectangle, use the following code:

```
drawRoundRect(x, y, w, h, aw, ah);
```

To draw a rounded rectangle filled with color, use the following code:

```
fillRoundRect(x, y, w, h, aw, ah);
```

The components x, y, w, and h are the same as in the drawRect() method, the parameter aw is the horizontal diameter of the arcs at the corner, and ah is the vertical diameter of the arcs at the corner (see Figure 8.19).

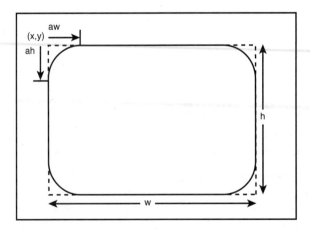

Figure 8.19   *The* drawRoundRect() *method draws a rounded-corner rectangle.*

To draw a 3D rectangle, use

```
draw3DRect(x, y, w, h, raised);
```

in which x, y, w, and h are the same as in drawRect(). The last parameter, a Boolean value, indicates whether the rectangle is raised or indented from the surface.

The following example demonstrates these methods. The output is shown in Figure 8.20.

```java
import java.awt.*;

public class TestRect extends MyFrameWithExitHandling
{
  public TestRect()
  {
    setTitle("Show Rectangles");
  }

  public static void main(String[] args)
  {
    TestRect f = new TestRect ();
    f.setSize(300,250);
    f.setVisible(true);
  }

  public void paint(Graphics g)
  {
    g.drawRect(30,30,100,100); //draw a rectangle

    //draw a rounded rectangle
    g.drawRoundRect(140, 30, 100, 100, 60, 30);
    g.setColor(Color.gray); //set new color

    //draw a 3D rectangle
    g.fill3DRect(30, 140, 100, 100, true);
  }
}
```

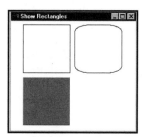

Figure 8.20   *The program draws a rectangle, a rounded rectangle, and a 3D rectangle.*

Ovals

You can use drawOval() or fillOval() to draw an oval in outline or filled solid. In Java, the oval is drawn based on its bounding rectangle; therefore, give the parameters as if you were drawing a rectangle.

To draw an oval, the syntax is as follows:

```
drawOval(x, y, w, h);
```

To draw an oval with color, you use the following code:

```
fillOval(x, y, w, h);
```

The parameters x and y indicate the top-left corner of the bounding rectangle, and w and h indicate the width and height, respectively, of the bounding rectangle, as shown in Figure 8.21.

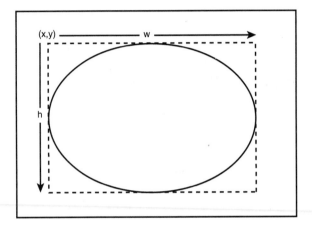

Figure 8.21   *The* drawOval() *method draws an oval based on its bounding rectangle.*

Following is an example of how to draw ovals, with the output in Figure 8.22.

```java
import java.awt.*;

public class TestOvals extends MyFrameWithExitHandling
{
  public TestOvals()
  {
    setTitle("Show Ovals");
  }

  public static void main(String[] args)
  {
    Frame f = new TestOvals();
    f.setSize(250,250);
    f.setVisible(true);
  }

  public void paint(Graphics g)
  {
    g.drawOval(10, 30, 100, 60);
    g.drawOval(130, 30, 60, 60);
    g.setColor(Color.gray);
    g.fillOval(10, 130, 100, 60);
  }
}
```

Figure 8.22   *The program draws an oval, a circle, and a filled oval.*

Arcs

Like an oval, an arc is drawn based on its bounding rectangle. An arc is conceived as part of an oval. The syntax to draw or fill an arc is as follows:

```
drawArc(x, y, w, h, angle1, angle2);

fillArc(x, y, w, h, angle1, angle2);
```

The parameters x, y, w, and h are the same as in the drawOval() method; the parameter angle1 is the starting angle; angle2 is the spanning angle (that is, the ending angle is angle1+angle2). Angles are measured in degrees and follow the usual mathematical conventions (that is, 0 degrees is at 3 o'clock, and positive angles indicate counterclockwise rotation; see Figure 8.23).

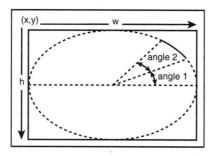

Figure 8.23   *The* drawArc() *method draws an arc based on an oval with specified angles.*

Following is an example of how to draw arcs, and the output is shown in Figure 8.24.

```
import java.awt.*;

public class TestArcs extends MyFrameWithExitHandling
{
  public TestArcs()
  {
    setTitle("Show Arcs");
  }

  public static void main(String[] args)
```

```
  {
    Frame f = new TestArcs();
    f.setSize(250,300);
    f.setVisible(true);
  }

  public void paint (Graphics g)
  {
    g.drawArc(10, 30, 100, 60, 20, 120); //draw an arc
    g.setColor(Color.gray); //set new color
    g.fillArc(10, 150, 100, 60, 120, 300); //draw another arc
  }
}
```

Figure 8.24   *The program draws an arc and a filled arc.*

Polygons

The `Polygon` class encapsulates a description of a closed, two-dimensional region within a coordinate space. This region is bounded by an arbitrary number of line segments, each of which is one side (or edge) of the polygon. Internally, a polygon comprises a list of (x, y) coordinate pairs, in which each pair defines a vertex of the polygon, and two successive pairs are the endpoints of a line that is a side of the polygon. The first and final pairs of (x, y) points are joined by a line segment that closes the polygon.

Java enables you to draw a polygon in two ways: by using the direct method or by using the `Polygon` object.

The direct method draws a polygon by specifying all the points in the `drawPolygon()` method. The syntax is as follows:

```
drawPolygon(x, y, n);

fillPolygon(x, y, n);
```

The parameters x and y are arrays of x-coordinates and y-coordinates, and n indicates the number of points. For example:

```
int x[] = {40, 70, 60, 45, 20};
int y[] = {20, 40, 80, 45, 60};
g.drawPolygon(x, y, x.length);
g.fillPolygon(x, y, x.length);
```

The drawing method opens the polygon by drawing lines between point (x(i), y(i)) and point (x(i+1), y(i+1)) for i = 0, ... , length-1; it closes the polygon by drawing a line between the first point and the last point (see Figure 8.25).

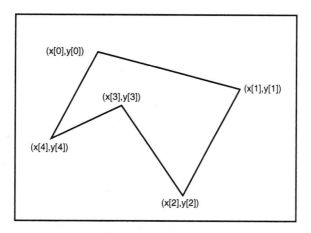

Figure 8.25 *The* drawPolygon() *method draws a polygon with specified points.*

You can also draw a polygon by first creating a Polygon object, adding points to it, and finally displaying it. To create a Polygon object, use

```
Polygon poly = new Polygon();
```

or

```
Polygon poly = new Polygon(x, y, n);
```

The parameters x, y, and n are the same as in the previous drawPolygon() method. Following is an example of how to draw a polygon in Graphics g:

```
Polygon poly = new Polygon();
poly.addPoint(20,30);
poly.addPoint(40,40);
poly.addPoint(50,50);
g.drawPolygon(poly);
```

The addPoint() method adds a point to the polygon. The drawPolygon() method also takes a Polygon object as a parameter.

Following is an example of how to draw a polygon with the output in Figure 8.26.

```
import java.awt.*;

public class TestPolygons extends MyFrameWithExitHandling
{
  public TestPolygons()
  {
    setTitle("Show Polygons");
  }

  public static void main(String[] args)
  {
    TestPolygons f = new TestPolygons ();
    f.setSize(200,250);
    f.setVisible(true);
  }

  public void paint(Graphics g)
```

```
    {
      //create a Polygon object
      Polygon poly = new Polygon();

      //add points to the polygon
      poly.addPoint(10, 30);
      poly.addPoint(60, 45);
      poly.addPoint(35, 55);
      poly.addPoint(90, 85);
      poly.addPoint(100, 155);
      poly.addPoint(50, 155);
      g.drawPolygon(poly);
    }
  }
```

Figure 8.26   *The program draws a polygon by using the* drawPolygon() *method.*

NOTE

Prior to JDK 1.1, a polygon was a sequence of lines that were not necessarily closed. But in JDK 1.1, a polygon is always closed. Nevertheless, you can draw a nonclosed polygon using the drawPolyline(int[] x, int[] y, int nPoints) method, which draws a sequence of connected lines defined by arrays of x and y coordinates. The figure is not closed if the first point differs from the last point.

Following is an example of combining various drawing methods to draw a clock.

Example 8.10   Drawing a Clock

This example presents a program that uses drawing and trigonometric methods to draw a clock showing the current time in a frame. The program displays the current time based on the specified locale and time zone. The language, country, and time zone are passed to the program as command-line arguments like this:

```
java CurrentTimeFrame en US CST
```

The program is given next, and its output is shown in Figure 8.27.

```
import java.awt.*;
import java.util.*;
import java.text.*;
```

```java
public class CurrentTimeFrame extends MyFrameWithExitHandling
{
  private int xcenter, ycenter;
  private int clockRadius;

  static Locale locale = Locale.getDefault();
  static TimeZone tz = TimeZone.getTimeZone("CST");
  static DateFormat myFormat;

  private GregorianCalendar cal = new GregorianCalendar();

  public static void main(String[] args)
  {
    //check usage and get language, country and time zone
    if (args.length > 3)
    {
      System.out.println(
        "Usage: java DisplayTime language country timezone");
      System.exit(0);
    }
    else if (args.length == 3)
    {
      locale = new Locale(args[0], args[1]);
      tz = TimeZone.getTimeZone(args[2]);
    }
    else if (args.length == 2)
    {
      locale = new Locale(args[0], args[1]);
      tz = TimeZone.getDefault();
    }
    else if (args.length == 1)
    {
      System.out.println(
        "Usage: java DisplayTime language country timezone");
      System.exit(0);
    }
    else
    {
      locale = Locale.getDefault();
      tz = TimeZone.getDefault();
    }

    //set display format in specified style, locale and timezone
    myFormat = DateFormat.getDateTimeInstance
      (DateFormat.MEDIUM, DateFormat.LONG, locale);
    myFormat.setTimeZone(tz);
    CurrentTimeFrame f = new CurrentTimeFrame();
    f.setSize(300,350);
    f.setVisible(true);
  }

  public CurrentTimeFrame()
  {
    setTitle("Clock Frame");
  }

  public void paint (Graphics g)
  {
    clockRadius =
      (int)(Math.min(getSize().width, getSize().height)*0.7*0.5);
```

continues

Example 8.10   continued

```
        xcenter = (getSize().width)/2;
        ycenter = (getSize().height)/2;

        //draw circle
        g.setColor(Color.black);
        g.drawOval(xcenter - clockRadius,ycenter - clockRadius,
          2*clockRadius, 2*clockRadius);
        g.drawString("12",xcenter-5, ycenter-clockRadius);
        g.drawString("9",xcenter-clockRadius-10,ycenter+3);
        g.drawString("3",xcenter+clockRadius,ycenter+3);
        g.drawString("6",xcenter-3,ycenter+clockRadius+10);

        //get current time using GregorianCalendar
        cal = new GregorianCalendar(tz);

        //draw second hand
        int s = (int)cal.get(GregorianCalendar.SECOND);
        int sLength = (int)(clockRadius*0.9);
        int secondx = (int)(Math.cos((s/60.0)*2*Math.PI - Math.PI/2)
          *sLength + xcenter);
        int secondy = (int)(Math.sin((s/60.0)*2*Math.PI - Math.PI/2)
          *sLength + ycenter);
        g.setColor(Color.red);
        g.drawLine(xcenter, ycenter, secondx, secondy);

        //draw minute hand
        int m = (int)cal.get(GregorianCalendar.MINUTE);
        int mLength = (int)(clockRadius*0.8);
        int minutex = (int)(Math.cos((m/60.0)*2*Math.PI - Math.PI/2)
          *mLength + xcenter);
        int minutey = (int)(Math.sin((m/60.0)*2*Math.PI - Math.PI/2)
          *mLength + ycenter);
        g.setColor(Color.blue);
        g.drawLine(xcenter, ycenter, minutex, minutey);

        //draw hour hand
        int h = (int)cal.get(GregorianCalendar.HOUR_OF_DAY);
        int hLength = (int)(clockRadius*0.7);
        double hourAngle = (h/12.0)*2*Math.PI +
          (m/60.0)*(2*Math.PI/60.0) - Math.PI/2;
        int hourx = (int)(Math.cos(hourAngle) * hLength + xcenter);
        int houry = (int)(Math.sin(hourAngle) * hLength + ycenter);
        g.setColor(Color.green);
        g.drawLine(xcenter, ycenter, hourx, houry);

        //display current date
        String today = myFormat.format(cal.getTime());
        FontMetrics fm = g.getFontMetrics();
        g.drawString(today, (getSize().width -
          fm.stringWidth(today))/2, ycenter+clockRadius+30);
    }
  }
```

Example Review

This program enables the clock size to adjust as the frame resizes. Every time you resize the window, paint() is automatically called to paint the new window. The paint() method displays the clock in proportion to the window size.

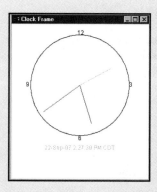

Figure 8.27   *The program displays a clock to show the current time with specified locale and time zone.*

You learned to process the date and time in Chapter 7, "Class Inheritance." This program used the GregorianCalendar class to extract the hour, minute, and second from the current time, and the DateFormat class to format date and time in a string, with the locale and time zone specified by the user.

To draw a clock, you need to draw the circle and three hands for second, minute, and hour. Remember that when drawing the second hand, you need to specify the two ends of the line. One end is the center of the clock at (xcenter, ycenter), and the other end (secondx, secondy) is determined by the following formula:

```
int s = (int)cal.get(GregorianCalendar.SECOND);
int sLength = (int)(clockRadius*0.9);
int secondx = (int)(Math.cos((s/60.0)*2*Math.PI -
                         Math.PI/2) * sLength + xcenter);
int secondy = (int)(Math.sin((s/60.0)*2*Math.PI -
                         Math.PI/2) * sLength + ycenter);
```

The variable s is a number ranging from 0 to 59. The coordinate xcenter, ycenter is the center of the clock. The coordinate secondx, secondy is the tip of the second hand. The line from (xcenter, ycenter) to (secondx, secondy) is the second hand. For example, consider the following code:

```
when s=0,  (secondx, secondy) = (xcenter, -slength+ycenter);
when s=15, (secondx, secondy) = (slength+xcenter, ycenter);
when s=30, (secondx, secondy) = (xcenter, slength+ycenter);
when s=45, (secondx, secondy) = (-slength+xcenter, ycenter).
```

The date is displayed below the clock. The program uses font metrics to determine the size of the date/time string and display it in the center.

Chapter Summary

In this chapter, you learned Java graphics programming using the AWT classes. These classes can be classified into three categories: container classes, UI component classes, and helper classes.

The container classes, such as `Frame`, `Panel`, and `Applet`, are subclasses of `Container`. They are used to contain other components.

The UI component classes, such as `Button`, `Canvas`, `TextField`, `TextArea`, `Choice`, `List`, `Checkbox`, `CheckboxGroup`, and `Menu`, are subclasses of `Component`. They are used to facilitate user interaction.

The helper classes, such as `Graphics`, `Color`, `Font`, `FontMetrics`, and `LayoutManager`, are used by components and containers to draw and place objects.

AWT programming is event driven. The code is executed upon activation of events. An event is generated by user actions such as mouse movements, keystrokes, or clicking buttons. Java uses the delegation-based model to register listeners and handle events. The external user actions on the source object generate events. The source object notifies listener objects of events by invoking the handlers implemented by the listener class.

Chapter Review

1. Describe the AWT class hierarchy. Find the `java.awt` package and `java.awt.event` package from the JDK documentation on the companion CD.

2. Browse `java.awt` and describe the methods in `Component`, `Container`, `Frame`, and `Panel`.

3. Describe AWT platform independence. Does it mean that the Java GUI looks the same as other GUI applications in the same platform? Does it mean that the GUI looks identical on different platforms?

4. Which of the following are containers?

   Button

   Canvas

   TextArea

   Window

   Panel

   Dialog

   Applet

5. Determine whether the following statements are true or false.

- You can add a component to a button.

- You can add a button to a frame.

- You can add a frame to a panel.

- You can add a panel to a frame.

- You can add any number of components to a panel, to a frame, or to an applet.

- You can derive a class from `Panel`, `Frame`, or `Applet`.

- You can derive a class from `Canvas`.

- You can derive a class from `Button`.

6. Describe how to register a listener object and how to implement a listener interface.

7. Describe the information contained in an AWTEvent object and an object of its subclasses. Find variables, constants, and methods defined in these Event classes.

8. How do you override a method defined in the listener interface? Do you need to override all the methods defined in the listener interface?

9. What is the event type for a mouse movement? What is the event type for getting key input?

10. Describe the `paint()` method. Where is it defined? How is it invoked?

11. Why do you need to use the layout managers?

12. Can you use the `setTitle()` method in a panel? Is a panel visible?

13. Describe `FlowLayout`. How do you create a `FlowLayout` manager? How do you add a component to a `FlowLayout` container? Is the number of components that can be added to a `FlowLayout` container limited?

14. Describe `GridLayout`. How do you create a `GridLayout` manager? How do you add a component to a `GridLayout` container? Is the number of components to be added to a `GridLayout` container limited?

15. Describe `BorderLayout`. How do you create a `BorderLayout` manager? How do you add a component to a `BorderLayout` container? List the exact names of the five sections in a `BorderLayout`. Can you add multiple components in the same section?

16. Suppose that you want to draw a new message below an existing message. Should the x, y coordinate increase or decrease?

17. How do you set colors and fonts in a graphics context? How do you find the current color and font style?

18. Describe the drawing methods for lines, rectangles, ovals, arcs, and polygons.

19. What methods do you use to detect mouse movements?

20. What methods do you use to obtain an input character from a keyboard event?

21. Write a statement to draw the following shapes:

- Draw a thick line from (10, 10) to (70, 30). You must draw several lines next to each other to create the effect of one thick line.

- Draw a rectangle of width 100 and height 50 with the upper-left corner at (10, 10).

- Draw a rounded rectangle with width 100, height 200, corner horizontal diameter 40, and corner vertical diameter 20.

- Draw a circle with radius 30.

- Draw an oval with width 50 and height 100.

- Draw the upper half of a circle with radius 50.

- Draw a polygon connecting the following points: (20, 40), (30, 50), (40, 90), (90, 10), (10, 30).

- Draw a 3D cube like the one in Figure 8.28.

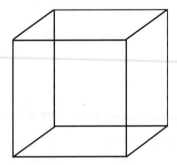

Figure 8.28   *Use the* drawLine *method to draw a 3D cube.*

Programming Exercises

1. Write a program to meet the following requirements (see Figure 8.29):

- Create a frame with FlowLayout.

- Create two panels and add the panels to the frame.

- Each panel contains three buttons. The panel uses FlowLayout.

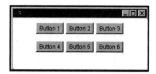

Figure 8.29 *The first three buttons are placed in one panel, and the remaining three buttons are placed in another panel.*

2. Rewrite the preceding program to create the same user interface. Instead of creating buttons and panels separately, you must define your Panel class that extends the Panel class. Place three buttons in your Panel class, and create three panels from the user-defined Panel class.

3. Write a program to display the mouse position when the mouse is pressed (see Figure 8.30).

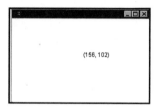

Figure 8.30 *When you click the mouse, the pixel coordinates are shown.*

4. Write a program to display the calendar, as shown in Figure 8.31.

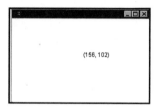

Figure 8.31 *The program displays a calendar for the month specified in the text field.*

The user specifies the month/year in the text field. Press the Show Calendar button to display the calendar for the month of the year in a canvas, using the drawing methods.

5. Write a program to display a multiplication table in a frame using the drawing methods, as shown in Figure 8.32.

Figure 8.32   *The program displays a multiplication table.*

6. Write a generic class to draw the diagram for a function. The class is defined as follows:

```
abstract public class DrawFunction extends Canvas
{
  abstract double f(double x);

  //draw the function
  public void drawFunction()
  {
  }
}
```

Implement the drawFunction() method. (Hint: Create arrays x[] and y[] for coordinates and use drawPolyLine() to connect the points.) Test the class with the following functions (see Figure 8.33):

$f(x) = x^2$;

$f(x) = \cos(x) + 5\sin(x)$;

$f(x) = \log(x) + x^2$;

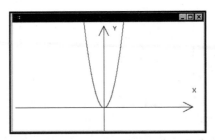

Figure 8.33   *The program draws a diagram for function $f(x) = x^2$.*

7. Example 8.9 displays the message on the frame. Rewrite Example 8.9 to display the message on a canvas and place the canvas in the center of the frame. Compare this exercise with Example 8.9. As you reduce the height of the frame to about the size of the frame title bar, the message disappears in Example 8.9, but the message is shown in this exercise.

8. Write a program to draw a fan with four blades, as shown in Figure 8.34. Draw the circle in blue and the blades in red.

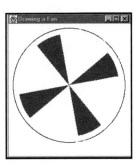

Figure 8.34   *The drawing methods are used to draw a fan with four blades.*

Hint: Use the `fillArc()` method to draw the blades.

CHAPTER 9

CREATING USER INTERFACES

Objectives

- ◉ Describe various user interface components: Button, Label, TextField, TextArea, Choice, List, Checkbox, CheckboxGroup, Dialog, MenuBar, Menu, MenuItem, and Scrollbar.

- ◉ Create interactive graphical user interfaces using these components.

- ◉ Implement the listener interface for the user interface components.

- ◉ Create multiple windows in an application.

Introduction

A graphical user interface (GUI) makes the system easy and fun to use. Creating a GUI requires creativity and a knowledge of how the GUI components work. The GUI components in Java are very flexible to enable the user to create an extensive array of different user interfaces.

This chapter concentrates on creating user interfaces. In particular, it discusses a variety of GUI components that make up a user interface and how to make those components work.

Button

A *button* is a component that triggers an event when clicked. The following are Button class constructors:

```
public Button()
```

This creates an empty button with no label.

```
public Button(String s)
```

This creates a button labeled with the specified string. The following example creates a button with My Button as the label (see Figure 9.1):

```
Button bt = new Button("My Button");
```

Figure 9.1   *A button looks like a 3D rectangle with a label.*

You can get the label or reset the label of a button using the following methods:

```
public String getLabel()
```

This returns the label of a button.

```
public void setLabel(String str)
```

This changes the label of the button with the new specified string str.

Buttons generate ActionEvent. In order to make a button responsive, you must implement the actionPerformed() method in the ActionListener interface. The following code is an example of handling a button event. The code prints out Button pressed! on the console when the button is pressed.

```
public void actionPerformed(ActionEvent e)
{
  String actionCommand = e.getActionCommand();  //get the button label.
```

```
    //make sure the event source is a button.
  if (e.getSource() instanceof Button)
    //make sure it is the right button
    if (actionCommand.equals("My Button"))
      System.out.println("Button pressed!");
}
```

Example 9.1   Using Buttons

This example gives a program to display a message in a canvas and uses two buttons, <= and =>, to move the message on the canvas to the left or right. The output of the program is shown in Figure 9.2.

```java
import java.awt.*;
import java.awt.event.*;

public class ButtonDemo extends MyFrameWithExitHandling
  implements ActionListener
{
  //declare a canvas for displaying message
  private MovingMessageCanvas c;

  //buttons to move the message left and right
  private Button btLeft, btRight;

  public static void main(String[] args)
  {
    ButtonDemo f = new ButtonDemo();
    f.setSize(300, 200);
    f.setVisible(true);
  }

  public ButtonDemo()
  {
    setTitle("Button Demo");

    //create a MovingMessageCanvas instance and set colors
    c = new MovingMessageCanvas("Welcome to Java");
    c.setBackground(Color.yellow);
    c.setForeground(Color.black);

    //create Panel p to hold two Buttons "<=" and "right =>"
    Panel p = new Panel();
    p.setLayout(new FlowLayout());
    p.add(btLeft = new Button("<="));
    p.add(btRight = new Button("=>"));

    //place c and p in the frame
    setLayout(new BorderLayout());
    add("Center", c);
    add("South", p);

    //register listener with the buttons
    btLeft.addActionListener(this);
    btRight.addActionListener(this);
  }
```

continues

275

Example 9.1   continued

```java
      //handler for button events
      public void actionPerformed(ActionEvent e)
      {
        String actionCommand = e.getActionCommand();
        if (e.getSource() instanceof Button)
          if ("<=".equals(actionCommand))
            c.left(); //shift the message to the left
          else if ("=>".equals(actionCommand))
            c.right();  //shift the message to the left
      }
    }

    class MovingMessageCanvas extends Canvas
    {
      private String message; //message to display

      //(x, y) coordinates where the message is displayed
      private int x = 10;
      private int y = 10;

      /*construct a canvas with the specified message to
        display in the canvas
      */
      public MovingMessageCanvas(String s)
      {
        message = s;
        repaint();
      }

      //shift the message left
      public void left()
      {
        if (x > 10) x -= 10;
        repaint();
      }

      //shift the message right
      public void right()
      {
        if (x < getSize().width - 20) x += 10;
        repaint();
      }

      public void paint(Graphics g)
      {
        g.drawString(message, x, y);
      }
    }
```

Figure 9.2 *Clicking the <= and => buttons causes the message on the canvas to move to the left or right, respectively.*

Example Review

The program displays a message in a canvas and places two buttons, <= and =>, below the canvas. The MovingMessageCanvas class that extends Canvas contains two methods: left() and right(). When you click the <= button, the message on the canvas is moved to the left by invoking the left() method. When you click the => button, the message is moved to the right by invoking the right() method.

When you click a button, the handler, actionPerformed(), determines which button is pressed and invokes left() or right() to move the message.

Label

Labels are simple text strings used to label other components (usually text fields). As with other components, the layout managers can place labels inside a container. The constructors for labels are as follows:

```
public Label(String s, int alignment)
```

This creates a label with the specified string and alignment (Label.LEFT, Label.RIGHT, or Label.CENTER).

```
public Label(String s)
```

This creates a label with string s using the default left alignment.

```
public Label()
```

This creates an empty label.

For example, the following statement creates a label with the string "Interest Rate":

```
Label myLabel = new Label("Interest Rate");
```

The following methods are often used for the Label object:

```
public String getText()
```

This returns a string for the label.

```
public void setText(String s)
```

This changes the text string of the label.

```
public int getAlignment()
```

This returns the alignment of the label.

```
public void setAlignment(int Alignment)
```

This resets the alignment of the label.

TextField

A *text field* is an input area where the user can type in characters. Text fields are useful in that they enable the user to enter variable data such as a name or a description.

To create a text field, use the following constructors:

```
public TextField(int width)
```

This creates an empty text field with the specified number of columns.

```
public TextField(String s)
```

This creates a text field initialized with the specified string s.

```
public TextField(String s, int width)
```

This creates a text field initialized with the specified string s and the column size width.

The following methods are often used to operate on text fields:

```
public String getText()
```

This returns the string from the text field.

```
public void setText(String s)
```

This puts the given string in the text field.

```
public void setEditable(boolean editable)
```

This enables or disables the text field to be edited. By default, editable is true.

```
public void setColumns(int)
```

This sets the number of columns in this text field. The length of the text field is changeable.

TextField might generate ActionEvent and ItemEvent. Pressing Enter in a text field triggers the ActionEvent. Changing contents in a text field triggers the ItemEvent.

Here is an example of how to get input from a text field using ActionEvent:

```
public void actionPerformed(ActionEvent e)
{
  String actionCommand = e.getActionCommand();

  //make sure it is a TextField
  if (e.getSource() instanceof TextField)
    //retrieves the value on the TextField to s
    String s = actionCommand;
}
```

Example 9.2 Using Labels and Text Fields

This example gives a program that enters two numbers in two text fields and displays their sum in the third text field when you press the Add button. The output of the program is shown in Figure 9.3.

```java
import java.awt.*;
import java.awt.event.*;

public class TextFieldDemo extends MyFrameWithExitHandling
  implements ActionListener
{
  //declare three text fields
  private TextField tfNum1, tfNum2, tfResult;
  private Button btAdd; //declare "Add" button

  public static void main(String[] args)
  {
    TextFieldDemo f = new TextFieldDemo();
    f.pack();
    f.setVisible(true);
  }

  public TextFieldDemo()
  {
    setTitle("TextFieldDemo");
    setBackground(Color.yellow);
    setForeground(Color.black);

    //use panel p1 to group text fields
    Panel p1 = new Panel();
    p1.setLayout(new FlowLayout());
    p1.add(new Label("Number 1"));
    p1.add(tfNum1 = new TextField(3));
    p1.add(new Label("Number 2"));
    p1.add(tfNum2 = new TextField(3));
    p1.add(new Label("Result"));
    p1.add(tfResult = new TextField(4));
    tfResult.setEditable(false);    //set tfResult noneditable

    //use panel p2 for the button
    Panel p2 = new Panel();
    p2.setLayout(new FlowLayout());
    p2.add(btAdd = new Button("Add"));

    //set FlowLayout for the frame
    setLayout(new BorderLayout());
    add("Center", p1);
    add("South", p2);

    //register listener
    btAdd.addActionListener(this);
  }

  //handling add operation
  public void actionPerformed(ActionEvent e)
  {
    String actionCommand = e.getActionCommand();
```

continues

Example 9.2   continued

```
            if (e.getSource() instanceof Button)
            {
              if ("Add".equals(actionCommand))
              { /*get int values from text fields and use trim() to
                   trim extraneous space in the text field
                */
                int num1 = (Integer.parseInt(tfNum1.getText().trim()));
                int num2 = (Integer.parseInt(tfNum2.getText().trim()));
                int result = num1 + num2;

                //set result in TextField tfResult
                tfResult.setText(String.valueOf(result));
              }
            }
          }
      }
```

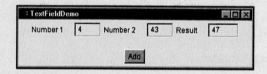

Figure 9.3   *The addition of Number 1 and Number 2 shows in Result when you click the Add button.*

Example Review

The program uses two panels, p1 and p2, to contain the components. The panel p1 is for the labels and text fields, and p2 is for the Add button. You can place the button directly in the frame instead of placing it in p2. However, the button will look very long because it stretches to fill in the entire south area in the BorderLayout.

Instead of using the setSize() method to set the size for the frame, this program uses the pack() method, which automatically sizes up the frame according to the size of the components that are placed in the frame.

The tfNum1.getText() method returns the text in the text field tfNum1, and tfResult.setText(s) sets the specified string into the text field tfResult.

The trim() method is useful to remove blank space from both ends of a string. If you run the program without applying trim() to the string, a runtime error may occur when converting the string to an integer.

Using tfResult.setEditable(false) prevents the user from editing the Result text field. By default, editing is enabled on all text fields.

TextArea

If you want to let the user enter multiple lines of text, you cannot use TextField unless you create several of them. The solution is to use TextArea, which enables the user to enter multiple lines of text.

To create a text area, use the following constructors:

```
public TextArea(int rows, int columns)
```

This creates a text area with the specified number of rows and columns.

```
public TextArea(String s, int rows, int columns)
```

This creates a text area with the specified text and the number of rows and columns specified.

```
public TextArea(String s, int rows, int columns, int scrollbars)
```

This constructs a new text area with the specified text, the number of rows and columns, and the type of scrollbars. The type of the scrollbars can be one of the following:

- **SCROLLBARS_BOTH**—Create and display both vertical and horizontal scrollbars.

- **SCROLLBARS_VERTICAL_ONLY**—Create and display vertical scrollbar only.

- **SCROLLBARS_HORIZONTAL_ONLY**—Create and display horizontal scrollbar only.

- **SCROLLBARS_NONE**—Do not create or display any scrollbars for the text area.

For example, the following statement creates a text area with two lines with a length of 10 characters per line (see Figure 9.4):

```
TextArea ta = new TextArea("My TextArea", 2, 10);
```

Figure 9.4   *A text area can have several lines with vertical and horizontal scrollbars.*

To create a text area with line wrapping, you should use a constructor like this:

```
TextArea ta = new TextArea
  ("My TextArea", 2, 10, TextArea.SCROLLBARS_VERTICAL_ONLY);
```

You can use the following methods to insert, append, and replace text:

```
public void insert(String s, int pos)
```

This inserts string s in the specified position in the text area.

```
public void append(String s)
```

This appends string s to the end of the text.

```
public void replaceRange(String s, int start, int end)
```

This replaces partial texts in the range from position start to position end with string s.

```
public int getRows()
```

This returns the number of rows in the text area.

Example 9.3   Using Text Areas

This example gives a program to let the user enter text from a text field and then append it to a text area. A sample run of the program is shown in Figure 9.5.

```java
import java.awt.*;
import java.awt.event.*;

public class TextAreaDemo extends MyFrameWithExitHandling
  implements ActionListener
{
  private TextField tf;
  private Button bt;
  private TextArea ta;

  public static void main(String[] args)
  {
    TextAreaDemo f = new TextAreaDemo();
    f.pack();
    f.setVisible(true);
  }

  public TextAreaDemo()
  {
    setTitle("Test TextArea");

    //create panel p to hold the text field and button
    Panel p = new Panel();
    p.setLayout(new FlowLayout());
    p.add(tf = new TextField(20));
    p.add(bt = new Button("Store"));

    //set FlowLayout for the frame
    setLayout(new BorderLayout());
    add("North",ta = new TextArea());
    add("South",p);

    //register listener
    bt.addActionListener(this);
  }

  //ActionEvent handler
  public void actionPerformed(ActionEvent e)
  {
    String actionCommand = e.getActionCommand();
    if ("Store".equals(actionCommand))
      ta.append(tf.getText().trim());
  }
}
```

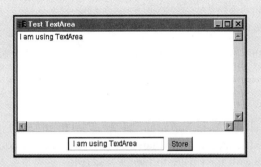

Figure 9.5   *The text in the text field is appended to the text area when you click the Store button.*

Example Review

The program groups the text field and the button in a panel and places the panel below the text area.

When you click the Store button, the handler, `actionPerformed()`, takes the string from the text field and appends it to the text area using the `append()` method.

The text area is editable. You can type characters or delete characters directly into the text area. You also can highlight to select characters in the text area.

Choice

A *choice* is a simple list of items from which the user can choose. It is useful in limiting a user's range of choices and avoids the cumbersome validation of data input. You can easily choose and extract the value in a choice box.

To create a `Choice`, use the following constructor:

```
public Choice()
```

This creates a `Choice` component.

The following methods are useful to operate a `Choice` object:

```
public void add(String s)
```

This adds the item s into the choice.

```
public String getItem(int index)
```

This gets an item from the choice at the specified index.

```
public int getSelectedIndex()
```

This gets the index of the selected item.

```
public String getSelectedItem()
```

This gets the selected item.

```
public void select(int index)
```

This sets the selected item in this Choice menu to be the item at the specified index.

```
public void select(String  str)
```

This sets the selected item in this Choice menu to be the item whose name is equal to the specified string. If more than one item matches (is equal to) the specified string, the one with the smallest index is selected.

Here is an example of how to create a Choice object and to add items to the object:

```
Choice cho = new Choice();
cho.add("item 1");
cho.add("item 2");
cho.add("item 3");
add(cho);
```

This creates a Choice with three choices (see Figure 9.6).

Figure 9.6 *A choice box enables you to choose one item from a list.*

To get data from a Choice menu, you can use getSelectedItem() to return a string representation of the currently selected item, or you can get the item from the itemStateChanged(ItemEvent e) handler, using the e.getItem() method.

Choice generates ItemEvent, and the itemStateChanged(ItemEvent e) handler processes a choice. Here is an example of how to get data from the itemStateChanged (ItemEvent e) handler:

```
public void itemStateChanged(ItemEvent e)
{
  //make sure the source is a choice
  if (e.getSource() instanceof Choice)
    String s = (String)e.getItem();
}
```

Example 9.4   Using Choices

This example gives a program to let users enter their name, department, university, state, and zip code and store the information in a text area. The state is a Choice item. Figure 9.7 shows a sample run for the program.

```java
import java.awt.*;
import java.awt.event.*;

public class ChoiceDemo extends MyFrameWithExitHandling
  implements ItemListener, ActionListener
{
  private Choice choState;
  private TextField tfName = new TextField(32);
  private TextField tfDepartment = new TextField(32);
  private TextField tfUniversity = new TextField(20);
  private TextField tfZip = new TextField(5);
  private TextArea ta = new TextArea(5, 30);
  private Button btStore = new Button("Store");
  private String state;

  public static void main(String[] args)
  {
    Frame f = new ChoiceDemo();
    f.setSize(400,350);
    f.setVisible(true);
  }

  public ChoiceDemo()
  {
    setTitle("ChoiceDemo");

    //panel p1 to hold name field
    Panel p1 = new Panel();
    p1.setLayout(new FlowLayout(FlowLayout.LEFT));
    p1.add(new Label("Name"));
    p1.add(tfName);

    //panel p2 to hold department field
    Panel p2 = new Panel();
    p2.setLayout(new FlowLayout(FlowLayout.LEFT));
    p2.add(new Label("Department"));
    p2.add(tfDepartment);

    //panel p3 to hold university field
    Panel p3 = new Panel();
    p3.setLayout(new FlowLayout(FlowLayout.LEFT));
    p3.add(new Label("University"));
    p3.add(tfUniversity);

    //panel p4 to hold state and zip field
    Panel p4 = new Panel();
    p4.setLayout(new FlowLayout(FlowLayout.LEFT));
    p4.add(new Label("State"));
    p4.add(choState = new Choice());
    p4.add(new Label("  Zip"));
    p4.add(tfZip);

    //initialize choice items
    choState.add("MA");
    choState.add("IN");
    choState.add("OK");
    choState.add("PA");

    //panel p5 to hold text area and button
    Panel p5 = new Panel();
```

continues

285

Example 9.4   continued

```
        p5.setLayout(new FlowLayout(FlowLayout.LEFT));
        p5.add(ta);
        p5.add(btStore);

        //add panels to the frame
        setLayout(new FlowLayout(FlowLayout.LEFT));
        add(p1);
        add(p2);
        add(p3);
        add(p4);
        add(p5);

        //set foreground and background colors
        setForeground(Color.red);
        setBackground(Color.yellow);

        //register listener
        choState.addItemListener(this);
        btStore.addActionListener(this);
    }

    //obtain state code
    public void itemStateChanged(ItemEvent e)
    {
      if (e.getSource() instanceof Choice)
      {
        state = (String)e.getItem();
      }
    }

    //respond to the button action
    public void actionPerformed(ActionEvent e)
    {
      String actionCommand = e.getActionCommand();
      if (e.getSource() instanceof Button)
        if ("Store".equals(actionCommand))
          storeToTextArea();
    }

    //store information to the text area
    private void storeToTextArea()
    {
      ta.append(tfName.getText()+'\n');
      ta.append(tfDepartment.getText()+'\n');
      ta.append(tfUniversity.getText()+'\n');
      ta.append(state+", "+tfZip.getText());
    }
  }
```

Example Review

The frame listens to ActionEvent for the Store button and ItemEvent for the Choice item, so it implements ActionListener and ItemListener.

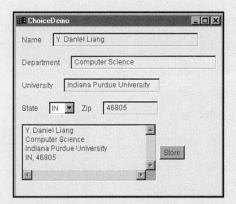

Figure 9.7   *When the Store button is clicked, the name, department, university, state, and zip code are displayed in the text area.*

The program uses several panels to organize the user interface. The state field is a `Choice` item with sample values `MA`, `IN`, `OK`, and `PA`. When the user selects a choice, the handler, `itemStateChanged(ItemEvent e)`, gets the selected item and stores it in the `state` string.

When the user clicks the Store button, the program gets the name, department, university, and zip code from the text fields and gets the state from the `state` variable, which contains a `Choice` item. The program stores the information to the text area.

You can simply use `choice.getSelectedItem()` to get the `Choice` item currently being selected, instead of using the `e.getItem()` method to retrieve the choice in the handler. If you run the program replacing `state` with `choice.getSelectedItem()` inside the `storeToTextArea()` method, the program will work just fine.

List

A `List` is a component that performs basically the same function as a `Choice`, but it enables the user to choose a single value or multiple values.

You can use the following constructors to create a `List`:

```
public List(int rows, boolean multipleSelection)
```

This creates a new scrolling list with the specified number of visible rows; the parameter `multipleSelection` indicates whether multiple selection is enabled.

```
public List(int rows)
```

This creates a new single-selection scrolling list initialized with the specified number of visible rows.

```
public List()
```

This creates a new scrolling list initialized with no visible lines or multiple selections.

The List object has the following methods:

```
public void add(String s)
```

adds the item s into the list.

```
public String getItem(int row)
```

This gets an item from the list at the specified row.

```
public int getSelectedIndex()
```

This gets the index of the selected item.

```
public String getSelectedItem()
```

This gets the selected item.

```
public String[] getSelectedItems()
```

This returns an array of strings containing the selected items.

Here is an example of how to create a List object and add items to the list:

```
List lst = new List(2, false);
lst.add("Item1");
lst.add("Item2");
lst.add("Item3");
add(lst);
```

This code creates a List object with three items, without multiple selection. The visible window of choices is 2, meaning that the user can see only two choices at a time (see Figure 9.8).

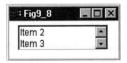

Figure 9.8   *A list box enables multiple selections.*

List can generate ActionEvent and ItemEvent. Clicking a list item triggers the ItemEvent. To trigger the ActionEvent, you need to double-click the selected item.

Here is an example of how to get input from a list using ActionEvent:

```
public void actionPerformed(ActionEvent e)
{
  String actionCommad = e.getActionCommand();
  if (e.getSource() instanceof List) //make sure it is a List
    String s = actionCommand;  //assigns the selected value to s
}
```

Here is an example of how to get all selected items from a list using `ItemEvent`:

```java
public void itemStateChanged(ItemEvent e)
{
  if (e.getSource() instanceof List) //make sure it is a list
  {
    //get all selected items in an array of strings
    String[] items = lst.getSelectedItems();
  }
}
```

Example 9.5   Using Lists

This example gives a program to store several states (Georgia, Indiana, Michigan, Ohio, Oklahoma, and Texas) in a list. When the states in the list are selected, they are displayed on a canvas. A sample output of the program is shown in Figure 9.9.

```java
import java.awt.*;
import java.awt.event.*;

public class ListDemo extends MyFrameWithExitHandling
  implements ItemListener
{
  private List lst; //declare a list

  //declare a canvas for displaying messages
  private DisplayMessage c;

  public static void main(String[] args)
  {
    Frame f = new ListDemo();
    f.setSize(300, 200);
    f.setVisible(true);
  }

  public ListDemo()
  {
    setTitle("ListDemo");

    //create and add canvas and list to the frame
    setLayout(new BorderLayout());
    add("Center", c = new DisplayMessage());
    add("South", lst = new List(3,true));

    //set background and foreground colors in canvas
    c.setBackground(Color.yellow);
    c.setForeground(Color.red);

    //add items to the list
    lst.add("Georgia");
    lst.add("Indiana");
    lst.add("Michigan");
    lst.add("Ohio");
    lst.add("Oklahoma");
    lst.add("Texas");
```

continues

Example 9.5   continued

```
      //register listener
      lst.addItemListener(this);
    }

    //listener handler for ItemEvent
    public void itemStateChanged(ItemEvent e)
    {
      if (e.getSource() instanceof List)
      {
        String[] items = lst.getSelectedItems();
        String selection = new String();
        for (int i=0; i<items.length; i++)
          selection = selection + "   " + items[i];
        c.setMessage("You have selected : "+ selection);
      }
    }
}

class DisplayMessage extends Canvas
{
  private String message = " ";

  public DisplayMessage()
  {
    super();
  }

  public String getMessage()
  {
    return message;
  }

  public void setMessage(String s)
  {
    message = s;
    repaint();
  }

  public void paint(Graphics g)
  {
    g.drawString(message, 20, 20);
  }
}
```

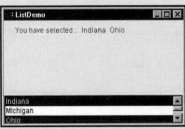

Figure 9.9   *State names that are selected from the list are displayed on the canvas.*

Example Review

The program creates a multiple-selection list with a visible window of three. There are six items on the list, but only three consecutive items are visible at a time. You can scroll the list to see other items.

Every time you click an item on the list, it triggers an `ItemEvent`. The handler for the event, `itemStateChanged(ItemEvent e)`, retrieves all the currently selected items and displays them on the canvas.

The `DisplayMessage`, a subclass of `Canvas`, displays a new message. The message is sent to the `DisplayMessage` through the `setMessage()` method. The `setMessage()` method sets the message and repaints the canvas.

NOTE

A choice box lets the user see all the choice items, but the number of items you see in a list at one time is specified by the list window size. The window size is fixed when the list is created.

TIP

If you have a short list of choices and only a single selection is needed, it is better to use `Choice` than `List`. If you want to select multiple items, you must use `List`.

Checkbox

A *check box* is a component that enables the user to toggle a choice on or off, like a light switch.

The following constructor is used to create a check box:

```
public Checkbox(String label)
```

This creates a check box with the specified label.

Here is how to create a check box:

```
Checkbox chk = new Checkbox("My Checkbox");
add(chk);
```

This creates a check box with the label "My Checkbox" (see Figure 9.10).

Figure 9.10   *A check box enables you to check or uncheck a selection.*

Checkbox can generate ItemEvent. The following code shows you how to implement isStateChanged() to determine whether a box is checked or unchecked:

```
public void itemStateChanged(ItemEvent e)
{
  //make sure the source is a checkbox
  if (e.getSource() instanceof Checkbox)
    boolean b = chk.getState(); //get state of the checkbox
}
```

This code simply gets the state of the Checkbox cb and saves it in boolean variable b.

You can also set the state of certain check boxes with the setState(boolean state) method. This is useful when you want to set the default state of check boxes.

Example 9.6   Using Check Boxes

This example gives a program to display a message in overlapping font styles. The message can be displayed in bold and in italic at the same time, for example. The output of a sample run of the program is given in Figure 9.11.

```
import java.awt.*;
import java.awt.event.*;

public class CheckboxDemo extends MyFrameWithExitHandling
   implements ItemListener
{
  //declare checkboxes
  private Checkbox chkPlain, chkBold, chkItalic;

  //declare a canvas for displaying message
  private DisplayMessageWithSelectedFonts c;

  public static void main(String[] args)
  {
    Frame f = new CheckboxDemo();
    f.setSize(400, 200);
    f.setVisible(true);
  }

  public CheckboxDemo()
  {
    setTitle("Checkbox Demo");

    //create the canvas
    c = new DisplayMessageWithSelectedFonts();
    c.setMessage("Welcome to Java!");
    c.setBackground(Color.red);

    //put three check boxes in Panel p
    Panel p = new Panel();
    p.setLayout(new FlowLayout());
    p.add(chkPlain = new Checkbox("Plain"));
    p.add(chkBold = new Checkbox("Bold"));
    p.add(chkItalic = new Checkbox("Italic"));

    //place c and p in the frame
    setLayout(new BorderLayout());
```

```
      add("Center", c);
      add("South", p);

      //register listeners on chkPlain, chkBold, and chkItalic
      chkPlain.addItemListener(this);
      chkBold.addItemListener(this);
      chkItalic.addItemListener(this);
    }

    public void itemStateChanged(ItemEvent e)
    {
      if (e.getSource() instanceof Checkbox)
      {
        int selection = 0;
        if (chkPlain.getState())
          selection = selection+Font.PLAIN;
        if (chkBold.getState())
          selection = selection+Font.BOLD;
        if (chkItalic.getState())
          selection = selection+Font.ITALIC;

        c.setFont(selection);
      }
    }
}

class DisplayMessageWithSelectedFonts extends DisplayMessage
{
  private int font = 0;

  public DisplayMessageWithSelectedFonts()
  {
    super();
  }

  public void setFont(int font)
  {
    this.font = font;
    repaint();
  }

  public void paint(Graphics g)
  {
    //create font
    Font f =new Font("Courier", font, 18);

    //set font
    g.setFont(f);
    displayAtCenter(g, getMessage(), f);
  }

  void displayAtCenter(Graphics g, String message, Font f)
  {
    //get font metrics for the font
    FontMetrics fm = g.getFontMetrics(f);

    //find the center location to display
    int w = fm.stringWidth(message);
    int h = fm.getAscent();
```

continues

293

Example 9.6   continued

```
        int x = (getSize().width-w)/2;
        int y = (getSize().height+h)/2;

        //draw string at the center
        g.drawString(message, x, y);
      }
    }
```

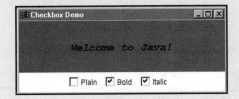

Figure 9.11   *The program uses three* Checkbox *components to let the user choose the font style for the message displayed at the center of the canvas.*

Example Review

The program displays the message in the center of a canvas and places three check boxes below the canvas. The check boxes are for three font styles: plain, bold, and italic. The user can toggle a check box on and off to select or deselect the item.

Upon selecting a check box, the handler, itemStateChanged(ItemEvent e), is invoked to determine the state of each check box and combines all selected fonts. The font styles are int constants: Font.PLAIN, Font.BOLD, and Font.ITALIC. Combining font styles is simply adding together the selected integers representing the fonts.

The state of the check box is true or false (indicating checked or unchecked), which is obtained by applying the getState() method on the check box instance.

The DisplayMessageWithSelectedFonts class extends DisplayMessage defined in Example 9.5 with additional methods that allow font selections (setFont()) and display a message on the center of the canvas (displayAtCenter()).

CheckboxGroup

Check box groups, also known as *option buttons* or *radio buttons*, are variations of check boxes, but only one box in the group can be checked at a time. Its appearance is similar to a check box. Check boxes display a square that is either checked or blank, and a check box in the group displays a circle that is either filled (if selected) or blank (not selected).

To create a `CheckboxGroup`, use the following:

```
CheckboxGroup cbg = new CheckboxGroup();
```

This creates the `CheckboxGroup` object `cbg`.

Here is an example of how to add choice boxes into the check box group `cbg`.

```
Checkbox chk;
add(chk = new Checkbox("Choice Name 1", cbg, true));
```

The last statement creates a choice box and places it in the `cbg` group. The choice box is labeled `Choice Name 1`, and the value `true` indicates the box is initially selected.

You can get the state of the individual box in the group using the `getState()` method. For example, `chk.getState()` indicates whether `cb1` is selected (`true`) or not selected (`false`).

Example 9.7   Using *CheckboxGroup*

This example gives a program to simulate traffic lights. The program lets the user select one of the three lights: red, yellow, or green. Upon selecting a check box, the light is turned on, and there is only one light on at a time. No light is on when the program starts. Figure 9.12 contains the output of a sample run for the program.

```java
import java.awt.*;
import java.awt.event.*;

public class CheckboxGroupDemo extends MyFrameWithExitHandling
  implements ItemListener
{
  //check boxes to be grouped in a check box group
  private Checkbox chkRed, chkYellow, chkGreen;
  //canvas to show traffic lights
  private Light light;

  public static void main(String[] args)
  {
    Frame f = new CheckboxGroupDemo();
    f.setSize(250,170);
    f.setVisible(true);
  }

  public CheckboxGroupDemo()
  {
    setTitle("CheckboxGroup Demo");

    //add traffic light canvas to panel p1
    Panel p1 = new Panel();
    p1.setSize(200,200);
    p1.setLayout(new FlowLayout(FlowLayout.CENTER));
    p1.add(light = new Light());
    light.setSize(40,90);
```

continues

295

Example 9.7   continued

```
        //put the check box in Panel p2
        Panel p2 = new Panel();
        p2.setLayout(new FlowLayout());
        CheckboxGroup cbg = new CheckboxGroup();
        p2.add(chkRed = new Checkbox("Red", cbg, false));
        p2.add(chkYellow = new Checkbox("Yellow", cbg, false));
        p2.add(chkGreen = new Checkbox("Green", cbg, false));

        //place p1 and p2 in the frame
        setLayout(new BorderLayout());
        add("Center", p1);
        add("South", p2);

        //register listeners for check boxes
        chkRed.addItemListener(this);
        chkYellow.addItemListener(this);
        chkGreen.addItemListener(this);
    }

    //handling checkbox events
    public void itemStateChanged(ItemEvent e)
    {
      if (chkRed.getState())
        light.red(); //set red light
      if (chkYellow.getState())
        light.yellow(); //set chkYellow light
      if (chkGreen.getState())
        light.green(); //set chkGreen light
    }
}

//Three traffic lights shown in a canvas
class Light extends Canvas
{
  private boolean red;
  private boolean yellow;
  private boolean green;

  public Light()
  {
    red = false;
    yellow = false;
    green = false;
  }

  //set red light on
  public void red()
  {
    red = true;
    yellow = false;
    green = false;
    repaint();
  }

  //set yellow light on
  public void yellow()
  {
    red = false;
```

```
        yellow = true;
        green = false;
        repaint();
    }

    //set green light on
    public void green()
    {
        red = false;
        yellow = false;
        green = true;
        repaint();
    }

    //display lights
    public void paint(Graphics g)
    {
        if (red)
        {
            g.setColor(Color.red);
            g.fillOval(10,10,20,20);
            g.setColor(Color.black);
            g.drawOval(10,35,20,20);
            g.drawOval(10,60,20,20);
            g.drawRect(5,5,30,80);
        }
        else if (yellow)
        {
            g.setColor(Color.yellow);
            g.fillOval(10,35,20,20);
            g.setColor(Color.black);
            g.drawRect(5,5,30,80);
            g.drawOval(10,10,20,20);
            g.drawOval(10,60,20,20);
        }
        else if (green)
        {
            g.setColor(Color.green);
            g.fillOval(10,60,20,20);
            g.setColor(Color.black);
            g.drawRect(5,5,30,80);
            g.drawOval(10,10,20,20);
            g.drawOval(10,35,20,20);
        }
        else
        {
            g.setColor(Color.black);
            g.drawRect(5,5,30,80);
            g.drawOval(10,10,20,20);
            g.drawOval(10,35,20,20);
            g.drawOval(10,60,20,20);
        }
    }
}
```

continues

297

Example 9.7   continued

Figure 9.12   *The* CheckboxGroup *enables you to check one color in the group and causes the corresponding traffic light to be shown on the canvas.*

Example Review

The lights are displayed on a canvas. The program groups the check boxes in a panel and places the panel below the canvas. The BorderLayout is used to arrange these components.

The Light class, a subclass of Canvas, contains the methods red(), yellow(), and green() to control lights. For example, use light.red() to turn on the red light, where light is an instance of Light.

The program creates a CheckboxGroup cbg and puts three Checkbox instances (red, yellow, and green) in the group. When the user checks a box in the group, the handler, itemStateChanged(ItemEvent e) determines which check box is checked using the getState() method and turns on the corresponding light.

Dialog

A *dialog box* is normally used as a temporary window to receive additional information from the user, or to provide notification that some event has occurred. The Dialog is a subclass of Window (just like Frame), but a Dialog instance must be associated with a frame. You may create a Dialog instance using the following constructor:

```
public Dialog(Frame parent, String title, boolean modal)
```

This constructs an initially invisible dialog box with a title under the specified frame. The modal parameter (true or false) indicates whether other windows can be accessed before the dialog is dismissed. The parent parameter is required, and the other two parameters are optional.

Example 9.8   Using Dialogs

This example gives a program to display student exam scores. The user enters the last name and the password, then clicks the Find Score button (see Figure 9.13) to show the full name and the score. If the last name is incorrect, a message dialog box displays the message Last name not found, as shown in Figure 9.14. If the password is incorrect, a message dialog box displays Password does not match last name, as shown in Figure 9.15. In either case, the user must click the OK button in the message dialog box to go back to the main frame.

```java
import java.awt.*;
import java.awt.event.*;

public class DialogDemo extends MyFrameWithExitHandling
  implements ActionListener
{
  //create sample student information in arrays
  private String[] fname =
    {"John", "Jim", "Bill", "George", "Michael"};
  private String[] mi = {"A", "B", "C", "E", "F"};
  private String[] lname =
    {"Willow", "Brown", "Kim", "Wall","Fong"};
  private String[] password = {"a450", "b344", "3342csa",
    "343rea2","34g"};
  private float[] score = {50.5f, 100, 23.5f, 90, 99};
  private TextField tfLastName; //declare text field for last name
  private TextField tfPassword; //declare text field for password
  private TextField tfFullName; //declare text field for full name
  private TextField tfScore; //declare text field for score
  private Button btFind; //declare button for "Find"
  private MessageDialog dialog;

  public static void main(String[] args)
  {
    DialogDemo f = new DialogDemo();
    f.pack();
    f.setVisible(true);
  }

  public DialogDemo()
  {
    setTitle("Find The Score");

    //enter last name
    Panel p1 = new Panel();
    p1.setLayout(new FlowLayout(FlowLayout.LEFT));
    p1.add(new Label("Enter Last Name"));
    p1.add(tfLastName = new TextField(25));

    //enter password
    Panel p2 = new Panel();
    p2.setLayout(new FlowLayout(FlowLayout.LEFT));
    p2.add(new Label("Enter Password"));
    p2.add(tfPassword = new TextField(25));

    //Set the echo character * for password text field
    tfPassword.setEchoChar('*');
```

continues

299

Example 9.8   continued

```
                    //display full name
                    Panel p3 = new Panel();
                    p3.setLayout(new FlowLayout(FlowLayout.LEFT));
                    p3.add(new Label("Name"));
                    p3.add(tfFullName = new TextField(25));

                    //display score
                    Panel p4 = new Panel();
                    p4.setLayout(new FlowLayout(FlowLayout.LEFT));
                    p4.add(new Label("Score"));
                    p4.add(tfScore = new TextField(5));

                    //place panels and a button in the frame
                    setLayout(new GridLayout(5, 1));
                    add(p1);
                    add(p2);
                    add(p3);
                    add(p4);
                    add(btFind = new Button("Find Score"));

                    //register listener for btFind
                    btFind.addActionListener(this);

                    //create a dialog box
                    dialog = new MessageDialog(this, "Error", true);
                }

                public void actionPerformed(ActionEvent e)
                {
                  int index = find(tfLastName.getText().trim(),
                    tfPassword.getText().trim());
                  if (index == -1)
                  {
                    dialog.setMessage("Last name not found");
                    dialog.pack();
                    dialog.setVisible(true);
                  }
                  else if (index == -2)
                  {
                    dialog.setMessage("Password does not match last name");
                    dialog.pack();
                    dialog.setVisible(true);
                  }
                  else
                  {
                    tfFullName.setText(fname[index]+" "+mi[index]+"
                      "+lname[index]);
                    tfScore.setText(Float.toString(score[index]));
                  }
                }

                /* find the username and password
                   return the index if found;
                   return -1 if last name does not match, and
                   return -2 if last name matches but password does not.
                */
                public int find(String username, String pw)
                {
                  for (int i=0; i<lname.length; i++)
```

```
        if (lname[i].equals(username) && password[i].equals(pw))
          return i;
      for (int i=0; i<lname.length; i++)
        if (lname[i].equals(username))
          return -2;
      return -1;
  }
}

class MessageDialog extends Dialog
  implements ActionListener
{
  private Label lblMessage; //for showing message
  private Button btOk;

  public MessageDialog(Frame parent, String title, boolean modal)
  {
    super(parent, title, modal);

    //Create panel to hold the button
    Panel p = new Panel();
    p.setLayout(new FlowLayout(FlowLayout.RIGHT));
    p.add(btOk = new Button("Ok"));

    //place label and panel p in the dialog
    setLayout(new BorderLayout());
    add("Center", lblMessage = new Label());
    add("South", p);

    //register listener
    btOk.addActionListener(this);
  }

  //respond to the button action
  public void actionPerformed(ActionEvent e)
  {
    setVisible(false);
  }

  public void setMessage(String message)
  {
    lblMessage.setText(message);
  }
}
```

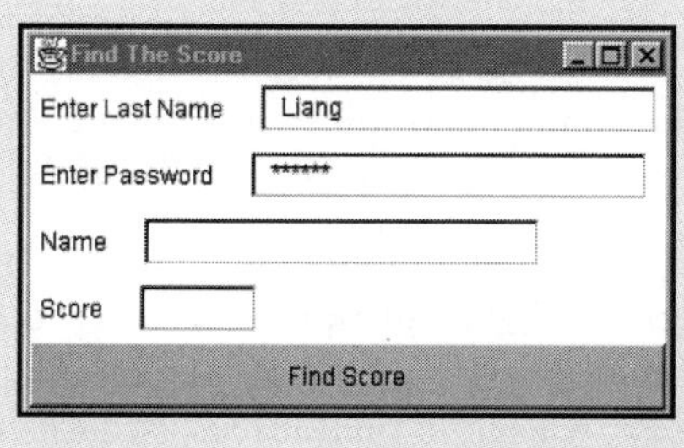

Figure 9.13 *The main frame lets the user enter his or her name and password and then click the Find Score button to display full name and score.*

continues

Example 9.8   continued

Figure 9.14   *The message box displays the error message* Last name not found

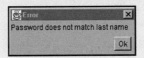

Figure 9.15   *The message box displays the error message* Password does not match last name

Example Review

The student information is stored in the arrays `fname[]`, `mi[]`, `lname[]`, `password[]`, and `score[]` for first name, middle name initial, last name, password, and the score. If the username and password in the dialog box match `lname[i]` and `password[i]`, the full name (`fname[i]+" "+mi[i]+" "+lname[i]`) and the score (`score[i]`) are displayed in the main frame.

When the program starts, the main frame comes up first, as shown in Figure 9.13. If the user enters the wrong username, the message Last name not found appears in the dialog box, as shown in Figure 9.14. If the user enters a correct last name, but wrong password, the message Password does not match last name appears in the dialog box, as shown in Figure 9.15. Upon receiving the correct username and password, the user's full name and the score are displayed in the dialog box, as shown in Figure 9.13.

The statement `dialog = new MessageDialog(this, "Error", true)` creates a `Dialog` object, dialog, from the frame (`this`). The value `true` indicates it is a modal dialog box, so no other frames can be accessed until the dialog box is dismissed.

The `pack()` method in the `Window` class automatically sets the size for the window so that all the components are packed in the window automatically. `dialog.pack()` is used to cause the dialog box to layout the label in its preferred size, which is dependent on the label text size.

The `tfPassword.setEchoChar('*')` method sets the echo character, *, for the password. This is useful for fields in which the user input shouldn't be echoed to the screen (as in this case, where the `TextField` is used for entering a password).

The `MessageDialog` class extends `Dialog`. It is a common practice to define a user dialog derived from the `Dialog` class. `Dialog` can be used like a frame. It is a window with a title.

The find(username, pw) method defined in the main frame returns the index of the student array element that matches the username and the password, returns –1 if last name is not found, and returns –2 if password does not match the last name.

Menu

Menus make selection easier, and are widely used in window applications. In Java, menus can only appear on a frame. Java provides three classes—MenuBar, Menu, and MenuItem—to implement menus in a frame.

A frame can hold a *menu bar* to which the *pull-down menus* are attached. Menus consist of *menu items* that the user can select (or toggle on or off). Menu bars can be viewed as a structure to support menus.

The sequence of implementing menus in Java is as follows:

1. Create a menu bar and associate it with a frame.

```
Frame f = new Frame();
f.setSize(300, 200);
f.setVisible(true);
MenuBar mb = new MenuBar();
f.setMenuBar(mb);
```

This code creates a frame and a menu bar, and sets the menu bar in the frame.

2. Create menus.

You can use the following constructors to create a menu:

```
public Menu(String label, boolean tearOff)
```

This constructs a new Menu instance with the specified label and tearOff. The true tearOff enables the programmer to create a menu that displays even when the mouse button is released.

```
public Menu(String label)
```

This constructs a new menu instance with the specified label. It is equivalent to Menu(label, false).

NOTE
The tearOff function may not be supported by all AWT implementations. If a particular implementation doesn't support tear-offs, this value will be ignored.

The following is an example of creating menus:

```
Menu fileMenu = new Menu("File", true);
Menu helpMenu = new Menu("Help", true);
mb.add(fileMenu);
mb.add(helpMenu);
```

This creates two menus labeled File and Help, as shown in Figure 9.16. The menus will not be seen until they are added to `MenuBar`.

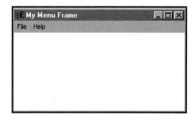

Figure 9.16   *The menu bar appears below the title bar on the frame.*

3. Create menu items and add them to menus.

```
fileMenu.add(new MenuItem("new"));
fileMenu.add(new MenuItem("open"));
fileMenu.add(new MenuItem("-"));
fileMenu.add(new MenuItem("print"));
fileMenu.add(new MenuItem("-"));
fileMenu.add(new MenuItem("exit"));
```

This code adds the menu items new, open, -, print, -, and exit, in this order, to the File menu, as shown in Figure 9.17.

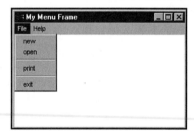

Figure 9.17   *Clicking a menu on the menu bar reveals the items under the menu.*

The character "-" separates menu items. You can also use the `addSeparator()` method to separate menu items:

```
file.addSeparator();
```

You can also embed menus inside menus so that the embedded menus become submenus. Here is an example:

```
Menu softwareHelpSubMenu = new Menu("Software");
Menu hardwareHelpSubMenu = new Menu("Hardware");
helpMenu.add(softwareHelpSubMenu);
helpMenu.add(hardwareHelpSubMenu);
softwareHelpSubMenu.add(new MenuItem("Unix"));
softwareHelpSubMenu.add(new MenuItem("NT"));
softwareHelpSubMenu.add(new MenuItem("Win95"));
```

This code adds two submenus: softwareHelpMenu and hardwareHelpMenu in helpMenu. The items Unix, NT, and Win95 are added into softwareHelpMenu (see Figure 9.18).

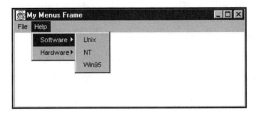

Figure 9.18   *Clicking a menu item reveals the secondary items under the menu item.*

You can also add a CheckboxMenuItem to a Menu. CheckboxMenuItem is a subclass of MenuItem that adds a Boolean state to the MenuItem, and displays a check when its state is true. You can click the menu item to turn it on and off. For example, the following statement adds the check box menu item Check it (see Figure 9.19).

```
helpMenu.add(new CheckboxMenuItem("Check it"));
```

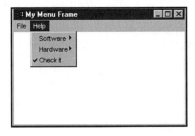

Figure 9.19   *A check box menu item lets you check or uncheck a menu item just like a check box.*

4. The menu items generate ActionEvent. Your program must implement the actionPerformed() handler to respond to the menu selection. The following is an example:

```
public void actionPerformed(ActionEvent e)
{
  String actionCommand = e.getActionCommand();

  //make sure the source is MenuItem
  if (e.getSource() instanceof MenuItem)
    if ("new".equals(actionCommand))
      respondToNew();
}
```

This code executes the method respondToNew() when the menu item labeled "new" is selected.

Example 9.9   Using Menus

This example gives a program to create a user interface that performs arithmetic. The interface contains labels and text fields for Number 1, Number 2, and Result. The Result text field displays the result of the arithmetic operation between Number 1 and Number 2.

The program has four buttons labeled Add, Subtract, Multiply, and Divide. The program will also create a menu to perform the same operation. The user can choose the operation either from buttons or from menu selections. Figure 9.20 contains a sample run for the example.

```java
import java.awt.*;
import java.awt.event.*;

public class MenuDemo extends MyFrameWithExitHandling
   implements ActionListener
{
  //text fields for Number 1, Number 2, and Result
  private TextField tfNum1, tfNum2, tfResult;
  //declare buttons
  private Button btAdd, btSub, btMul, btDiv;
  //declare menu items
  private MenuItem miAdd, miSub, miMul, miDiv, miClose;

  public static void main(String[] args)
  {
    MenuDemo f = new MenuDemo();
    f.setSize(400,150);
    f.setVisible(true);
  }

  public MenuDemo()
  {
    setTitle("Test Menus");
    setBackground(Color.yellow);
    setForeground(Color.red);

    //create MenuBar mb
    MenuBar mb = new MenuBar();
    setMenuBar(mb);

    //add a Menu "Operation" in mb
    Menu operationMenu = new Menu("Operation");
    mb.add(operationMenu);

    //add a Menu "Exit" in mb
    Menu exitMenu = new Menu("Exit");
    mb.add(exitMenu);

    //add MenuItems
    operationMenu.add(miAdd = new MenuItem("Add"));
    operationMenu.add(miSub = new MenuItem("Subtract"));
    operationMenu.add(miMul = new MenuItem("Multiply"));
    operationMenu.add(miDiv = new MenuItem("Divide"));
    exitMenu.add(miClose = new MenuItem("Close"));

    //set FlowLayout for p1
    Panel p1 = new Panel();
```

```
          p1.setLayout(new FlowLayout());
          p1.add(new Label("Number 1"));
          p1.add(tfNum1 = new TextField(3));
          p1.add(new Label("Number 2"));
          p1.add(tfNum2 = new TextField(3));
          p1.add(new Label("Result"));
          p1.add(tfResult = new TextField(4));
          tfResult.setEditable(false);

          //set FlowLayout for p2
          Panel p2 = new Panel();
          p2.setLayout(new FlowLayout());
          p2.add(btAdd = new Button("Add"));
          p2.add(btSub = new Button("Subtract"));
          p2.add(btMul = new Button("Multiply"));
          p2.add(btDiv = new Button("Divide"));

          //set BorderLayout for the frame
          setLayout(new BorderLayout());
          add("Center", p1);
          add("South", p2);

          //register listeners
          btAdd.addActionListener(this);
          btSub.addActionListener(this);
          btMul.addActionListener(this);
          btDiv.addActionListener(this);
          miAdd.addActionListener(this);
          miSub.addActionListener(this);
          miMul.addActionListener(this);
          miDiv.addActionListener(this);
          miClose.addActionListener(this);
        }

        //handling ActionEvent from buttons and menu items
        public void actionPerformed(ActionEvent e)
        {
          String actionCommand = e.getActionCommand();

          //handling button events
          if (e.getSource() instanceof Button)
          {
            if ("Add".equals(actionCommand))
              calculate('+');
            else if ("Subtract".equals(actionCommand))
              calculate('-');
            else if ("Multiply".equals(actionCommand))
              calculate('*');
            else if ("Divide".equals(actionCommand))
              calculate('/');
          }
          else if (e.getSource() instanceof MenuItem)
          {
            //handling menu item events
            if ("Add".equals(actionCommand))
              calculate('+');
            else if ("Subtract".equals(actionCommand))
              calculate('-');
```

continues

Example 9.9   continued

```
            else if ("Multiply".equals(actionCommand))
              calculate('*');
            else if ("Divide".equals(actionCommand))
              calculate('/');
            else if ("Close".equals(actionCommand))
              System.exit(0);
        }
    }

    //divide Number 1 by Number 2 the result in tfResult
    private void calculate(char operator)
    {
      //obtain Number 1 and Number 2
      int num1 = (Integer.parseInt(tfNum1.getText().trim()));
      int num2 = (Integer.parseInt(tfNum2.getText().trim()));
      int result = 0;

      //perform selected operation
      switch (operator)
      {
        case '+': result = num1 + num2;
                  break;
        case '-': result = num1 - num2;
                  break;
        case '*': result = num1 * num2;
                  break;
        case '/': result = num1 / num2;
      }

      //set result in TextField tfResult
      tfResult.setText(String.valueOf(result));
    }
}
```

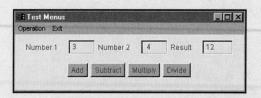

Figure 9.20   *The arithmetic operations can be performed by clicking buttons or choosing the menu items from the Operation menu.*

Example Review

The program creates a menu bar, mb, that holds two menus: operationMenu and exitMenu. The operationMenu contains four menu items: Add, Subtract, Multiply, and Divide for performing arithmetic. The exitMenu contains the menu item Close for exiting the program.

The user enters two numbers in the number fields. When choosing an operation from the menu, the result of the operation involving two numbers is displayed in the Result field. The user may also click the buttons to perform the same operation.

The private method `calculate(char operator)` retrieves operands from the text fields in Number 1 and Number 2, and applies the binary operator on the operands and sets the result in the Result text field.

Creating Multiple Windows

Occasionally, you may want to create multiple windows in an application. Suppose that your application has two tasks: displaying traffic lights and performing arithmetic calculation. You can design a main frame with two buttons representing the two tasks for the user to choose. When the user clicks a button, the application opens a new window for performing the specified task. The new windows are called subwindows and the main frame is called the main window.

To create a subwindow from an application, you usually need to create a subclass of `Frame` that defines the task and tells the new window what to do. You can then create an instance of subclass in the application and launch the new window by setting the frame instance to be visible.

Example 9.10   Creating Multiple Windows

This example creates a main window with two buttons: Simple Calculator and Traffic Lights. When the user clicks Simple Calculator, a new window appears to let the user perform add, subtract, multiply, and divide operations. When the user clicks Traffic Lights, another window appears to display traffic lights.

The Simple Calculator frame named `MenuDemo` is given in Example 9.9, and the Traffic Lights frame named `CheckboxGroupDemo` is given in Example 9.7. They can be directly used in this example without modification.

Figure 9.21 contains the output of a sample run for the program.

```
import java.awt.*;
import java.awt.event.*;

public class MultipleWindowsDemo
  extends MyFrameWithExitHandling implements ActionListener
{
  //declare and create a frame: an instance of MenuDemo
  MenuDemo calcFrame = new MenuDemo();

  //declare and create a frame: an instance of CheckboxGroupDemo
  CheckboxGroupDemo lightsFrame = new CheckboxGroupDemo();
```

continues

Example 9.10   continued

```
       //declare buttons to be put in the frame
       private Button btCalc;
       private Button btLights;

       public static void main(String[] args)
       {
         MultipleWindowsDemo f = new MultipleWindowsDemo();
         f.setSize(300,200);
         f.setVisible(true);
       }

       public MultipleWindowsDemo()
       {
         setLayout(new FlowLayout());

         //add buttons to the main frame
         add(btCalc = new Button("Simple Calculator"));
         add(btLights = new Button("Traffic Lights"));

         //register the main frame as listener for the buttons
         btCalc.addActionListener(this);
         btLights.addActionListener(this);
       }

       public void actionPerformed(ActionEvent e)
       {
         String actionCommand = e.getActionCommand();
         if (e.getSource() instanceof Button)
           if ("Simple Calculator".equals(actionCommand))
           {
             //show the MenuDemo frame
             calcFrame.setSize(300,200);
             calcFrame.setVisible(true);
           }
           else if ("Traffic Lights".equals(actionCommand))
           {
             //show the CheckboxGroup frame
             lightsFrame.setSize(300,200);
             lightsFrame.setVisible(true);
           }
       }
     }
```

Example Review

The program creates calcFrame to be an instance of MenuDemo, and creates lightsFrame to be an instance of CheckboxGroupDemo. The classes MenuDemo and CheckboxGroupDemo are given in Example 9.9 and Example 9.7, respectively.

The program creates two buttons—Simple Calculator and Traffic Lights—and adds them to the main frame. When a button is clicked, the ActionEvent handler determines which source object triggers the event. If the source object is the Simple Calculator button, the window for performing arithmetic calculation is launched with calcFrame.setSize() and calcFrame.setVisible(true). If the source object is the Traffic Lights button, the window for displaying lights is launched.

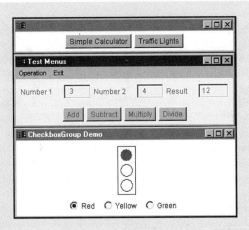

Figure 9.21   *Multiple windows can be displayed simultaneously, as shown in this program.*

It is interesting to see that the MenuDemo class and the CheckboxGroupDemo class are used in this application without any changes. What about the main() method in the MenuDemo and in the CheckboxGroupDemo? The main() method is ignored because the bytecode for MenuDemo or CheckboxGroupDemo is not directly invoked by the Java interpreter.

The program has an annoying problem. When you close a subwindow, the whole program exits. This is because the subwindows are the frames that extend MyFrameWithExitHandling. How do you close the new windows without terminating the whole program? There are several ways to fix the problem.

One way is to replace system.exit(0) in MyFrameWithExitHandling with setVisible(false), which in effect closes the subwindow but does not terminate the main frame. The other approach is to change the label of the buttons in the main frame. For example, when you click the Simple Calculator button, the Calculator window appears, and the name of the button changes to Hide Calculator. When you click the Hide Calculator button, the window is closed and the name of the button changes back to Simple Calculator (see Exercise 8 at the end of this chapter).

CAUTION
You cannot add a frame to a container. For example, adding calcFrame or lightsFrame to the main frame would cause a runtime error. However, you can create a frame instance and set it to be visible to launch a new window.

Scrollbar

A *scrollbar* is a control that enables the user to select from a range of values. The scrollbar appears in two styles: *horizontal* and *vertical*, as shown in Figure 9.22.

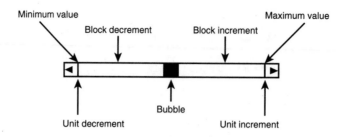

Figure 9.22   *A scrollbar represents a range of values graphically.*

You can use the following constructors to create a scrollbar:

```
public Scrollbar()
```

This constructs a new vertical scrollbar.

```
public Scrollbar(int orientation)
```

This constructs a new scrollbar with the specified orientation (`Scrollbar.HORIZONTAL` or `Scrollbar.VERTICAL`).

```
public Scrollbar(int orientation, int value,
                 int visible, int minimum, int maximum)
```

This constructs a new scrollbar with the specified orientation, initial value, visible bubble size, and minimum and maximum values.

The scrollbar has the following properties with the associated getter and setter methods.

- **orientation**—Specifies horizontal or vertical style, with 0 for horizontal and 1 for vertical.

- **maximum**—The maximum value the scrollbar represents when the bubble reaches to the right end of the scrollbar for horizontal style or the bubble reaches to the bottom of the scrollbar for vertical style.

- **minimum**—The minimum value the scrollbar represents when the bubble reaches to the left end of the scrollbar for horizontal style or the bubble reaches to the top of the scrollbar for vertical style.

- **visibleAmount**—The relative width of the scrollbar's bubble. The actual width appearing on the screen is determined by the maximum value and the value of `visibleAmount`.

- **value**—Represents the current value of the scrollbar. Normally, a program should change a scrollbar's value by calling `setValue()`. The `setValue()` method simultaneously and synchronously sets the minimum, maximum, visible amount, and value properties of a scrollbar, so that they are mutually consistent.

- **blockIncrement**—The value that is added (subtracted) when the user activates the block increment (decrement) area of the scrollbar as shown in

Figure 9.22. The `blockIncrement` property, which is new in JDK 1.1, supercedes the `pageIncrement` property used in JDK 1.02.

■ **`unitIncrement`**—The value that is added (subtracted) when the user activates the unit increment (decrement) area of the scrollbar, as shown in Figure 9.22. The `unitIncrement` property, which is new in JDK 1.1, supercedes the `lineIncrement` property used in JDK 1.02.

NOTE

The actual width of the scrollbar's track is `maximum+visibleAmount`. When the scrollbar is set to its maximum value, the left side of the bubble is at `maximum`, and the right side is at `maximum+visibleAmount`.

Normally, the user changes the value of the scrollbar by making a gesture with the mouse. For example, the user can drag the scrollbar's bubble up and down, or click in the scrollbar's unit increment or block increment areas. Keyboard gestures can also be mapped to the scrollbar. By convention, the Page Up and Page Down keys are equivalent to clicking in the scrollbar's block increment and block decrement areas.

When the user changes the value of the scrollbar, the scrollbar generates an instance of `AdjustmentEvent`, which is passed to any registered listeners. Any object that wishes to be notified of changes to the scrollbar's value should implement `adjustmentValueChanged` method in the `AdjustmentListener` interface defined in the package `java.awt.event`.

Example 9.11   Using Scrollbars

This example uses a horizontal scrollbar and a vertical scrollbar to control a message displayed in a canvas. You can move the message to the left or to the right using the horizontal scrollbar and move the message up and down using the vertical scrollbar. The output of the program is shown in Figure 9.23.

```java
import java.awt.*;
import java.awt.event.*;

public class ScrollbarDemo
   extends MyFrameWithExitHandling implements AdjustmentListener
{
  //declare scrollbars
  Scrollbar scbHort, scbVert;

  //declare a canvas
  ScrollMessageCanvas c;

  public static void main(String[] args)
  {
    ScrollbarDemo f = new ScrollbarDemo();
```

continues

Example 9.11   continued

```java
        f.setSize(300,200);
        f.setVisible(true);
    }

    public ScrollbarDemo()
    {
      setLayout(new BorderLayout());

      //create scrollbars
      scbVert = new Scrollbar();
      scbVert.setOrientation(Scrollbar.VERTICAL);
      scbHort = new Scrollbar();
      scbHort.setOrientation(Scrollbar.HORIZONTAL);

      add("Center", c = new ScrollMessageCanvas());
      add("East", scbVert);
      add("South", scbHort);

      //register listener for the scrollbars
      scbHort.addAdjustmentListener(this);
      scbVert.addAdjustmentListener(this);
    }

    public void adjustmentValueChanged(AdjustmentEvent e)
    {
      if (e.getSource() == scbHort)
      {
        /*getValue() and getMaximumValue() return int, but for better
          precision, use double
        */
        double value = scbHort.getValue();
        double maximumValue = scbHort.getMaximum();
        double newX = (value*c.getSize().width/maximumValue);
          c.setX((int)newX);
      }
      else if (e.getSource() == scbVert)
      {
        /*getValue() and getMaximumValue() return int, but for better
          precision, use double
        */
        double value = scbVert.getValue();
        double maximumValue = scbVert.getMaximum();
        double newY = (value*c.getSize().height/maximumValue);
          c.setY((int)newY);
      }
    }
  }

  class ScrollMessageCanvas extends Canvas
  {
    private int x = 10;
    private int y = 20;
    private String message = "Welcome to Java!";

    public ScrollMessageCanvas()
    {
      repaint();
    }
```

```java
      public void setX(int x)
      {
        this.x = x;
        repaint();
      }

      public void setY(int y)
      {
        this.y = y;
        repaint();
      }

      public void paint(Graphics g)
      {
        g.drawString(message, x, y);
      }
    }
```

Figure 9.23   *The scrollbars move the message in the canvas horizontally and vertically.*

Example Review

The program creates an instance of `ScrollMessageCanvas` (c) and two scrollbars (scbVert and scbHort). c is placed in the center of the frame; scbVert and scbHort are placed in the east and south sections of the frame, respectively.

You can specify the orientation of the scrollbar in the constructor or use the setOrientation() method. By default, the property value for maximum is 100, for minimum is 0, for pageIncrement is 10, and for visibleAmount is 10.

When the user drags the bubble, or clicks the increment or decrement unit, the value of the scrollbar changes. An instance of AdjustmentEvent is generated and passed to the listener by invoking the adjustmentValueChanged() method. Since there are two scrollbars in the frame, the e.getSource() method is used to determine the source of the event. The vertical scrollbar moves the message up and down, and the horizontal bar moves the message to the right and to the left.

The maximum value of the vertical scrollbar corresponds to the height of the canvas, and the maximum value of the horizontal scrollbar corresponds to the width of the canvas. The ratio between current value and the maximum of the horizontal scrollbar is the same as the ratio between the x value and the width of the canvas. Similarly, the ratio between current value and the maximum of the vertical scrollbar is the same as the ratio between the y value and the height of the canvas.

Chapter Summary

In this chapter, you learned how to create graphical user interfaces using Button, Label, TextField, TextArea, Choice, List, Checkbox, CheckboxGroup, Dialog, MenuBar, Menu, MenuItem, and Scrollbar.

Buttons are used to activate actions. The user expects something to happen when a button is clicked. Clicking a button generates the ActionEvent and triggers the listener to invoke the actionPerformed() method.

Label is plain text used to label other GUI components. TextField is used to accept user input into a string. TextArea can accept multiple lines of strings.

List is a simple list of values to choose from. The user can choose one or more values at a time, depending on how the list is constructed. Choice is similar to List, but you can get only one value from a Choice. Checkbox is for specifying whether the item is selected or not. Usually, you will have many items, each of which is in a check box. CheckboxGroup groups all items in a group. You can select one item from the group at a time.

A dialog box is commonly used to gather information from the user or show information to the user. A dialog box is a window constructed using the Dialog class. Dialog is a subclass of Window (just like Frame), but a Dialog instance must be associated with a frame.

Menus can be placed in a frame. A menu bar is used to hold the menus. You must add a menu bar to the frame using the setMenuBar() method, add menus into the menu bar, and add menu items into a menu.

Scrollbars are the controls for selecting from a range of values. You can create scrollbars using the Scrollbar class and specify horizontal or vertical scrollbars using the setOrientation() method.

To handle events generated by button, list, choice, check box, check box group, menu, or scrollbar, you must register the listener object with the source object and implement the corresponding listener interface.

You cannot add an instance of the Window class to a container. Therefore, a frame or a dialog box cannot be put into a frame or a dialog box. However, you can create a frame or a dialog box and set it to visible to launch a separate window in the program.

Chapter Review

1. How do you create a button labeled "OK"? How do you change a label on a button?

2. How do you create a label named "Address"? How do you change the name on a label?

3. How do you create a text field with a width of 10 characters and the default text "Welcome to Java"?

4. How do you create a text area with 10 rows and 20 columns? How do you insert three lines into the text area?

5. How do you create a choice, add three items into the choice, and retrieve the choice items?

6. How do you create a list with 10 rows and allow multiple selections? How do you add three items to the list and retrieve the list items?

7. How do you create a check box? How do you determine if a box is checked?

8. How do you create a check box group with three items? How do you determine if a box in the group is checked?

9. How do you create the menus File, Edit, View, Insert, Format, and Help, and add menu items Toolbar, Format Bar, Ruler, Status Bar and Options to the View menu? (See Figure 9.24.)

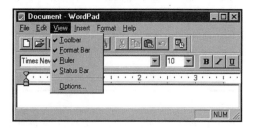

Figure 9.24   *Create a menu like this in WordPad, with menus and menu items.*

10. Can you specify the size for GUI components such as buttons, labels, text fields, text areas and lists?

11. Sometimes you get a blank frame. Your frame is displayed, but no contents are in it. Give some reasons. (Either the layout manager is not specified, no components are added to the frame, or there is another reason.)

12. Can you remove a component from a container? Find the remove() method in the Container class from the Java API and use this method to remove a component.

13. Can you remove a menu item from the menu?

14. Describe how to create a dialog box. Describe the modal parameter in the dialog box.

15. Describe how to create and show multiple frames in an application.

Programming Exercises

1. Rewrite Example 9.1 to add a check box group to select background colors. The available colors are red, yellow, white, gray, and green (see Figure 9.25).

Figure 9.25   *The <= and => buttons move the message on the canvas, and you can also set the color for the message.*

2. Rewrite Example 9.2 to handle double values and perform subtract, multiply, and divide operations in addition to the add operation (see Figure 9.26).

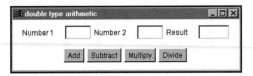

Figure 9.26   *The program performs addition, subtraction, multiplication, and division on double numbers.*

3. Write a project to meet the following requirements:

- Create a text field, a text area, a list, and a choice in a panel using the `FlowLayout`.

- Create a button labeled Store and place it in a panel using the `FlowLayout`.

- Place the preceding two panels in a frame.

- The action of the Store button is to retrieve the item from the text field and store it in a text area, a list, or a choice.

- When an item in the list box is selected, the item is displayed in the text field.

- When an item in the choice box is selected, the item is displayed in the text field.

4. Modify Exercise 2 from Chapter 8, "Getting Started with Graphics Programming" as follows. Create your own button class named NewButton that extends `java.awt.Button`. When you click an instance of `NewButton`, the label is changed to new if the current label is not new. If the current label *is* new, the label is changed back to its original name. You need to implement the actionPerformed() method in the NewButton class and use the setLabel() method to change the label (see Figure 9.27).

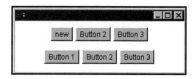

Figure 9.27 *NewButton, a subclass of Button, changes the label to new and restores the original label alternately.*

5. Write a program to draw various figures on a canvas. The user selects figures from a check box group. The selected figure is then displayed in the canvas (see Figure 9.28).

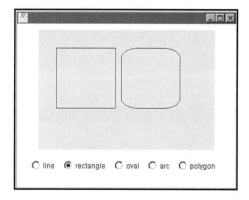

Figure 9.28 *This program displays lines, rectangles, ovals, arcs, or polygons when you select a shape type.*

6. Write a program to calculate the future value of an investment at a given interest rate for a specified number of years. The formula for the calculation is as follows:

futureValue = investmentAmount $\times$ (1 + interestRate)^{years}

Use text fields for interest rate, investment amount, and years. Display the future amount in a text field when the user clicks the Calculate button, or chooses Calculate from the Operation menu (see Figure 9.29).

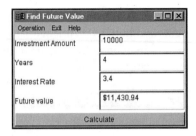

Figure 9.29   *The user enters the investment amount, years, and interest rate to compute future value.*

7. Write a program to display a calendar as follows (see Figure 9.30).

   ■ The user specifies a month and a year on the text field, then clicks the Show button to display the calendar for the month of the year. Each day on the calendar is shown on a button, and the weekday names are labels.

   ■ Place all the buttons for the calendar in a panel with GridLayout with 5 rows and 7 columns.

   ■ Place the text field and the Show button in a panel with FlowLayout.

   ■ Place the first panel in the North and the second panel in the South in the frame with BorderLayout.

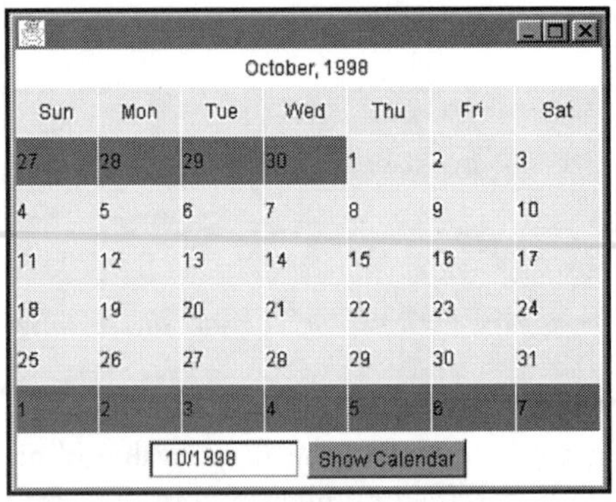

Figure 9.30   *The program is similar to the one in Exercise 4 in Chapter 8, except that the day names are displayed on labels and the days are displayed as labels on buttons.*

8. Rewrite Example 9.10 as follows:

   ■ When the user clicks the Simple Calculator button, the Calculator window appears and the name of the button changes to Hide Calculator. When the user clicks the Hide Calculator button, the window is closed, and the name of the button changes back to Simple Calculator.

- Modify the function of the Traffic Lights button in the same way as in the preceding item.

9. Write a program to use the scrollbars to select the background color for a canvas, as shown in Figure 9.31. Three horizontal scrollbars are used for selecting red, green, and blue components of the color.

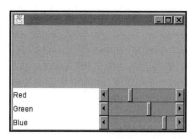

Figure 9.31   *The background color changes in the canvas as you change the values in the scrollbar.*

CHAPTER 10

APPLETS AND ADVANCED GRAPHICS

Objectives

@ Understand how the Web browser controls and executes the applet.

@ Become familiar with the `init()`, `start()`, `stop()`, and `destroy()` methods in the `Applet` class.

@ Pass parameters to applets from HTML.

@ Convert between applications and applets.

@ Write a Java program that can run as an application and as an applet.

@ Understand and handle mouse events and keystrokes.

@ Know when to use `CardLayout` and `GridBagLayout`, or use no layout managers.

Introduction

Java's early success was attributed to applets. Applets can run from a Java-enabled Web browser and can bring dynamic interaction and live animation to an otherwise static HTML page. It is safe to say that Java would be nowhere today without applets. Applets make Java appealing, attractive, and popular.

In this book so far, you have mostly used Java applications in examples that introduce Java programming. Everything you have learned about writing applications, however, also applies to writing applets. Because applets are invoked from a Web page, Java provides special features to enable applets to run from a Web browser.

In this chapter, you will learn how to write Java applets, discover the relationship between applets and the Web browser, and explore the similarities and differences of applications and applets. You also will see more complex examples of handling mouse events and keystrokes and of using advanced layout managers.

The *Applet* Class

As shown in Chapter 1, "Introduction to Java," every Java applet extends the `java.applet.Applet` class. The `Applet` class provides the essential framework to enable your applets to be run by a Web browser. Every Java application has a `main()` method, which is executed when the application starts. Unlike applications, applets do not have a `main()` method. Applets depend on the browser to call the methods. Every applet has a structure like the following:

```
public class MyApplet extends java.applet.Applet
{
  ...
  /*called by the browser when the Web page containing
    this applet is loaded
  */
  public void init()
  {
    ...
  }

  /*called by the browser after the init() method and
    every time the Web page is visited.
  */
  public void start()
  {
    ...
  }

  /*called by the browser when the page containing this
    applet becomes inactive.
  */
  public void stop()
  {
    ...
  }

  //called by the browser when the Web browser exits.
  public void destroy()
```

```
    {
      ...
    }
      //other methods if necessary...
  }
```

The browser controls the applets using the `init()`, `start()`, `stop()`, and `destroy()` methods. By default, these methods do nothing. To perform specific functions, they need to be modified in the user's applet so that the browser can call your code properly. Figure 10.1 shows how the browser calls these methods.

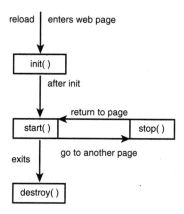

Figure 10.1   *The Web browser controls the applet using the `init()`, `start()`, `stop()`, and `destroy()` methods.*

The *init()* Method

The `init()` method is invoked when the applet is first loaded and again if it is reloaded.

A subclass of `Applet` should override this method if the subclass has an initialization to perform. Common functions implemented using this method include creating new threads, loading images, setting up user interface components, and getting parameters from the `<applet>` tag in the HTML page. Chapter 12, "Multithreading," discusses threads in more detail; passing `Applet` parameters is discussed later in this chapter.

The *start()* Method

The `start()` method is invoked after the `init()` method. It also is called whenever the applet becomes active again after a period of inactivity. The `start()` method is called, for example, when the user returns to the Web page containing the applet after surfing other pages.

A subclass of `Applet` should override this method if the subclass has any operation that needs to be performed each time the Web page containing the applet is visited. An applet with animation, for example, might want to use the `start()` method to resume animation.

The *stop()* Method

The `stop()` method is the opposite of the `start()` method. The `start()` method is called when the user moves back to the page containing the applet. The `stop()` method is invoked when the user moves off the page.

A subclass of `Applet` should override this method if the subclass has any operation that needs to be performed each time the Web page containing the applet is no longer visible. When the user leaves the page, any threads the applet has started—but not completed—will continue to run. You should override the `stop()` method to suspend the running threads so the applet does not take up system resources when it is not active.

The *destroy()* Method

The `destroy()` method is invoked when the browser exits normally to inform the applet that it is no longer needed and that it should release any resources it has allocated. The `stop()` method always is called before the `destroy()` method.

A subclass of `Applet` should override this method if the subclass has any operation that needs to be performed before it is destroyed. Usually, you won't need to override this method unless you need to release specific resources, such as threads that the applet created.

Example 10.1   Using Applets

This example shows an applet to compute mortgages. The applet enables the user to enter the interest rate, the number of years, and the loan amount. Clicking the Compute button displays the monthly payment and the total payment. The applet and the HTML code containing the applet are provided in the following code. Figure 10.2 contains a sample run of the applet.

```
//MortgageApplet.java source code
import java.applet.*;
import java.awt.*;
import java.awt.event.*;

public class MortgageApplet extends Applet
  implements ActionListener
{
  private TextField tfInterestRate; //interest rate
  private TextField tfYear; //loan period
  private TextField tfLoan; //loan amount
  private TextField tfMonthlyPay; //monthly payment
```

```
private TextField tfTotalPay; //total payment
private Button btCompute; //compute mortgage button

//initialize user interface
public void init()
{
  //create text fields and the compute button
  tfInterestRate = new TextField(10);
  tfYear = new TextField(10);
  tfLoan = new TextField(10);
  tfMonthlyPay = new TextField(10);
  tfMonthlyPay.setEditable(false);
  tfTotalPay = new TextField(10);
  tfTotalPay.setEditable(false);
  btCompute = new Button("Compute");

  //set background and foreground colors
  setBackground(Color.yellow);
  setForeground(Color.red);

  //create panel p to hold labels and text fields
  Panel p = new Panel();
  p.setLayout(new GridLayout(5,2));

  //add labels and text fields to p
  p.add(new Label("Interest Rate"));
  p.add(tfInterestRate);
  p.add(new Label("Years "));
  p.add(tfYear);
  p.add(new Label("Loan Amount"));
  p.add(tfLoan);
  p.add(new Label("Monthly Payment"));
  p.add(tfMonthlyPay);
  p.add(new Label("Total Payment"));
  p.add(tfTotalPay);

  //set Layout for the applet
  setLayout(new FlowLayout());

  //add p and the compute button to the frame
  add(p);
  add(btCompute);

  //register listener
  btCompute.addActionListener(this);
}

//handle "Compute" button
public void actionPerformed(ActionEvent e)
{
  String actionCommand = e.getActionCommand();
  if (e.getSource() instanceof Button)
    if (actionCommand.equals("Compute"))
    {
      //get values from text fields.
      double interest =
        (Double.valueOf(tfInterestRate.getText())).doubleValue();
      int year =
        (Integer.valueOf(tfYear.getText())).intValue();
```

continues

327

Example 10.1   continued

```
              double loan =
                (Double.valueOf(tfLoan.getText())).doubleValue();

              //create a mortgage object
              Mortgage m = new Mortgage(interest, year, loan);

              //display monthly pay and total pay
              tfMonthlyPay.setText(String.valueOf(m.monthlyPay()));
              tfTotalPay.setText(String.valueOf(m.totalPay()));
          }
      }
  }

  <-- HTML code, this code is separated from the preceding Java code>
  <html>
  <head>
  <title>Mortgage Applet</title>
  </head>
  <body>
  This is a mortgage calculator, enter your input for interest, year
  and loan amount, click the "Compute" button, you will get the
  payment information.<p>
  <applet
    code = "MortgageApplet.class"
    width = 300
    height = 150
    alt="You must have a JDK1.1-enabled browser to view the applet">
  </applet>
  </body>
  </html>
```

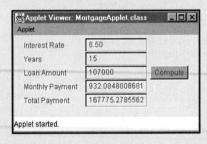

Figure 10.2   *The applet computes the monthly payment and the total payment when provided with the interest rate, number of years, and loan amount.*

Example Review

You need to import `java.applet.*` since every applet extends `Applet`.

You need to use the `public` modifier for the `MortgageApplet`; otherwise, the Web browser cannot load the applet.

`MortgageApplet` implements `ActionListener` because it listens for button actions.

The init() method initializes the user interface. The program overrides this method to create user interface components (labels, text fields, and a button), and places them in the applet.

The only event handled is the Compute button. When this button is clicked, the actionPerformed() method gets the interest rate, year, and loan from the text fields. It then creates a Mortgage object to obtain the monthly pay and the total pay. Finally, it displays the monthly and total payments in their respective text fields.

The monthly and total payments are not displayed in currency format. To display a number as currency, you can use the java.text.NumberFormat class to format numbers in the desired locale and style. For example, replacing the highlighted code in this program with the following code will display a monthly payment, such as $932.08.

```
NumberFormat nf = NumberFormat.getCurrencyInstance(Locale.US);
monthlyPayDisplay.setText(nf.format(m.monthlyPay()));
```

The Mortgage class is responsible for computing the payments. This class was discussed in Example 5.8, "Using the Rational Class" (see Chapter 5, "Programming with Objects and Classes").

Applets are embedded in HTML using the <applet> tag, which is discussed in the next section. The code parameter specifies the location of the applet bytecode file. The width and height, both in pixels, specify the initial size of the applet.

The applet must be viewed by a JDK 1.1–enabled Web browser or by the Applet Viewer utility. The message You must have a JDK1.1–enabled browser to view the applet is displayed if your browser is not capable of viewing applets. Please download the HotJava browser from **www.javasoft.com**, Internet Explorer 4.0 from **www.microsoft.com**, or Netscape Navigator 4.05 from **www.netscape.com** if your browser is not JDK1.1–compatible.

The *<applet>* HTML Tag

To run applets, you must create an HTML file with the <applet> tag to specify the applet bytecode file, the applet viewing area dimension (width and height), and other associated parameters. The syntax of the <applet> tag is as follows:

```
<applet
  code=classfilename.class
  width=applet_viewing_width_in_pixels
  height=applet_viewing_height_in_pixels
  [archive=archivefile]
  [codebase=applet_url]
  [vspace=vertical_margin]
  [hspace=horizontal_margin]
  [align=applet_alignment]
  [alt=alternative_text]
>
<param name=param_name1 value=param_value1>
```

```
<param name=param_name2 value=param_value2>
...
<param name=param_name3 value=param_value3>
</applet>
```

The `code`, `width`, and `height` attributes are required; all others are optional. The `<param>` tag is introduced in the section "Passing Parameters to Applets." The meanings of other attributes are described as follows:

- **archive**—You can use this attribute to instruct the browser to load an archive file that contains all the class files needed to run the applet. To create such a file, use the JDK `jar` command, as in the following example:

  ```
  jar -cf des.jar A1.class A2.class
  ```

  This command creates an archive file named **des.jar** for classes A1 and A2. For more information on the use of the `jar` command, refer to the JDK 1.2 Documentation included in the companion CD or online at **java.sun.com/ products/jdk/1.2/docs/**. The archiving allows the Web browser to load all the classes from a single compressed file only once—thus reducing loading time and improving performance.

- **codebase**—If this attribute is not used, the Web browser loads the applet from the directory in which the HTML page is located. If your applet is located in a different directory from the HTML page, you must specify the `applet_url` for the browser to load the applet. This attribute enables you to load the class from anywhere on the Internet. The classes used by the applet are dynamically loaded when needed.

- **vspace** and **hspace**—These two attributes specify the size of the blank margin to leave around the applet vertically and horizontally in pixels.

- **align**—This attribute specifies how the applet will be aligned in the browser. One of nine values is used: `left`, `right`, `top`, `texttop`, `middle`, `absmiddle`, `baseline`, `bottom`, and `absbottom`.

- **alt**—This attribute specifies the text to be displayed in case the browser cannot run Java.

Passing Parameters to Applets

In Chapter 6, "Arrays and Strings," you learned how to pass parameters to Java applications from a command line. The parameters were entered when using the Java interpreter and were passed as an array of strings to the `main()` method. When the application starts, the `main()` method can use these arguments. There is no `main()` method in an applet, however, and applets are not run from the command line by the Java interpreter.

How, then, can applets accept arguments? In this section, you will learn how to pass parameters to Java applets.

To pass parameters to an applet, the parameters must be declared before the applet starts, and they must be read by the applet when the applet is initialized. The parameters are declared using the <param> tag in the HTML page. The <param> tag must be embedded in the <applet> tag, and it has no end tag. The syntax for the <param> tag is as follows:

```
<param name=parametername value=parametervalue>
```

This tag specifies a parameter and its corresponding value.

NOTE

There is not a comma to separate the parameter name from the parameter value in the HTML code.

Suppose you want to write an applet to display a message. The message is passed as a parameter. In addition, you want the message to be displayed at a specific location. The start location of the message also is passed as a parameter in two values, x coordinate and y coordinate. Assume the applet is named DisplayMessage.class. The parameters and their values are listed in Table 10.1.

TABLE 10.1   Parameter Names and Values for *DisplayMessage.class*

Parameter Name	Parameter Value
MESSAGE	"Welcome to Java"
X	20
Y	30

The HTML source file might look like this:

```
<html>
<head>
<title>Passing Parameters to Java Applets</title>
</head>
<body>
This applet gets a message from the HTML page and displays it.
<p>
<applet
  code = "DisplayMessage.class"
  width = 200
  height = 50
  alt="You must have a JDK1.1-enabled browser to view the applet"
>
<param name=MESSAGE value="Welcome to Java">
<param name=X value=20>
<param name=Y value=30>
</applet>
</body>
</html>
```

To read the parameter from the applet, use the following method:

```
public String getParameter("parametername");
```

This returns the value of the specified parameter.

Example 10.2   Passing Parameters to Java Applets

This example shows an applet to display a message at a specified location. The message and the location (x, y) are obtained from the HTML source. The program creates a Java source file named **DisplayMessage.java**, as shown in the following. The output of a sample run is shown in Figure 10.3.

```java
//DisplayMessage.java
import java.applet.Applet;
import java.awt.*;

public class DisplayMessage extends Applet
{
  private String message; //message to display
  private int x = 20; //default x coordinate
  private int y = 20; //default y coordinate

  public void init()
  {
    //getting parameter values from the HTML file
    message = getParameter("MESSAGE");
    x = Integer.parseInt(getParameter("X"));
    y = Integer.parseInt(getParameter("Y"));
  }

  public void paint(Graphics g)
  {
    g.setColor(Color.red);
    g.drawString(message, x, y);
  }
}
```

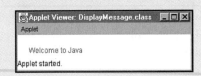

Figure 10.3   *The applet displays the message Welcome to Java passed from the HTML page.*

Example Review

The program gets the parameter values from HTML in the init() method. The values are strings obtained using the getParameter() method. Because x and y are int, the program uses Integer.parseInt(string) to convert a digital string into an int value.

If you change "Welcome to Java" to "Welcome to HTML" in the HTML file and reload the HTML file in the Web browser, you should see Welcome to HTML displayed. Similarly, x and y values can be changed to display the message in the desired location.

Conversions Between Applications and Applets

The Frame class and the Applet class have a lot in common despite some differences. They both are subclasses of the Container class. Therefore, all the user interface components, layout managers, and event-handling features are the same for both classes. Application frames, however, are invoked by the Java interpreter, and applets are invoked by the Web browser. In this section, you will learn how to convert between applets and applications.

In general, you can convert an applet to an application. The following are the steps for conversion:

1. Eliminate the import java.applet.* statement.

2. Eliminate the HTML page that invokes the applet. If the applet gets parameters from the HTML page, you can handle these parameters from the command line.

3. Derive the main class named NewClass, for instance, from Frame or MyFrameWithExitHandling instead of from Applet.

4. Write a constructor in the new class to contain the code in the init() and start() methods.

5. Place the codes from the stop() and destroy() methods in the windowClosing() method that handles the window-closing event.

6. Add a main() method as follows:

```
public static void main()
{
  NewClass f = new NewClass();
  //width and height are from the <applet> tag
  f.resize(width, height);
  f.setVisible(true);
}
```

7. Because applets do not have title bars, you can add a title for the window using the setTitle() method.

NOTE

When using frames in applications, specify an initial size in width and height using the setSize() method. After the frame is displayed, you can resize it. With applets, the viewing area is fixed on a Web page by the width and height values in the <applet> tag.

Often you want the frame to be displayed in a specified location on the screen; you can use the setLocation(x, y) method to specify the upper-left corner x and y coordinates. To center the frame on the screen, you need to know the width and height of the screen and the frame in order to determine the upper-left coordinates of the frame. The screen width and height can be obtained using the java.awt.Toolkit class as follows:

```
Dimension screenSize = Toolkit.getDefaultToolkit().getScreenSize();
int screenWidth = screenSize.width;
int screenHeight = screenSize.height;
```

Therefore, the upper left x and y coordinates of the frame f can be as follows:

```
Dimension frameSize = f.getSize();
int x = (screenWidth - frameSize.width)/2;
int y = (screenHeight - frameSize.height)/2;
```

Example 10.3   Converting Applets into Applications

This example converts the Java applet MortgageApplet (from Example 10.1) to a Java application and displays the frame in the center of the screen. The following is the program, and its output is shown in Figure 10.4.

```
import java.awt.*;
import java.awt.event.*;

public class MortgageApplication
  extends MyFrameWithExitHandling implements ActionListener
{
  private TextField tfInterestRate;
  private TextField tfYear;
  private TextField tfLoan;
  private TextField tfMonthlyPay;
  private TextField tfTotalPay;
  private Button btCompute;

  /*add a main method to create the frame instance and show
    it on the screen
  */
  public static void main(String[] arg)
  {
    Frame f = new MortgageApplication();
    //width and height from the <applet> tag
    f.setSize(400,200);
    f.setVisible(true);

    //Center the window
    Dimension screenSize =
      Toolkit.getDefaultToolkit().getScreenSize();
    int screenWidth = screenSize.width;
    int screenHeight = screenSize.height;

    Dimension frameSize = f.getSize();
    int x = (screenWidth - frameSize.width)/2;
    int y = (screenHeight - frameSize.height)/2;

    if (x < 0)
    {
      x = 0;
      frameSize.width = screenWidth;
    }

    if (y < 0)
```

```
      {
        y = 0;
        frameSize.height = screenHeight;
      }

      f.setLocation(x, y);
}

//add a constructor to replace the init() method
//in the applet
public MortgageApplication()
{
    //set title for the window
    setTitle("Mortgage Application");

    tfInterestRate = new TextField(10);
    tfYear = new TextField(10);
    tfLoan = new TextField(10);
    tfMonthlyPay = new TextField(10);
    tfMonthlyPay.setEditable(false);
    tfTotalPay = new TextField(10);
    tfTotalPay.setEditable(false);
    btCompute = new Button("Compute");

    setBackground(Color.yellow);
    setForeground(Color.red);

    Panel p = new Panel();
    p.setLayout(new GridLayout(5,2));
    p.add(new Label("Interest Rate"));
    p.add(tfInterestRate);
    p.add(new Label("Years "));
    p.add(tfYear);
    p.add(new Label("Loan Amount"));
    p.add(tfLoan);

    p.add(new Label("Monthly Payment"));
    p.add(tfMonthlyPay);
    p.add(new Label("Total Payment"));
    p.add(tfTotalPay);

    setLayout(new FlowLayout());
    add(p);
    add(btCompute);

    btCompute.addActionListener(this);
}

//handle the "Compute" button
public void actionPerformed(ActionEvent e)
{
    String actionCommand = e.getActionCommand();
    if (e.getSource() instanceof Button)
      if (actionCommand.equals("Compute"))
      {
        double interest = (Double.valueOf(
          tfInterestRate.getText())).doubleValue();
        int year = (Integer.valueOf(
          tfYear.getText())).intValue();
```

continues

335

Example 10.3   continued

```
            double loan = (Double.valueOf(
              tfLoan.getText())).doubleValue();
            Mortgage m = new Mortgage(interest, year, loan);
            tfMonthlyPay.setText(String.valueOf(m.monthlyPay()));
            tfTotalPay.setText(String.valueOf(m.totalPay()));
          }
        }
      }
```

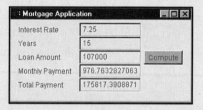

Figure 10.4   *The program is the same as Example 10.1 except it is written as an application.*

Example Review

The program extends MyFrameWithExitHandling, a subclass of Frame with window-closing capability, instead of extending Applet.

The program uses a constructor to initialize the user interface instead of using the init() method. The setTitle() method is used to set a title for the frame in the constructor.

The program creates a main() method to start the program by the Java interpreter.

The frame is centered on the screen. If the screen width is smaller than the frame width, the frame width is set to the screen width; similarly, frame height is set to the screen height if the screen height is smaller than the frame height.

In Chapter 1, you learned that certain limitations are imposed on applets for security reasons. Applets, for example, are not allowed to access local files. If the conversion from applications to applets does not violate the security constraints imposed on applets, you can perform the following steps to convert an application to an applet:

1. Add the import java.applet.* statement.

2. Create an HTML page with the <applet> tag that invokes the applet. If command-line parameters are used in the application, add the parameters in the <applet> tag and get the parameters using getParameter() in the init() method.

3. Derive the main class from `Applet` instead of from `Frame`.

4. Replace the application's constructor by the `init()` method.

5. Eliminate the `main()` method. The `main()` method usually contains the method to create and display the frame. The applet is automatically displayed in the size specified by the width and height in the `<applet>` tag. This step is optional. If you leave the `main()` method intact, the `main()` method is simply ignored.

6. Because applets do not have title bars, eliminate the `setTitle()` method (if it is in the application). Because the applet does not support menus, replace menus with buttons or other user interface components (if menus are used in the application).

Example 10.4   Converting Applications into Applets

This example converts the Java application `CurrentTimeFrame`, which displays a clock (Example 8.10, "Drawing a Clock," from Chapter 8, "Getting Started with Graphics Programming"), into a Java applet.

Example 8.10 passes command-line parameters for language code, country code, and time zone code to the program. In a Java applet, these parameters are passed from HTML. Therefore, you need to create an HTML file with the `<param>` tags inside the `<applet>` tag. The following is the HTML file:

```
<html>
<head>
<title>Display Current Time Applet</title>
</head>
<body>
<applet
  code = "CurrentTimeApplet.class"
  width = 200
  height = 220
  alt ="You must have a Java-enabled browser to view the applet">
<param name=language value=en>
<param name=country value=US>
<param name=timezone value=CST>
</applet>
</body>
</html>
```

The following Java applet `CurrentTimeApplet` is converted from the application `CurrentTimeFrame`. A sample run of this applet is shown in Figure 10.5.

```
import java.awt.*;
import java.util.*;
import java.text.*;
import java.applet.*;

public class CurrentTimeApplet extends Applet
{
  private int xcenter, ycenter;
```

continues

337

Example 10.4   continued

```
private int clockRadius;
static Locale locale = Locale.getDefault();
static TimeZone tz = TimeZone.getTimeZone("CST");
static DateFormat myFormat;
private GregorianCalendar cal = new GregorianCalendar();

public void init()
{
  //get parameters from the HTML
  String language = getParameter("language");
  String country = getParameter("country");
  String timezone = getParameter("timezone");

  //Set default values if parameters are not given in the HTML file
  if (language == null)
    language = "en";

  if (country == null)
    country = "US";

  if (timezone == null)
    timezone = "CST";

  //set locale and timezone
  locale = new Locale(language, country);
  tz = TimeZone.getTimeZone(timezone);

  /*set display format in specified style,
    locale and timezone */
  myFormat = DateFormat.getDateTimeInstance
    (DateFormat.MEDIUM, DateFormat.LONG, locale);
  myFormat.setTimeZone(tz);

  //get clock radius and center
  clockRadius =
    (int)(Math.min(getSize().width, getSize().height)*0.7*0.5);
  xcenter = (getSize().width)/2;
  ycenter = (getSize().height)/2;
}

public void paint(Graphics g)
{
  //draw circle
  g.setColor(Color.black);
  g.drawOval(xcenter - clockRadius,ycenter - clockRadius,
    2*clockRadius, 2*clockRadius);
  g.drawString("12",xcenter-5, ycenter-clockRadius);
  g.drawString("9",xcenter-clockRadius-10,ycenter+3);
  g.drawString("3",xcenter+clockRadius,ycenter+3);
  g.drawString("6",xcenter-3,ycenter+clockRadius+10);

  //get current time using GregorianCalendar
  cal = new GregorianCalendar(tz);

  //draw second hand
  int s = (int)cal.get(GregorianCalendar.SECOND);
  int sLength = (int)(clockRadius*0.9);
```

```
        int secondx = (int)(Math.cos((s/60.0)*2*Math.PI -
          Math.PI/2) * sLength + xcenter);
        int secondy = (int)(Math.sin((s/60.0)*2*Math.PI -
          Math.PI/2) * sLength + ycenter);
        g.setColor(Color.red);
        g.drawLine(xcenter, ycenter, secondx, secondy);

        //draw minute hand
        int m = (int)cal.get(GregorianCalendar.MINUTE);
        int mLength = (int)(clockRadius*0.8);
        int minutex = (int)(Math.cos((m/60.0)*2*Math.PI -
          Math.PI/2)*mLength+xcenter);
        int minutey = (int)(Math.sin((m/60.0)*2*Math.PI -
          Math.PI/2)*mLength+ycenter);
        g.setColor(Color.blue);
        g.drawLine(xcenter, ycenter, minutex, minutey);

        //draw hour hand
        int h = (int)cal.get(GregorianCalendar.HOUR_OF_DAY);
        int hLength = (int)(clockRadius*0.7);
        double hourAngle = (h/12.0)*2*Math.PI +
          (m/60.0)*(2*Math.PI/60.0) - Math.PI/2;
        int hourx = (int)(Math.cos(hourAngle) * hLength + xcenter);
        int houry = (int)(Math.sin(hourAngle) * hLength + ycenter);
        g.setColor(Color.green);
        g.drawLine(xcenter, ycenter, hourx, houry);

        //display current date
        String today = myFormat.format(cal.getTime());
        FontMetrics fm = g.getFontMetrics();
        g.drawString(today, (getSize().width -
          fm.stringWidth(today))/2, ycenter+clockRadius+30);
    }
  }
```

Example Review

The program implements the init() method, which incorporates the code in the main() method and in the constructor from the CurrentTimeFrame application in Example 8.10.

The getParameter() method gets parameters language, country, and timezone from the HTML file. These are the same parameters used by the application and passed from the command line.

Because the viewing area of an applet never changes, the program obtains the applet width and height in the init() method and initializes the clock radius and the center. Note these operations are performed in the paint() method in the CurrentTimeFrame class; therefore, you might get a new clock radius and center when the frame is resized.

continues

Example 10.4   continued

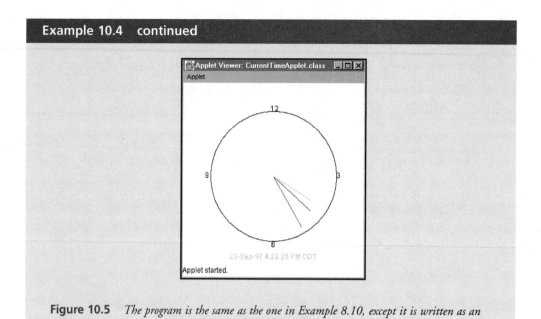

Figure 10.5 *The program is the same as the one in Example 8.10, except it is written as an applet.*

Running a Program as an Applet and as an Application

You can implement a main() method in an applet to run the applet as an application or to run it as an applet using the same program. This feature has both theoretical and practical implications. Theoretically, it blurs the difference between applets and applications. You can write a class that is both an applet and application. Practically, it is convenient to be able to run a program in two ways.

It is not difficult to write such types of programs on your own. Suppose you have an applet named TestApplet. To enable it to run as an application, all you need to do is add a main() method in the applet with the implementation as follows:

```
public static void main(String[] args)
{
  //create a Frame object f
  Frame f = new MyFrameWithExitHandling(
    "Running a program as applet and frame");

  //create an instance of TestApplet
  TestApplet testApplet = new TestApplet();

  //add the applet instance to the frame
  f.setLayout(new BorderLayout());
  f.add("Center", testApplet);
  f.setSize(300, 300);

  //invoke init() and start()
  testApplet.init();
```

```
        testApplet.start();

        //display the frame
        f.setVisible(true);
    }
```

The Applet class is a subclass of Panel. Therefore, it can be placed in a frame. You can invoke the init() and start() methods of the applet to run an Applet object in an application.

Example 10.5   Running a Program as an Applet and as an Application

This example modifies the MortgageApplet to enable it to run both as an applet and as an application. The program is identical to MortgageApplet except it adds a new main() method. Figure 10.6 contains a sample run of the program as an applet, and Figure 10.7 contains a sample run of the program as an application.

```
import java.applet.*;
import java.awt.*;
import java.awt.event.*;

public class MortgageAppletAndFrameDemo extends Applet
  implements ActionListener
{
  private TextField tfInterestRate; //interest rate
  private TextField tfYear; //loan period
  private TextField tfLoan; //loan amount
  private TextField tfMonthlyPay; //monthly payment
  private TextField tfTotalPay; //total payment
  private Button btCompute; //compute mortgage button

  /*add a main method to enable the applet to run
    as an application*/
  public static void main(String[] args)
  {
    //create a Frame object f
    Frame f = new MyFrameWithExitHandling(
      "Running a program as applet and frame");

    //create an instance of MortgageAppletAndFrameDemo
    MortgageAppletAndFrameDemo mort =
      new MortgageAppletAndFrameDemo();

    //add the applet instance to the frame
    f.setLayout(new BorderLayout());
    f.add("Center", mort);
    f.setSize(300, 300);

    //invoke init() and start()
    mort.init();

    //display the frame
    f.setVisible(true);
  }
```

continues

Example 10.5   continued

```
          //initialize user interface
          public void init()
          {
            //create text fields and the compute button
            tfInterestRate = new TextField(10);
            tfYear = new TextField(10);
            tfLoan = new TextField(10);
            tfMonthlyPay = new TextField(10);
            tfMonthlyPay.setEditable(false);
            tfTotalPay = new TextField(10);
            tfTotalPay.setEditable(false);
            btCompute = new Button("Compute");

            //set background and foreground colors
            setBackground(Color.yellow);
            setForeground(Color.red);

            //create panel p to hold labels and text fields
            Panel p = new Panel();
            p.setLayout(new GridLayout(5,2));

            //add labels and text fields to p
            p.add(new Label("Interest Rate"));
            p.add(tfInterestRate);
            p.add(new Label("Years"));
            p.add(tfYear);
            p.add(new Label("Loan Amount"));
            p.add(tfLoan);
            p.add(new Label("Monthly Payment"));
            p.add(tfMonthlyPay);
            p.add(new Label("Total Payment"));
            p.add(tfTotalPay);

            //set Layout for the applet
            setLayout(new FlowLayout());

            //add p and the compute button to the frame
            add(p);
            add(btCompute);

            //register listener
            btCompute.addActionListener(this);
          }

          //handle "Compute" button
          public void actionPerformed(ActionEvent e)
          {
            String actionCommand = e.getActionCommand();
            if (e.getSource() instanceof Button)
              if (actionCommand.equals("Compute"))
              {
                //get values from text fields.
                double interest =
                  (Double.valueOf(tfInterestRate.getText())).doubleValue();
                int year =
                  (Integer.valueOf(tfYear.getText())).intValue();
                double loan =
                  (Double.valueOf(tfLoan.getText())).doubleValue();
```

```
                    //create a mortgage object
                    Mortgage m = new Mortgage(interest, year, loan);

                    //display monthly pay and total pay
                    tfMonthlyPay.setText(String.valueOf(m.monthlyPay()));
                    tfTotalPay.setText(String.valueOf(m.totalPay()));
                }
            }
        }
```

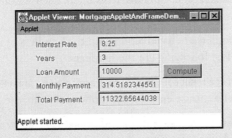

Figure 10.6   *The* `MortgageAppletAndFrameDemo` *class runs as an applet.*

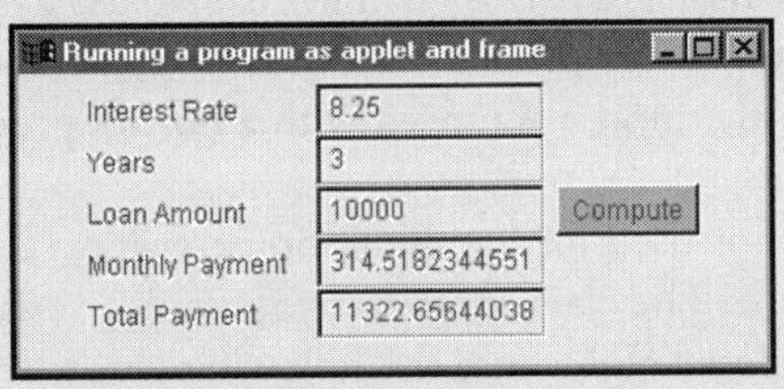

Figure 10.7   *The* `MortgageAppletAndFrameDemo` *class runs as an application.*

Example Review

When you run the program as an applet, the `main()` method is ignored. When you run it as a frame, the `main()` method is invoked.

The `main()` method creates a frame object `f` and creates `mort`, an instance of the applet. The `main()` method then places the applet `mort` into the frame `f` and invokes the applet's `init()` method. The application runs just like an applet.

The `setVisible(true)` method was invoked *after* the components had been added into the applet and the applet has been added into the frame to ensure the components to be visible. Otherwise, the components are not shown when the frame starts.

Drawing with the Mouse

A mouse event is generated whenever a mouse is clicked, released, moved, or dragged. The mouse event object captures the nature of the event, such as the number of clicks associated with the event or the location (x and y coordinates) of the mouse. Java provides two listener interfaces, `MouseListener` and `MouseMotionListener`, to handle mouse events. You should implement the `MouseListener` interface to listen for such actions as when the mouse is pressed, released, entered, exited, or clicked, and implement the `MouseMotionListener` interface to listen for such actions as dragging or moving the mouse.

The `MouseEvent` handlers are listed along with the handlers of other events in Table 8.2 in Chapter 8. The following are the handlers:

- The `mouseEntered(MouseEvent e)` and `mouseExit(MouseEvent e)` handlers are invoked when a mouse enters a component or exits the component.

- The `mousePressed(MouseEvent e)` and `mouseReleased(MouseEvent e)` handlers are invoked when a mouse is pressed or released. The `mouseClicked(MouseEvent e)` handler is invoked when a mouse is pressed and then released.

- The `mouseMoved(MouseEvent e)` handler is invoked when the mouse is moved without a button being pressed. The `mouseDragged(MouseEvent e)` handler is invoked when the mouse is moved with a button pressed.

The `Point` class often is used for handling mouse events. The `Point` class encapsulates a point in a plane. The class contains two instance variables, x and y, for coordinates. To create a point object, use the following constructor:

```
Point(int x, int y)
```

This constructs a `Point` object with the specified x and y coordinates.

You can use the `move(int x, int y)` method to move the point to the specified x and y coordinates. You can use the following properties from a `MouseEvent` object when a mouse event occurs:

```
public int getClickCount()
```

This returns the number of mouse clicks associated with this event.

```
public Point getPoint()
```

This returns the x and y coordinates of the event relative to the source component.

```
public int getX()
```

This returns the x coordinate of the event relative to the source component.

```
public int getY()
```

This returns the y coordinate of the event relative to the source component.

The `MouseEvent` class inherits `InputEvent`. Therefore, you can use the methods defined in the `InputEvent` class on a `MouseEvent` object. The following methods in `InputEvent` are often useful for handling mouse events:

```
public long getWhen()
```

This returns the time stamp of when this event occurred.

```
public boolean isAltDown()
```

This returns whether the Alt modifier is down on this event.

```
public boolean isControlDown()
```

This returns whether the Control modifier is down on this event.

```
public boolean isMetaDown()
```

This returns true if the right mouse button is pressed.

```
public boolean isShiftDown()
```

This returns whether the Shift modifier is down on this event.

Example 10.6   Handling Complex Mouse Events

This example shows a program for drawing using a mouse. You can use this program to draw anything on a canvas by dragging with the left mouse button pressed. You can erase the drawing by dragging with the right button pressed. A sample run of the program is shown in Figure 10.8.

```java
import java.awt.*;
import java.applet.*;
import java.awt.event.*;

public class MouseDrawingDemo extends Applet
{
  /*This main method enables the applet to run
    as an application
  */
  public static void main(String[] args)
  {
    //create a frame
    Frame f = new
      MyFrameWithExitHandling("Mouse Event Demo");

    //create an instance of MouseDrawingDemo
    MouseDrawingDemo mdd = new MouseDrawingDemo();

    //invoke init()
    mdd.init();

    //add the applet to the frame
    f.add("Center", mdd);
    f.setSize(300, 300);
    f.setVisible(true);
  }
```

continues

Example 10.6   continued

```java
        public void init()
        {
          Canvas c = new PaintCanvas(); //create a canvas
          c.setBackground(Color.yellow);

          //add canvas to the frame
          setLayout(new BorderLayout());
          add("Center", c);
        }
      }

      class PaintCanvas extends Canvas
        implements MouseListener, MouseMotionListener
      {
        final int CIRCLESIZE = 20; //circle diameter
        private Point lineStart = new Point(0, 0); //line start point
        private Graphics g; //creating a Graphics object for drawing

        public PaintCanvas()
        {
          //register listener for the mouse event
          addMouseListener(this);
          addMouseMotionListener(this);
        }

        public void mouseClicked(MouseEvent e)
        {
        }

        public void mouseEntered(MouseEvent e)
        {
        }

        public void mouseExited(MouseEvent e)
        {
        }

        public void mouseReleased(MouseEvent e)
        {
        }

        public void mousePressed(MouseEvent e)
        {
          lineStart.move(e.getX(), e.getY());
        }

        public void mouseDragged(MouseEvent e)
        {
          g = getGraphics(); //get graphics context

          if (e.isMetaDown()) //detect right button pressed
          {
            //erase the drawing using an oval
            g.setColor(getBackground());
            g.fillOval(e.getX() - (CIRCLESIZE/2),
                e.getY() - (CIRCLESIZE/2), CIRCLESIZE, CIRCLESIZE);
          }
          else
          {
```

```
        g.setColor(Color.black);
        g.drawLine(lineStart.x, lineStart.y,
          e.getX(), e.getY());
      }

    lineStart.move(e.getX(), e.getY());

    //dispose this graphics context
    g.dispose();
  }

  public void mouseMoved(MouseEvent e)
  {
  }
}
```

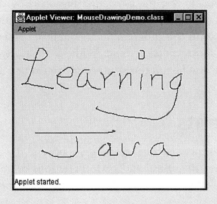

Figure 10.8   *The program enables you to draw anything using the mouse.*

Example Review

The program can run as an application and as an applet. The program creates a PaintCanvas instance to capture mouse movements on the canvas. It creates or erases lines by dragging the mouse with the left or right button pressed.

When a button is pressed, the mousePressed() handler is invoked. This handler sets the Point lineStart to the current mouse point as the starting point. When the mouse is dragged with the left button pressed, drawing starts. In this case, the mouseDragged() handler sets the foreground color to black, and draws a line along the path of the mouse movement.

When the mouse is dragged with the right button pressed, erasing occurs. In this case, the mouseDragged() handler sets the foreground color to the background color and draws an oval filled with the background color at the mouse pointer to erase the area covered by the oval.

continues

Example 10.6   continued

The program does not use the paint(Graphics g) method. Instead, the program uses getGraphics() to obtain a Graphics instance and draws on this Graphics instance.

Because mousePressed() is defined in the MouseListener interface and mouseDragged() is defined in the MouseMotionListener interface, the program implements both interfaces.

The dispose() method disposes of this graphics context and releases any system resources that it is using. Although the finalization process of the Java runtime system automatically disposes of the object after it is no longer used, I recommend that you manually free the associated resources by calling this method rather than relying on a finalization process that may not run to completion for a long period of time. In this program, a large number of Graphics objects can be created within a short period of time. Without manually disposing of these objects, the program would run fine, but would consume a lot of memory.

Keyboard Events

Keyboard events are generated whenever a key is pressed. By using keyboard events, users can use the keys to control and perform actions or get input from the keyboard.

The keyboard event object describes the nature of the event (a key is pressed, released, or typed) and the value of the key. To process a keyboard event, use the following handlers from the KeyListener interface:

```
public void keyPressed(KeyEvent e)
```

This handler is called when a key is pressed.

```
public void keyReleased(KeyEvent e)
```

This handler is called when a key is released.

```
public void keyTyped(KeyEvent e)
```

This handler is called when a key is pressed and then released.

The keys captured in the event are integers representing Unicode character values, which include alphanumeric characters, function keys, the Tab key, the Enter key, and so on. Every keyboard event has an associated key character or key code, which is returned by the getKeyChar() or getKeyCode() method in KeyEvent, respectively.

Java has defined many constants for normal keys and function keys in the KeyEvent class. Table 10.2 shows the most common ones.

TABLE 10.2   Key Constants

Constant	Description
VK_HOME	The Home key
VK_End	The End key
VK_PGUP	The Page Up key
VK_PGDN	The Page Down key
VK_UP	The up-arrow key
VK_DOWN	The down-arrow key
VK_LEFT	The left-arrow key
VK_RIGHT	The right-arrow key
VK_ESCAPE	The Esc key
VK_TAB	The Tab key
VK_BACK_SPACE	The Backspace key
VK_CAPS_LOCK	The Caps Lock key
VK_NUM_LOCK	The Num Lock key
VK_ENTER	The Enter key
VK_F1 to VK_F12	The function keys F1 to F12
VK_0 to VK_9	The number keys from 0 to 9
VK_A to VK_Z	The letter keys from A to Z

Example 10.7   Keyboard Events Demo

This example shows a program that displays a user-input character. The user can move the character up, down, left, and right using arrow keys VK_UP, VK_DOWN, VK_LEFT, and VK_RIGHT. Figure 10.9 contains a sample run of the program.

```
import java.awt.*;
import java.awt.event.*;
import java.applet.*;

public class KeyboardEventDemo extends Applet
{
  public static void main(String[] args)
  {
    //create a frame
    Frame f = new
      MyFrameWithExitHandling("Keyboard Event Demo");

    //create an instance of MouseDrawingDemo
    KeyboardEventDemo applet = new KeyboardEventDemo();

    //invoke init()
    applet.init();
```

continues

Example 10.7   continued

```java
        //add the applet to the frame
        f.add("Center", applet);
        f.setSize(300, 300);
        f.setVisible(true);
    }

    public void init()
    {
        //create a canvas to accept and display user input
        Canvas c = new KeyboardCanvas();
        c.setBackground(Color.yellow);

        //place canvas c in the frame
        setLayout(new BorderLayout());
        add("Center", c);

        c.requestFocus();
    }
}

class KeyboardCanvas extends Canvas implements KeyListener
{
    private int x = 100;
    private int y = 100;
    private char keyChar = 'A'; //default key

    public KeyboardCanvas()
    {
        addKeyListener(this); //add listener
    }

    public void keyReleased(KeyEvent e)
    {
    }

    public void keyTyped(KeyEvent e)
    {
    }

    public void keyPressed(KeyEvent e)
    {
        switch (e.getKeyCode())
        {
            case e.VK_DOWN: y += 10; break;
            case e.VK_UP: y -= 10; break;
            case e.VK_LEFT: x -= 10; break;
            case e.VK_RIGHT: x += 10; break;
            default: keyChar = e.getKeyChar();
        }
        repaint();
    }

    public void paint(Graphics g)
    {
        g.setFont(new Font("TimesRoman", Font.PLAIN, 24));
        g.drawString(String.valueOf(keyChar), x, y);
    }
}
```

Figure 10.9   *The program responds to the keyboard events, displaying a character and moving it up, down, left, and right.*

Example Review

When a non-arrow key is pressed, the key is displayed. When an arrow key is pressed, the character moves in the direction indicated by the arrow key.

Because the program gets input from the keyboard, it listens for KeyEvent and implements KeyListener to handle key input.

When a key is pressed, the keyPressed() method is invoked. The program uses e.getKeyCode() to obtain the int value for the key and uses e.getKeyChar() to get the character for the key. In fact, (int)e.getKeyChar() is the same as e.getKeyCode().

In the init() method, c.requestFocus() is used to request input focus, which is needed to get attention from the Web browser for keyboard input.

The *CardLayout* Manager (Optional)

Layout managers arrange components in a container. You have used the FlowLayout manager, the GridLayout manager, and the BorderLayout manager. Java has two other layout managers: CardLayout and GridBagLayout. Java also enables you to directly place components in a specific position without using a layout manager. This section discusses the CardLayout manager, and the following sections discuss the GridBagLayout manager and using no layout manager.

The CardLayout manager arranges components in a queue of cards. You can only see one card at a time. To construct a CardLayout, simply use the constructor CardLayout().

Cards are usually placed in a container such as a panel. Components are placed into the card queue in the order in which they are added. To add a component in the CardLayout container, use the following method:

```
void add(Component com, String name)
```

This adds the specified component to this container. The `String` argument of the method, `name`, gives an explicit identity to the component in the queue.

To make a component visible in the container with `CardLayout`, you can use the following instance methods in the `CardLayout` object:

```
public void first(Container container)
```

This method views the first card in the container.

```
public void last(Container container)
```

This method views the last card in the container.

```
public void next(Container container)
```

This method views the next card in the container.

```
public void previous(Container container)
```

This method views the previous card in the container.

```
public void show(Container container, String name)
```

This method views the component with the specified name in the container. You can use this method to directly display the component.

Example 10.8   Testing *CardLayout* Manager

This example shows a program that creates two panels in a frame. The first panel uses `CardLayout` to hold 15 labels named `Component` i (for i=1 through 15). The second panel uses `FlowLayout` to group four buttons named `First`, `Next`, `Previous`, and `Last`, and a choice box labeled `Component`.

These buttons control which component will be shown in the `CardLayout` panel. When the user clicks on the First button, for example, the first button in the `CardLayout` panel appears. The choice box enables the user to directly select a component.

The program follows, and the output of a sample run is shown in Figure 10.10.

```java
import java.awt.*;
import java.awt.event.*;
import java.applet.*;

public class ShowCardLayout extends Applet
  implements ActionListener, ItemListener
{
  private CardLayout queue = new CardLayout();
  private Panel cardPanel = new Panel();
  private Button btFirst, btNext, btPrevious, btLast;
  private Choice choComponent;

  public void init()
  {
```

```
      //add 15 buttons into cardPanel
      cardPanel.setLayout(queue);
      cardPanel.setBackground(Color.yellow);
      cardPanel.setForeground(Color.red);
      for (int i=1; i<=15; i++)
        cardPanel.add
          (new Label("Component "+i,Label.CENTER), String.valueOf(i));

      //add action buttons
      Panel buttonPanel = new Panel();
      buttonPanel.setLayout(new FlowLayout());
      buttonPanel.add(btFirst = new Button("First"));
      buttonPanel.add(btNext = new Button("Next"));
      buttonPanel.add(btPrevious= new Button("Previous"));
      buttonPanel.add(btLast = new Button("Last"));

      //add choice
      buttonPanel.add(new Label("Component"));
      buttonPanel.add(choComponent = new Choice());
      for (int i=1; i<=15; i++)
        choComponent.addItem(String.valueOf(i));

      //place panels in the frame
      setLayout(new BorderLayout());
      add("Center", cardPanel);
      add("South", buttonPanel);

      //register listener with the source objects
      btFirst.addActionListener(this);
      btNext.addActionListener(this);
      btPrevious.addActionListener(this);
      btLast.addActionListener(this);
      choComponent.addItemListener(this);
    }

    public static void main(String[] args)
    {
      //create a frame
      Frame f = new
        MyFrameWithExitHandling("Show CardLayout");

      //create an instance of MouseDrawingDemo
      ShowCardLayout applet = new ShowCardLayout();

      //invoke init()
      applet.init();

      //add the applet to the frame
      f.add("Center", applet);
      f.setSize(400, 200);
      f.setVisible(true);
    }

    public void actionPerformed(ActionEvent e)
    {
      String actionCommand = e.getActionCommand();
      if (e.getSource() instanceof Button)
        if ("First".equals(actionCommand))
          //show the first component in queue
          queue.first(cardPanel);
```

continues

Example 10.8   continued

```
            else if ("Last".equals(actionCommand))
              //show the last component in queue
              queue.last(cardPanel);
            else if ("Previous".equals(actionCommand))
              //show the previous component in queue
              queue.previous(cardPanel);
            else if ("Next".equals(actionCommand))
              //show the next component in queue
              queue.next(cardPanel);
    }

    //handling choice item events
    public void itemStateChanged(ItemEvent e)
    {
      if (e.getSource() instanceof Choice)
        //show the component at specified index
        queue.show(cardPanel, (String)e.getItem());
    }
  }
```

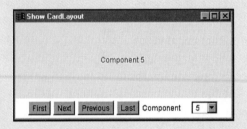

Figure 10.10   *The program shows components in a panel of* CardLayout.

Example Review

The program creates an instance of CardLayout, queue = new CardLayout(). The statement cardPanel.setLayout(queue) sets the cardPanel with the CardLayout; cardPanel is an instance of Panel. You have used such statements as setLayout(new FlowLayout()) to directly set the layout for a container, instead of declaring and creating a separate instance of the layout manager, as in this program. The object queue, however, is useful later in the program to show components in cardPanel. You have to use queue.first(cardPanel), for example, to view the first component in cardPanel.

The statement cardPanel.add(new Label("Component "+i,Label.CENTER), String.valueOf(i)) adds the label with identity String.valueOf(i). Later, when the user selects a component with number i, this identity String.valueOf(i) is used in the queue.show() method to view the component with the specified identity.

Example 10.9   Using Menus to Select Cards

This example shows a program that does arithmetic on integers and rationals. The program uses two panels in a CardLayout manager, one for integer arithmetic and the other for rational arithmetic.

The program provides a menu labeled Operation that has two menu items, Integer and Rational, for selecting the two panels. When the user chooses the Integer menu item from the Operation menu, the integer panel is activated. When the user chooses the Rational menu item, the rational panel is activated.

The program follows. Its output of a sample run for integer arithmetic is shown in Figure 10.11; its output for rational arithmetic is shown in Figure 10.12.

```java
import java.awt.*;
import java.awt.event.*;
import java.util.*;

public class IntAndRatCalc extends MyFrameWithExitHandling
  implements ActionListener
{
  private CardLayout queue = new CardLayout();
  private Panel cardPanel = new Panel();
  private MenuItem miInt, miRat, miClose;

  public static void main(String[] args)
  {
    IntAndRatCalc f = new IntAndRatCalc();
    f.setSize(400,200);
    f.setVisible(true);
  }

  public IntAndRatCalc()
  {
    super("Use CardLayout for Integer and Rational Calculation");

    //create MenuBar mb
    MenuBar mb = new MenuBar();
    setMenuBar(mb);

    //add a menu "Operation" in mb
    Menu operationMenu = new Menu("Operation", false);
    mb.add(operationMenu);

    //add a menu "Exit" in mb
    Menu exitMenu = new Menu("Exit", true);
    mb.add(exitMenu);

    //add MenuItems
    operationMenu.add(miInt = new MenuItem("Integer"));
    operationMenu.add(miRat = new MenuItem("Rational"));
    exitMenu.add(miClose = new MenuItem("Close"));

    //create intPanel for integer arithmetic
    Panel intPanel = new IntPanel();

    //create rationalPanel for rational arithmetic
    Panel rationalPanel = new RationalPanel();
```

continues

355

Example 10.9   continued

```java
        cardPanel.setLayout(queue);
        cardPanel.add(intPanel, "Integer");
        cardPanel.add(rationalPanel, "Rational");

        //set FlowLayout in the frame
        setLayout(new FlowLayout());
        add(cardPanel);

        //register listener with the munu items
        miInt.addActionListener(this);
        miRat.addActionListener(this);
        miClose.addActionListener(this);
    }

    //handling menu selection
    public void actionPerformed(ActionEvent e)
    {
        String actionCommand = e.getActionCommand();
        if (e.getSource() instanceof MenuItem)
        {
            if ("Integer".equals(actionCommand))
                queue.first(cardPanel);
            else if ("Rational".equals(actionCommand))
                queue.last(cardPanel);
            else if ("Close".equals(actionCommand))
                System.exit(0);
        }
    }
}

class IntPanel extends CalculationPanel
{
    IntPanel()
    {
        super("Integer Calculation");
    }

    void add()
    {
        int result = getNum1() + getNum2();
        //set result in TextField tf3
        tfResult.setText(String.valueOf(result));
    }

    void subtract()
    {
        int result = getNum1() - getNum2();
        //set result in TextField tf3
        tfResult.setText(String.valueOf(result));
    }

    void multiply()
    {
        int result = getNum1() * getNum2();
        //set result in TextField tfResult
        tfResult.setText(String.valueOf(result));
    }
```

```java
    void divide()
    {
      int result = getNum1() / getNum2();
      //set result in TextField tfResult
      tfResult.setText(String.valueOf(result));
    }

    private int getNum1()
    {
      //use trim() to trim extraneous space in the text field
      int num1 = Integer.parseInt(tfNum1.getText().trim());
      return num1;
    }

    private int getNum2()
    {
      //use trim() to trim extraneous space in the text field
      int num2 = Integer.parseInt(tfNum2.getText().trim());
      return num2;
    }
}

class RationalPanel extends CalculationPanel
{
  RationalPanel()
  {
    super("Rational Calculation");
  }

  void add()
  {
    Rational num1 = getNum1();
    Rational num2 = getNum2();
    Rational result = num1.add(num2);

    //set result in TextField tfResult
    tfResult.setText(result.toString());
  }

  void subtract()
  {
    Rational num1 = getNum1();
    Rational num2 = getNum2();
    Rational result = num1.subtract(num2);

    //set result in TextField tfResult
    tfResult.setText(result.toString());
  }

  void multiply()
  {
    Rational num1 = getNum1();
    Rational num2 = getNum2();
    Rational result = num1.multiply(num2);

    //set result in TextField tfResult
    tfResult.setText(result.toString());
  }
```

continues

357

Example 10.9   continued

```
            void divide()
            {
              Rational num1 = getNum1();
              Rational num2 = getNum2();
              Rational result = num1.divide(num2);

              //set result in TextField tfResult
              tfResult.setText(result.toString());
            }

          Rational getNum1()
          {
            StringTokenizer st1 = new
              StringTokenizer(tfNum1.getText().trim(), "/");
            int numer1 = Integer.parseInt(st1.nextToken());
            int denom1 = Integer.parseInt(st1.nextToken());
            return new Rational(numer1,denom1);
          }

          Rational getNum2()
          {
            StringTokenizer st2 = new
              StringTokenizer(tfNum2.getText().trim(), "/");
            int numer2 = Integer.parseInt(st2.nextToken());
            int denom2 = Integer.parseInt(st2.nextToken());
            return new Rational(numer2,denom2);
          }
        }

        /*design a generic calculation user interface for int and
          rational arithmetic
        */
        abstract class CalculationPanel extends Panel
          implements ActionListener
        {
          private Panel p0 = new Panel();
          private Panel p1 = new Panel();
          private Panel p2 = new Panel();
          TextField tfNum1, tfNum2, tfResult;
          private Button btAdd, btSub, btMul, btDiv;

          public CalculationPanel(String title)
          {
            p0.add(new Label(title));

            //add labels and text fields
            p1.setLayout(new FlowLayout());
            p1.add(new Label("Number 1"));
            p1.add(tfNum1 = new TextField(" ", 3));
            p1.add(new Label("Number 2"));
            p1.add(tfNum2 = new TextField(" ", 3));
            p1.add(new Label("Result"));
            p1.add(tfResult = new TextField(" ", 4));
            tfResult.setEditable(false);

            //set FlowLayout for p2
            Panel p2 = new Panel();
            p2.setLayout(new FlowLayout());
            p2.add(btAdd = new Button("Add"));
```

```
      p2.add(btSub = new Button("Subtract"));
      p2.add(btMul = new Button("Multiply"));
      p2.add(btDiv = new Button("Divide"));

      //add panels into CalculationPanel
      setLayout(new BorderLayout());
      add("North",p0);
      add("Center",p1);
      add("South",p2);

      //register listener for source objects
      btAdd.addActionListener(this);
      btSub.addActionListener(this);
      btMul.addActionListener(this);
      btDiv.addActionListener(this);
    }

    public void actionPerformed(ActionEvent e)
    {
      String actionCommand = e.getActionCommand();
      if (e.getSource() instanceof Button)
      {
        if ("Add".equals(actionCommand))
          add();
        else if ("Subtract".equals(actionCommand))
          subtract();
        else if ("Multiply".equals(actionCommand))
          multiply();
        else if ("Divide".equals(actionCommand))
          divide();
      }
    }

    abstract void add();

    abstract void subtract();

    abstract void multiply();

    abstract void divide();
  }
```

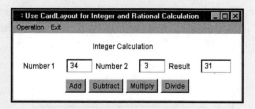

Figure 10.11   *You can perform integer arithmetic by choosing Integer from the Operation menu.*

continues

Example 10.9 continued

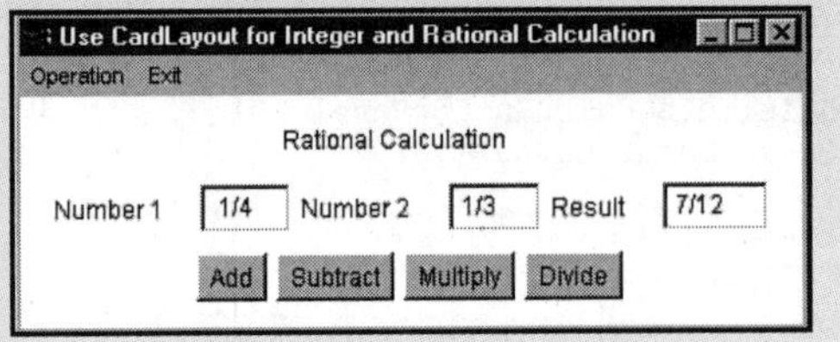

Figure 10.12 *You can perform rational arithmetic by choosing Rational from the Operation menu.*

Example Review

The `Rational` class was presented in Example 5.8, "Using the `Rational` Class" (see Chapter 5), and was used here for rational number arithmetic.

Because the user interface is the same for both integer and rational arithmetic, the program defines the `CalculationPanel` class as the basis for GUI layout. This class encapsulates the common features and actions. The `IntPanel` and `RationalPanel` extend the `CalculationPanel` class and implement the `add()`, `subtract()`, `multiply()`, and `divide()` methods that are specific to integers and rationals.

The `IntPanel` and `RationalPanel` are placed in the `CardPanel` using `CardLayout`. The `CardPanel` is then placed in the frame.

The *GridBagLayout* Manager (Optional)

The `GridBagLayout` manager is the most flexible and the most complex. It is similar to the `GridLayout` manager in the sense that both layout managers arrange components in a grid. The components can vary in size, however, and can be added in any order in `GridBagLayout`. For example, you can create the layout shown in Figure 10.13 using `GridBagLayout`.

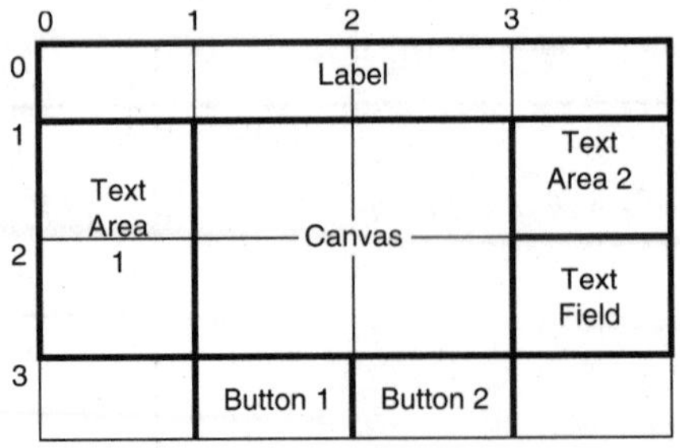

Figure 10.13 *A `GridBagLayout` manager divides the container into cells. A component can occupy several cells.*

The constructor `GridBagLayout()` is used to create a new `GridBagLayout`. In the `GridLayout`, the grid size (the number of rows and columns) is specified in the constructor. The size is unspecified, however, in the `GridBagLayout`.

Each `GridBagLayout` uses a dynamic rectangular grid of cells, with each component occupying one or more cells called its display area. Each component managed by a `GridBagLayout` is associated with a `GridBagConstraints` instance that specifies how the component is laid out within its display area. How a `GridBagLayout` places a set of components depends on each component's `GridBagConstraints` and minimum size, as well as the preferred size of the component's container.

To use a `GridBagLayout` effectively, you must customize one or more of its component's `GridBagConstraints`. You customize a `GridBagConstraints` object by setting one or more of its instance variables:

- **gridx** and **gridy**—Specifies the cell at the upper left of the component's display area. Note that `gridx` specifies the column in which the component will be placed, and `gridy` specifies the row in which the component will be placed. In Figure 10.13, Button 1 has a `gridx` value of `1` and a `gridy` value of `3` and Label has a `gridx` value of `0` and a `gridy` value of `0`.

- **gridwidth** and **gridheight**—Specifies the number of cells in a row (for `gridwidth`) or column (for `gridheight`) in the component's display area. The default value is `1`. In Figure 10.13, the canvas in the center occupies two columns and two rows and text area 2 occupies one row and one column.

- **weightx** and **weighty**—Specifies the extra space to allocate horizontally and vertically for the component when the window is resized. Unless you specify a weight for at least one component in a row (`weightx`) and a column (`weighty`), all the components clump together in the center of their container. This is because when the weight is zero (the default), the `GridBagLayout` puts any extra space between its grid of cells and the edges of the container. You will see the effect of these parameters in Example 10.10.

- **fill**—Specifies how the component should be resized if the component's viewing area is larger than its current size. Valid values are `GridBagConstraints.NONE` (the default), `GridBagConstraints.HORIZONTAL` (makes the component wide enough to fill its display area horizontally, but doesn't change its height), `GridBagConstraints.VERTICAL` (makes the component tall enough to fill its display area vertically, but doesn't change its width), and `GridBagConstraints.BOTH` (makes the component fill its display area entirely).

- **anchor**—Specifies where in the area the component is placed when the component does not fill in the entire area. Valid values are as follows:

`GridBagConstraints.CENTER` (the default)

`GridBagConstraints.NORTH`

```
GridBagConstraints.NORTHEAST

GridBagConstraints.EAST

GridBagConstraints.SOUTHEAST

GridBagConstraints.SOUTH

GridBagConstraints.SOUTHWEST

GridBagConstraints.WEST

GridBagConstraints.NORTHWEST
```

The `fill` and `anchor` parameters deal with how to fill and place the component when the viewing area is larger than the requested area. The `fill` and `anchor` parameters are class variables, while `gridx`, `gridy`, `width`, `height`, `weightx`, and `weighty` are instance variables.

Example 10.10   Testing the *GridBagLayout* Manager

This example shows a program that creates a layout for Figure 10.13 using the GridBagLayout manager. The output of the program is shown in Figure 10.14.

```
import java.awt.*;
import java.awt.event.*;

public class ShowGridBagLayout extends MyFrameWithExitHandling
{
  private Label lbl;
  private TextArea ta1, ta2;
  private TextField tf;
  private Canvas c;
  private Button bt1, bt2;
  private GridBagLayout gbLayout;
  private GridBagConstraints gbConstraints;

  public static void main(String[] args)
  {
    Frame f = new ShowGridBagLayout();
    f.setSize(350,200);
    f.setVisible(true);
  }

  // add a component to the container
  private void addComp(Component c, GridBagLayout gbLayout,
                       GridBagConstraints gbConstraints,
                       int row, int column, int numRows,
                       int numColumns, int weightx, int weighty)
  {
    //set parameters
    gbConstraints.gridx = column;
    gbConstraints.gridy = row;
    gbConstraints.gridwidth = numColumns;
    gbConstraints.gridheight = numRows;
    gbConstraints.weightx = weightx;
    gbConstraints.weighty = weighty;
```

```
            //set constraints in the GridBagLayout
            gbLayout.setConstraints(c, gbConstraints);

            //add component to the container
            add(c);
        }

        public ShowGridBagLayout()
        {
            setTitle("Show GridBagLayout");

            //initialize UI components
            lbl = new Label("Resize the Window and Study GridBagLayout",
                            Label.CENTER);
            c = new Canvas();
            ta1 = new TextArea("Text Area", 5, 15 );
            ta2 = new TextArea("Text Area", 5, 15 );
            tf = new TextField("TextField");
            bt1 = new Button("Cancel" );
            bt2 = new Button("Ok" );

            //create GridBagLayout and GridBagConstraints object
            gbLayout = new GridBagLayout();
            gbConstraints = new GridBagConstraints();
            setLayout(gbLayout);

            //place label to occupy row 0 (the first row)
            gbConstraints.fill = GridBagConstraints.BOTH;
            gbConstraints.anchor = GridBagConstraints.CENTER;
            addComp(lbl, gbLayout, gbConstraints, 0, 0, 1, 4, 0, 0);

            //place text area 1 in row 1 and 2, and column 0
            addComp(ta1, gbLayout, gbConstraints, 1, 0, 2, 1, 0, 0);

            //place canvas in row 1 and 2, and column 1 and 2
            addComp(c, gbLayout, gbConstraints, 1, 1, 2, 2, 100, 100);
            c.setBackground(Color.red);

            //place text area 2 in row 1 and column 3
            addComp(ta2, gbLayout, gbConstraints, 1, 3, 1, 1, 0, 100);

            //place text field in row 2 and column 3
            addComp(tf, gbLayout, gbConstraints, 2, 3, 1, 1, 0, 0);

            //place button 1 in row 3 and column 1
            addComp(bt1, gbLayout, gbConstraints, 3, 1, 1, 1, 0, 0);

            //place button 2 in row 3 and column 2
            addComp(bt2, gbLayout, gbConstraints, 3, 2, 1, 1, 0, 0);
        }
    }
```

Example Review

The program defines the addComp() method to add a component to the GridBagLayout with the specified constraints parameters.

continues

Example 10.10   continued

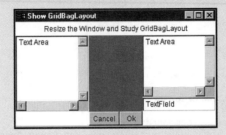

Figure 10.14   *The components are placed in the frame of* GridBagLayout.

The program creates a canvas with a weightx of 100 and a weighty of 100, so this component has extra space to grow horizontally and vertically up to 100 pixels. If you resize the window, you will see that the canvas's viewing area increases or shrinks as the window grows and shrinks.

The program creates the second text area ta2 with weightx 0 and weighty 100 so that this text area can grow vertically, but not horizontally when resizing the window.

The weightx and weighty for all the other components are 0. Whether the size of these components grows or shrinks depends on the fill and anchor parameters. The program defines fill = BOTH and anchor = CENTER.

Because the fill and anchor parameters are class variables, their values are for all components. Consider this scenario: Suppose you enlarge the window. The canvas is expanded, which causes the display area for text area ta1 to increase. Because fill is BOTH for ta1, ta1 fills in its new display area.

Using No Layout Manager (Optional)

Java enables you to place components in a container without using any layout manager. In this case, the component must be placed using the component's instance method setBounds(), as follows:

```
void setBounds(int x, int y, int width, int height);
```

This sets the location and size for the component, as in the following example:

```
Button bt = new Button("Help");
bt.setBounds(10, 10, 40, 20);
```

The upper-left corner of the Help button is placed at (10, 10); the button width is 40 and the height is 20.

You can perform the following steps to use no layout manager:

1. Use the following statement to specify no layout manager:

   ```
   setLayout(null);
   ```

2. Add the component to the container:

   ```
   add(component);
   ```

3. Specify the location to place the component, using the setBounds() method as follows:

   ```
   Button bt = new Button("Help");
   bt.setBounds(10, 10, 40, 20);
   ```

Example 10.11   Using No Layout Manager

This example shows a program that places the same components in the same layout as in the previous example, but without using a layout manager. Figure 10.15 contains the sample output.

```java
import java.awt.*;
import java.awt.event.*;

public class ShowNoLayout extends MyFrameWithExitHandling
{
  private Label lbl;
  private TextArea ta1, ta2;
  private TextField tf;
  private Canvas c;
  private Button bt1, bt2;
  private GridBagLayout gbLayout;
  private GridBagConstraints gbConstraints;

  public static void main(String[] args)
  {
    Frame f = new ShowNoLayout();
    f.setSize(400,200);
    f.setVisible(true);
  }

  public ShowNoLayout()
  {
    setTitle("Show No Layout");

    //specify no layout manager
    setLayout(null);

    //initialize UI components
    lbl = new Label("Resize the Window and Study No Layout",
              Label.CENTER);
    c = new Canvas();
    ta1 = new TextArea("Text Area", 5, 10 );
    ta2 = new TextArea("Text Area", 5, 10 );
    tf = new TextField("TextField");
    bt1 = new Button("Cancel" );
    bt2 = new Button("Ok" );
```

continues

365

Example 10.11 continued

```
        //add components to frame
        add(lbl);
        add(c);
        c.setBackground(Color.red);
        add(ta1);
        add(ta2);
        add(tf);
        add(bt1);
        add(bt2);

        //put components in the right place
        lbl.setBounds(0, 10, 400, 40);
        ta1.setBounds(0, 50, 100, 100);
        c.setBounds(100, 50, 200, 100);
        ta2.setBounds(300, 50, 100, 50);
        tf.setBounds(300, 100, 100, 50);
        bt1.setBounds(100, 150, 100, 50);
        bt2.setBounds(200, 150, 100, 50);
    }
}
```

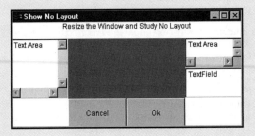

Figure 10.15 *The components are placed in the frame without using a layout manager.*

Example Review

If you run this program on Windows with 640×480 resolution, the layout size is desirable. If you run the program on Windows with a higher resolution, the components appear very small and clump together. If you run the program on Windows with a lower resolution, the components cannot be shown in their entirety.

If you resize the window, you will see that the components' location and size are not changed, as shown in Figure 10.16.

NOTE
Microsoft Visual J++ 6.0 uses the no-layout approach to generate code. JBuilder allows you to use FlowLayout, GridLayout, BorderLayout, CardLayout, GridBagLayout, and JBuilder-supplied layout managers.

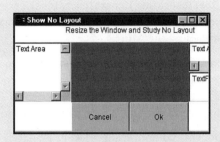

Figure 10.16 *The components' size and positions are fixed with no layout, and can be changed in the frame only with a layout manager.*

> **TIP**
> You should avoid using the no layout manager option to develop platform-independent applications.

Chapter Summary

In this chapter, you learned about applets and advanced graphics programming using mouse and keyboard events, `CardLayout` manager, `GridBagLayout` manager, and using no layout manager.

The Web browser controls and executes applets through the `init()`, `start()`, `stop()`, and `destroy()` methods in the `Applet` class. Applets always extend the `Applet` class and implement these methods if applicable, so they can be run by the Web browser. The applet bytecode must be specified using the `<applet>` tag in an HTML file to tell the Web browser where to find the applet. The applet can accept parameters from HTML using the `<param>` tag.

Writing applications and writing applets are very similar. You can easily convert an applet into an application or convert an application into an applet. You can also write an applet with the capability to run as an application as well as an applet.

Two examples were given in this chapter to demonstrate handling mouse and keyboard events. Mouse events and keyboard events often are useful in graphics programming. Clicking, pressing, or releasing a mouse button generates a `MouseEvent`; dragging or moving a mouse generates a `MouseMotionEvent`. Entering a key generates a `KeyEvent`. `MouseEvent`, `MouseMotionEvent`, and `KeyEvent` are subclasses of `InputEvent`, which contains several common methods useful in processing mouse and keyboard events.

The `CardLayout` manager arranges components in a queue of cards. You can see one component at a time. To add a component into the container, you need to use `add(component, string)`. You can see the components using the methods first(container), last(container), next(container), previous(container), or show(container, string). The show(container, string) method directly displays the component identified by the string.

The GridBagLayout manager gives you the most flexible way to arrange components. It is similar to GridLayout in the sense that the components are placed into cells. The GridBagLayout, however, enables a component to occupy multiple cells. The components can vary in size and can be placed in any order.

You can place components without using a layout manager. In this case, the components are placed at a hard-coded location. Using this approach, your program might look fine on one machine and be useless on other machines. It is recommended that you use the layout managers to develop a platform-independent graphical user interface.

Chapter Review

1. How do you run an applet?

2. Describe the init(), start(), stop(), and destroy() methods in the Applet class.

3. Is the getParameter() method defined in Applet? Is the paint() method defined in Applet? Find where these methods are originally defined.

4. Describe how the paint() method works in an applet.

5. Describe the <applet> HTML tag. How do you pass parameters to an applet?

6. Describe the procedure to convert an application to an applet and vice versa.

7. How do you create a frame from an applet?

8. Can you place an applet in a frame?

9. Describe CardLayout. How do you create a CardLayout? How do you add a component to a CardLayout? How do you show a card in the CardLayout container?

10. Describe GridBagLayout. How do you create a GridBagLayout? How do you create a GridBagConstraints object? What are the constraints you learned in this chapter? Describe their functions. How do you add a component to a GridBagLayout container?

11. Is the order in which the components are added important for certain layout managers? Identify those layout managers.

12. Which layout manager allows the components in the container to be moved to other rows when the window is resized?

13. Can you place components without using a layout manager? What are the disadvantages of not using a layout manager?

Programming Exercises

1. Convert Example 9.7, "Using CheckboxGroup," into an applet.

2. Rewrite Example 10.2 to display a message with specified color, font, and size. The message, color, font, and size are parameters in the `<applet>` tag, like this:

```
<applet
  code = "DisplayMessage.class"
  width = 200
  height = 50
  alt="You must have a JDK1.1-enabled browser to view the applet"
>
<param name=message value="Welcome to Java">
<param name=color value="red">
<param name=font value="TimesRoman">
<param name=size value=20>
</applet>
```

3. Write an applet to display the calendar for a given month of a year. The month and the year are the parameters in the `<applet>` tag (see Figure 10.17).

   Can you make this applet run as an application? (Hint: You need to declare a `boolean` variable `isApplet` with a default value in the program as `true`.) In the `main()` method, assign `false` to `isApplet`. The `main()` method gets the parameters `month` and `year` from the command line.

   The applet's `init()` method receives the parameter from the HTML only if `isApplet` is true. With the `isApplet` variable, your program gets command-line parameters if invoked as an application and gets HTML parameters if invoked as an applet.

Figure 10.17   *The applet receives month and year as HTML parameters and displays the calendar.*

4. Write an applet to find a path in a maze, as shown in Figure 10.18. The maze is represented by an 8×8 board. The path must meet the following conditions:

   ■ The path is between the upper-left corner cell and the lower-right corner cell in the maze.

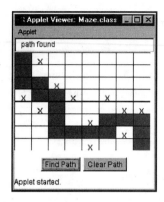

Figure 10.18 *The program finds a path from the upper-left corner to the bottom-right corner.*

■ The applet enables the user to insert or remove a mark on a cell. A path consists of adjacent unmarked cells. Two cells are said to be adjacent if they are horizontal or vertical neighbors, but not diagonal neighbors.

■ The path does not contain cells that form a square. The path in Figure 10.19, for example, does not meet this condition. (The condition makes a path easy to identify on the board.)

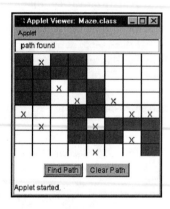

Figure 10.19 *The path does not meet the third condition for this exercise.*

5. Write an applet to play the tick-tack-toe game, as shown in Figure 10.20. The game lets two players alternately enter "X" and "O" in the cells. A winner is declared if a player occupies three cells in a line vertically, horizontally, or diagonally. A tie is declared if all cells are occupied without a winner.

Figure 10.20 *The applet implements the tick-tack-toe game.*

6. Write an applet that contains two buttons called Simple Calculator and Mortgage. When you click Simple Calculator, a frame for Example 9.9, "Using Menus," appears in a new window so that you can perform arithmetic (see Chapter 9, "Creating User Interfaces"). When you click Mortgage, a frame for Example 10.4 appears in a separate new window so that you can calculate a mortgage (see Figure 10.21).

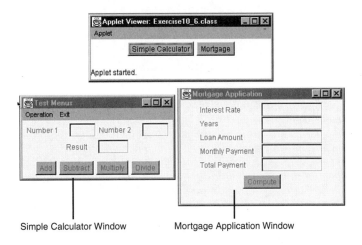

Figure 10.21 *You can show frames in the applets.*

7. Use `GridBagLayout` to lay out the following calculator and to implement addition (+), subtraction (–), division (/), square root (sqrt), and modulus (%) functions (see Figure 10.22).

8. Use no layout to lay out the preceding calculator.

9. Write a program to get character input from the keyboard and to put the characters where the mouse points.

10. Write an applet to emulate a paint utility. Your program should enable the user to choose options, draw shapes, and get characters from the keyboard (see Figure 10.23).

Figure 10.22 *You can use* GridBagLayout *to design the interface for the calculator.*

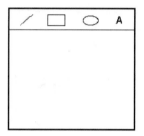

Figure 10.23 *This exercise produces a prototype drawing utility that enables you to draw lines, rectangles, ovals, and characters.*

PART IV

DEVELOPING COMPREHENSIVE PROJECTS

This Part is devoted to several advanced features of Java programming. You will learn to develop comprehensive programs using these features, such as using exception handling to make your program robust, using multithreading to make your program more responsive and interactive, incorporating sound and images to make your program user friendly, using input and output to manage and process a large quantity of data, and creating client/server applications with Java networking support.

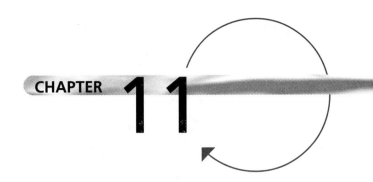

CHAPTER 11

EXCEPTION HANDLING

Objectives

- Understand the concept of exception handling.
- Become familiar with exception types.
- Claim exceptions in a method.
- Throw exceptions in a method.
- Use the `try-catch` block to handle exceptions.
- Create your own exception classes.
- Rethrow exceptions in a `try-catch` block.
- Use the `finally` clause in a `try-catch` block.
- Know when to use exceptions.

Introduction

So far, you have seen program examples without runtime errors. Runtime errors are unavoidable, even for experienced programmers, and cause exceptions in Java: events that occur during the execution of a program and disrupt the normal flow of control.

If the program does not provide the code to handle the exceptions, the program might terminate abnormally, causing serious problems. For example, if your program attempts to transfer money from a savings account to a checking account but, because of a runtime error, is terminated after the money is drawn from the savings account and before the money is deposited to the checking account, the customer loses money.

Java provides the capability to let the programmer handle runtime errors. With this capability, referred to as exception handling, you can develop robust programs for mission-critical computing.

This chapter introduces Java's exception-handling model. The chapter covers error types, claiming exceptions, throwing exceptions, catching exceptions, creating exception classes, rethrowing exceptions, and the `finally` clause.

Exceptions and Exception Types

Runtime errors occur for various reasons. For example, the user enters an invalid input, the program attempts to open a file that doesn't exist, the network connection hangs up, or the program attempts to access an out-of-bounds array element. When a runtime error occurs, Java raises an exception.

Exceptions are handled differently from the events of AWT programming. (In Chapter 8, "Getting Started with Graphics Programming," you learned the events used in AWT.) An event may be ignored in AWT programming, but an exception cannot be ignored. In AWT, a listener must register with the source object. The external user action on the source object generates an event that triggers the Java runtime system to invoke the handlers implemented by the listener. If no listener is registered with the source object, the event is ignored. However, when an exception occurs, the program may terminate if no handler can be used to deal with the exception.

A Java exception is an instance of a class derived from `Throwable`. The `Throwable` class is contained in the `java.lang` package, and subclasses of `Throwable` are contained in various packages. For example, errors related to AWT are included in the `java.awt` package; the numeric exceptions are included in the `java.lang` package because they are related to the `java.lang.Number` class. You can create your own exception classes by extending `Throwable` or a subclass of `Throwable`. Figure 11.1 shows some predefined exception classes in Java.

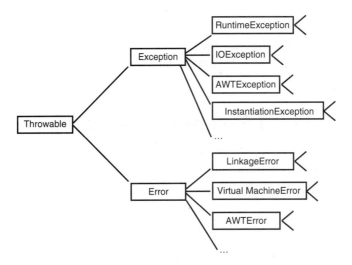

Figure 11.1   *The exceptions are the instances of the classes shown in this diagram.*

The class names `Error`, `Exception`, and `RuntimeException` are somewhat confusing. All the classes are exceptions. `Exception` is just one of these classes, and all errors discussed here occur at runtime.

The `Error` class describes internal system errors, which rarely occur. If such an error occurs, there is little you can do beyond notifying the user and trying to terminate the program gracefully. Examples of subclasses of `Error` are `LinkageError`, `VirtualMachineError`, and `AWTError`. Subclasses of `LinkageError` indicate that a class has some dependency on another class; however, the latter class has incompatibly changed after the compilation of the former class. Subclasses of `VirtualMachineError` indicate that the Java Virtual Machine is broken or has run out of resources necessary for it to continue operating. `AWTError` is caused by a fatal error in AWT programs.

The `Exception` class describes the errors caused by your program and external circumstances. These errors can be caught and handled by your program. `Exception` has many subclasses. Examples are `RuntimeException`, `IOException`, `AWTException`, and `InstantiationException`.

The `RuntimeException` class describes programming errors such as bad casting, accessing an out-of-bound array, and numeric errors. Examples of subclasses of `RuntimeException` are `ArithmeticException`, `NullPointerException`, `IllegalArgumentException`, `ArrayStoreException`, and `IndexOutOfBoundsException`.

The `IOException` class describes errors related to input/output operations such as invalid input, reading past the end of a file, and opening a nonexistent file. Examples of subclasses of `IOException` are `InterruptedIOException`, `EOFException`, and `FileNotFoundException`.

The AWTException class describes errors caused by AWT operations.

The InstantiationException class describes class instantiation errors. For example, this exception is thrown if attempting to instantiate an abstract class or an interface.

Understanding Exception Handling

Java's exception-handling model is based on three operations: claiming an exception, throwing an exception, and catching an exception.

In Java, the statement currently being executed belongs to a method; the statement belongs either to main() or to a method invoked by another method. The main method is invoked by the system. In general, every method must state the types of exceptions it can encounter. This process is called *claiming an exception*, which simply tells the compiler what can go wrong.

When a statement causes errors, the method containing the statement creates an exception object and passes it to the system. The exception object contains information about the exception, including its type and the state of the program when the error occurred. This process is called *throwing an exception*.

After a method throws an exception, the Java runtime system begins the process of finding the code to handle the error. The code that handles the error is called the *exception handler*, which is found by searching backward through a chain of method calls, starting from the current method. The handler must match the type of exception thrown. If no such handler is found, the program terminates. The process of finding a handler is called *catching an exception*.

Claiming Exceptions

To claim an exception is to tell the compiler what might go wrong during the execution of a method. Because system errors and runtime errors can happen to any code, Java does not require you to claim Error and RuntimeException in the method. However, all the other exceptions must be explicitly claimed in the method declaration if they are thrown by the method.

To claim an exception in a method, you use the throws keyword in the method declaration, as in this example:

```
public void myMethod() throws IOException
```

The throws keyword indicates that myMethod() might throw an IOException. If the method might throw multiple exceptions, you can add a list of the exceptions, separated by commas, after throws:

```
MethodDeclaration throws Exception1, Exception2, ..., ExceptionN
```

Throwing Exceptions

In the method that has claimed the exception, you can throw an object of that exception if the exception arises. The following is the syntax to throw an exception:

```
throw new TheException();
```

Or if you prefer, you can use the following:

```
TheException e = new TheException();
throw e;
```

NOTE

The keyword to claim an exception is `throws`, and the keyword to throw an exception is `throw`.

A method can only throw the exceptions claimed in the method declaration or throw `Error`, `RuntimeException`, or subclasses of `Error` and `RuntimeException`. For example, the method cannot throw `IOException` if it is not claimed in the method declaration, but a method can always throw `RuntimeException` or a subclass of it even if it is not claimed by the method.

Example 11.1   Throwing Exceptions

This example demonstrates the throwing of an exception by modifying the `Rational` class defined in Example 5.8, "Using the `Rational` Class" (see Chapter 5, "Programming with Objects and Classes"), so that it can handle the zero denominator exception.

The new `Rational` class is the same except that the `divide()` method throws a zero-denominator exception if the client attempts to call the method with a zero denominator. The new `divide()` method is as follows:

```
public Rational divide(Rational r) throws Exception
{
  if (r.numer == 0)
    throw new Exception("denominator cannot be zero");

  long n = numer*r.denom;
  long d = denom*r.numer;
  return new Rational(n,d);
}
```

Example Review

The original class `Rational` remains intact except for the `divide()` method. The `divide()` method now claims an exception and throws the exception if the divisor is zero.

continues

379

Example 11.1   continued

The `divide()` method claims the exception to be an instance of `Exception` by using `throws Exception` in the method signature. The method throws the exception by using the following statement:

```
throw new Exception("denominator cannot be zero");
```

You should only compile the `Rational` class, not the `TestRationalClass` class, from Example 5.8. If you compiled the `Rational` class with the `TestRationalClass` class, you would get a syntax error, indicating that the exception is not caught. You will learn how to catch exceptions in the next section.

Catching Exceptions

You now know how to claim an exception and how to throw an exception. Next, you learn to handle exceptions.

When calling a method that explicitly claims an exception, you must use the `try-catch` block to wrap the statement, as shown in the following lines:

```
try
{
  statements;   //statements that may throw exceptions
}
catch (Exception1 ex)
{
  handler for exception1;
}
catch (Exception2 ex)
{
  handler for exception2;
}
...
catch (ExceptionN ex)
{
  handler for exceptionN;
}
```

If no exceptions arise during the execution of the `try` clause, the `catch` clauses are skipped.

If one of the statements inside the `try` block throws an exception, Java skips the remaining statements and starts to search for a handler for the exception. If the exception type matches one listed in a `catch` clause, the code in the `catch` clause is executed. If the exception type does not match any exception in the `catch` clauses, Java exits this method and passes the exception to the method that invoked this method and continues the same process to find a handler. If no handler is found in the chain of the calling method, the program terminates and prints an error message on the console.

Consider the scenario in Figure 11.2. Suppose that an exception occurs in the `try-catch` block that contains a call to `method3`. If the exception type is `Exception3`, it is caught by the catch clause for handling exception ex3. If the exception type is Exception2, it is caught by the catch clause for handling exception ex2. If the exception type is Exception1, it is caught by the catch clause for handling exception ex1 in the main() method. If the exception type is not Exception1, Exception2, or Exception3, the program terminates immediately.

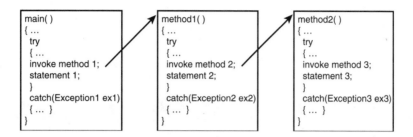

Figure 11.2 *If an exception is not caught in the current method, it is passed to its caller. The process is repeated until the exception is caught or passed to the* main() *method.*

If the exception type is Exception3, statement3 is skipped. If the exception type is Exception2, statement2 and statement3 are skipped. If the exception type is Exception1, statement1, statement2, and statement3 are skipped.

NOTE

If an exception of a subclass of Exception occurs in a graphics program, Java prints the error message on the console, but the program goes back to its user-interface processing loop to run continuously. The exception is ignored.

The exception object contains valuable information about the exception. This object may use the following instance methods in the java.lang.Throwable class to get the information related to the exception.

```
public String getMessage()
```

This returns the detailed message of the Throwable object.

```
public String toString()
```

This returns a short description of the Throwable object, whereas getMessage() returns a detailed message.

```
public String getLocalizedMessage()
```

This returns a localized description of the Throwable object. Subclasses of Throwable can override this method in order to produce a locale-specific message. For subclasses that do not override this method, the default implementation returns the same result as getMessage().

```
public void printStackTrace()
```

This prints the Throwable object and its trace information on the console.

> **NOTE**
>
> Various exception classes can be derived from a common superclass. If a `catch` clause catches `exception` objects of a superclass, the clause can catch all exception objects of subclasses of that superclass.

> **CAUTION**
>
> The order in which the exceptions are specified in a `catch` clause is important. You should specify an exception object of a class before the exception object of the superclass of that class; otherwise, it results in a compilation error.

Example 11.2   Catching Exceptions

This program demonstrates catching exceptions, using the new `Rational` class given in Example 11.1. Figure 11.3 shows the output of a sample run of the program.

```java
public class TestRationalException
{
  public static void main(String[] args)
  {
    Rational r1 = new Rational(4,2);
    Rational r2 = new Rational(2,3);
    Rational r3 = new Rational(0,1);

    try
    {
      System.out.println(r1+" + "+ r2 +" = "+r1.add(r2));
      System.out.println(r1+" - "+ r2 +" = "+r1.subtract(r2));
      System.out.println(r1+" * "+ r2 +" = "+r1.multiply(r2));
      System.out.println(r1+" / "+ r2 +" = "+r1.divide(r2));
      System.out.println(r1+" / "+ r3 +" = "+r1.divide(r3));
      System.out.println(r1+" + "+ r2 +" = "+r1.add(r2));
    }
    catch(Exception ex)
    {
      System.out.println(ex);
    }

    System.out.println(r1+" - "+r2+" = "+r1.subtract(r2));
  }
}
```

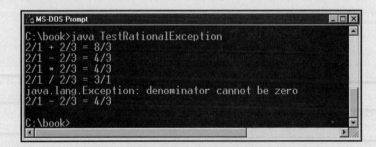

```
C:\book>java TestRationalException
2/1 + 2/3 = 8/3
2/1 - 2/3 = 4/3
2/1 * 2/3 = 4/3
2/1 / 2/3 = 3/1
java.lang.Exception: denominator cannot be zero
2/1 - 2/3 = 4/3

C:\book>
```

Figure 11.3   *The exception is raised when the divisor is zero.*

Example Review

The program creates two Rational numbers, r1 and r2, to test numeric methods (add(), subtract(), multiply(), and divide()) on rational numbers.

Invoking the divide() method with divisor 0 causes the method to throw an exception object. In the catch clause, the type of the object ex is Exception (catch Exception ex), which matches the object thrown by the divide() method. So this exception is caught by the catch clause.

The exception handler simply prints a short message, ex.toString(), about the exception, using System.out.println(ex).

Note that the execution continues in the event of the zero denominator. If the handlers had not caught the exception, the program would have abruptly terminated.

Example 11.3   Exceptions in GUI Applications

Here Example 9.9, "Using Menus," (from Chapter 9, "Creating User Interfaces") is used to demonstrate the effect of exceptions in GUI applications. Run the program and enter any number in the Number 1 field and 0 in the Number 2 field; then click the Divide button (see Figure 11.4). You will see nothing in the Result field, but an error message appears on the console, as shown in Figure 11.5. The GUI application continues.

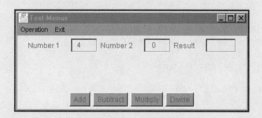

Figure 11.4   *In GUI programs, if an exception of the Exception class is not caught, it is ignored, and the program continues.*

```
Command Prompt - java MenuDemo
C:\book>java MenuDemo
Exception occurred during event dispatching:
java.lang.ArithmeticException: / by zero
        at MenuDemo.divide(MenuDemo.java:133)
        at MenuDemo.actionPerformed(MenuDemo.java:86)
        at java.awt.Button.processActionEvent(Button.java:172)
        at java.awt.Button.processEvent(Button.java:153)
        at java.awt.Component.dispatchEventImpl(Component.java:1442)
        at java.awt.Component.dispatchEvent(Component.java:1382)
        at java.awt.EventDispatchThread.run(EventDispatchThread.java:63)
```

Figure 11.5   *In GUI programs, if an exception of the Exception class is not caught, an error message appears on the console.*

continues

Example 11.3   continued

Example Review

When Java graphics programs are running, if exceptions of the type Exception are not caught, the error messages are displayed on the console, but the program continues to run.

If you rewrite the calculate() method in the MenuDemo program of Example 9.9 with a try-catch block to catch RuntimeException as follows, the program will display Error in the Result text field in the case of a numerical error. No errors are shown on the console because they are handled in the program.

```java
private void calculate(char operator)
{
  //obtain Number 1 and Number 2
  int num1 = (Integer.parseInt(tfNum1.getText().trim()));
  int num2 = (Integer.parseInt(tfNum2.getText().trim()));
  int result = 0;

  try
  {
    //perform selected operation
    switch (operator)
    {
      case '+': result = num1 + num2;
                break;
      case '-': result = num1 - num2;
                break;
      case '*': result = num1 * num2;
                break;
      case '/': result = num1 / num2;
    }

    //set result in TextField tfResult
    tfResult.setText(String.valueOf(result));
  }
  catch (RuntimeException ex)
  {
    tfResult.setText("Error"+ex);
  }
}
```

Creating Exception Classes

Java provides quite a few exception classes. You should use them whenever possible instead of creating your own exception classes. However, you may run into a problem that cannot be adequately described by these predefined exception classes. In this case, you can create your own exception class, derived from Exception or from a subclass of Exception, such as IOException. This section shows how to create your own exception class.

Example 11.4   Creating Your Own Exception Classes

This program creates 10 accounts and transfers funds among the accounts. If a transaction amount is negative, the program raises a negative-amount exception. If the account's balance is less than the requested transaction amount, an insufficient-funds exception is raised.

The example consists of four classes: Account, NegativeAmountException, InsufficientAmountException, and TestMyException. The Account class provides the information and operations pertaining to the account. NegativeAmountException and InsufficientAmountException are the exception classes dealing with transactions of negative or insufficient amounts. The TestMyException class utilizes all these classes to perform transactions, transferring funds among accounts.

The code for the Account class follows. This class contains two data fields: id (for account ID) and balance (for current balance). The methods for Account are deposit() and withdraw(). Both methods will throw NegativeAmountException if the transaction amount is negative. The withdraw() method will also throw InsufficientFundException if the current balance is less than the requested transaction amount.

```
class Account
{
  private int ID;
  private double balance;

  Account(int ID, double balance)
  {
    this.ID = ID;
    this.balance = balance;
  }

  public int accountID()
  {
    return ID;
  }

  public void setBalance(double balance)
  {
    this.balance = balance;
  }

  public double accountBalance()
  {
    return balance;
  }

  public void deposit(double amount)
    throws NegativeAmountException
  {
    if (amount < 0)
      throw new NegativeAmountException
        (this, amount, "deposit");
```

continues

Example 11.4   continued

```
      balance = balance + amount;
   }

   public void withdraw(double amount)
     throws NegativeAmountException, InsufficientFundException
   {
     if (amount < 0)
       throw new NegativeAmountException
         (this, amount, "withdraw");
     if (balance < amount)
       throw new InsufficientFundException(this, amount);
     balance = balance - amount;
   }
}
```

The NegativeAmountException exception class follows. It contains information about the attempted transaction type (deposit or withdrawal), the account, and the negative amount passed from the method.

```
class NegativeAmountException extends Exception
{
  //declare information that will be passed to the handlers
  private Account account;
  private double amount;
  private String transactionType;

  public NegativeAmountException(Account account,
                                 double amount,
                                 String transactionType)
  {
    super("Negative amount");
    this.account = account;
    this.amount = amount;
    this.transactionType = transactionType;
  }
}
```

The InsufficientFundException exception class follows. It contains information about the account and the amount passed from the method.

```
class InsufficientFundException extends Exception
{
  //declare fields that will be passed to handlers
  private Account account;
  private double amount;

  public InsufficientFundException(Account account, double amount)
  {
    super("Insufficient amount");
    this.account = account;
    this.amount = amount;
  }

  //override the "toString" method
  public String toString()
  {
    return "account balance is "+account.accountBalance();
  }
}
```

The TestMyException class follows. It creates 10 accounts with account id 0, 1, and so on, to 9. Each account has an initial balance of $1,000. The program first attempts to deposit –$10 into account 0, raising the negative amount exception. The program then continuously withdraws $9 from account 0. When the balance of account 0 falls below $9, the program begins to withdraw from the next account, and finally the program terminates when all the accounts' balances are below $9. The output of the test program is shown in Figure 11.6.

```java
public class TestMyException
{
  //create 10 accounts with id 0 .. 9 and initial balance 1000
  public static void main(String[] args)
  {
    //create and initialize 10 accounts
    Account[] account = new Account[10];
    for (int i=0; i<10; i++)
      account[i] = new Account(i, 1000);

    //test negative deposit exception
    try
    {
      account[0].deposit(-10);
    }
    catch (NegativeAmountException ex)
    {
      System.out.println(ex);
    }

    //test negative withdraw exception
    try
    {
      account[0].withdraw(-10);
    }
    catch (NegativeAmountException ex)
    {
      System.out.println(ex);
    }
    catch (InsufficientFundException ex)
    {
      System.out.println(ex);
    }

    //keep withdraw $9 dollars from the accounts
    for (int j=0; j<10; j++)
    {
      boolean enoughFund = true;
      while (enoughFund)
        try
        {
          account[j].withdraw(9);
        }
        catch (InsufficientFundException ex)
        {
          enoughFund = false;
          System.out.println(ex);
        }
```

continues

Example 11.4   continued

```
                    catch (NegativeAmountException ex)
                    {
                      System.out.println(ex);
                    }
                }
            }
        }
```

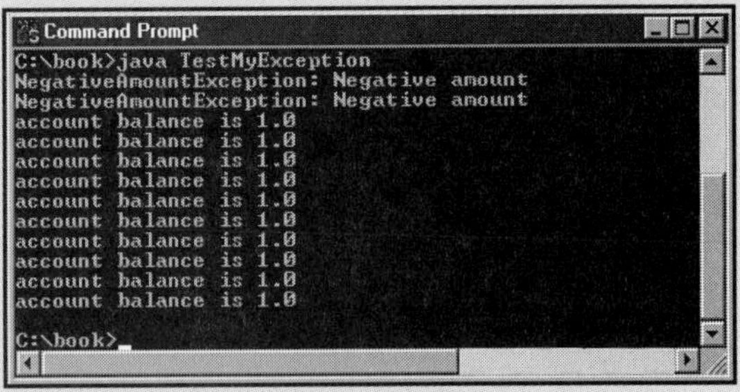

Figure 11.6   *The* TestMyException *program tests* NegativeAmountException *and* InsufficientFundException.

Example Review

You need to create and save all the programs, either in one combined file or in separate files, then compile the TestMyException class. The Java compiler will compile all the classes on which TestMyException depends. Therefore, the classes Account, NegativeAmountException, and InsufficientFundException will be compiled along with TestMyException.

In the Account class, the deposit() method throws NegativeAmountException if the amount to be deposited is less than 0. The withdraw() method throws a NegativeAmountException if the amount to be withdrawn is less than 0 and throws an InsufficientFundException if the amount to be withdrawn is less than the current balance.

The user-defined exception class always extends Exception or a subclass of Exception. Therefore, both NegativeAmountException and InsufficientFundException extend Exception.

Storing relevant information in the exception object is useful, enabling the handler to retrieve the information from the exception object. For example, NegativeAmountException contains the account, the amount, and the transaction type.

The NegativeAmountException occurs when the test program deposits –$10, using account[0].deposit(–10). The NegativeAmountException again occurs when the program withdraws –$10, using `account[0].withdraw(-10)`. The exception handler in the test program displays the first two lines of the output to tell the user that these exceptions have occurred and were caught and properly handled.

The test program then repeatedly withdraws $9 from each account until the account balance is below $9. When the program attempts to withdraw from an account with a balance below $9, an exception is raised and caught by the handler, which displays the account balance.

Note that the test program continues its normal execution after an exception is handled. In the `while` loop, if the balance of one account is below $9, an exception is raised and handled in the `try-catch` block; then the program continues to stay in the `for` loop to withdraw from the next account until the balance of every account is below $9.

Example 11.5   Using Exceptions in Applets

This example demonstrates the use of exceptions in GUI applications. The applet presented here handles account transactions. It displays the account ID and balance and lets the user deposit to or withdraw from the account. For each transaction, a message is displayed to indicate the status of the transaction: successful or failed. In case of failure, the failure reason is reported. A sample run of the program is shown in Figure 11.7.

```java
import java.awt.*;
import java.awt.event.*;

public class AccountApplet extends java.applet.Applet
  implements ActionListener
{
  //declare text fields
  private TextField tfID, tfBalance, tfDeposit, tfWithdraw;
  private Button btDeposit, btWithdraw; //action buttons
  private Account a; //declare the account
  private DisplayStatusCanvas c; //canvas for displaying status

  public void init()
  {
    //group ID, Balance in p1
    Panel p1 = new Panel();
    p1.setLayout(new FlowLayout());
    p1.add(new Label("ID"));
    p1.add(tfID = new TextField(4));
    p1.add(new Label("Balance"));
    p1.add(tfBalance = new TextField(4));
    tfID.setEditable(false);
    tfBalance.setEditable(false);
```

continues

Example 11.5   continued

```java
            //group deposit amount and button in p2
            Panel p2 = new Panel();
            p2.setLayout(new FlowLayout());
            p2.add(new Label("Deposit"));
            p2.add(tfDeposit = new TextField(4));
            p2.add(btDeposit = new Button("Deposit"));

            //group withdraw amount and button in p3
            Panel p3 = new Panel();
            p3.add(new Label("Withdraw"));
            p3.add(tfWithdraw = new TextField(4));
            p3.add(btWithdraw = new Button("Withdraw"));

            //display canvas in p4
            Panel p4 = new Panel();
            p4.setLayout(new FlowLayout());
            p4.add(c = new DisplayStatusCanvas());
            c.setBackground(Color.red);
            c.setForeground(Color.black);
            c.setSize(400,50);

            //set FlowLayout for the frame
            setLayout(new FlowLayout());
            add(p1);
            add(p2);
            add(p3);
            add(p4);

            //create an account with initial balance $1000
            a = new Account(1, 1000);

            //refresh ID and Balance fields
            refreshFields();

            //register listener
            btDeposit.addActionListener(this);
            btWithdraw.addActionListener(this);
        }

        public void actionPerformed(ActionEvent evt)
        {
          String actionCommand = evt.getActionCommand();
          if (evt.getSource() instanceof Button)
            if ("Deposit".equals(actionCommand))
            {
              try
              {
                double depositValue = (Double.valueOf(
                  tfDeposit.getText().trim())).doubleValue();
                a.deposit(depositValue);
                refreshFields();
                c.setMessage("Transaction Processed");
              }
              catch(NegativeAmountException ex)
              {
                c.setMessage("Negative Amount");
              }
            }
            else if ("Withdraw".equals(actionCommand))
```

```
          {
            try
            {
              double withdrawValue = (Double.valueOf(
                tfWithdraw.getText().trim())).doubleValue();
              a.withdraw(withdrawValue);
              refreshFields();
              c.setMessage("Transaction Processed");
            }
            catch(NegativeAmountException ex)
            {
              c.setMessage("Negative Amount");
            }
            catch(InsufficientFundException ex)
            {
              c.setMessage("Insufficient Funds");
            }
          }
        }

    public void refreshFields()
    {
      tfID.setText(String.valueOf(a.accountID()));
      tfBalance.setText(String.valueOf(a.accountBalance()));
    }
  }

class DisplayStatusCanvas extends Canvas
{
  private String message;

  public DisplayStatusCanvas()
  {
    setMessage(" ");
  }

  public void setMessage(String s)
  {
    message = s;
    repaint();
  }

  public void paint(Graphics g)
  {
    g.drawString(message, 10, 10);
  }
}
```

Example Review

The program creates an applet with three panels (p1, p2, and p3) and a canvas to display messages. The panel p1 contains ID and account information; the panel p2 contains the deposit amount and the Deposit action button; the panel p3 contains the withdrawal amount and the Withdraw button.

continues

Example 11.5   continued

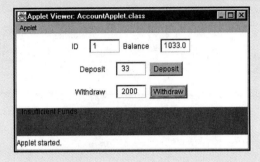

Figure 11.7   *The program lets you deposit and withdraw funds and display transaction status on the canvas.*

With a click of the Deposit button, the amount in the `Deposit` text field is added to the balance. With a click of the Withdraw button, the amount in the `Withdraw` text field is subtracted from the balance.

For each successful transaction, the message `Transaction Processed` is displayed. For a negative amount, the message `Negative Amount` is displayed; for insufficient funds, the message `Insufficient Funds` is displayed.

Rethrowing Exceptions

When an exception occurs in a method, the method exits immediately if the exception is not caught by the method. If the method is required to perform some tasks before exiting, you can catch the exception in the method and then rethrow it to the real handler in a structure like this:

```
try
{
  statements;
}
catch(TheException ex)
{
  perform operations before exits;
  throw ex;
}
```

The statement `throw ex` rethrows the exception so that other handlers get a chance to process the exception ex.

The *finally* Clause

Occasionally, you may want some code to be executed regardless of whether the exception occurs and whether it is caught. Java has a `finally` clause that you can use to accomplish this objective. The syntax for the `finally` clause might look like this:

```
try
{
  statements;
}
catch(TheException ex)
{
  handling ex;
}
finally
{
  finalStatements;
}
```

The code in the `finally` block is executed under all circumstances, regardless of whether an exception occurs in the `try` block and whether it is caught. Consider three possible cases:

- If no exception arises in the `try` block, `finalStatements` is executed, and the next statement after the `try-catch` block is executed.

- If one of the statements causes an exception in the `try` block that is caught in a `catch` clause, the rest of the statements in the `try` block are skipped, the `catch` clause is executed, and the `finally` clause is executed. If the `catch` clause does not rethrow an exception, the next statement after the `try-catch` block is executed. If it does, the exception is passed to the caller of this method.

- If one of the statements causes an exception that is not caught in any `catch` clause, the rest of the statements in the `try` block are skipped, the `finally` clause is executed, and the exception is passed to the caller of this method.

Cautions When Using Exceptions

Exception handling separates error-handling code from normal programming tasks, thus making programs easier to read and to modify. However, you should be aware that exception handling usually requires more time and resources because it requires instantiating a new exception object, rolling back the call stack, and propagating the errors to the calling methods.

Exception handling should not be used to replace simple tests. You should test simple exceptions whenever possible, and let exception handling deal with circumstances that cannot be handled with `if` statements.

Example 11.4 demonstrates the use of exception handling; however, it is a bad example in the sense that its implementation is inefficient. Instead of letting the exceptions be caught by the other programs, you could simply check for a negative amount and insufficient balance before calling the `deposit()` and `withdraw()` methods in the test program. This would significantly improve the performance of the program.

Example 11.6   Demonstrating Performance Differences With and Without Exception Handling

This example compares the performance of the program in Example 11.4, which uses exception handling, with the performance of the same program without exception handling. Example 11.4 uses exception handlers for processing negative amounts and insufficient funds. Here, that program is rewritten without the use of exceptions and compares the execution time of these two programs. The output of a sample run of the program is shown in Figure 11.8.

```java
import java.util.*;

public class UsingNoException
{
  //create 10 accounts with id 0 .. 9 and initial balance 1000
  public static void main(String[] args)
  {
    //create and initialize 10 accounts
    Account[] account = new Account[10];
    for (int i=0; i<10; i++)
      account[i] = new Account(i, 1000);

    //get start time
    Date startTime = new Date();

    //keep withdrawing $9 dollars from the accounts
    for (int j=0; j<10; j++)
    {
      boolean enoughFund = true;
      while (enoughFund)
        try
        {
          if (account[j].accountBalance() < 9)
          {
            System.out.println("Account balance is "+
              account[j].accountBalance());
            enoughFund = false;
          }
          else
            account[j].withdraw(9);
        }
        catch (InsufficientFundException ex)
        {
          enoughFund = false;
          System.out.println(ex);
        }
        catch (NegativeAmountException ex)
        {
          System.out.println(ex);
        }
    }

    //get end time
    Date endTime = new Date();
    long elapseTime = endTime.getTime() - startTime.getTime();
    System.out.println("Elapsed time: "+ elapseTime
      "Milliseconds");
  }
}
```

To compare the execution time with exception handling, replace the if statement (set in bold in the code) with the following code:

```
account[j].withdraw(9);
```

For convenience, rename the program TestMyExceptionWithTiming. A sample run of the output of the program is shown in Figure 11.9.

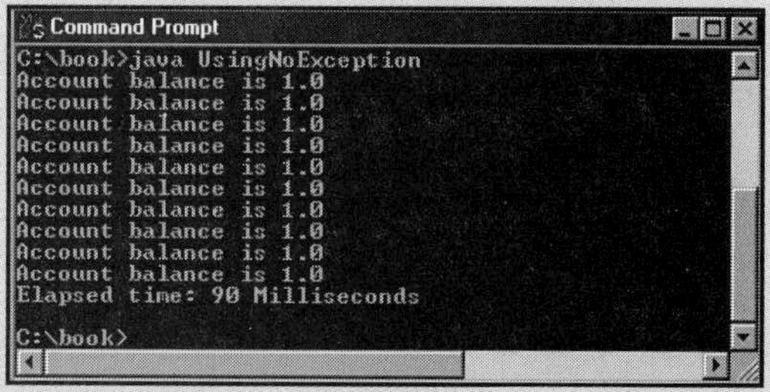

Figure 11.8 *The program uses* if *statements to test for negative amounts and insufficient funds.*

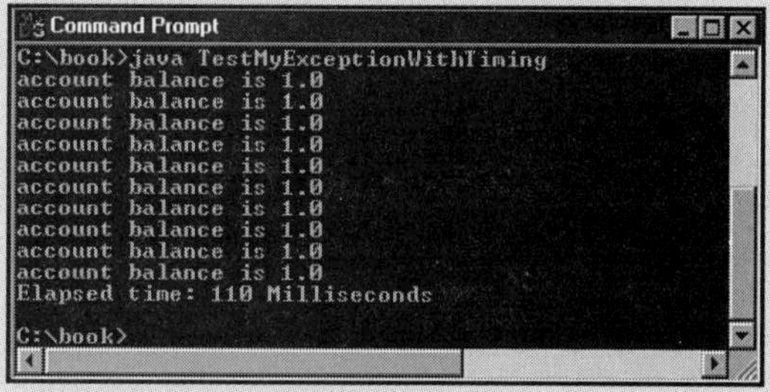

Figure 11.9 *Because the program uses exceptions to test for negative amounts and insufficient funds, it takes a little more time.*

Example Review

The UsingNoException program uses the if statement to check whether the account has a sufficient balance before invoking the withdraw() method, whereas the TestMyExceptionWithTiming program lets the catch block handle the case. The try-catch block is required because the program invokes withdraw(), which claims two exceptions. Whenever you use a method that claims an exception, the try-catch block must be used. However, no exceptions are raised in the UsingNoException program because the program uses a simple if statement to check the account balance.

continues

Example 11.6   continued

You want to see the time spent on the `for` loop, so the program obtains the `startTime` before the `for` loop starts and the `endTime` after the `for` loop finishes. The elapsed time is

```
endTime.getTime() - startTime.getTime()
```

Note that this elapsed time is not the exact CPU time spent on the loop, and every time you run the program, you might get a different elapsed time, depending on your system load when the program is executed.

The result of comparing running time of these two programs clearly shows the performance benefits of not using exceptions. You should avoid using exception handling if a simple `if` statement will work instead.

TIP

Do not use exception handling to validate user input. The input can be validated with the use of simple `if` statements.

Chapter Summary

In this chapter, you learned how Java handles exceptions. When an exception occurs, Java creates an object that contains the information for the exception. You can use the information to handle the exception.

A Java exception is an instance of a class derived from `java.lang.Throwable`. You can create your own exception classes by extending `Throwable` or a subclass of `Throwable`. The Java system provides a number of predefined exception classes such as `Error`, `Exception`, `RuntimeException`, and `IOException`. You can also define your own exception class.

Exceptions occur during the execution of a method. When defining the method, you have to claim an exception if the method might throw that exception, thus telling the compiler what can go wrong. These processes are called claiming and throwing an exception.

To use the method that claims exceptions, you need to enclose the method call in the `try` clause of a `try-catch` block. When the exception occurs during the execution of the method, the `catch` clause catches and handles the exception.

Exception handling takes time because it requires instantiating a new exception object. Exceptions are not meant to substitute for simple tests. You should avoid using exception handling if an alternative solution can be found. Using an alternative would significantly improve the performance of the program.

Chapter Review

1. Describe the Java `Throwable` class, its subclasses, and the types of exceptions.

2. What is the purpose of claiming exceptions? How do you claim an exception, and where? Can you claim multiple exceptions in a method declaration?

3. How do you throw an exception? Can you throw multiple exceptions in one `throw` statement?

4. What is the keyword `throw` used for? What is the keyword `throws` used for?

5. What does the Java runtime system do when an exception occurs?

6. How do you catch an exception?

7. Does the presence of the `try-catch` block impose overhead when no exception occurs?

8. Suppose that `statement2` causes an exception in the following `try-catch` block:

   ```
   try
   {
     statement1;
     statement2;
     statement3;
   }
   catch (Exception1 ex1)
   {
   }
   catch (Exception2 ex2)
   {
   };

   statement4;
   ```

   Answer the following questions:

   - Will `statement3` be executed?

   - If the exception is not caught, will `statement4` be executed?

   - If the exception is caught in the catch clause, will `statement4` be executed?

   - If the exception is passed to the caller, will `statement4` be executed?

9. Suppose that `statement2` causes an exception in the following `try-catch` block:

   ```
   try
   {
     statement1;
     statement2;
     statement3;
   }
   catch (Exception1 ex1)
   {
   }
   catch (Exception2 ex2)
   ```

```
    {
    }
    catch (Exception3 ex3)
    {
      throw ex3;
    }
    finally
    {
      statement4;
    };

    statement4;
```

Answer the following questions:

- Will statement5 be executed?

- If the exception is of type Exception3, what will happen? Will statement5 be executed? Will statement4 be executed?

10. If an exception were not caught in a non-GUI application, what would happen? If an exception were not caught in a GUI application, what would happen?

Programming Exercises

1. Example 6.10, "Using Command-Line Parameters," in Chapter 6, "Arrays and Strings," is a simple command-line calculator. Note that the program terminates if any operand is non-numeric. Write a program with an exception handler to deal with non-numeric operands; then write another program without using an exception handler to achieve the same objective. Your program should display a message to inform the user of the wrong operand type before exiting (see Figure 11.10).

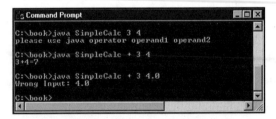

Figure 11.10 *The program performs arithmetic operations and detects input errors.*

2. Example 9.9 is a GUI calculator. Note that if Number 1 or Number 2 were a non-numeric string, the program would display errors on the console. Add a canvas to the GUI and write a program with an exception handler to display a wrong operand type message on the canvas; then write a program to achieve the same objective without using exception handling.

3. Write a program to meet the following requirements:

- Create an array with 100 elements that are randomly chosen.

- Create a text field to enter an array index and another text field to display the array element at the specified index (see Figure 11.11).

- Create a Show button to cause the array element to be displayed. If the specified index is out-of-bound, display the message Out of Bound.

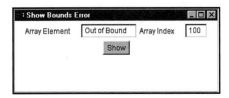

Figure 11.11 *The program displays the array element at the specified index or displays a message Out of Bound if the index is out-of-bound.*

CHAPTER 12

MULTITHREADING

Objectives

- ℮ Understand the concept of multithreading and apply it to developing animation.

- ℮ Write threads by extending the Thread class.

- ℮ Write threads by implementing the Runnable interface in case of multiple inheritance.

- ℮ Understand the life cycle of thread states.

- ℮ Understand and set thread priorities.

- ℮ Use thread groups to manage a group of similar threads.

- ℮ Use thread synchronization to avoid resource conflicts.

Introduction

A *thread* is a flow of execution of a task in a program, which has a beginning and an end. The programs you have seen so far run in a single thread; that is, at any given time, a single statement is being executed. With Java, you can launch multiple threads from a program concurrently. These threads can be executed simultaneously in multiprocessor systems, as shown in Figure 12.1.

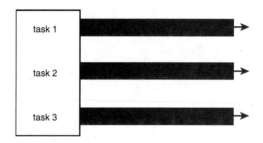

Figure 12.1   *Here, multiple threads run on multiple CPUs.*

In single-processor systems, as shown in Figure 12.2, the multiple threads share the CPU time, and the operating system is responsible for scheduling and allocating resources to the threads. This arrangement is practical because most of the time the CPU is idle. For example, the CPU does nothing while the user enters data.

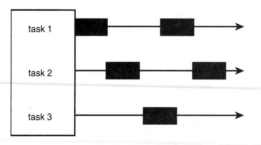

Figure 12.2   *Here, multiple threads share a single CPU.*

Multithreading can make your program more responsive and interactive, as well as enhance performance. For example, a good word processor lets you print or save the file while you are typing. In some cases, multithreaded programs run faster than single-threaded programs even on single-processor systems. Multithreading is particularly useful for animation in Java, which is designed to make computer animation easy. Java also provides exceptionally good support for programming with multiple threads of execution, including built-in support for creating threads and for locking resources to prevent conflicts.

You can create threads by extending the Thread class or implementing the Runnable interface. Both Thread and Runnable are defined in the java.lang package. Thread actually implements `Runnable`. In this chapter, you learn how to write multithreaded programs, using the `Thread` class and the `Runnable` interface.

The *Thread* Class

The `Thread` class contains the constructor `Thread()`, as well as many useful methods to run, start, suspend, resume, interrupt, and stop threads. To create and run a thread, first define a class that extends the `Thread` class. Your thread class must override the `run()` method, which tells the system how the thread will be executed when it runs. You then need a client class that creates an object running on the thread. This object is referred to as a runnable object. Figure 12.3 illustrates the structure of a thread class and its client class.

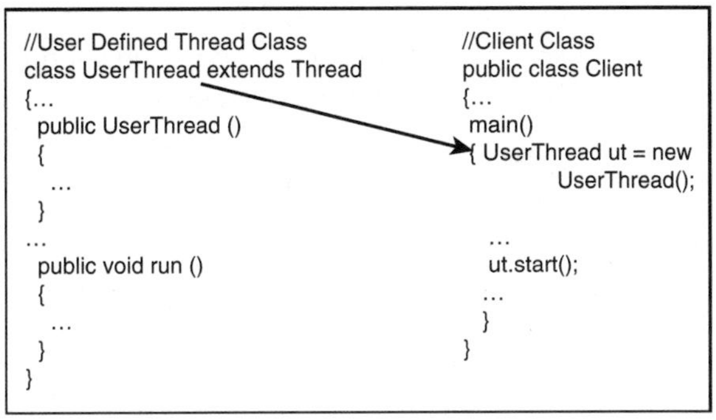

```
//User Defined Thread Class          //Client Class
class UserThread extends Thread      public class Client
{...                                 {...
    public UserThread ()               main()
    {                                  { UserThread ut = new
        ...                                   UserThread();
    }
    ...                                    ...
    public void run ()                     ut.start();
    {                                      ...
        ...                                }
    }                                  }
}
```

Figure 12.3   *A thread is defined as a subclass of the* `Thread` *class.*

You create a runnable object by using the `Thread()` constructor. The `start()` method tells the system that the thread is ready to run. The constructor and several methods in the `Thread` class are described in the following paragraphs. The following constructs a new thread:

```
public Thread()
```

Usually, it is called from the client class to create a runnable object. If the user-defined thread class is used, the client program creates a thread by using the user-defined thread class constructor, as shown in Figure 12.3.

```
public void run()
```

This method is invoked by the Java runtime system to execute the thread. You must override this method and provide the code you want your thread to execute in your thread class. This method is never directly invoked by the runnable object in the program, although it is an instance method of a runnable object.

```
public void start()
```

This method starts the thread, which causes the `run()` method to be invoked. This method is called by the runnable object in the client class.

```
public void stop()
```

This method stops the thread. As of JDK 1.2, this method is deprecated, because it is known to be inherently unsafe. You should assign `null` to a `Thread` variable to indicate it is stopped instead of using the `stop()` method.

```
public void suspend()
```

This method suspends the thread. As of JDK 1.2, this method is deprecated, because it is known to be deadlock-prone. You should use the `wait()` method along with a `boolean` variable to indicate whether a thread is suspended instead of using the `suspend()` method. An example of implementing the `suspend()` method is introduced in the next section, "The `Runnable` Interface."

```
public void resume()
```

This method resumes the thread. As of JDK 1.2, this method, along with the `suspend()` method, has been deprecated because it is deadlock-prone. You should use the `notify()` method along with a `boolean` variable to indicate whether a thread is resumed instead of using the `resume()` method. An example of implementing the `resume()` method will be introduced in the next section, "The `Runnable` Interface."

```
public static void sleep(long millis) throws InterruptedException
```

This method puts the runnable object to sleep for a specified time in milliseconds. Note that `sleep()` is a class method.

```
public void interrupt()
```

This method interrupts the running thread.

```
public static boolean interrupted()
```

This method tests to see whether the current thread has been interrupted.

```
public boolean isAlive()
```

This method tests to see whether the thread is currently running.

```
public void setPriority(int p)
```

This method sets priority p (ranging from 1 to 10) for this thread.

The `wait()` and `notify()` methods in the `Object` class are often used with threads.

```
public final void wait() throws InterruptedException
```

This method puts the thread to wait for notification by another thread of a change in this object.

```
public final void notify()
```

This method awakens a single thread that is waiting on this object.

Example 12.1   Using the *Thread* Class to Create and Launch Threads

This program creates and runs the following three threads:

- The first thread prints the letter *a* 100 times.

- The second thread prints the letter *b* 100 times.

- The third thread prints the integers 1 through 100.

The program has three independent tasks. To run them concurrently, the program needs to create a runnable object for each task. Because the first two threads have similar functionality, they can be defined in one thread class.

The program is given here and its output is shown in Figure 12.4.

```
public class TestThreads
{
  public static void main(String[] args)
  {
    //declare and create threads
    PrintChar printA = new PrintChar('a',100);
    PrintChar printB = new PrintChar('b',100);
    PrintNum  print100 = new PrintNum(100);

    //start threads
    print100.start();
    printA.start();
    printB.start();
  }
}

/*The thread class for printing a specified character
  in specified times
*/
class PrintChar extends Thread
{
  private char charToPrint;  //the character to print
  private int times;  //the times to repeat

  //The thread class constructor
  public PrintChar(char c, int t)
  {
    charToPrint = c;
    times = t;
  }

  /*override the run() method to tell the system
    what the thread will do
  */
  public void run()
  {
    for (int i=1; i < times; i++)
      System.out.print(charToPrint);
  }
}
```

continues

405

Example 12.1   continued

```
//The thread class for printing number from 1 to n for a given n
class PrintNum extends Thread
{
  private int lastNum;

  public PrintNum(int i)
  {
    lastNum = i;
  }

  public void run()
  {
    for (int i=1; i <= lastNum; i++)
      System.out.print(" "+i);
  }
}
```

Example Review

If you run this program on a multiple CPU system, all three threads will be executing simultaneously. If you run this program on a single CPU system, all three threads will share the CPU because they take turns printing letters and numbers on the console.

Figure 12.4   *The threads* printA, printB, *and* print100 *are executed simultaneously to display the letter a 100 times, the letter b 100 times, and the numbers from 1 to 100.*

The program creates thread classes by extending the Thread class. The PrintChar class, derived from the Thread class, overrides the run() method with the print character action. This class provides a framework for printing any single character a given number of times. The runnable objects printA and printB are instances of the user-defined thread class PrintChar.

The PrintNum class overrides the run() method with the print number action. This class provides a framework for printing numbers from *1* to *n*, for any integer *n*. The runnable object print100 is an instance of the user-defined thread class printNum.

In the client program, the program creates a thread, printA, for printing the letter *a*; and a thread, printB, for printing the letter *b*. Both are objects of the PrintChar class. The print100 thread object is created from the PrintNum class.

The start() method is invoked to start a thread, which causes the run() method to execute. When the run() method completes, the thread terminates.

> **NOTE**
>
> On some systems, the program might not terminate or print out all the characters and numbers. The problem has nothing to do with your program. It might be an OS problem or a Java Virtual Machine implementation problem. If the program does not seem to terminate, press Ctrl+C to stop it.

The *Runnable* Interface

In the preceding section, you created and ran a thread by declaring a user thread class that extends the Thread class. This approach works well if the user thread class inherits only from the Thread class, but it does not work if the user thread class inherits multiple classes, as in the case of an applet. To inherit multiple classes, you have to implement interfaces. Java provides the Runnable interface as an alternative to the Thread class.

In Chapter 10, "Applets and Advanced Graphics," you drew a clock to show the current time in an applet. The clock is not ticking after it is displayed. What can you do to let the clock display a new current time every second? The key to making the clock tick is to repaint the clock every second with a new current time. You could attempt to override the start() method with the following code:

```
public void start()
{
  while (true)
  {
    repaint();
    try
    {
      Thread.sleep(1000);
    }
    catch(InterruptedException ex)
    {
    }
  }
}
```

The start() method is called when the applet begins. The infinite loop repeatedly repaints the clock every 1,000 milliseconds (which equals 1 second). This appears to refresh the clock every second, but if you run the program, the browser hangs up. The problem is that as long as the while loop is running, the browser cannot serve any of the other events that might be occurring. Therefore, the paint() method is not called. The solution to the problem is to move the while loop to another thread, which can be executed in parallel with the paint() method.

To create a new thread for the applet, you need to implement the Runnable interface in the applet. The following are the implementation guidelines for the Runnable interface:

1. Add implements Runnable in the applet class declaration:

   ```
   public class MyApplet extends Applet implements Runnable
   ```

2. Declare a thread in MyApplet. For example, the following statement declares a thread instance, timer, with the initial value null:

   ```
   private Thread timer = null;
   ```

   By default, the initial value is null, so assigning null in this statement is not necessary.

3. Create a new thread in the applet's init() method and start it right away in MyApplet:

   ```
   public void init()
   {
     timer = new Thread(this);  //create a thread
     timer.start();  //start the thread
   }
   ```

   The this argument in the Thread constructor is required, which specifies that the run function of MyApplet should be called when the thread executes an instance of MyApplet.

4. Resume the thread in the applet's start() method by invoking the resume() like this in MyApplet:

   ```
   public void start()
   {
     resume();
   }
   ```

   The resume() method resumes this thread if it was suspended. This method is ignored if the thread was not suspended. Since the resume() method in the Thread class has been deprecated, you have to create a new one in the program.

5. Create resume() and suspend() methods as follows:

   ```
   public synchronized void resume()
   {
     if (suspended)
     {
       suspended = false;
       notify();
     }
   }

   public synchronized void suspend()
   {
     suspended = true;
   }
   ```

The variable `suspended` should be declared as a data member of the class, which indicates the state of the thread. The `synchronized` keyword ensures that the `resume()` and `suspend()` methods are serialized to avoid race conditions that could result in an inconsistent value for the variable `suspended`. The `synchronized` keyword is further discussed in the section titled "Synchronization," later in this chapter.

6. Write the code you want the thread to execute in the `run()` method:

```
public void run()
{
  while (true)
  {
    repaint();

    try
    {
      timer.sleep(1000);
      synchronized (this)
      {
        while (suspended)
        wait();
      }
    }
    catch (InterruptedException ex)
    {
    }
  }
}
```

The `run()` method is invoked by the Java runtime system when the applet starts. The `while` loop repeatedly calls the `repaint()` method every second if the thread is not suspended. If `suspended` is true, the `wait()` method causes the thread to suspend and wait for notification by the `notify()` method invoked from the `resume()` method. The `repaint()` method runs on the system default thread, which is separate from the thread on which the `while` loop is running. The `synchronized` keyword eliminates potential conflicts that could cause the suspended thread to miss a notification and remain suspended.

7. Override the `stop()` method to suspend the running thread:

```
public void stop()
{
  suspend();
}
```

This code suspends the thread so that it does not consume CPU time while the Web page containing this applet becomes inactive.

8. Override the `destroy()` method to kill the thread:

```
public void destroy()
{
  timer = null;
}
```

This code releases all the resources associated with the thread when the Web browser exits.

Example 12.2   Implementing the *Runnable* Interface in an Applet

The applet presented here displays a clock. To simulate the clock running, a separate thread is used to repaint the clock. The output of the program is shown in Figure 12.5.

```java
import java.applet.*;
import java.awt.*;

public class ClockApplet extends CurrentTimeApplet
  implements Runnable
{
  //declare a thread
  private Thread timer = null;
  private boolean suspended = false;

  public void init()
  {
    super.init();

    //create the thread
    timer = new Thread(this);

    //start the thread
    timer.start();
  }

  //implement the start() method to resume the thread
  public void start()
  {
    resume();
  }

  //implement the run() method to dictate what the thread will do
  public void run()
  {
    while (true)
    {
      repaint();
      try
      {
        timer.sleep(1000);
        synchronized (this)
        {
          while (suspended)
            wait();
        }
      }
      catch (InterruptedException ex)
      {
      }
    }
  }

  //implement the stop method to suspend the thread
  public void stop()
  {
    suspend();
  }
```

```
            //destroy the thread
            public void destroy()
            {
              timer = null;
            }

            public synchronized void resume()
            {
              if (suspended)
              {
                suspended = false;
                notify();
              }
            }

            public synchronized void suspend()
            {
              suspended = true;
            }
          }
```

Figure 12.5 *The control of the clock drawing runs a thread separately from the* paint() *method that draws the clock.*

Example Review

The CurrentTimeApplet class is presented in Example 10.4, "Converting Applications into Applets," to display the current time (see Chapter 10, "Applets and Advanced Graphics"). The ClockApplet class extends CurrentTimeApplet with a control loop running on a separate thread to make the clock tick.

The run() method comes from the Runnable interface and is modified to specify what the separate thread will do. The paint() method is called every second by the repaint() method to display the current time.

The init(), start(), stop(), and destroy() methods in the Applet class are modified for this program to work with the Web browser. The init() method is invoked to start the thread when the Web page is loaded. The stop() method

continues

Example 12.2   continued

is invoked to suspend the thread when the Web page containing the applet becomes inactive. The `start()` method is invoked to resume the thread when the Web page containing the applet becomes active. The `destroy()` method is invoked to terminate the thread when the Web browser exits.

The separate thread named `timer` is created and started in the applet's `init()` method:

```
timer = new Thread(this);
timer.start();
```

The `ClockApplet`'s `init()` method calls `super.init()` defined in the `CurrentTimeApplet` class, which gets parameters for country, language, and time zone from HTML. Therefore, the `ClockApplet` class can get these parameters from HTML.

The `resume()` method sets the variable `suspended` to `false` and awakens the thread that is waiting on the notification by invoking the `notify()` method. The `suspend()` method sets the variable `suspended` to `true`, which causes the thread to suspend and wait for notification to resume.

NOTE

The `start()` method in `timer.start()` is different from the `start()` method in the applet. The former starts the thread and causes the `run()` method to execute, and the latter is executed by the Web browser when the applet starts for the first time or is reactivated.

TIP

Because it is easier and simpler to use the `Thread` class, I recommend that you use it unless your class uses multiple inheritance.

CAUTION

I recommend that you suspend the threads in the Applet's `stop()` method so that the applet does not consume CPU time while the Web page is inactive.

The preceding example shows how to implement the `Runnable` interface in an applet. You can implement the `Runnable` interface in any class. The next example shows you how to use the `Runnable` interface in a class other than applets.

Example 12.3   Controlling a Group of Clocks

This program displays three clocks in a group. Each clock has individual Resume and Suspend control buttons. You can also resume or suspend all the clocks by using group control Resume All and Suspend All buttons. Figure 12.6 contains the output of a sample run of the program.

```java
import java.awt.*;
import java.awt.event.*;
import java.util.*;
import java.text.*;

public class ClockGroup extends MyFrameWithExitHandling
    implements ActionListener
{
  //declare three clock panels
  private ClockPanel c1, c2, c3;

  //declare group control buttons
  private Button btResumeAll, btSuspendAll;

  public static void main(String[] args)
  {
    Frame f = new ClockGroup();
    f.setSize(500,260);
    f.setVisible(true);
  }

  public ClockGroup()
  {
    setTitle("Clock Group");

    //create a Panel for ClockPanels
    Panel p1 = new Panel();
    p1.setLayout(new FlowLayout());
    p1.add(c1 = new ClockPanel());
    c1.setBackground(Color.yellow);
    p1.add(c2 = new ClockPanel());
    c2.setBackground(Color.white);
    p1.add(c3 = new ClockPanel());
    c3.setBackground(Color.gray);

    //create a Panel for group control
    Panel p2 = new Panel();
    p2.setLayout(new FlowLayout());
    p2.add(btResumeAll = new Button("Resume All"));
    p2.add(btSuspendAll = new Button("Suspend All"));

    //add panels in the frame
    setLayout(new BorderLayout());
    add("North",p1);
    add("South",p2);

    //register this frame as a listener on the buttons
    btResumeAll.addActionListener(this);
    btSuspendAll.addActionListener(this);
  }
```

continues

413

Example 12.3   continued

```java
        //for group control
        public void actionPerformed(ActionEvent e)
        {
          String actionCommand = e.getActionCommand();
          if (e.getSource() instanceof Button)
          {
            if ("Resume All".equals((String)actionCommand))
            {
              //start all clocks
              c1.resume();
              c2.resume();
              c3.resume();
            }
            else if ("Suspend All".equals((String)actionCommand))
            {
              //stop all clocks
              c1.suspend();
              c2.suspend();
              c3.suspend();
            }
          }
        }
      }
    }

    class ClockPanel extends Panel implements ActionListener
    {
      private ClockCanvas clock  = null;
      private Button btResume, btSuspend;  //individual control buttons

      ClockPanel()
      {
        //create a Panel for grouping buttons
        Panel forButton = new Panel();
        forButton.add(btResume = new Button("Resume"));
        forButton.add(btSuspend = new Button("Suspend"));

        //set BorderLayout for the ClockPanel
        setSize(100,170);
        setLayout(new BorderLayout());

        //add Clock to this panel (ClockPanel)
        add("Center", clock = new ClockCanvas());
        clock.setSize(100,160);

        //add forButton to this panel (ClockPanel)
        add("South", forButton);

        //register ClockPanel as a listener to the buttons
        btResume.addActionListener(this);
        btSuspend.addActionListener(this);
      }

      //buttons "Resume" and "Suspend" for individual control
      public void actionPerformed(ActionEvent e)
      {
        String actionCommand = e.getActionCommand();
        if (e.getSource() instanceof Button)
        {
          if ("Resume".equals((String)actionCommand))
```

```
        {
          clock.resume();
        }
        else if ("Suspend".equals((String)actionCommand))
        {
          clock.suspend();
        }
      }
    }

  public void resume()
  {
    if (clock != null) clock.resume();
  }

  public void suspend()
  {
    if (clock != null) clock.suspend();
  }
}

class ClockCanvas extends Canvas implements Runnable
{
  private Thread timer = null;
  private int xcenter, ycenter;
  private int clockRadius;
  static Locale locale = Locale.getDefault();
  static TimeZone tz = TimeZone.getTimeZone("CST");
  static DateFormat myFormat;
  private GregorianCalendar cal;
  private boolean suspended = false;

  public ClockCanvas()
  {
    //set display format in specified style, locale, and time zone
    myFormat = DateFormat.getDateTimeInstance
      (DateFormat.SHORT, DateFormat.SHORT, locale);
    myFormat.setTimeZone(tz);

    //create the thread
    timer = new Thread(this);

    //start the thread
    timer.start();
  }

  public void run()
  {
    while (true)
    {
      repaint();
      try
      {
        timer.sleep(1000);
        synchronized (this)
        {
          while (suspended)
            wait();
        }
      }
```

continues

415

Example 12.3   continued

```
            catch (InterruptedException ex)
            {
            }
        }
    }

    public synchronized void resume()
    {
      if (suspended)
      {
        suspended = false;
        notify();
      }
    }

    public synchronized void suspend()
    {
      suspended = true;
    }

    //paint the clock
    public void paint(Graphics g)
    {
      //set clock radius, and center
      clockRadius =
        (int)(Math.min(getSize().width, getSize().height)*0.7*0.5);
      xcenter = (getSize().width)/2;
      ycenter = (getSize().height)/2;

      //draw circle
      g.setColor(Color.black);
      g.drawOval(xcenter - clockRadius,ycenter - clockRadius,
        2*clockRadius, 2*clockRadius);
      g.drawString("12",xcenter-5, ycenter-clockRadius);
      g.drawString("9",xcenter-clockRadius-10,ycenter+3);
      g.drawString("3",xcenter+clockRadius,ycenter+3);
      g.drawString("6",xcenter-3,ycenter+clockRadius+10);

      //get current time using GregorianCalendar
      cal = new GregorianCalendar(tz);

      //draw second hand
      int s = (int)cal.get(GregorianCalendar.SECOND);
      int sLength = (int)(clockRadius*0.9);
      int secondx = (int)(Math.cos((s/60.0)*2*Math.PI -
        Math.PI/2) * sLength + xcenter);
      int secondy = (int)(Math.sin((s/60.0)*2*Math.PI -
        Math.PI/2) * sLength + ycenter);
      g.setColor(Color.red);
      g.drawLine(xcenter, ycenter, secondx, secondy);

      //draw minute hand
      int m = (int)cal.get(GregorianCalendar.MINUTE);
      int mLength = (int)(clockRadius*0.8);
      int minutex = (int)(Math.cos((m/60.0)*2*Math.PI -
        Math.PI/2)*mLength+xcenter);
      int minutey = (int)(Math.sin((m/60.0)*2*Math.PI -
        Math.PI/2)*mLength+ycenter);
      g.setColor(Color.blue);
      g.drawLine(xcenter, ycenter, minutex, minutey);
```

```
//draw hour hand
int h = (int)cal.get(GregorianCalendar.HOUR_OF_DAY);
int hLength = (int)(clockRadius*0.7);
double hourAngle = (h/12.0)*2*Math.PI + (m/60.0)*
  (2*Math.PI/60.0) - Math.PI/2;
int hourx = (int)(Math.cos(hourAngle) * hLength + xcenter);
int houry = (int)(Math.sin(hourAngle) * hLength + ycenter);
g.setColor(Color.green);
g.drawLine(xcenter, ycenter, hourx, houry);

//display current date
String today = myFormat.format(cal.getTime());
FontMetrics fm = g.getFontMetrics();
g.drawString(today, (getSize().width -
  fm.stringWidth(today))/2, ycenter+clockRadius+30);
  }
}
```

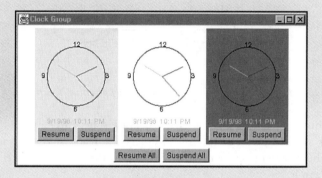

Figure 12.6   *Three clocks run independently with individual control and group control.*

Example Review

The program creates and places three clock panels above two group control buttons, Resume All and Suspend All, in the frame. You can use these two buttons to resume or suspend all the clocks.

The ClockPanel contains a clock and its control buttons, Resume and Suspend. You can use these two buttons to resume or suspend an individual clock.

The clock is encapsulated in the ClockCanvas class. ClockCanvas extends Canvas and implements Runnable. Each instance of ClockCanvas runs on a separate thread to draw a clock on a canvas. The program uses the default locale and CST time zone to format the current time into a string and displays the string below the clock.

The program defines the resume() and suspend() methods in the ClockCanvas to resume and suspend the individual clock. The statement c1.resume() resumes the clock in Panel c1, and c1.suspend() suspends the clock in Panel c1.

Thread States

Threads can be in one of five states: new, ready, running, inactive, or finished (see Figure 12.7).

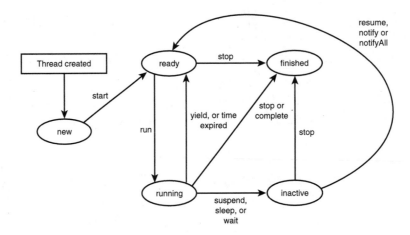

Figure 12.7   *A thread can be in one of five states: new, ready, running, inactive, or finished.*

When a thread is newly created, it enters the new state. After a thread is started by calling its start() method, the thread enters the ready state. A ready thread is runnable but may not yet be running. It is up to the operating system to allocate CPU time to it.

When the ready thread begins executing, it enters the running state. A running thread may enter the ready state if its given CPU time expires or its yield() method is called.

A thread may enter the inactive state for several reasons. It may have invoked the sleep(), wait(), or suspend() method. Some other thread may have invoked its sleep() or suspend() method. It may be waiting for an I/O operation to finish. An inactive thread may become reactivated when the action inactivating the thread is reversed. For example, if a thread has been put to sleep and the sleep time has expired, the thread is reactivated and enters the ready state.

Finally, a thread is finished if it completes the execution of its run() method or if its stop() method is invoked.

To find out the state of a thread, you can use the isAlive() method. It returns true if the thread is in the ready, inactive, or running state; it returns false if the thread is new and has not started or if the thread is finished.

Thread Priority

Every thread in Java is assigned a priority. By default, a thread inherits the priority from the thread that spawned it. You can increase or decrease the priority of any thread by using the setPriority() method, and you can get the thread's priority by using the getPriority() method. Priorities are the numbers ranging from 1 to 10. The Thread class has int constants MIN_PRIORITY, NORM_PRIORITY, and MAX_PRIORITY, representing 1, 5, and 10, respectively. The priority of the main thread is Thread.NORM_PRIORITY.

TIP

In a future version of Java, the priority numbers might change. You should use the constants in the Thread class to specify the thread priorities to minimize the impact of any changes.

The Java runtime system always picks the thread with the highest priority that is currently runnable. If several runnable threads have equal highest priority, the CPU is allocated to all of them, in a round-robin fashion. A lower priority thread can run only when no higher priority threads are currently running.

Example 12.4   Testing Thread Priorities

This program creates three threads named printA, printB, and printC that print the letters *a*, *b*, and *c*, respectively. The program sets priority NORM_PRIORITY for printA, NORM_PRIORITY + 1 for printB, and NORM_PRIORITY + 2 for printC. Figure 12.8 contains the output of a sample run for the program.

```
public class TestThreadPriority
{
  public static void main(String[] args)
  {
    //declare and create threads
    PrintChar printA = new PrintChar('a',200);
    PrintChar printB = new PrintChar('b',200);
    PrintChar printC = new PrintChar('c',200);

    //set priorities
    printA.setPriority(Thread.NORM_PRIORITY);
    printB.setPriority(Thread.NORM_PRIORITY+1);
    printC.setPriority(Thread.NORM_PRIORITY+2);

    //start threads
    printA.start();
    printB.start();
    printC.start();
  }
}
```

Example Review

The PrintChar class for repeatedly printing a character in a separate thread was given in Example 12.1.

continues

Example 12.4   continued

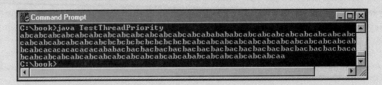

Figure 12.8 *The threads* printA, printB, *and* printC *are assigned with different priorities.*

The three threads are started in this order: printA, printB, and printC. The priority of these threads is printC, printB, and printA, so printC will be the first to get CPU time after it is ready to run.

In theory, printC should finish first; however, the actual execution depends on the system load. You may get different output with different times on different systems.

Thread Groups

A *thread group* is a set of threads. Some programs contain quite a few threads with similar functionality. For convenience, you can group them together and perform operations on all the threads in the group. For example, you can suspend or resume all the threads at the same time if the threads belong to a group.

The following are the guidelines for using the thread group:

1. Construct a thread group, using the ThreadGroup constructor:

   ```
   ThreadGroup g = new ThreadGroup("timer thread group");
   ```

   This creates a thread group g named "timer thread group". The name is a string and must be unique.

2. Place a thread in a thread group, using the Thread constructor:

   ```
   Thread t = new Thread(g, new ThreadClass(), "This thread");
   ```

   The statement new ThreadClass() creates a runnable instance for the ThreadClass. You can also add a thread group under another thread group to form a tree in which every thread group except the initial thread group has a parent.

3. To find out how many threads in a group are currently running, use the activeCount() method. For example, the following statement displays the active number of threads in the group g:

   ```
   System.out.println("The number of runnable threads in the group "
     + g.activeCount());
   ```

4. Each thread belongs to a thread group. By default, a newly created thread becomes a member of the current thread group that spawned it. To find which group a thread belongs to, use the getThreadGroup() method.

NOTE

You have to start each thread individually. There is no start() method in ThreadGroup. As of JDK 1.2, the stop(), suspend() and resume() methods are deprecated. You implemented the stop(), suspend(), and resume() methods in the Thread class. Similarly, you can implement these methods in the ThreadGroup class.

In the next section, you see an example that uses the ThreadGroup class.

Synchronization

When multiple threads access a shared resource simultaneously, the shared resource may be corrupted. The following example demonstrates the problem.

Example 12.5   Showing Resource Conflict

This program demonstrates the problem of resource conflict. Suppose that you launch 100 threads to transfer money from a savings account to a checking account, and 100 threads to transfer money from the checking account to the savings account, with each thread transferring $1. Assume that the savings account has an initial balance of $10,000 and the checking account has $0. The output of the program is shown in Figure 12.9.

```
public class TestTransferWithoutSync
{
  public static void main(String[] args)
  {
    boolean done = false; //to check if all threads are finished

    //create a savings account with ID 1 and balance 10000
    Account saving = new Account(1, 10000);
    //create a checking account with ID 2 and balance 0
    Account checking = new Account(2, 0);

    /*create 100 threads in t1 to transfer money from
      savings to checking
    */
    Thread t1[] = new Thread[100];

    //create a thread group g1 for grouping t1's
    ThreadGroup g1 = new ThreadGroup("from savings to checking");

    /*create 100 threads in t2 to transfer money from
      checking to savings
    */
    Thread t2[] = new Thread[100];
```

continues

Example 12.5   continued

```java
      //create a thread group g2 grouping t2's
      ThreadGroup g2 = new ThreadGroup("from checking to savings");

      //add t1[i] to g1, and start t1[i]
      for (int i=0; i<100; i++)
      {
        t1[i] = new Thread(g1,
          new TransferThread(saving, checking, 1),"t1");
        t1[i].start();
      }

      //add t2[i] to g2, and start t2[i]
      for (int i=0; i<100; i++)
      {
        t2[i] = new Thread(g2,
          new TransferThread(checking, saving, 1),"t2");
        t2[i].start();
      }

      //exit the loop when all threads finished
      while (!done)
        if ((g1.activeCount() == 0) && (g2.activeCount() == 0))
          done = true;

      //show the balance in the savings and checking accounts
      System.out.println("Savings account balance "+
        saving.accountBalance());
      System.out.println("Checking account balance "+
        checking.accountBalance());
  }
}

//define the thread to transfer money between accounts
class TransferThread extends Thread
{
  private Account fromAccount, toAccount;
  private double amount;

  /*constructing a thread transferring amount
    from account s to account
  */
  public TransferThread(Account s, Account c, double amount)
  {
    fromAccount = s;
    toAccount = c;
    this.amount = amount;
  }

  public void run()
  {
    transfer(fromAccount, toAccount, amount);
  }

  public void transfer(Account fromAccount,
                       Account toAccount,
                       double amount)
  {
    //record the balance before transaction for use in recovery
    double fromAccountPriorBalance = fromAccount.accountBalance();
    double toAccountPriorBalance = toAccount.accountBalance();
```

```
        try
        {
          toAccount.deposit(amount);
          sleep(10);
          fromAccount.withdraw(amount);
        }
        catch (NegativeAmountException ex)
        {
          //reset the balance to the value prior to the exception
          fromAccount.setBalance(fromAccountPriorBalance);
          toAccount.setBalance(toAccountPriorBalance);
        }
        catch (InsufficientFundException ex)
        {
          //reset the balance to the value prior to the exception
          fromAccount.setBalance(fromAccountPriorBalance);
          toAccount.setBalance(toAccountPriorBalance);
        }
        catch (InterruptedException ex)
        {
        }
      }
    }
```

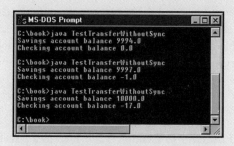

Figure 12.9 *The* `TestTransferWithoutSync` *program causes data inconsistency.*

Example Review

The program creates an `Account` object for a savings account with an initial balance of $10,000, and an `Account` object for the checking account with an initial balance of $0.00. The `Account` class was given in Example 11.4, "Creating Your Own Exception Classes" (see Chapter 11, "Exception Handling").

The program creates 100 identical threads in array `t1` to transfer $1 from the savings account to the checking account, and then creates 100 identical threads to transfer $1 from the checking account to the savings account. The program groups all the threads in `t1` in a thread group `g1`, and then groups all the threads in `t2` in a thread group `g2` (see Figure 12.10).

The `transfer()` method is used by all the threads to transfer money from one account to the other.

continues

Example 12.5   continued

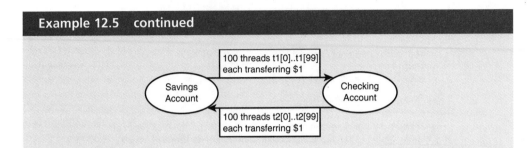

Figure 12.10   *The threads transfer funds between the savings account and the checking account.*

When all the threads finish, the correct result should be that the sum of the balances of the two accounts is 10,000; however, the output is unpredictable. Apparently the answers are wrong in the sample run, as shown in Figure 12.9. The sample run demonstrates the data corruption problem caused by unsynchronized threads with access to the same data source.

Interestingly, it is not easy to replicate the problem. The sleep() method in the transfer() method causes the transfer operation to pause for 10 milliseconds. The sleep() method is added deliberately to magnify the data corruption problem, making it easy to see. If you run the program for several times, but still do not see the problem, put the transfer() method in a for loop to run 100 times in the run() method. This would dramatically increase the chances for resource contention.

So, what caused the error in Example 12.5? Here is a possible scenario:

1. A thread t1[i] reads the savings account balances and checking account balances and loses CPU time to a thread t1[j].

2. A thread t1[j] reads the savings account balances and checking account balances and completes a transfer.

3. A thread t1[i] regains the CPU time and completes a transfer.

The effect of this scenario is that thread t1[j] did nothing, because thread t1[i] overrides t1[j]'s result in Step 3. Obviously, the problem is that t1[i] and t1[j] access the common resource, causing conflict.

To avoid resource conflict, Java uses the keyword synchronized to synchronize method invocation so that only one thread can be in that method at a time. To correct the data corruption problem in the previous example, put the keyword synchronized on the transfer() method and make transfer() static, as follows:

```
public static synchronized void transfer(Account saving,
                                         Account checking,
                                         double amount)
```

With the keywords static synchronized in the method, the preceding scenario cannot happen. If thread t1[i] starts to enter the method and thread t1[j] is already in the method, thread t1[j] is blocked until thread t1[i] finishes the method.

A synchronized method acquires a lock before it executes. For an instance method, the lock is on the object for which the method was invoked. For a class (static) method, the lock is on all the objects of the same class. The synchronized keyword in the suspend() and resume() methods in Example 12.2 ensures that the variable suspended is updated serially without corruption within the object. Adding the keywords static synchronized in the transfer() method in Example 12.5 ensures that only one object can transfer funds among all the objects in the array t1 and t2, which avoids concurrent access of the checking and saving accounts that could corrupt these accounts.

▇▇▇ NOTE

In the run() method of Example 12.2, a synchronized block was used. A synchronized block obtains the lock in the same way as a synchronized method. If a synchronized block is inside a static method, the lock is associated with the class; if it is inside an instance method, the lock is associated with the object.

In operating systems and database systems, locks are often used to protect resources exclusively for write or shared read operations. Java does not have the mechanism that lets you lock data.

Chapter Summary

In this chapter, you learned multithreading programming, using the Thread class and the Runnable interface. You can derive your thread class from the Thread class and create a thread instance to run a task on a separate thread. If your class needs to inherit multiple classes, you can implement the Runnable interface to run multiple tasks in the program simultaneously.

After a thread object is created, you can use start() to start a thread; use sleep() to put a thread to sleep so that other threads can get a chance to run. Since the stop(), suspend(), and resume() methods are deprecated in JDK 1.2, you need to implement these methods to stop, suspend, and resume a thread.

Your thread object never directly invokes the run() method. The Java runtime system invokes the run() method when it is time to execute the thread. Your class must override the run() method to tell the system what the thread will do when it runs.

Threads can be assigned a priority. The Java runtime system always executes the ready thread with highest priority. You can use a thread group to put relevant threads together for group control. To prevent threads from corrupting a shared resource, you should put the synchronized keyword in the method that may cause corruption.

Chapter Review

1. Why do you need multithreading capability in applications? In a single-processor system, how can multiple threads run simultaneously?

2. What are two ways to create threads? When do you use the Thread class, and when do you use the Runnable interface? What are the differences between the Thread class and the Runnable interface?

3. How do you create a thread and launch a thread object? Which of the following methods are instance methods? Which of the following are deprecated in JDK 1.2?

   run(), start(), stop(), suspend(), resume(), sleep(), interrupted()

4. Will the program behave differently if timer.sleep() is replaced by Thread.sleep() in Example 12.2?

5. Describe the life cycle of a thread object.

6. How do you set a priority for a thread? What is the default priority?

7. Describe a thread group. How do you create a thread group? Can you control an individual thread in a thread group (suspend, resume, stop, and so on)?

8. Give some examples of possible resource corruption when running multiple threads. How do you synchronize conflict threads?

Programming Exercises

1. Write an applet to display a flashing label.

   Hint: To make the label flash, you need to repaint the window alternately with the label and without the label (blank screen). You can use a boolean variable to control the alternation.

2. Write an applet to display a moving label. The label moves from the right to the left continuously in the applet's viewing area. When the label disappears from the viewing area, it starts moving again from the right to the left. The label freezes when the mouse is clicked on the label, and the label moves again when the button is released.

   Hint: Repaint the window with a new x coordinate.

3. Rewrite Example 12.1 to display the output on a text area, as shown in Figure 12.11.

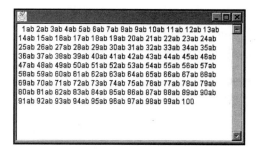

1ab 2ab 3ab 4ab 5ab 6ab 7ab 8ab 9ab 10ab 11ab 12ab 13ab
14ab 15ab 16ab 17ab 18ab 19ab 20ab 21ab 22ab 23ab 24ab
25ab 26ab 27ab 28ab 29ab 30ab 31ab 32ab 33ab 34ab 35ab
36ab 37ab 38ab 39ab 40ab 41ab 42ab 43ab 44ab 45ab 46ab
47ab 48ab 49ab 50ab 51ab 52ab 53ab 54ab 55ab 56ab 57ab
58ab 59ab 60ab 61ab 62ab 63ab 64ab 65ab 66ab 67ab 68ab
69ab 70ab 71ab 72ab 73ab 74ab 75ab 76ab 77ab 78ab 79ab
80ab 81ab 82ab 83ab 84ab 85ab 86ab 87ab 88ab 89ab 90ab
91ab 92ab 93ab 94ab 95ab 96ab 97ab 98ab 99ab 100

Figure 12.11 *The output from three threads is displayed on a text area.*

4. Write a program to launch 100 threads. Each thread is to add 1 to a variable `sum`. The variable `sum` is zero initially. You need to pass `sum` by reference to each thread. In order to pass it by reference, you need to define an `Integer` wrapper object to hold `sum`. Run the program with and without synchronization to see its effect.

5. Write a program to simulate an elevator going up and down (see Figure 12.12). The buttons on the left indicate the floor where the rider is now located. The rider must first click a button on the left to request that the elevator move to his or her floor. When the rider gets inside the elevator, the rider clicks a button on the right to request that the elevator go to the specified floor.

Elevator Simulation
getting passengers
F8
F7
F6
F5
F4
F3
F2
F1
Elevator Simulation
sending passengers

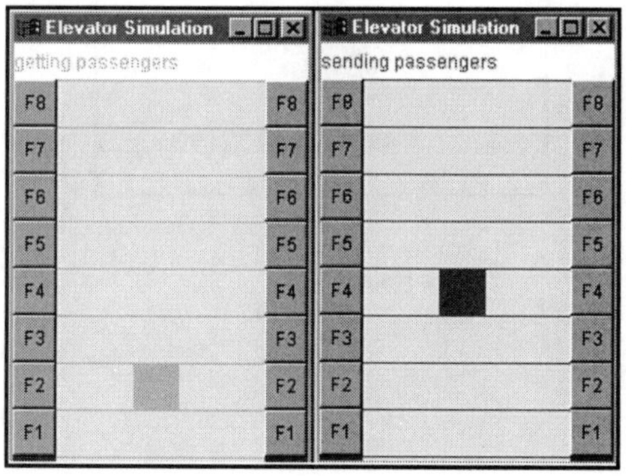

Figure 12.12 *The program simulates elevator operations.*

6. Write a Java applet to display a stock index ticker (see Figure 12.13). The stock index information is passed from the `<param>` tag in the HTML file. Each index has four parameters: Index Name (for example, S&P 500), Current Time (for example, 15:54), the index from the previous day (for example, 919.01), and Change (for example, 4.54).

   Use at least five indexes, such as Dow Jones, S & P 500, NASDAQ, NIKKEI, and Gold & Silver Index. Display positive change in green and negative change in red. The indexes move from the right to the left in the applet's view area. Clicking anywhere on the applet freezes the ticker, and the ticker moves again when the mouse button is released.

Figure 12.13 *The program displays a stock index ticker.*

7. Write a Java applet to simulate a running fan, as shown in Figure 12.14. Create a subclass of `Canvas` to display the fan. This subclass also contains the methods to suspend and resume the fan and the method for setting the fan's speed and reversing the fan's direction.

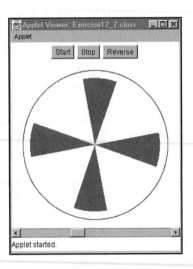

Figure 12.14 *The program simulates a running fan.*

13

MULTIMEDIA

Objectives

- Develop multimedia applications with audio and images.

- Get audio files and play sound.

- Get image files and display graphics.

- Override the update() method, and use double buffering to reduce flickering.

- Use MediaTracker to ensure that images are completely loaded before they are displayed.

Introduction

Welcome to the fascinating world of *multimedia*. You have seen computer animation used every day on TV and in movies. When surfing the Web, you have seen sites with text, images, sound, animation, and movie clips. These are examples of multimedia at work.

Multimedia is a broad term that describes making, storing, retrieving, transferring, and presenting various types of information, such as text, graphics, pictures, videos, and sound. Multimedia involves a complex weave of communications, electronics, and computer technologies. It is beyond the scope of this book to cover multimedia in great detail. This chapter concentrates on the presentation of multimedia in Java.

Java was designed with multimedia in mind. Most programming languages have no built-in multimedia capabilities. But Java provides extensive built-in support to enable you to develop powerful multimedia applications easily. Java's multimedia capabilities include animation that uses drawings, audio, and images.

You have already used animation with drawings, such as simulating a clock. In this chapter, you will learn how to develop Java programs with audio and images. You will also be introduced to various animation techniques that reduce flickering.

Playing Audio

Audio is stored in files. There are several formats of audio files. Prior to JDK 1.1, Java could only play the format used on UNIX machines. These are the sound files with the .au extension. With JDK 1.2, you can also play the popular .wav format audio files commonly used on Windows. If you have a sound file in a format other than the .au and .wav formats, you can use audio-processing utilities to convert that file to the .au or .wav format so that you can use it in Java.

You can play an audio clip in an applet simply by using the following play() method:

```
play(URL url, String filename);
```

This method downloads the audio file from the url and plays the audio clip.

The URL (Universal Resource Locator) describes the location of a resource on the Internet. Java provides a class that is used to manipulate URLs: java.net.URL. The URL of the applet and its containing HTML file can be located in different directories. You can use getCodeBase() to get the URL of the applet, or getDocumentBase() to get the HTML file that contains the applet. These two methods are defined in the Applet class:

```
play(getCodeBase(), "soundfile.au");

play(getDocumentBase(), "soundfile.au");
```

The former method plays the sound file **soundfile.au**, which is located in the applet's directory. The latter method plays the sound file **soundfile.au**, which is located in the HTML file's directory.

The play(url, filename) statement will download the audio file every time you play the audio. If you want to play the audio many times, you can create an *audio clip object* for the file. The audio clip is created once and can be played repeatedly without reloading the file. To create an audio clip, you can use the following methods:

```
public AudioClip getAudioClip(URL url);

public AudioClip getAudioClip(URL url, String  name);
```

The former requires an absolute URL address for it to specify a sound file; the latter enables you to use a relative URL with the filename. The relative URL is obtained using getCodeBase() or getDocumentBase(). For example, the following statement creates an audio clip for the file **soundfile.au** that is stored in the same directory as the applet that contains the statement.

```
AudioClip ac = getAudioClip(getCodeBase(), "soundfile.au");
```

To manipulate a sound for an audio clip, you can use the following methods. The following method starts playing the clip:

```
public void play()
```

Each time this method is called, the clip is restarted from the beginning. The following method starts playing the clip repeatedly:

```
public void loop()
```

The following method stops playing the clip:

```
public void stop()
```

Example 13.1   Incorporating Sound in Applets

This program displays a running clock, as shown in Example 12.2, "Implementing the Runnable Interface in an Applet" (see Chapter 12, "Multithreading"). Additionally, the program plays sound files to announce the time at every minute.

```
import java.applet.*;
import java.awt.*;
import java.util.*;

public class ClockAppletWithAudio extends ClockApplet
{
  //declare audio files
  private AudioClip[] hourAudio = new AudioClip[12];
```

continues

Example 13.1   continued

```java
private AudioClip minuteAudio;
private AudioClip amAudio;
private AudioClip pmAudio;

public void init()
{
  super.init();

  //create audio clips for pronouncing hours
  for (int i=0; i<12; i++)
    hourAudio[i] = getAudioClip(getCodeBase(),
      "timeaudio/hour"+i+".au");

  //create audio clips for pronouncing am and pm
  amAudio = getAudioClip(getCodeBase(), "timeaudio/am.au");
  pmAudio = getAudioClip(getCodeBase(), "timeaudio/pm.au");
}

//paint the clock
public void paint(Graphics g)
{
  super.paint(g);

  //get current time using GregorianCalendar
  GregorianCalendar cal = new GregorianCalendar(tz);

  //draw second hand
  int s = (int)cal.get(GregorianCalendar.SECOND);
  int m = (int)cal.get(GregorianCalendar.MINUTE);
  int h = (int)cal.get(GregorianCalendar.HOUR_OF_DAY);

  //announce current time
  announceTime(s, m, h);
}

//announce the current time at every minute
public void announceTime(int s, int m, int h)
{
  if (s == 0)
  {
    //load the minute file
    minuteAudio = getAudioClip(getCodeBase(),
      "timeaudio/minute"+m+".au");

    hourAudio[h%12].play();   //announce hour

    //time lap to allow hourAudio play to finish
    try
    {
      Thread.sleep(1500);
    }
    catch(InterruptedException ex)
    {
    }

    minuteAudio.play(); //announce minute
```

```
                    //time delay to allow minuteAudio play to finish
                    try
                    {
                      Thread.sleep(1500);
                    }
                    catch(InterruptedException ex)
                    {
                    }

                    //announce am or pm
                    if (h < 12)
                      amAudio.play();
                    else
                      pmAudio.play();
                }
            }
        }
```

Example Review

The program extends the ClockApplet class with the capability to announce time. The hourAudio is an array of 12 audio clips that are used to pronounce the 12 hours of the day; the minuteAudio is an array of 60 audio clips that are used to pronounce the 60 minutes in an hour. The amAudio pronounces A.M.; the pmAudio pronounces P.M.

For example, if the current time is 6:30:00, the applet announces "The time is six-thirty A.M." If the current time is 20:20:00, the applet announces, "The time is eight-twenty P.M." The audio clips are played in sequence in order to announce a time.

The init() method invokes super.init() defined in the ClockApplet class, and creates audio clips for pronouncing time. super.init() gets country, language, and time zone parameters from HTML, and starts a thread to control the clock.

All of the audio files are stored in the directory timeaudio, a subdirectory of the applet's directory. The 12 audio clips that are used to pronounce the hours are stored in the files **hour0.au**, **hour1.au**, and so on, to **hour11.au**. They are loaded using the following loop:

```
        for (int i=0; i<12; i++)
          hourAudio[i] = getAudioClip(getCodeBase(),
            "timeaudio/hour"+i+".au");
```

Similarly, the amAudio clip is stored in the file **am.au**, and the pmAudio clip is stored in the file **pm.au**; they are loaded along with the hour clips in the init() method.

The program created an array of 12 audio clips for pronouncing each hour, but did not create 60 audio clips for pronouncing each minute. Instead, the program

continues

Example 13.1   continued

created and loaded the minute audio clip when needed in the announceTime() method. The audio files are very large. Loading all the 60 audio clips at once may cause an OutOfMemoryError exception.

The paint() method invokes super.paint() and announceTime(). super.paint() defined in ClockApplet draws a clock for the current time. announceTime(h, m, s) announces the current hour, minute, and A.M. or P.M. if the second s is 0.

In the announceTime() method, the sleep() method is purposely invoked to ensure that the clip finishes before the next clip starts so that the clips do not interfere with each other.

▬ NOTE

For all the programs in this chapter, you need the associated audio or image files in order to run the programs. These files are on the companion CD-ROM. The image files are in the \book\images directory and the audio files are in the \book\timeaudio directory.

Running Audio on a Separate Thread

If you had run the previous program, you would have noticed that the second hand did not display at the first, second, and third second of the minute. This is caused by invoking sleep(1500) twice in the announceTime() method, which takes three seconds to announce time at the beginning of each minute.

Because of this delay, the paint() method does not have time to draw the clock during the first three seconds of each minute. Clearly, the announceTime() method for playing audio interferes with repainting the clock. To avoid the conflict, you should announce the time on a separate thread. This problem can be fixed in the following program.

Example 13.2   Announcing the Time on a Separate Thread

To avoid the conflict between painting the clock and announcing time, the program in this example runs these tasks on separate threads.

```
import java.applet.*;
import java.awt.*;
import java.util.*;

public class ClockAppletWithAudioOnSeparateThread extends
  ClockApplet
{
  //declare audio files
```

```
        private AudioClip[] hourAudio = new AudioClip[12];
        private AudioClip minuteAudio;
        private AudioClip amAudio;
        private AudioClip pmAudio;

        //declare a thread for announcing time
        AnnounceTime a;

        public void init()
        {
          super.init();
          //create audio clips and load audio files for pronouncing hours
          for (int i=0; i<12; i++)
            hourAudio[i] = getAudioClip(getCodeBase(),
              "timeaudio/hour"+i+".au");

          /*create audio clips and load audio files
            for pronouncing am and pm
          */
          amAudio = getAudioClip(getCodeBase(), "timeaudio/am.au");
          pmAudio = getAudioClip(getCodeBase(), "timeaudio/pm.au");
        }

        //paint the clock
        public void paint(Graphics g)
        {
          super.paint(g);

          //get current time using GregorianCalendar
          GregorianCalendar cal = new GregorianCalendar(tz);

          //draw second hand
          int s = (int)cal.get(GregorianCalendar.SECOND);
          int m = (int)cal.get(GregorianCalendar.MINUTE);
          int h = (int)cal.get(GregorianCalendar.HOUR_OF_DAY);


          //announce current time
          if (s == 0)
          {
            minuteAudio = getAudioClip(getCodeBase(),
              "timeaudio/minute"+m+".au");
            if (h < 12)
              a = new AnnounceTime(hourAudio[h%12],
                minuteAudio, amAudio);
            else
              a = new AnnounceTime(hourAudio[h%12],
                minuteAudio, pmAudio);
            a.start();
          }
        }
      }

//define a thread class for announcing time
class AnnounceTime extends Thread
{
  private AudioClip hourAudio, minuteAudio, amPM;

  //get Audio clips
```

continues

435

Example 13.2   continued

```
    public AnnounceTime(AudioClip hourAudio,
                        AudioClip minuteAudio,
                        AudioClip amPM)
{
  this.hourAudio = hourAudio;
  this.minuteAudio = minuteAudio;
  this.amPM = amPM;
}

public void run()
{
  hourAudio.play(); //announcing hour

  /*time delay to allow hourAudio play to finish
    before playing the clip
  */
  try
  {
    Thread.sleep(1500);
  }
  catch(InterruptedException ex)
  {
  }

  minuteAudio.play();

  //time delay to allow minuteAudio play to finish
  try
  {
    Thread.sleep(1500);
  }
  catch(InterruptedException ex)
  {
  }

  amPM.play(); //announcing am or pm
}
  }
```

Example Review

The program extends `ClockApplet` with the capability to announce time without interfering with the `paint()` method. The program defines a new thread class, `AnnounceTime`, which is derived from the `Thread` class. This new class plays audio.

To create an instance of the `AnnounceTime` class, you would need to pass three audio clips. These three audio clips are used to announce the hour, the minute, and A.M. or P.M. This instance is created only when s equals 0 at the beginning of each minute.

When running this program, you discover that the audio does not interfere with the clock animation because an instance of `AnnounceTime` starts on a separate thread to announce the current time. This thread is independent of the thread on which the `paint()` method runs.

Reducing Animation Flickering

If you ran the preceding clock example for a while, you would probably observe occasional flickering in the animation. There would be nothing wrong with the program if this occurred. The flickering problem is caused by the update() method, which is invoked by the repaint() method. By default, the update() method clears the viewing area and then invokes the paint() method.

The parts of the viewing area that do not change rapidly after they are cleared but before they are painted cause flickering to occur. It is not necessary to repaint the entire viewing area. To reduce flickering, you can just repaint the affected area. For example, if the clock does not enter a new hour, the clock circle and the hour hand do not need to be repainted. Two major techniques reduce flickering:

- Override the update() method so that the viewing area is not cleared, and repaint only the parts of the area you have changed.

- Use double buffering to build the next frame offscreen. Place the entire painting onscreen together.

You will learn the double-buffering technique later in this chapter. Following is an example of reducing flickering by overriding the update() method.

Example 13.3 Reducing Flickering by Overriding the *update()* Method

This example rewrites the program in the preceding example. This rewritten program will override the update() method so that the viewing area is not cleared when repaint() is called. The paint() method will only paint the affected area. As a result of this program, flickering will be reduced.

```
import java.awt.*;
import java.util.*;
import java.text.*;

public class ClockAppletReducingFlickering extends ClockApplet
{
  private int xcenter, ycenter;
  private int clockRadius;
  private int lastsecondx=0, lastsecondy=0,
    lastminutex=0, lastminutey=0, lasthourx=0, lasthoury=0;
  private int secondx, secondy, minutex, minutey, hourx, houry;
  private String lastdate = new String();

  //declare audio files
  private AudioClip[] hourAudio = new AudioClip[12];
  private AudioClip minuteAudio;
  private AudioClip amAudio;
  private AudioClip pmAudio;

  //declare a thread for announcing time
  AnnounceTime a;
```

continues

Example 13.3   continued

```
public void init()
{
  super.init();

  //get clock radius and center
  clockRadius =
    (int)(Math.min(getSize().width, getSize().height)*0.7*0.5);
  xcenter = (getSize().width)/2;
  ycenter = (getSize().height)/2;

  //create audio clips
  for (int i=0; i<12; i++)
    hourAudio[i] = getAudioClip(getCodeBase(),
      "timeaudio/hour"+i+".au");

  amAudio = getAudioClip(getCodeBase(), "timeaudio/am.au");
  pmAudio = getAudioClip(getCodeBase(), "timeaudio/pm.au");
}

//override update
public void update(Graphics g)
{
  paint(g);
}

//paint the clock
public void paint(Graphics g)
{
  //draw circle
  g.setColor(Color.black);
  g.drawOval(xcenter - clockRadius,ycenter - clockRadius,
    2*clockRadius, 2*clockRadius);
  g.drawString("12",xcenter-5, ycenter-clockRadius);
  g.drawString("9",xcenter-clockRadius-10,ycenter+3);
  g.drawString("3",xcenter+clockRadius,ycenter+3);
  g.drawString("6",xcenter-3,ycenter+clockRadius+10);

  //get current time using GregorianCalendar
  GregorianCalendar cal = new GregorianCalendar(tz);

  //redraw second hand, erase previous drawing if necessary
  int s = (int)cal.get(GregorianCalendar.SECOND);
  int sLength = (int)(clockRadius*0.9);
  secondx = (int)(Math.cos((s/60.0)*2*Math.PI -
    Math.PI/2) * sLength + xcenter);
  secondy = (int)(Math.sin((s/60.0)*2*Math.PI -
    Math.PI/2) * sLength + ycenter);

  //display current date
  String today = myFormat.format(cal.getTime());
  FontMetrics fm = g.getFontMetrics();

  if ((lastsecondx != secondx) || (lastsecondy != secondy))
  {
    g.setColor(getBackground());
    g.drawLine(xcenter, ycenter, lastsecondx, lastsecondy);
    g.drawString(lastdate, (getSize().width -
      fm.stringWidth(today))/2, ycenter+clockRadius+30);
  }
```

```
g.setColor(Color.red);
g.drawLine(xcenter, ycenter, secondx, secondy);
g.drawString(today, (getSize().width -
  fm.stringWidth(today))/2, ycenter+clockRadius+30);

//redraw minute hand, erase previous drawing if necessary
int m = (int)cal.get(GregorianCalendar.MINUTE);
int mLength = (int)(clockRadius*0.8);
minutex = (int)(Math.cos((m/60.0)*2*Math.PI -
  Math.PI/2)*mLength+xcenter);
minutey = (int)(Math.sin((m/60.0)*2*Math.PI -
  Math.PI/2)*mLength+ycenter);

if ((lastminutex != minutex) || (lastminutey != minutey))
{
  g.setColor(getBackground());
  g.drawLine(xcenter, ycenter, lastminutex, lastminutey);
}

g.setColor(Color.blue);
g.drawLine(xcenter, ycenter, minutex, minutey);

//redraw hour hand, erase previous drawing if necessary
int h = (int)cal.get(GregorianCalendar.HOUR_OF_DAY);
int hLength = (int)(clockRadius*0.7);
double hourAngle = (h/12.0)*2*Math.PI +
  (m/60.0)*(2*Math.PI/60.0) - Math.PI/2;
hourx = (int)(Math.cos(hourAngle) * hLength + xcenter);
houry = (int)(Math.sin(hourAngle) * hLength + ycenter);

if ((lasthourx != hourx) || (lasthoury != houry))
{
  g.setColor(getBackground());
  g.drawLine(xcenter, ycenter, lasthourx, lasthoury);
}

g.setColor(Color.black);
g.drawLine(xcenter, ycenter, hourx, houry);

lastsecondx = secondx;
lastsecondy = secondy;
lastminutex = minutex;
lastminutey = minutey;
lasthourx = hourx;
lasthoury = houry;
lastdate = today;

//announce current time
if (s == 0)
{
  //get minute audio clip
  minuteAudio = getAudioClip(getCodeBase(),
    "timeaudio/minute"+m+".au");

  if (minuteAudio == null) return;

  if (h < 12)
    a = new AnnounceTime(hourAudio[h%12],
      minuteAudio, amAudio);
```

continues

Example 13.3   continued

```
        else
          a = new AnnounceTime(hourAudio[h%12],
            minuteAudio, pmAudio);
        a.start();
      }
    }
  }
```

Example Review

The program overrides the update() method in order to call the paint() method without clearing the screen. If you want to try this program, you are encouraged to remove the update() method so that you can see the effect of its absence.

Because the previous screen is not the cleared, you have to erase the old drawing manually, if necessary. Therefore, the program needs to store the previous drawing information in lastsecondx, lastsecondy, lastminutex, lastminutey, lasthourx, lasthoury, and lastdate. When the second hand ticks, the previous second hand is erased. (The background color is used to redraw the previous second hand.)

The date, the minute hand, and the hour hand can be erased and repainted in a similar way.

Displaying Images

Java currently supports two image formats: GIF (Graphics Interchange Format) and JPEG (Joint Photographic Experts Group). Image filenames for each of these types end with .gif and .jpg, respectively. If you have a bitmap file, or image files in other formats, you can use image-processing utilities to convert these files into GIF or JPEG format for use in Java.

To display an image, you need to perform the following steps:

1. Retrieve the image from a file or from an Internet source.

2. Draw the image.

To load an image from a local file or download it from an Internet source, you need to use the getImage() method in the Applet class. When this method is invoked, it launches a separate thread to load the image, which enables the program to continue while the image is being retrieved. This method returns an Image object. The following code loads the image from the specified URL:

```
public Image getImage(URL url)
```

The following code loads the image file from the specified file at the given URL:

```
public Image getImage(URL url, String filename)
```

You need to draw an image in a graphics context. The Graphics class has the drawImage() method for displaying an image. The following code draws the specified image:

```
drawImage(Image img, int x, int y, Color bgcolor, ImageObserver observer)
```

The image's top-left corner is at (x, y) in the graphics context's coordinate space. Transparent pixels in the image are drawn in the specified color bgcolor. The observer is the object on which the image is displayed. The following code draws as much of the specified image as is currently available at the specified coordinate (x, y):

```
drawImage(Image img, int x, int y, ImageObserver observer)
```

The following code draws a scaled version of the image so that the image can fill all of the available space in the specified rectangle:

```
drawImage(Image img, int x, int y, int width, int height,
    ImageObserver observer)
```

Example 13.4   Displaying Images in an Applet

The program in this example will display an image in an applet. The image is stored in a file that is located in the same directory as the applet. The user enters the filename in a text field and displays the image on a canvas. Figure 13.1 contains the output of a sample run of the program.

```
import java.applet.*;
import java.awt.*;
import java.awt.event.*;

public class DisplayImageApplet extends Applet
  implements ActionListener
{
  private ImageCanvas c;  //the canvas for displaying image
  private TextField tfFilename; //the name of the image file
  private Button btShow;  //the "Show" button

  public void init()
  {
    //create Panel p1 to hold a text field and a button
    Panel p1 = new Panel();
    p1.setLayout(new FlowLayout());
    p1.add(new Label("Filename"));
    p1.add(tfFilename = new TextField(10));
    p1.add(btShow = new Button("Show"));

    //place an ImageCanvas object and p1 in the frame
    setLayout(new BorderLayout());
    add("Center", c = new ImageCanvas());
```

continues

Example 13.4   continued

```
            add("South", p1);
            c.setBackground(Color.gray);

            //register listener
            btShow.addActionListener(this);
            tfFilename.addActionListener(this);
        }

        //handling the "Show" button
        public void actionPerformed(ActionEvent e)
        {
            if ((e.getSource() instanceof Button) ||
                (e.getSource() instanceof TextField))
                displayImage();
        }

        private void displayImage()
        {
            //retrieving image
            Image image = getImage(getCodeBase(),
                tfFilename.getText().trim());
            //show image in the canvas
            c.showImage(image);
        }
    }

    //define the canvas for showing an image
    class ImageCanvas extends Canvas
    {
        private String filename;
        private Image image = null;

        public ImageCanvas()
        {
        }

        //set image
        public void showImage(Image image)
        {
            this.image = image;
            repaint();
        }

        public void paint(Graphics g)
        {
            if (image != null)
                g.drawImage(image, 0, 0,
                    getSize().width, getSize().height, this);
        }
    }
```

Example Review

The image is loaded by using the getImage() method from the file that is in the same directory as the applet. The showImage() method that is defined in ImageCanvas passes the image to the canvas so that it can be drawn by the paint() method.

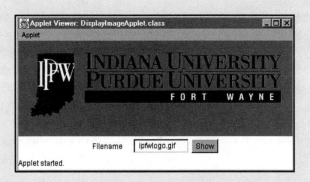

Figure 13.1   *Given the image filename, the applet displays an image.*

The statement g.drawImage(image, 0, 0, getSize().width, getSize().height, this) displays the image in the Graphics context g on the ImageCanvas object. You can display the image by entering the filename in the text field, then pressing the Enter key or clicking the Show button. The filename you enter must be located in the same directory as the applet.

ImageObserver is an asynchronous update interface for receiving notifications about image information as the image is constructed. The Component class implements ImageObserver. Therefore, ImageCanvas (this) is an instance of ImageObserver.

The getImage() method used in Example 13.4 is defined in the Applet class, thus only available with the applet. When writing Java applications, you can load an image by using the getImage() method in the Toolkit class, as shown in the following example.

Example 13.5   Displaying Images in a Frame

This program is the same as the one in the preceding example, except that it uses a frame instead of an applet. The output of a sample run for the program is shown in Figure 13.2.

```
import java.awt.*;
import java.awt.event.*;

public class DisplayImageFrame extends MyFrameWithExitHandling
  implements ActionListener
{
  private ImageCanvas c;
  private TextField tfFilename;
  private Button btShow;

  public static void main(String[] args)
  {
    DisplayImageFrame f = new DisplayImageFrame();
```

continues

Example 13.5   continued

```
            f.setSize(350,250);
            f.setVisible(true);
        }

        public DisplayImageFrame()
        {
          setTitle("Image Demo");

          //create Panel p1 and put in a text field and a button
          Panel p1 = new Panel();
          p1.setLayout(new FlowLayout());
          p1.add(new Label("Filename"));
          p1.add(tfFilename = new TextField(10));
          p1.add(btShow = new Button("Show"));

          //place an ImageCanvas object and p1 in the frame
          setLayout(new BorderLayout());
          add("Center", c = new ImageCanvas());
          add("South", p1);
          c.setBackground(Color.gray);

          btShow.addActionListener(this);
          tfFilename.addActionListener(this);
        }

        //handling the "Show" button
        public void actionPerformed(ActionEvent e)
        {
          if ((e.getSource() instanceof Button) ||
             (e.getSource() instanceof TextField))
             displayImage();
        }

        private void displayImage()
        {
          Toolkit tk = Toolkit.getDefaultToolkit();

          /*get image using the getImage() method from the
            Toolkit class
          */
          Image image = tk.getImage(tfFilename.getText().trim());
          c.showImage(image);
        }
      }
```

Figure 13.2   *The application uses the* Toolkit *class to display an image.*

Example Review

The only important difference between Example 13.4 and Example 13.5 is that they do not get images in the same way. In this example, the program uses the `getImage()` method in the `Toolkit` class. The `Toolkit` class is an abstract class, so the program uses `getDefaultToolkit()` to create a Toolkit instance.

The `getImage()` method used here has a different signature from the one defined in the `Applet` class. You must always give an URL when using the `getImage()` in the `Applet` class.

Displaying a Sequence of Images

In the preceding section, you learned how to display a single image. Now you will learn how to display a sequence of images, which will simulate a movie. You can use a control loop to paint the viewing area with different images continuously. As in the clock example, the loop and the `paint()` method should run on separate threads so that the `paint()` method can execute while the loop controls how the images are drawn. The two images should not be drawn at the same time. The first image should be seen before the next image is drawn.

Example 13.6   Using Image Animation

This example presents a program that will display a sequence of images in order to create a movie. The images are files stored in the `Images` directory that are named **L1.gif**, **L2.gif**, and so on, to **L52.gif**. When you run the program, you will see a label entitled "Learning Java" rotate. Figure 13.3 contains the output of a sample run of the program.

```java
import java.applet.Applet;
import java.awt.*;

public class ImageAnimation extends Applet
  implements Runnable
{
  private Thread imageThread = null;
  private Image imageToDisplay;
  private Image imageArray[]; //hold images
  private int numOfImages = 52, //total number of images
              currentImage = 0, //current image subscript
              sleepTime = 1000/6; //milliseconds to sleep

  //declare suspend for holding thread status
  private boolean suspended = false;

  //load the image, the image files are L1 - L52 in Images directory
  public void init()
  {
    imageArray = new Image[numOfImages];
```

continues

Example 13.6   continued

```java
            for (int i=0; i<imageArray.length; i++ )
            {
              imageArray[i] = getImage(getDocumentBase(),
                "Images/L" + (i+1) + ".gif" );
            }

            //start with the first image
            currentImage = 0;

            imageThread = new Thread(this);
            imageThread.start();
        }

        public void start()
        {
          resume();
        }

        public void stop()
        {
          suspend();
        }

        public synchronized void resume()
        {
          if (suspended)
          {
            suspended = false;
            notify();
          }
        }

        public synchronized void suspend()
        {
          suspended = true;
        }

        public void destroy()
        {
          imageThread = null;
        }

        public void run()
        {
          while (true)
          {
            imageToDisplay = imageArray[currentImage%numOfImages];
            currentImage++;
            repaint();

            try
            {
              imageThread.sleep(sleepTime);
              synchronized (this)
              {
                while (suspended)
                  wait();
              }
            }
```

```
          catch (InterruptedException ex)
          {
          }
      }
  }

  //display an image
  public void paint(Graphics g)
  {
    if (imageToDisplay != null)
      g.drawImage(imageToDisplay, 0, 0, getSize().width,
        getSize().height, this);
  }
}
```

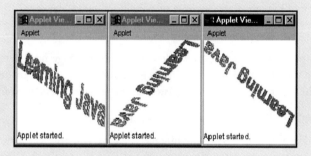

Figure 13.3   *The applet displays a sequence of images.*

Example Review

Fifty-two image files are located in the Images directory, which is a subdirectory of the getDocumentBase() directory. The images in these files are first loaded to imageArray and then are painted continuously on the applet on a separate thread.

The image is drawn to occupy the entire applet viewing area in a rectangle. The image is scaled to fill in the area.

The imageThread for drawing images is created and started in the applet's init() method, and it is suspended in the applet's stop() method. Therefore, the images are not displayed when the browser leaves the applet's page. From then on, the thread releases the CPU time when it is not active. When the applet becomes active again, the imageThread is resumed in the applet's start() method to display images.

You can adjust the sleepTime to control animation speed.

You can add a simple function to suspend a running imageThread with a mouse click. You can resume a suspended imageThread with another click. (See the fourth exercise in the "Programming Exercises" section at the end of this chapter.)

Using *MediaTracker*

One problem you might face if you run the preceding example is that when the images are initially loaded, they are only partially displayed. This occurs because the image has not yet been loaded completely. The problem is particularly annoying when you are downloading the image over a slow modem.

To resolve the problem, Java provides the MediaTracker class to track the status of a number of media objects. Media objects could include audio clips as well as images, though currently only images are supported.

You can use MediaTracker to determine if an image has been completely loaded. To use it, you must first create an instance of MediaTracker for a specific AWT component. The following is an example of creating a MediaTracker:

```
MediaTracker imageTracker = new MediaTracker(this);
```

To enable imageTracker (in order to determine if the image has been loaded), you need to use the addImage() method to register the image with imageTracker. For example, the following statement registers anImage with imageTracker:

```
imageTracker.addImage(Image anImage, int num);
```

The second argument, num, is an integer ID that controls the priority order in which the images are fetched. Images with a lower ID are loaded in preference to those with a higher ID number. The ID can be used to query imageTracker about the status of the registered image. To query, use the checkID() method. For example, the following method returns true if the image with the ID num is completely loaded:

```
checkID(num)
```

Otherwise, it returns false.

You can use the waitForID(num) method to force the program to wait until the image registered with the ID num is completely loaded, or you can use the waitForAll() method to wait for all of the registered images to be loaded completely. The following methods block the program until the image is completely loaded:

```
waitForID(int id) throws InterruptedException
```

```
waitForAll() throws InterruptedException
```

TIP

To track multiple images as a group, you can register them with a media tracker using the same ID.

Example 13.7   Using *MediaTracker*

This example uses `MediaTracker` to improve upon the preceding example. Using `MediaTracker`, the user of this program can ensure that all of the images are fully loaded before they are displayed.

```java
import java.applet.Applet;
import java.awt.*;

public class ImageAnimationUsingMediaTracker
  extends Applet implements Runnable
{
  private Thread imageThread;
  private Image imageToDisplay;
  private Image imageArray[];
  private int numOfImages = 52, //total number of images
              currentImageIndex = 0, //current image subscript
              sleepTime = 1000/6; //milliseconds to sleep
  private MediaTracker imageTracker;

  //declare suspend for holding thread status
  private boolean suspended = false;

  //load the image and register image with imageTracker
  public void init()
  {
    //create an instance of MediaTracker
    imageTracker = new MediaTracker(this);

    //create images
    imageArray = new Image[numOfImages];

    for (int i=0; i<imageArray.length; i++)
    {
      imageArray[i] = getImage(getDocumentBase(),
        "Images/L" + (i+1) + ".gif" );

      //register images with the  imageTracker
      imageTracker.addImage(imageArray[i], i);
    }

    //wait for all the images to be completely loaded
    try
    {
      imageTracker.waitForAll();
    }
    catch (InterruptedException ex)
    {
    }

    //dispose of imageTracker since it is no longer needed
    imageTracker = null;

    imageThread = new Thread(this);
    imageThread.start();
  }

  public void start()
  {
```

continues

Example 13.7   continued

```java
      resume();
    }

    public void stop()
    {
      suspend();
    }

    public synchronized void resume()
    {
      if (suspended)
      {
        suspended = false;
        notify();
      }
    }

    public synchronized void suspend()
    {
      suspended = true;
    }

    public void destroy()
    {
      imageThread = null;
    }

    public void run()
    {
      while (true)
      {
        imageToDisplay = imageArray[currentImageIndex%numOfImages];
        currentImageIndex++;
        repaint();

        try
        {
          imageThread.sleep(sleepTime);
          synchronized (this)
          {
            while  (suspended)
              wait();
          }
        }
        catch (InterruptedException ex)
        {
        }
      }
    }

    public void paint(Graphics g)
    {
      if (imageToDisplay != null)
        g.drawImage(imageToDisplay, 0, 0, getSize().width,
          getSize().height, this );
    }
  }
```

Example Review

The program creates an instance of MediaTracker, imageTracker, and registers images with imageTracker in order to track image loading. The program uses imageTracker to ensure that all of the images are completely loaded before they are displayed.

The waitForAll() method forces the program to wait for all of the images to be loaded before displaying any. Because the program needs to load 52 images, using waitForAll() results in a long delay before images are displayed. You should display something while the image is loaded to keep the user attentive and/or informed. A simple approach is to use the showStatus() method in the Applet class to display some information on the Web browser's status bar, such as the following:

```
showStatus("Please wait while loading images");
```

You should put this statement before the try/catch block for waitForAll() in the program.

The imageTracker object is no longer needed after the images are loaded. The statement imageTracker = null notifies the garbage collector of the Java runtime system to reclaim the memory space previously occupied by the imageTracker object.

Double-Buffering Technique

If you ran the preceding example, you might have observed flickering in the images. In Example 13.3, you learned a simple way to reduce flickering: repainting only the viewing area that has changed. This method is effective if a small part of the viewing area was changed. In this section, you will learn how to use the *double-buffering* technique to reduce flickering in image animation.

With double buffering, you first create a graphics context offscreen. You then draw graphics on the context. Finally, you display the whole context on the real screen. There is no flickering within an image because all of the drawing is done in the background and all of it is displayed at the same time. Double buffering reduces flickering. However, it requires substantial memory and additional processing time to store the image offscreen. Therefore, double buffering could slow the speed of the animation.

To use double buffering, you need to first create an image buffer and then create a graphics context, which is used to draw images. You can draw things on the graphics context. To display the drawing, paste that graphics context on the real screen.

The buffer image is created using the createImage() method in the Component class. Applet is a subclass of Component, so this method can be used in the applet.

The following code creates an offscreen drawable `Image` that has the specified viewing area needed for double buffering:

```
Image bufferImage = createImage(width, height);
```

To get a `Graphics` object that you can draw into the image, you can use the following method:

```
Graphics gContext = bufferImager.getGraphics();
```

NOTE

There are two `getGraphics()` methods in Java; one is defined in the `Component` class, and the other is defined in the `Image` class. The `getGraphics()` method in the `Component` class returns an image that is currently on the screen. Therefore, what you draw on the image is displayed directly on the screen. However, the `getGraphics()` method in the `Image` class will only work for offscreen images.

Example 13.8   Using Double Buffering

This example, which rewrites the preceding example, uses the double-buffering technique to fix animation flickering.

```java
import java.applet.Applet;
import java.awt.*;

public class ImageAnimationUsingDoubleBuffering
    extends Applet implements Runnable
{
  private Thread imageThread = null;
  private Image imageToDisplay;
  private Image imageArray[];
  private int numOfImages = 52, //total number of images
              currentImageIndex = 0, //current image subscript
              sleepTime = 1000/6; //milliseconds to sleep
  private MediaTracker imageTracker;
  private Image bufferImage;
  private Graphics gContext;

  //declare suspend for holding thread status
  private boolean suspended = false;

  //load the image and register image with imageTracker
  public void init()
  {
    //create an instance of MediaTracker
    imageTracker = new MediaTracker(this);

    //create images
    imageArray = new Image[numOfImages];

    for (int i=0; i<imageArray.length; i++)
    {
      imageArray[i] = getImage(getDocumentBase(),
        "Images/L" + (i+1) + ".gif" );
```

```
         //register images with the imageTracker
         imageTracker.addImage(imageArray[i], i);
      }

      //inform the user that images are being loaded
      showStatus("Please wait while loading images");

      //wait for the first image to complete loading
      try
      {
        imageTracker.waitForAll();
      }
      catch (InterruptedException ex)
      {
      }

      //create an image buffer
      bufferImage = createImage(getSize().width, getSize().height);
      gContext = bufferImage.getGraphics();
      gContext.setColor(Color.white);

      imageThread = new Thread(this);
      imageThread.start();
   }


   public void start()
   {
     resume();
   }

   public void stop()
   {
     suspend();
   }

   public synchronized void resume()
   {
     if (suspended)
     {
       suspended = false;
       notify();
     }
   }

   public synchronized void suspend()
   {
     suspended = true;
   }

   public void destroy()
   {
     imageThread = null;
   }

   public void run()
   {
     while (true)
     {
       imageToDisplay = imageArray[currentImageIndex%numOfImages];
       currentImageIndex++;
```

continues

Example 13.8 continued

```
                   //clear image
                   gContext.fillRect(0, 0, getSize().width, getSize().height);

                   //draw image on graphic context
                   gContext.drawImage(imageToDisplay, 0, 0,
                     getSize().width, getSize().height, this);

                   repaint();
                   try
                   {
                     imageThread.sleep(sleepTime);
                     synchronized (this)
                     {
                       while (suspended)
                         wait();
                     }
                   }
                   catch (InterruptedException ex)
                   {
                   }
                 }
               }
             }
```

Example Review

The program creates an image buffer that holds the graphics context, as follows:

```
//create an image buffer
bufferImage = createImage(getSize().width, getSize().height);
gContext = bufferImage.getGraphics();
```

This code creates a graphics object `gContext` on the offscreen image buffer `bufferImage`. You can draw things on the graphics object and store the object that contains the complete drawings in the buffer.

While the current image is being displayed on the real screen, the next image is being built in the buffer offscreen using the following code:

```
gContext.drawImage(imageToDisplay, 0, 0,
          getSize().width, getSize().height, this);
```

Before drawing the next image, the program needs to clear the context in the image. The `fillRect()` method paints the area with the color white, as follows:

```
gContext.fillRect(0, 0, getSize().width, getSize().height);
```

The following statemen in the `paint()` method displays the image on the real screen:

```
g.drawImage(bufferImage, 0, 0,
  getSize().width, getSize().height, this);
```

Chapter Summary

In this chapter, you learned how to play audio and display images in Java multimedia programming. You also learned various animation techniques (overriding the update() method, double buffering, and media tracking) that are used to sharpen and track images.

The multimedia methods are provided in the Applet class. The audio and images files are accessible through an URL. The getDocumentBase() method returns the URL of the HTML file that invokes the applet. The getCodeBase() method returns the URL of the applet.

The applet method getAudioClip() gets an audio file and returns it as an AudioClip instance. You can use the methods play(), loop(), and stop() in the AudioClip class to play, repeatedly play, or stop sound.

You can use getImage() in the Applet class or in the Toolkit class to retrieve an image and return it as an instance of Image. You can then draw the image in a graphics context using the drawImage() method in the Graphics class.

The MediaTracker class is used to determine if one image or all of the images are completely loaded. The MediaTracker obtains this information in order to ensure that the images will be displayed fully.

You learned two approaches to reduce animation flickering. One approach is to override the update() method and repaint part of the viewing area. The other approach is to use double buffering to draw the image offscreen and then paint the entire drawing on the actual viewing area. The former approach is often used for drawing geometric objects in which only a small part of the drawing needs to be repainted. The latter approach is used for drawing graphics images, in which the entire image needs to be repainted.

Chapter Review

1. What types of audio files are used in Java?

2. How do you get an audio file? How do you play, repeatedly play, and stop an audio clip?

3. The getAudioClip() method is defined in the Applet class. If you want to use audio in Java applications, what options do you have?

4. What is the difference between getDocumentBase() and getCodeBase()?

5. What is the difference between the getImage() method in the Applet class and the getImage() method in the Toolkit class?

6. What is the difference between getImage() and createImage()? Where are they defined?

7. Describe the `drawImage()` method.

8. How do you display an offscreen image on the real screen?

9. What is the difference between `getGraphics()` in the `Component` class and `getGraphics()` in the `Image` class?

10. Why do you use `MediaTracker`? How do you add images to a media tracker? How do you know that an image or all of the images are completely loaded? Can you assign images the same ID in order to register them with a media tracker?

11. Describe animation flickering and the techniques used to reduce it.

12. Why would overriding the `update()` method help reduce flickering?

Programming Exercises

1. Write an applet to meet the following requirements:

   ■ Get an audio file from the URL of the HTML base code.

   ■ Place three buttons labeled Play, Loop, and Stop, as shown in Figure 13.4.

   ■ If you click the Play button, the audio file is played once. If you click the Loop button, the audio file keeps playing repeatedly. If you click the Stop button, the play stops.

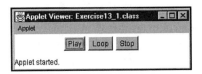

Figure 13.4   *Click Play to play an audio clip once, click Loop to play an audio repeatedly, and click Stop to terminate playing.*

2. Modify the elevator program in the fifth exercise in the "Programming Exercises" section of Chapter 12, using an applet. Add sound to the program. When the elevator goes up, play a sound indicating that it is going up. When the elevator goes down, play a sound indicating that it is going down. And when the elevator stops on a floor, announce which floor the elevator is on.

3. Write an applet to display the temperatures of each hour during the last 24 hours in a histogram. Suppose that the temperatures between 50 and 90 degrees Fahrenheit are obtained randomly and that they are updated every hour. The temperature of the current hour needs to be redisplayed, while others remain unchanged. You should override the `update()` method to repaint the current hour. Use a unique color to highlight the temperature for the current hour (see Figure 13.5).

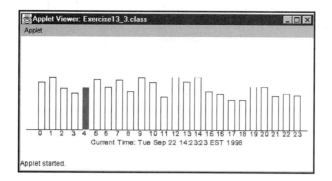

Figure 13.5 *The histogram displays the average temperature of every hour in the last 24 hours.*

4. Rewrite Example 13.8 to add the following new functions:

- The applet gets sleepTime from the HTML <param> tag.

- The animation is suspended when the mouse is clicked and resumed when the mouse is clicked again.

- The applet displays a flashing label to advise the user that the images are being loaded. The label disappears after the images are completely loaded.

- Sound is incorporated into the applet so that it is played while images are displayed.

5. Write an applet that will display a digital clock with a large display panel to show hour, minute, and second. This clock should allow the user to set an alarm. Figure 13.6 shows an example of such a clock. To turn on the alarm, check the Alarm check box. To specify the alarm time, click the "Set alarm" button to display a new frame, as shown in Figure 13.7. You can set the alarm time in the frame.

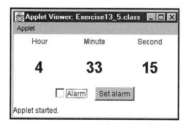

Figure 13.6 *The program displays the current hour, minute, and second and enables you to set an alarm.*

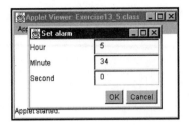

Figure 13.7   *You can set the alarm time by specifying the hour, minute, and second.*

6. Create animation using the applet, as follows:

- Allow the user to specify the animation speed. The user can enter the speed in a text field.

- Get the number of frames and the image filename prefix from the user. For example, if the user enters n for the number of the frames and T for the image prefix, then the files are **T1**, **T2**, and so on, to **Tn**. Assume that the images are stored in the Images directory, a subdirectory of the applet's directory.

- Allow the user to specify an audio filename. The audio file is stored in the same directory as the applet. The sound is played while the animation runs.

7. Write an applet that will display a sequence of images for a single image in different sizes. Initially, the viewing area for this image is of 300 width and 300 height. Your program should continuously shrink the viewing area by 1 in width and 1 in height until the viewing area reaches a width of 50 and a height of 50. At that point, the viewing area should continuously enlarge by 1 in width and 1 in height until it reaches a width of 300 and a height of 300. The viewing area should shrink and enlarge (alternately) to create animation for the single image.

8. Suppose that the instructor asks each student of a Java class to state in a short paragraph his/her personal objectives in taking the Java course. Write an applet to present each student with his or her photo, name, and paragraph (see Figure 13.8) along with audio that reads the paragraph. Your applet should repeatedly present each student, one after another.

Suppose there is a total of 10 students in the class. Assume that the audio files, named **a1.au**, **a2.au**, and so on, up to **a10.au**, are stored in a subdirectory named audio in the applet's directory, and the photo image files named **photo1.gif**, **photo2.gif**, and so on, up to **photo10.gif**, are stored in a subdirectory named photo in the applet's directory. Assume the name and paragraph of each student is passed from HTML. Here is an example for student a1.

```
<param name= "paragraph1"
value="I am taking the class because I want to
```

```
learn to write cool programs like this!">
<param name= "name1", value = "Michael Liang">
```

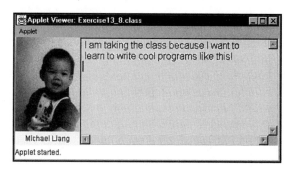

Figure 13.8   *This applet shows each student's photo, name, and paragraph, one after another, and reads the paragraph that is currently shown.*

9. Rewrite the seventh exercise in the "Programming Exercises" section at the end of Chapter 12. Use the double-buffering technique to reduce flickering.

CHAPTER 14

INPUT AND OUTPUT

Objectives

- ◎ Understand input and output streams and learn how to create them.

- ◎ Discover the uses of byte and character streams.

- ◎ Know how to read from or write to external files using file streams.

- ◎ Employ data streams for cross-platform data format compatibility.

- ◎ Identify print streams and use them to output data of primitive types in text format.

- ◎ Know how to parse text files using `StreamTokenizer`.

- ◎ Understand how to use `RandomAccessFile` for both read and write.

- ◎ Use `FileDialog` to open and save files.

- ◎ Become familiar with interactive I/O for input and output on the console.

Introduction

In previous chapters, you used input and output only on the console. In Chapter 2, "Java Building Elements," you created the `MyInput` class and used `MyInput.readInt()` and `MyInput.readDouble()` to receive data from the console. You used `System.out.print()` to display output on the console. In this chapter, you will learn about many other forms of input and output as well as how these methods work.

In Java, all I/Os are handled in streams. A *stream* is an abstraction of the continuous one-way flow of data. Imagine a swimming pool with tubes that connect it to another pool. Let's consider the water in the first pool as the data and the water in the second pool as your program. The flow of water through these tubes is called a *stream*. If you want input, just open the valve to let water out of the data pool and into the program pool. If you want output, just open the valve to let water out of the program pool and into the data pool.

It's a very simple concept, and a very efficient one. Java streams can be applied to any source of data, so a programmer can input from a keyboard or output to a console as easily as that programmer can input from a file or output to a file. Figure 14.1 shows input and output streams between a program and an external file. Java streams are used liberally. You can even have input and output streams between two programs.

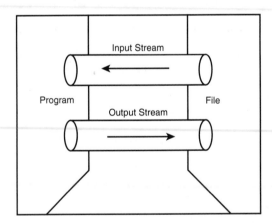

Figure 14.1   *The program receives data through the input stream and sends data through the output stream.*

In general, all streams except the random access file streams flow only in one direction; therefore, if you want to input and output, you need two separate stream objects. In Java, streams can be *layered*—that is, they can be connected to one another in a pipeline fashion. The output of a stream becomes the input of another stream.

This layering capability enables data to be filtered along the pipeline of streams so that you can get data in the desired format. For instance, suppose you want to get integers from an external file. You can use a file input stream to get raw data in binary format, then use a data input stream to extract integers from the output of the input stream.

Streams are objects. Stream objects have methods that read and write data and methods that do other useful things, such as flushing the stream, closing the stream, and counting the number of bytes in the stream.

Stream Classes

Java offers many stream classes for processing all kinds of data. Figures 14.2 and 14.3 show the hierarchical relationship of these classes.

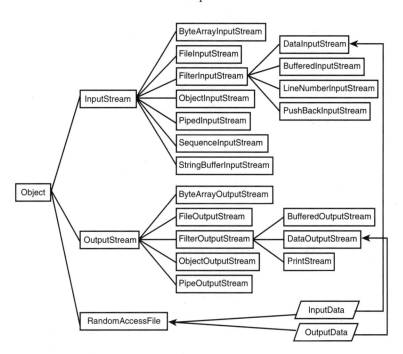

Figure 14.2 *InputStream, OutputStream, RandomAccessFile, and their subclasses deal with streams of bytes.*

The stream classes can be categorized into two types: *byte streams* and *character streams*. The InputStream/OutputStream class is the root of all byte stream classes, and the Reader/Writer class is the root of all character stream classes. The subclasses of InputStream/OutputStream are analogous to the subclasses of Reader/Writer.

Many of these subclasses have similar method signatures, and often you can use these subclasses in the same way. The RandomAccessFile class extends Object and implements the InputData and OutputData interfaces. This class can be used to open a file that allows both reading and writing. The StreamTokenizer class that extends Object can be used for parsing text files.

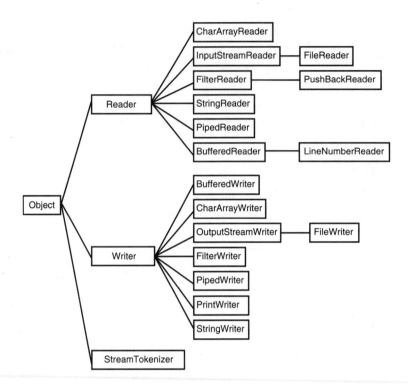

Figure 14.3   *Reader, Writer, StreamTokenizer, and their subclasses are concerned with streams of characters.*

InputStream and Reader

The abstract InputStream and Reader classes, extending Object, are the base classes for all the input streams of bytes and characters, respectively. These classes and their subclasses are very similar, except that InputStream uses bytes for its fundamental unit of information, and Reader uses characters. InputStream and Reader have many common methods that have identical signatures. These methods have similar functionality, but InputStream is designed to read bytes, and Reader is designed to read characters.

The following methods, which are defined in InputStream, are often useful. The following method reads the next byte and returns its value:

```
public abstract int read() throws IOException
```

The value of the byte is returned as an int that is in the range from 0 to 255. At the end of the stream, it returns -1. This method blocks the program from executing until input data is available, the end of the stream is detected, or an exception is thrown. A subclass of InputStream must provide an implementation of this method.

The following method reads b.length bytes into array b, returns b.length if the number of available bytes is more than b.length, returns the number of bytes read if the number of available bytes is less than b.length, and returns –1 at the end of the stream:

```
public int read(byte[] b) throws IOException
```

The following method closes the input stream:

```
public void close() throws IOException
```

The following method returns the number of bytes that can be read from this input stream without blocking:

```
public void int available() throws IOException
```

The following method skips over and discards n bytes of data from this input stream. The actual number of bytes skipped is returned:

```
public long skip(long n) throws IOException
```

NOTE

The read() method reads a byte from the stream. If no data is available, it blocks the program from executing the next statement. The program just sits there waiting for the read() method to finish.

The Reader class contains all of the methods listed previously except available(). These methods have the same functionality in Reader as they do in InputStream, but they are subject to character stream interpretation. For example, read() returns an integer that is in the range from 0 to 16,383, which represents a Unicode character.

OutputStream and Writer

Like InputStream and Reader, OutputStream and Writer are counterparts. They are the base classes for all output streams of bytes and characters, respectively. The following instance methods are in both OutputStream and Writer. The following method writes a byte (for OutputStream) or a character (for Writer):

```
public abstract void write(int b) throws IOException
```

The following method writes all bytes in the array b to the output stream (for OutputStream) or characters in the array of characters (for Writer):

```
void write(byte[] b) throws IOException
```

The following method closes the output stream:

```
public void close() throws IOException
```

The following method flushes the output stream (that is, it sends any buffered data in the stream to its destination):

```
public void flush() throws IOException
```

NOTE

In JDK 1.02, the methods in OutputStream do not throw exceptions. But all the methods in the OutputStream class throw IOException in JDK 1.1 and JDK 1.2.

Processing External Files

You must use file streams to read from or write to a disk file. You can use FileInputStream or FileOutputStream for byte streams, and you can use FileReader or FileWriter for character streams. To create a file stream, you can use the following constructors:

```
public FileInputStream(String fileNameString)

public FileOutputStream(String fileNameString)

public FileReader(String fileNameString)

public FileWriter(String fileNameString)
```

For example, the following statements create infile and outfile streams for the input file **in.dat** and the output file **out.dat**, respectively:

```
FileInputStream infile = new FileInputStream("in.dat");
FileOutputStream outfile = new FileOutputStream("out.dat");
```

Note that whenever a filename or a path is used, it is assumed that the host's filenaming conventions are used. For example, a filename with a path on Windows could be **c:\data\in.dat**. If it had a path on UNIX, the same file might be **/username/data/in.dat**.

You can also use a file object to construct a file stream. For example, see the following statement:

```
FileInputStream infile = new FileInputStream(new File("in.dat"));
```

The File class is intended to provide an abstraction that deals with most of the machine-dependent complexities of files and path names in a machine-independent fashion.

An abstract method, such as read(byte b) in InputStream, is implemented in FileInputStream, and the abstract write(int b) method in the OutputStream class is implemented in FileOutputStream.

Example 14.1   Processing External Files

This example gives a program that uses FileInputStream and FileOutputStream to copy files. The user needs to provide a source file and a target file as command-line arguments. The program copies the source file to the target file and displays the number of bytes in the file. The output of the sample run for the program is shown in Figure 14.4.

```java
import java.io.*;

public class CopyFileUsingByteStream
{
  public static void main(String[] args)
  {
    //declare input and output file streams
    FileInputStream fis = null;
    FileOutputStream fos = null;

    //check usage
    if (args.length !=2)
    {
      System.out.println(
        "Usage: java CopyFileUsingByteStream fromfile tofile");
      System.exit(0);
    }

    try
    {
      //create file input stream
      fis = new FileInputStream(new File(args[0]));

      //create file output stream if the file does not exist
      File outFile = new File(args[1]);
      if (outFile.exists())
      {
        System.out.println("file "+args[1]+" already exists");
        return;
      }
      else
        fos = new FileOutputStream(args[1]);

      System.out.println("The file "+args[0]+" has "+
        fis.available()+" bytes");

      int r;
      //continuously read a byte from fis and write it to fos
      while ((r = fis.read()) != -1)
        fos.write((byte)r);
    }
    catch (FileNotFoundException ex)
    {
      System.out.println("File not found: "+args[0]);
    }
    catch (IOException ex)
    {
      System.out.println(ex.getMessage());
    }
    finally
    {
      try
      {
        //close files
        if (fis != null) fis.close();
        if (fos != null) fos.close();
      }
```

continues

Example 14.1   continued

```
          catch (IOException ex)
          {
          }
        }
      }
   }
```

Figure 14.4   *The program copies a file using byte streams.*

Example Review

The program creates the `fis` and `fos` streams for the input file `args[0]` and the output file `args[1]` (see Figure 14.5).

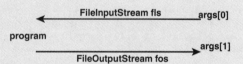

Figure 14.5   *The program uses `FileInputStream` to read data from the file and `FileOutputStream` to write data to the file.*

If the input file `args[0]` does not exist, new `FileInputStream(new File(args[0]))` will raise the exception `FileNotFoundException`. By contrast, new `FileOutputStream(new File(args[1]))` will always create a file output stream, whether or not the file `args[1]` exists.

To avoid writing in an existing file, the program uses the `exists()` method in the `File` class to determine whether `args[1]` exists. If the file already exists, the user should be notified; otherwise, the file should be created.

The program continuously reads a byte from the `fis` stream and sends it to the `fos` stream until all the bytes have been read. (The condition (`fis.read()` == -1) signifies the end of a file.)

The program closes any open file streams in the `finally` clause. The statements in the `finally` clause are always executed, whether or not exceptions occur.

The program could be rewritten using `FileReader` and `FileWriter`. The new program would be almost exactly the same. (See the first exercise in the "Programming Exercises" section at the end of this chapter.)

 TIP

Always close the files when they are not needed. In some cases, it would cause programming errors if they were not closed. Files are usually closed in the `finally` clause.

Array Streams

Streams were first used for file input/output in the C language; however, Java streams are not limited to this function. You can use array streams to read and write bytes or characters from arrays. These streams include `ByteArrayInputStream`, `CharArrayReader`, `ByteArrayOutputStream`, and `CharArrayWriter`. You can use the following constructors to create array streams:

```
public ByteArrayInputStream(byte[] byteArray)

public ByteArrayOutputStream(byte[] byteArray)

public ByteArrayReader(char[] byteArray)

public ByteArrayWriter(char[] byteArray)
```

For example, the following statements create the byte array input stream `bai` and the character array read stream `car`.

```
byte[] bArray = new byte[2048];
char[] cArray = new char[2048];
ByteArrayInputStream bai = new ByteArrayInputStream(bArray);
ByteArrayReader car = new ByteArrayReader(cArray);
```

You could now process the streams just as you would process file streams. For example, `bai.read()` reads a byte, and `car.read()` reads a character from the array streams.

Filter Streams

Filter streams are defined as streams that filter bytes or characters for some purpose. The basic input stream provides a read method that can only be used for reading bytes or characters. If you want to read integers, doubles, or strings, you can use a filter class to wrap an input stream. Using a filter class enables you to read integers, doubles, and strings instead of bytes and characters.

When you need to process primitive numeric types in JDK 1.1, you should use `FilterInputStream` and `FilterOutputStream` to filter bytes. You should use

BufferedReader and PushbackReader to filter characters when you need to process strings. FilterInputStream and FilterOutputStream are abstract classes; their subclasses (which are listed in Table 14.1 and Table 14.2) are often used.

TABLE 14.1 *FilterInputStream* Subclasses

Subclass	Class Usage
DataInputStream	Handles binary formats of all the primitive data types.
BufferedInputStream	Gets data from the buffer and then reads it from the stream if necessary.
LineNumberInputStream	Keeps track of how many lines are read.
PushbackInputStream	Allows single-byte look-ahead. After the byte is looked at, the byte is pushed back to the stream so that the next read method can read it.

TABLE 14.2 *FilterOutputStream* Subclasses

Subclass	Class Usage
DataOutputStream	Outputs the binary format of all the primitive types, which is useful if another program uses the output.
BufferedOutputStream	Outputs to the buffer first and then outputs to the stream if necessary. Programmers can also call the flush() method to write the buffer to the stream.
PrintStream	Outputs the Unicode format of all the primitive types, which is useful if the format is output to the console.

Data Streams

The data streams (DataInputStream and DataOutputStream) read and write Java primitive types in a machine-independent fashion, which enables you to write a data file on one machine and read it on another machine that has a different operating system or file structure.

DataInputStream extends FilterInputStream and implements the DataInput interface. DataOutputStream extends FilterOutputStream and implements the DataOutput interface. The DataInput and DataOutput interfaces are also implemented by the RandomAccessFile class, which is discussed in the section "Random Access Files," later in this chapter.

The following methods are defined in the DataInput interface:

```
public int readByte() throws IOException

public int readShort() throws IOException
```

```
public int readInt() throws IOException

public int readLong() throws IOException

public float readFloat() throws IOException

public double readDouble() throws IOException

public char readChar() throws IOException

public boolean readBoolean() throws IOException

public String readUTF() throws IOException
```

The following methods are defined in the DataOutput interface:

```
public void writeByte(byte b) throws IOException

public void writeShort(short s) throws IOException

public void writeInt(int i) throws IOException

public void writeLong(long l) throws IOException

public void writeFloat(float f) throws IOException

public void writeDouble(double d) throws IOException

public void writeChar(char c) throws IOException

public void writeBoolean(boolean b) throws IOException

public void writeBytes(String l) throws IOException

public void writeChars(String l) throws IOException

public void writeUTF(String l) throws IOException
```

The data streams are often used as wrappers on existing input and output streams to filter data in the original stream.

The data I/O stream constructors are the following:

```
public DataInputStream(InputStream instream)

public DataOutputStream(OutputStream outstream)
```

For example, the following statements create data streams. The first statement creates an input file for **in.dat**; the second statement creates an output file for **out.dat**.

```
DataInputStream infile =
  new DataInputStream(new FileInputStream("in.dat"));
DataOutputStream outfile =
  new DataOutputStream(new FileOutputStream("out.dat"));
```

Example 14.2   Using Data Streams

This example presents a program that creates 10 random integers, stores them in a data file, retrieves data from the file, and then displays the integers on the console. Figure 14.6 contains the output of a sample run of the program.

The program uses a temporary file to store data. The temporary file is named **mytemp.dat**.

```java
import java.io.*;

public class TestDataStreams
{
  public static void main(String[] args)
  {
    //declare data input and output streams
    DataInputStream dis = null;
    DataOutputStream dos = null;

    //construct a temp file
    File tempFile = new File("mytemp.dat");

    //check if the temp file exists
    if (tempFile.exists())
    {
      System.out.println("The file mytemp.dat already exists,"
        +" delete it, rerun the program");
      System.exit(0);
    }

    //write data
    try
    {
      //create data output stream for tempFile
      dos = new DataOutputStream(new
        FileOutputStream(tempFile));
      for (int i=0; i<10; i++)
        dos.writeInt((int)(Math.random()*1000));
    }
    catch (IOException ex)
    {
      System.out.println(ex.getMessage());
    }
    finally
    {
      try
      {
        //close files
        if (dos != null) dos.close();
      }
      catch (IOException ex)
      {
      }
    }

    //read data
    try
    {
      //create data input stream
      dis = new DataInputStream(new FileInputStream(tempFile));
```

```
        for (int i=0; i<10; i++)
          System.out.print("  "+dis.readInt());
      }
      catch (FileNotFoundException ex)
      {
        System.out.println("File not found");
      }
      catch (IOException ex)
      {
        System.out.println(ex.getMessage());
      }
      finally
      {
        try
        {
          //close files
          if (dis != null) dis.close();
        }
        catch (IOException ex)
        {
        }
      }
    }
  }
```

Figure 14.6 *The program creates 10 random numbers and stores them in a file named **mytemp.dat**. It then reads the data from the file and displays it on the console.*

Example Review

The program creates a `DataInputStream` object dis wrapped on `FileInputStream` and creates a `DataOutputStream` object dos wrapped on `FileOutputStream` (see Figure 14.7).

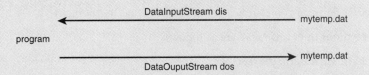

Figure 14.7 *The program uses `DataOutputStream` to write data to a file and `DataInputStream` to read the data from the file.*

continues

473

Example 14.2   continued

The program first creates **mytemp.dat** if it does not already exist. It then writes 10 random integers into **mytemp.dat** using the data output stream and then it closes the stream.

The program creates a data input stream for **mytemp.dat**, reads integers from it, and displays it.

■ NOTE

The data stored in **mytemp.dat** is in binary format, which is machine-independent and portable. If you need to transport data between different systems, you should use data input and data output streams.

Print Streams

The data output stream outputs a binary representation of data, so you cannot view its contents as text. As shown in Figure 14.6, when you attempt to view the **mytemp.dat** file on the console, strange symbols are displayed. In Java, you can use print streams to output data into files. These files can be viewed as text.

The PrintStream and PrintWriter classes provide this functionality. You have already used System.out.println() to display data on the console. An instance of PrintStream, out, is defined in the java.lang.System class. PrintStream and PrintWriter have similar method interfaces. PrintStream has been deprecated in JDK 1.1, but the System.out standard output stream has not been; therefore, you can continue to use it for output to the console.

The constructors for PrintWriter are the following:

```
public PrintWriter(Writer out)

public PrintWriter(Writer out, boolean autoFlush)

public PrintWriter(OutputStream out)

public PrintWriter(OutputStream out, boolean autoFlush)
```

The methods in PrintWriter are as follows:

```
public void print(Object o)

public void print(String s)

public void print(char c)

public void print(char[] cArray)

public void print(int i)
```

```
public void print(long l)

public void print(float f)

public void print(double d)

public void print(boolean b)
```

You can replace print with println. The println() method, which prints the object, is followed by a new line. When an object is passed to print() or println(), the object's toString() method converts it to a String object.

Example 14.3   Using Print Streams

The program in this example creates 10 random integers and stores them in a text data file. The file can be viewed on the console by using an OS command, such as type on Windows or cat on UNIX. Figure 14.8 contains the output of a sample run of the program.

```
import java.io.*;

public class TestPrintWriters
{
  public static void main(String[] args)
  {
    //declare print stream
    PrintWriter pw = null;

    //check usage
    if (args.length != 1)
    {
      System.out.println("Usage: java TestPrintWriters file");
      System.exit(0);
    }

    File tempFile = new File(args[0]);

    if (tempFile.exists())
    {
      System.out.println("The file " + args[0] +
        " already exists, delete it, rerun the program");
      System.exit(0);
    }

    //write data
    try
    {
      //create data output stream for tempFile
      pw = new PrintWriter(new FileOutputStream(tempFile), true);
      for (int i=0; i<10; i++)
        pw.print(" "+(int)(Math.random()*1000));
    }
    catch (IOException ex)
    {
      System.out.println(ex.getMessage());
    }
```

continues

475

Example 14.3   continued

```
        finally
        {
          //close files
          if (pw != null) pw.close();
        }
      }
    }
```

C:\book>java TestPrintWriters t.dat
The file t.dat already exists, delete it, rerun the program

C:\book>del t.dat

C:\book>java TestPrintWriters t.dat

C:\book>type t.dat
496 989 619 763 149 932 359 684 444 860
C:\book>

Figure 14.8   *The program creates 10 random numbers and stores them in a text file.*

Example Review

The program creates a print stream pw of `PrintWriter`—which is wrapped in `FileOutputStream`—for output data, which is in text format (see Figure 14.9).

program ————————————▸ args[0]
         PrintWriter   FileOutputStream

Figure 14.9   *The program uses the `PrintWriter` stream, which is wrapped in `FileOutputStream`, to write data in text format.*

The program first creates the file **args[0]** if that file does not already exist. It then writes 10 random integers into **args[0]** by using the data output stream; the program then closes the stream.

The output in **args[0]** is in text format. The data can be seen using the type command in DOS.

Buffered Streams

Java introduces buffered streams that speed input and output by reducing the number of reads and writes. The buffered streams employ a buffered array of bytes or characters that acts as a cache. In the case of input, the array reads a chunk of bytes or characters into the buffer before these individual bytes or characters are read. In the case of output, the array accumulates a block of bytes or characters before writing the entire block to the output stream.

By using buffered streams, you can read and write a chunk of bytes or characters at a time instead of reading or writing a single byte or character at a time. The `BufferedInputStream`, `BufferedOutputStream`, `BufferedReader`, and `BufferedWriter` classes provide this functionality.

You can use the following constructors to create a buffered stream:

```
public BufferedInputStream(InputStream in)

public BufferedInputStream(InputStream in, int bufferSize)

public BufferedOutputStream(OutputStream in)

public BufferedOutputStream(OutputStream in, int bufferSize)

public BufferedReader(Reader in)

public BufferedReader(Reader in, int bufferSize)

public BufferedWriter(Writer out)

public BufferedWriter(Writer out, int bufferSize)
```

If no buffer size is specified, the default size is 512 bytes or characters. A buffered input stream reads as much data into its buffer as possible in a single read call. By contrast, a buffered output stream calls the write method only when its buffer fills up or when the `flush()` method is called.

The buffered stream classes inherit methods from their superclasses. In addition to using the methods from their superclasses, `BufferedReader` has a `readLine()` method to read a line.

Example 14.4   Displaying a File in a Text Area

This example presents a program that views a file in a text area. The user enters a filename in a text field and clicks the View button; the file is then displayed in a text area. Figure 14.10 contains the output of a sample run of the program.

```java
import java.awt.*;
import java.awt.event.*;
import java.io.*;

public class ViewFile extends MyFrameWithExitHandling
  implements ActionListener
{
  private Button btView;
  private TextField tf; //text field to receive file name
  private TextArea ta; //text area to store file

  public static void main(String[] args)
  {
    ViewFile f = new ViewFile();
    f.setSize(400,300);
    f.setVisible(true);
  }
```

continues

Example 14.4   continued

```java
public ViewFile()
{
  setTitle("View File");

  //create a Panel to hold a label, a text field, and a button
  Panel p = new Panel();
  p.setLayout(new FlowLayout());
  p.add(new Label("Filename"));
  p.add(tf = new TextField(" ",12));
  tf.setBackground(Color.yellow);
  tf.setForeground(Color.red);
  p.add(btView = new Button("View"));

  //using BorderLayout for the frame
  setLayout(new BorderLayout());
  add("Center",ta = new TextArea());
  add("South",p);
  ta.setBackground(Color.yellow);
  ta.setForeground(Color.black);

  //register listener
  btView.addActionListener(this);
}

//handling the "View" button
public void actionPerformed(ActionEvent e)
{
  String actionCommand = e.getActionCommand();
  if (e.getSource() instanceof Button)
    if ("View".equals(actionCommand))
      showFile();
}

private void showFile()
{
  BufferedReader infile = null;  //declare buffered stream
  //get file name from the text field
  String filename = tf.getText().trim();
  String inLine;

  try
  {
    //create a buffered stream
    infile = new BufferedReader(new FileReader(filename));

    //read a line
    inLine = infile.readLine();

    boolean firstLine = true;

    //append the line to the text area
    while (inLine != null)
    {
      if (firstLine)
      {
        firstLine = false;
        ta.append(inLine);
      }
      else
      {
        ta.append("\n"+inLine);
```

```
        }
      inLine = infile.readLine();
    }
  }
  catch (FileNotFoundException ex)
  {
    System.out.println("File not found: "+filename);
  }
  catch (IOException ex)
  {
    System.out.println(ex.getMessage());
  }
  finally
  {
    try
    {
      if (infile != null) infile.close();
    }
    catch (IOException ex)
    {
    }
  }
  }
}
```

Figure 14.10   *The program displays the specified file in the text area.*

Example Review

The user enters a filename into the Filename text field. When the View button is pressed, the program gets the input filename from the text field; it then creates a data input stream. The data is read one line at a time and appended to the text area for display.

The program uses a `BufferedReader` stream to read lines from a buffer. Instead of using `BufferedReader` and `Reader` classes, the `BufferedInputStream` and `FileInputStream` can also be used in this example.

You are encouraged to rewrite the program without using buffers and then compare the performance of the two programs. You will see the performance improvement of using buffers when reading from a large file.

TIP

Typical physical input and output involving I/O devices are extremely slow compared with the CPU processing speeds, so you should use buffered input/output streams to improve performance.

Parsing Text Files

Occasionally you need to process a text file. For example, the Java source file is a text file. The compiler reads the source file and translates it into bytecode, which is a binary file. Java provides the StreamTokenizer class so that you can take an input stream and parse it into words, which are known as *tokens*. The tokens are read one at a time.

To construct an instance of StreamTokenizer, you can use StreamTokenizer(Reader is) on a given character input stream. The StreamTokenizer class contains useful constants, which are listed in the Table 14.3.

TABLE 14.3   *StreamTokenizer* Constants

Constant	Description
TT_WORD	The token is a word.
TT_NUMBER	The token is a number.
TT_EOL	The end of the line has been read.
TT_EOF	The end of the file has been read.

The StreamTokenizer class also contains some useful variables, which are listed in Table 14.4.

TABLE 14.4   *StreamTokenizer* Variables

Variable	Description
int ttype	Contains the current token type, which matches one of the constants listed previously.
double nval	Contains the value of the current token if that token is a number.
String sval	Contains a string that gives the characters of the current token if that token is a word.

Typically, you can use the nextToken() method to retrieve tokens one by one in a loop until TT_EOF is returned. The following method parses the next token from the input stream of a StreamTokenizer:

```
public int nextToken() throws IOException
```

The type of the next token is returned in the ttype field. If ttype == TT_WORD, the token is stored in sval; if ttype == TT_NUMBER, the token is stored in nval.

Example 14.5   Using *StreamTokenizer*

The program in this example demonstrates parsing text files. The program reads a text file containing students' exam scores. Each record in the input file consists of a student's name, two midterm exam scores, and a final exam score. The program reads the fields for each record and computes the total score. It then stores the result in a new file. The formula for computing the total score is the following:

```
total score = midterm1*30% + midterm2*30% + final*40%;
```

Each record in the output file consists of a student's name and his or her total score. Figure 14.11 contains the output of a sample run of the program.

```java
import java.io.*;

public class ParsingTextFile
{
  public static void main(String[] args)
  {
    //declare file reader and writer streams
    FileReader frs = null;
    FileWriter fws = null;

    //declare streamTokenizer
    StreamTokenizer in = null;

    //declare a print stream
    PrintWriter out = null;

    /*for input file fields: student name, midterm1,
      midterm2, and final exam score
    */
    String sname = null;
    double midterm1 = 0;
    double midterm2 = 0;
    double finalScore = 0;

    //computed totalscore
    double total = 0;

    try
    {
      //create file input and output streams
      frs = new FileReader("in.dat");
      fws = new FileWriter("out.dat");

      //create a stream tokenizer wrapping file input stream
      in = new StreamTokenizer(frs);
      out = new PrintWriter(fws);

      //read first token
      in.nextToken();

      //process a record
      while (in.ttype != in.TT_EOF)
      {
        //get student name
```

continues

Example 14.5   continued

```
        if (in.ttype == in.TT_WORD)
          sname = in.sval;
        else
          System.out.println("Bad file format");

        //get midterm1
        if (in.nextToken() == in.TT_NUMBER)
          midterm1 = in.nval;
        else
          System.out.println("Bad file format");

        //get midterm2
        if (in.nextToken() == in.TT_NUMBER)
          midterm2 = in.nval;
        else
          System.out.println("Bad file format");

        //get final score
        if (in.nextToken() == in.TT_NUMBER)
          finalScore = in.nval;

        total = midterm1*0.3 + midterm2*0.3 + finalScore*0.4;
        out.println(sname + " " +total);

        in.nextToken();
      }
    }
    catch (FileNotFoundException ex)
    {
      System.out.println("File not found: in.dat");
    }
    catch (IOException ex)
    {
      System.out.println(ex.getMessage());
    }
    finally
    {
      try
      {
        if (frs != null) frs.close();
        if (fws != null) fws.close();
      }
      catch (IOException ex)
      {
      }
    }
  }
}
```

Example Review

Before running this program, make sure you have created the text file **in.dat**. To parse the text file **in.dat**, the program uses StreamTokenizer to wrap a FileReader stream. The nextToken() method is used on a StreamTokenizer object to get one token at a time. The token value is stored in the nval field if the token is numeric, and it is stored in the sval field if the token is a string. The token type is stored in the ttype field.

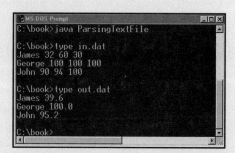

Figure 14.11   *The program uses* StreamTokenizer *to parse the text file into strings and numbers.*

For each record, the program reads the name and the three exam scores and then computes the total score. A FileWriter stream is then used to store the name and the total score in the text file **out.dat** (see Figure 14.12).

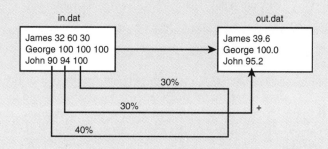

Figure 14.12   *The program reads two midterm scores and a final exam score and then computes a total score.*

Random Access Files

All the streams you have used so far are known as *read-only* or *write-only* streams. The external files of these streams are sequential files that cannot be updated without creating a new file. It is often necessary to modify files or to insert new records into the files. For this reason, Java provides the RandomAccessFile class to allow a file to be read and updated at the same time.

The RandomAccessFile class extends Object and implements DataInput and DataOutput interfaces. Because DataInputStream implements the DataInput interface and DataOutputStream implements the DataOutput interface, many methods in RandomAccessFile are the same as those in DataInputStream and DataOutputStream. For example, readInt(), readLong(), readDouble(), readUTF(), writeInt(), writeLong(), writeDouble(), and writeUTF() can be used in data input streams or data output streams as well as in RandomAccessFile streams.

Additionally, `RandomAccessFile` provides the following methods to deal with random access.

The following method sets the offset from the beginning of the `RandomAccessFile` stream to where the next read or write occurs:

```
public void seek(long pos) throws IOException
```

The following method returns the current offset, in bytes, from the beginning of the file to where the next read or write occurs:

```
public long getFilePointer() throws IOException
```

The following method returns the length of the file:

```
public long length() throws IOException
```

The following method writes a character to the file as a two-byte Unicode, with the high byte written first:

```
public final void writeChar(int v) throws IOException
```

The following method writes a string to the file as a sequence of characters:

```
public final void writeChars(String s) throws IOException
```

When creating a `RandomAccessFile` stream, you can specify one of the two modes (`"r"` or `"rw"`). The mode `"r"` means that the stream is read-only, and the mode `"rw"` indicates that the stream allows both read and write. For example, the following statement creates a new stream `raf` that allows the program to read from and write to the file **test.dat**:

```
RandomAccessFile raf = new RandomAccessFile("test.dat", "rw");
```

If **test.dat** already exists, `raf` is created to access **test.dat**; if **test.dat** does not exist, a new file named **test.dat** is created, and `raf` is created to access the new file. The method `raf.length()` indicates the number of bytes in **test.dat** at any given time. If you append new data into the file, `raf.length()` increases.

NOTE
When you use `writeChar()` to write a character or use `writeChars()` to write characters, a character occupies two bytes.

TIP
You should open the file with the `"r"` mode if the file is not intended to be modified. This prevents unintentional modification of the file.

Random access files are often used to process files of records. For convenience, fixed-length records are used in random access files so that a record can be located easily. A record consists of a fixed number of fields. A field can be a string or a primitive data type. A string in a fixed-length record has a maximum size. If a string size is smaller than the maximum size, the rest of the string is padded with blanks.

Example 14.6 Using Random Access Files

This example presents a program that registers students and displays student information. The program starts with two buttons, Register Students and View Students, which are displayed in a frame (see Figure 14.13). If the user clicks the Register Students button, a new frame opens that is used to enter student information, as shown in Figure 14.14. If the user clicks the View Students button, another frame opens that enables the user to browse through student information (see Figure 14.15).

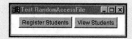

Figure 14.13 *The main frame contains the Register Students and View Students buttons.*

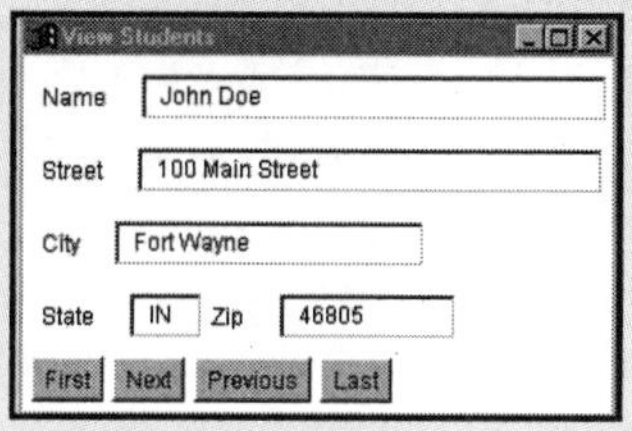

Figure 14.14 *The Register Students frame enables the user to register a student.*

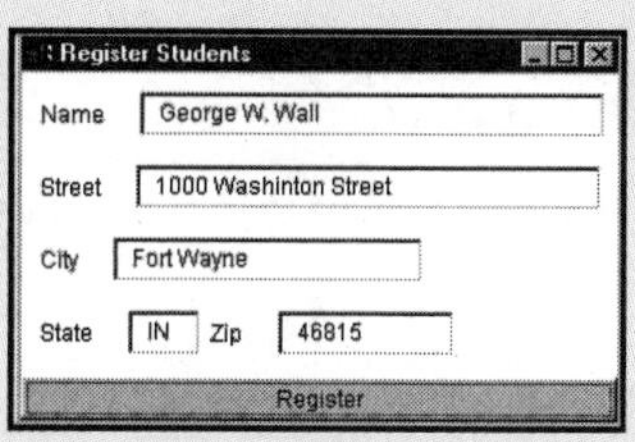

Figure 14.15 *The View Students frame displays student information.*

The program is presented in the following code and its sample run is shown in Figures 14.13, 14.14, and 14.15.

```
import java.io.*;
import java.awt.*;
import java.awt.event.*;

public class TestRandomAccessFile
  extends MyFrameWithExitHandling implements ActionListener
{
  private Button btRegister, btView;
  private RandomAccessFile raf;
```

continues

Example 14.6   continued

```java
        public static void main(String[] args)
        {
          TestRandomAccessFile f = new TestRandomAccessFile();
          f.pack();
          f.setVisible(true);
        }

        public TestRandomAccessFile()
        {
          setTitle("Test RandomAccessFile");

          //place buttons in the frame
          setLayout(new FlowLayout());
          add(btRegister = new Button("Register Students"));
          add(btView = new Button("View Students"));

          //register listener for buttons
          btRegister.addActionListener(this);
          btView.addActionListener(this);

          try
          {
            raf = new RandomAccessFile("student.dat", "rw");
          }
          catch(IOException ex)
          {
            System.out.print("Error: " + ex);
            System.exit(0);
          }
        }

        public void actionPerformed(ActionEvent evt)
        {
          String actionCommand = evt.getActionCommand();
          if (evt.getSource() instanceof Button)
          {
            if ("Register Students".equals(actionCommand))
            {
              //start a new frame for registering students
              RegisterStudent registrationFrame =
                new RegisterStudent(raf);
              registrationFrame.setSize(350,250);
              registrationFrame.setVisible(true);
            }
            else if ("View Students".equals(actionCommand))
            {
              //start a new frame for viewing students
              ViewStudent viewFrame = new ViewStudent(raf);
              viewFrame.setSize(350,250);
              viewFrame.setVisible(true);
            }
          }
        }
      }

      class RegisterStudent extends MyFrameWithHideHandling
        implements ActionListener
      {
        private Button btRegister;
```

```
      private InformationPanel registerPanel;
      private RandomAccessFile raf;

      public RegisterStudent(RandomAccessFile raf)
      {
        this.raf = raf;

        setTitle("Register Students");
        setLayout(new BorderLayout());

        //add components in the frame
        add("Center",registerPanel = new InformationPanel());
        add("South", btRegister = new Button("Register"));

        //register listener
        btRegister.addActionListener(this);
      }

      public void actionPerformed(ActionEvent evt)
      {
        String actionCommand = evt.getActionCommand();
        if (evt.getSource() instanceof Button)
        {
          if ("Register".equals(actionCommand))
          {
            Student s = registerPanel.getStudent();

            try
            {
              raf.seek(raf.length());
              s.writeStudent(raf);
            }
            catch(IOException ex)
            {
              System.out.print("Error: " + ex);
            }
          }
        }
      }
    }

class ViewStudent extends MyFrameWithHideHandling
  implements ActionListener
{
  private Button btFirst, btNext, btPrevious, btLast;
  private RandomAccessFile raf = null;
  private long lastPos;
  private Student s = new Student();
  private long currentPos;
  private InformationPanel viewPanel;

  public ViewStudent(RandomAccessFile raf)
  {
    this.raf = raf;

    setTitle("View Students");
    setLayout(new BorderLayout());

    viewPanel = new InformationPanel();
```

continues

Example 14.6   continued

```java
        Panel p = new Panel();
        p.setLayout(new FlowLayout(FlowLayout.LEFT));
        p.add(btFirst = new Button("First"));
        p.add(btNext = new Button("Next"));
        p.add(btPrevious = new Button("Previous"));
        p.add(btLast = new Button("Last"));

        add("Center",viewPanel);
        add("South",p);

        btFirst.addActionListener(this);
        btNext.addActionListener(this);
        btPrevious.addActionListener(this);
        btLast.addActionListener(this);
    }

    public void actionPerformed(ActionEvent evt)
    {
      String actionCommand = evt.getActionCommand();
      if (evt.getSource() instanceof Button)
      {
        if ("First".equals(actionCommand))
        {
          try
          {
            if (raf.length() > 0)
              retrieve(0);
          }
          catch(IOException ex)
          {
            System.out.print("Error: " + ex);
          }
        }
        else if ("Next".equals(actionCommand))
        {
          try
          {
            currentPos = raf.getFilePointer();
            if (currentPos < raf.length())
              retrieve(currentPos);
          }
          catch(IOException ex)
          {
            System.out.print("Error: " + ex);
          }
        }
        else if ("Previous".equals(actionCommand))
        {
          try
          {
            currentPos = raf.getFilePointer();
            if (currentPos > 0)
              retrieve(currentPos - 2*2*Student.RECORD_SIZE);
          }
          catch(IOException ex)
          {
            System.out.print("Error: " + ex); }
          }
        else if ("Last".equals(actionCommand))
```

```
        {
          try
          {
            lastPos = raf.length();
            if (lastPos > 0)
              retrieve(lastPos - 2*Student.RECORD_SIZE);
          }
          catch(IOException ex)
          {
            System.out.print("Error: " + ex);
          }
        }
      }
    }

    //retrieve a record at specified position
    public void retrieve(long pos)
    {
      try
      {
        raf.seek(pos);
        s.readStudent(raf);
        viewPanel.setStudent(s);
      }
      catch(IOException ex)
      {
        System.out.print("Error: " + ex);
      }
    }
}

class Student
{
  private String name;
  private String street;
  private String city;
  private String state;
  private String zip;

  //the size of five string fields in the record
  final static int NAME_SIZE = 32;
  final static int STREET_SIZE = 32;
  final static int CITY_SIZE = 20;
  final static int STATE_SIZE = 2;
  final static int ZIP_SIZE = 5;

  /*the total size of the record in bytes, a Unicode
    character is 2 bytes size.*/
  final static int RECORD_SIZE =
    (NAME_SIZE + STREET_SIZE + CITY_SIZE + STATE_SIZE + ZIP_SIZE);

  Student()
  {
  }

  Student(String name, String street, String city,
          String state, String zip  )
  {
    this.name = name;
    this.street = street;
```

continues

489

Example 14.6   continued

```java
        this.city = city;
        this.state = state;
        this.zip = zip;
    }

    public String getName()
    {
      return name;
    }

    public String getStreet()
    {
      return street;
    }

    public String getCity()
    {
      return city;
    }

    public String getState()
    {
      return state;
    }

    public String getZip()
    {
      return zip;
    }

    public void writeStudent(DataOutput out) throws IOException
    {
      FixedLengthStringIO.writeFixedLengthString(
        name, NAME_SIZE, out);
      FixedLengthStringIO.writeFixedLengthString(
        street, STREET_SIZE, out);
      FixedLengthStringIO.writeFixedLengthString(
        city, CITY_SIZE, out);
      FixedLengthStringIO.writeFixedLengthString(
        state, STATE_SIZE, out);
      FixedLengthStringIO.writeFixedLengthString(
        zip, ZIP_SIZE, out);
    }

    public void readStudent(DataInput in) throws IOException
    {
      name = FixedLengthStringIO.readFixedLengthString(
        NAME_SIZE, in);
      street = FixedLengthStringIO.readFixedLengthString(
        STREET_SIZE, in);
      city = FixedLengthStringIO.readFixedLengthString(
        CITY_SIZE, in);
      state = FixedLengthStringIO.readFixedLengthString(
        STATE_SIZE, in);
      zip = FixedLengthStringIO.readFixedLengthString(
        ZIP_SIZE, in);
    }
  }
```

```
class FixedLengthStringIO
{
  public static String readFixedLengthString(int size,
                                              DataInput in)
  throws IOException
  {
    char c[] = new char[size];

    for (int i=0; i<size; i++)
      c[i] = in.readChar();

    return new String(c);
  }

  public static void writeFixedLengthString(String s, int size,
    DataOutput out) throws IOException
  {
    char cBuffer[] = new char[size];
    s.getChars(0, s.length(), cBuffer, 0);
    for (int i=s.length(); i<cBuffer.length; i++)
      cBuffer[i] = ' ';
    String newS = new String(cBuffer);
    out.writeChars(newS);
  }
}

class InformationPanel extends Panel
{
  TextField tfName = new TextField(32);
  TextField tfStreet = new TextField(32);
  TextField tfCity = new TextField(20);
  TextField tfState = new TextField(2);
  TextField tfZip = new TextField(10);

  InformationPanel()
  {
    setLayout(new FlowLayout(FlowLayout.LEFT));

    Panel p1 = new Panel();
    p1.setLayout(new FlowLayout(FlowLayout.LEFT));
    p1.add(new Label("Name"));
    p1.add(tfName);
    add(p1);

    Panel p2 = new Panel();
    p2.setLayout(new FlowLayout(FlowLayout.LEFT));
    p2.add(new Label("Street"));
    p2.add(tfStreet);
    add(p2);

    Panel p3 = new Panel();
    p3.setLayout(new FlowLayout(FlowLayout.LEFT));
    p3.add(new Label("City"));
    p3.add(tfCity);
    add(p3);

    Panel p4 = new Panel();
    p4.setLayout(new FlowLayout(FlowLayout.LEFT));
    p4.add(new Label("State"));
```

continues

491

Example 14.6   continued

```
        p4.add(tfState);
        p4.add(new Label("Zip"));
        p4.add(tfZip);
        add(p4);
    }

    public Student getStudent()
    {
        return new Student(tfName.getText().trim(),
                           tfStreet.getText().trim(),
                           tfCity.getText().trim(),
                           tfState.getText().trim(),
                           tfZip.getText().trim());
    }

    public void setStudent(Student s)
    {
        tfName.setText(s.getName());
        tfStreet.setText(s.getStreet());
        tfCity.setText(s.getCity());
        tfState.setText(s.getState());
        tfZip.setText(s.getZip());
    }
}

class MyFrameWithHideHandling extends Frame implements
    WindowListener
{
    public MyFrameWithHideHandling()
    {
        super();
        addWindowListener(this);
    }

    public MyFrameWithHideHandling(String str)
    {
        super(str);
        addWindowListener(this);
    }

    public void windowClosed(WindowEvent event)
    {
    }

    public void windowDeiconified(WindowEvent event)
    {
    }

    public void windowIconified(WindowEvent event)
    {
    }

    public void windowActivated(WindowEvent event)
    {
    }

    public void windowDeactivated(WindowEvent event)
    {
    }
```

```
      public void windowOpened(WindowEvent event)
      {
      }

      public void windowClosing(WindowEvent event)
      {
        setVisible(false);
      }
    }
```

Example Review

The main frame consists of two buttons, Register Students and View Students. A random file, **student.dat**, is created to store student information if the file does not yet exist. If it does exist, the file is opened. The random file object, `raf`, is used in both registration and in the viewing part of the program. The user could add a new student record into the file in the Register frame and view it immediately in the View frame.

When the Register Students button is clicked, the registration frame is shown. When the View Students button is clicked, the viewing frame is shown. The main frame extends `MyFrameWithExitHandling`; the two subframes extend `MyFrameWithHideHandling`. When the main frame is closed, the program exits; when a subframe is closed, the frame becomes invisible.

Several classes are used in this example. The relationship between these classes is shown in Figure 14.16. The main class, `TestRandomAccessFile`, is a subclass of `MyFrameWithExitHandling` and creates an instance of the `RegisterStudent` class and an instance of the `ViewStudent` class.

The `RegisterStudent` class and the `ViewStudent` class have many things in common. They both extend the `MyFrameWithHideHandling` class, and they both use the `InformationPanel` class, the `Student` class, and the `FixedLengthStringIO` class.

The information panels for registering and viewing student information are identical. Therefore, the program creates one superclass, `InformationPanel`, to define the text fields in a panel. The class lays out the text fields and provides the method `getStudent()` for getting text fields and the method `setStudent()` for setting text fields.

The `Student` class defines the student record structure and provides methods for reading and writing a record into the file. The `FixedLengthStringIO` class defines the methods for reading and writing fixed-length strings.

The size of each field in the student record is fixed. For example, zip code is set to a maximum of five characters. If you entered a zip code of more than five characters by mistake, the `ArrayIndexOutofBounds` runtime error would occur when the program attempts to write the zip code into the file using the `writeFixedLengthString()` method defined in the `FixedLengthStringIO` class.

continues

Example 14.6   continued

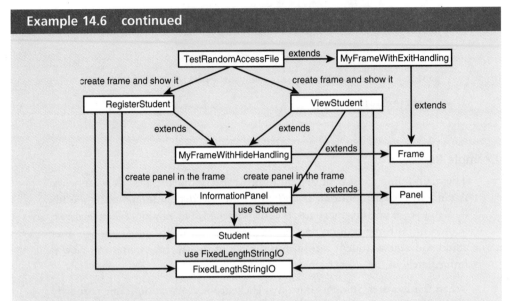

Figure 14.16   *TestRandomAccess creates instances of* RegisterStudent *and* ViewStudent. RegisterStudent *and its subclasses register student information in a random access file, and* ViewStudent *and its subclasses view student information from the same file.*

FileDialog

FileDialog is a subclass of Dialog that displays a dialog box from which the user can navigate through the file system and select files for loading or saving. The "look" of the file dialog box is determined by the native windowing system. A file dialog box under Windows looks the same as other file dialog boxes under Windows, and a file dialog box under Sun Solaris looks the same as other file dialog boxes under Sun Solaris.

The file dialog box is modal by default; when it is displayed, it blocks the rest of the application until it disappears. The file dialog box can appear in two modes: *open* and *save*. The *open mode* is for opening a file, and the *save mode* is used to save a file.

To construct a file dialog box, use one of the following constructors.

```
FileDialog(Frame parent, String title, int mode)
```

Creates a file dialog box with the specified title for loading or saving a file. The files shown in the dialog box are those in the current directory. If the value of mode is FileDialog.LOAD, then the file dialog is for selecting a file to read. If the value of mode is FileDialog.SAVE, the file dialog is for selecting a filename to write to it.

```
FileDialog(Frame parent, String title)
```

Creates a file dialog window with the specified title for loading a file.

```
FileDialog(Frame parent)
```

Creates a file dialog for loading a file. The title of the file dialog is initially empty.

The `FileDialog` class has the properties `file`, `directory`, and `mode` with the associated getter and setter methods. For example, you can use the `setFile()` method to specify a default file that you expect the user to use. You can use the `getFile()` method to obtain the file that is opened.

To display the dialog box, use the `show()` method in the `Dialog` class.

Example 14.7   Using *FileDialog*

This example gives a program that creates a simple notepad using `FileDialog` to open and save files. The notepad enables the user to open an existing file, edit the file, and save the note into the current file or to a specified file. You can display and edit the file in a text area.

A sample run of the program is shown in Figure 14.17. When you open a file, a file dialog box with the default title "Open" appears onscreen to let you select a file for loading, as shown in Figure 14.18. When you save a file, a file dialog box with the default title "Save As" appears to let you select a file for saving, as shown in Figure 14.19. The status label below the text area displays the status of the file operations.

```java
import java.awt.*;
import java.awt.event.*;
import java.io.*;

public class FileDialogDemo extends MyFrameWithExitHandling
  implements ActionListener
{
  private MenuItem miOpen, miSave,miExit, miAbout;
  private TextArea ta; //for display and edit file
  private Label lblStatus; //for showing operation status
  private FileDialog fileDialog; //file dialog box
  private MessageDialog messageDialog; //message dialog box

  public static void main(String[] args)
  {
    FileDialogDemo f = new FileDialogDemo();
    f.setSize(300,150);
    f.setVisible(true);
  }

  public FileDialogDemo ()
  {
    setTitle("Test FileDialog");

    //create MenuBar mb
    MenuBar mb = new MenuBar();
    setMenuBar(mb);
```

continues

Example 14.7   continued

```
                //add a Menu "File" in mb
                Menu fileMenu = new Menu("File");
                mb.add(fileMenu);

                //add a Menu "Help" in mb
                Menu helpMenu = new Menu("Help");
                mb.add(helpMenu);

                //add MenuItems
                fileMenu.add(miOpen = new MenuItem("Open"));
                fileMenu.add(miSave = new MenuItem("Save"));
                fileMenu.addSeparator();
                fileMenu.add(miExit = new MenuItem("Exit"));
                helpMenu.add(miAbout = new MenuItem("About"));

                //set BorderLayout for the frame
                setLayout(new BorderLayout());
                add("Center", ta = new TextArea());
                add("South", lblStatus = new Label());
                lblStatus.setBackground(Color.gray);

                //register listeners
                miOpen.addActionListener(this);
                miSave.addActionListener(this);
                miAbout.addActionListener(this);

                //create fileDialog
                fileDialog = new FileDialog(this);

                //create messageDialog
                messageDialog =
                  new MessageDialog(this, "FileDialog Demo", true);
                messageDialog.setMessage(
                  "A sample program to show file dialog box");
                messageDialog.pack();
              }

              //handle ActionEvent for menu items
              public void actionPerformed(ActionEvent e)
              {
                String actionCommand = e.getActionCommand();

                if (e.getSource() instanceof MenuItem)
                {
                  if ("Open".equals(actionCommand))
                    open();
                  else if ("Save".equals(actionCommand))
                    save();
                  else if ("About".equals(actionCommand))
                    messageDialog.show();
                  else if ("Exit".equals(actionCommand))
                    System.exit(0);
                }
              }

              //open file
              private void open()
              {
                fileDialog.setMode(FileDialog.LOAD);
                fileDialog.show();
```

```
      if (fileDialog.getFile() != null)
        open(fileDialog.getDirectory()+fileDialog.getFile());
    }

    private void open(String fileName)
    {
      try
      {
        BufferedInputStream in = new BufferedInputStream(
          new FileInputStream(new File(fileName)));
        byte[] b = new byte[in.available()];
        in.read(b,0,b.length);
        ta.append(new String(b,0,b.length));
        in.close();

        //Display the status of the Open file
        //operation in lblStatus.
        lblStatus.setText(fileName+ " Opened");
      }
      catch (IOException ex)
      {
        lblStatus.setText("Error opening "+fileName);
      }
    }

    //save file
    private void save()
    {
      fileDialog.setMode(FileDialog.SAVE);
      fileDialog.show();
      if (fileDialog.getFile() != null)
        save(fileDialog.getDirectory()+fileDialog.getFile());
    }

    private void save(String fileName)
    {
      try
      {
        BufferedOutputStream out = new BufferedOutputStream(
          new FileOutputStream(new File(fileName)));
        byte[] b = (ta.getText()).getBytes();
        out.write(b, 0, b.length);
        out.close();

        //Display the status of the Open file
        //operation in statusBar.
        lblStatus.setText(fileName + " Saved ");
      }
      catch (IOException ex)
      {
        lblStatus.setText("Error saving"+fileName);
      }
    }
}
```

continues

Example 14.7   continued

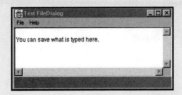

Figure 14.17   *The program enables you to open, save, and edit files.*

Figure 14.18   *The Open dialog box enables you to open an existing file.*

Figure 14.19   *The Save As dialog box enables you to save to a new file or an existing file.*

Example Review

The program creates the File and Help menus. The File menu contains menu commands Open for loading a file, Save for saving a file, and Exit for terminating the program. The Help menu contains a menu command About to display a message about the program.

The `MessageDialog` class was presented in Example 9.8, "Using Dialogs" (see Chapter 9, "Creating User Interfaces"). To use it, simply create an instance of `MessageDialog` and use the `setMessage()` method to set the message you want to display in the dialog box. To display the dialog box, use the `show()` method.

An instance `fileDialog` of `FileDialog` was created for displaying the file dialog box to open and save files. You can use the `setMode()` method to specify the type of the file dialog box used for loading or for saving files. The `getFile()` method returns the filename if a file is selected; otherwise, `getFile()` returns `null`.

The `open()` method is invoked when the user clicks the Open menu command. It sets the file dialog mode to `FileDialog.LOAD` and displays the dialog box using the `show()` method. Upon receiving the selected file, the method `open(filename)` is invoked to load the file to the text area using a `BufferedInputStream` wrapped on a `FileInputStream`.

The `save()` method is invoked when the user clicks the Save menu command. It sets the file dialog mode to `FileDialog.SAVE` and displays the dialog box using the `show()` method. Upon receiving the selected file, the method `save(filename)` is invoked to save the contents from the text area to the file using a `BufferedOutputStream` wrapped on an `FileOutputStream`.

Interactive Input and Output

There are two types of *interactive I/O*. One involves simple input from the keyboard and simple output in a pure text form. The other involves input from various input devices and output to a graphical environment on frames and applets. The former is referred to as *text interactive I/O*, and the latter is known as *graphical interactive I/O*.

The graphical interactive I/O takes an entirely different approach from the text interactive I/O. In the graphical environment, the input can be received from a UI component such as a text field, text area, list, choice, check box, or check box group. The input can also be received from a keystroke or a mouse movement. The output is usually displayed on the canvas, in text fields, or in text areas.

Now turn your attention to text I/O. In all the previous chapters, you used text input and output with the `System` class. The `System` class contains three I/O objects: `System.in`, `System.out`, and `System.err`. The objects `in`, `out`, and `err` are static variables. The variable `in` is of `InputStream` type, and `out` and `err` are of `PrintStream` type. These are the basic objects that all Java programmers use to input from the keyboard, output to the screen, and display error messages. Because this class is used in virtually all programs for simple console input and output, they are stored in the `java.lang` package, which is imported into a class automatically.

To perform console output, you can simply use any of the methods for `PrintStream` in `System.out`. However, keyboard input is more complicated. The `MyInput` class, which is used for getting `int` and `double` from the keyboard, was introduced in the section "Separate Classes" in Chapter 2. In this section, `MyInput` class, as well as input for other primitive types and strings, will be described in more detail.

You need to use BufferedReader and StringTokenizer to input from the keyboard. BufferedReader takes the input of the character format of all the primitive types, such as integer, double, string, and so on. The StringTokenizer class, introduced in Chapter 6, "Arrays and Strings," takes in a string, such as "Welcome to Java" and breaks it into little pieces, which are known as *tokens*.

The tokens are usually separated by spaces (but the programmer can dictate what delimiter should be used). The StringTokenizer objects are instantiated with the string, and each subsequent call to StringTokenizerObject.nextToken() returns a new token. In order to make input possible, you need to declare these two objects as follows:

```
static private BufferedReader br =
  new BufferedReader(new InputStreamReader(System.in),1);
static StringTokenizer stok;
```

NOTE

It is known to JavaSoft that some brands of PCs running Windows 95 and Windows 98 are prone to cause input problems if the buffer size for the BufferedReader stream br is not set to 1. Therefore, the buffer size of 1 is purposely chosen to help eliminate some of the input problems.

Table 14.5 shows the code for reading different primitive data types from the keyboard.

TABLE 14.5   Input and Output of Primitive Types on the Console

Data Type	How to Read It

int	`String str = br.readLine();`
	`stok = new StringTokenizer(str);`
	`int i = Integer.parseInt(stok.nextToken());`

byte	`String str = br.readLine();`
	`stok = new StringTokenizer(str);`
	`int i = Integer.parseInt(stok.nextToken());`
	`byte b = (byte)i;`

short	Same as the preceding entry, except that byte b = (byte)i; needs to be replaced with short b = (short)i;

boolean	`String str = br.readLine();`
	`stok = new StringTokenizer(str);`
	`boolean bo = new Boolean(stok.nextToken()).booleanValue();`

char	`char ch = br.readLine().charAt(0);`
long	`String str = br.readLine();` `long lg = Long.parseLong(st.nextToken());`

Data Type	How to Read It

float	`String str = br.readLine();`
	`stok = new StringTokenizer(str);`
	`float fl = new Float(stok.nextToken()).floatValue();`

double	`String str = br.readLine();`
	`stok = new StringTokenizer(str);`
	`double db = new Double(stok.nextToken()).doubleValue();`

String	`String str = br.readLine();`

Note that with the previous code, the programmer needs to add an exception handler in the try/catch wraparound because these I/O statements throw IOException.

Piped Streams, String Streams, Pushback Streams, Line Number Streams, and Object Streams

You have learned many I/O streams in this chapter. Each stream has its intended application. There are several other stream classes that you might find useful. For example, you can use object streams to read or write whole objects from or to files. A brief discussion of these streams follows:

- **Piped streams**—These streams could be thought of as the two ends of a pipe that connects two processes. One process sends data out through the pipe, and the other process receives data from the pipe. Piped streams are used in interprocess communication (IPC). Two processes running on separate threads can exchange data. Java provides `PipedInputStream`, `PipedOutputStream`, `PipedReader`, and `PipedWriter` to support piped streams.

- **String streams**—String streams (`StringReader` and `StringWriter`) are exactly like character array streams, except that the source of the string stream is a string, and the destination of the string stream is a string buffer.

- **Pushback streams**—Pushback streams are commonly used in parsers to "push back" a single byte or character in the input stream after reading from the input stream. The pushback stream's purpose is simply to preview the input to determine what to do next. The number of bytes or characters being pushed can be specified when the streams are constructed. By default, a single byte or a single character is pushed back. Java provides the classes `PushbackInputStream` and `PushbackReader` to support pushback streams.

- **Line number streams**—Line number streams allow you to track the current line number of an input stream. Java provides the `LineNumberReader` class for this purpose. The `LineNumberReader` class is useful for such applications as an editor or a debugger. You can use the `getLineNumber()` method to get the current line number of the input and the `getLine()` method to retrieve a line into a string.

- **Object streams**—Thus far, this chapter has covered input and output of bytes, characters, and primitive data types. Object streams enable you to perform input and output at the object level. This is particularly useful when dealing with a file of records. For example, you can save an array of student records. Each student is an object. The `ObjectInputStream` and `ObjectOutputStream` classes provide functionality to support object streams.

Chapter Summary

In this chapter, you learned about Java input and output. In Java, all I/O is handled in streams. Java offers many stream classes for processing all kinds of data.

Streams can be categorized into two types: byte streams and character streams. The `InputStream` and `OutputStream` classes are the root of all byte stream classes, and the `Reader` and `Writer` classes are the root of all character stream classes. The subclasses of `InputStream` and `OutputStream` are analogous to the subclasses of `Reader` and `Writer`. Many of them have similar method signatures, and you can use them in the same way.

The file streams—`FileInputStream` and `FileOutputStream` for byte streams, and `FileReader` and `FileWriter` for character streams—are used to read from or write data to external files. The data streams `DataInputStream` and `DataOutputStream` read or write Java primitive types in a machine-independent fashion, which enables you to write a data file on one machine and read it on a machine that has a different OS or file structure.

The data output stream outputs a binary representation of data. Therefore, you cannot view its content as text. The `PrintStream` and `PrintWriter` classes allow you to print streams in text format. `System.out`, `System.in`, and `System.err` are examples of `PrintStream` objects.

The `BufferedInputStream`, `BufferedOutputStream`, `BufferedReader`, and `BufferedWriter` classes can be used to speed input and output by reducing the number of reads and writes. Typical physical input/output involving I/O devices is extremely slow compared with CPU processing, so using buffered I/O can greatly improve performance.

The `StreamTokenizer` class is useful in processing text files. The `StreamTokenizer` class enables you to take an input stream, parse it into tokens, and allow those tokens to be read one at a time.

The `RandomAccessFile` class enables you to read and write data to a file at the same time. You can open a file with the `"r"` mode to indicate that the file is read only, or you can open a file with the `"rw"` mode to indicate that the file is updateable. The `RandomAccessFile` class implements `DataInput` and `DataOutput` interfaces.

Therefore, many methods in `RandomAccessFile` are the same as those in `DataInputStream` and `DataOutputStream`.

You can use the `FileDialog` class to display standard file dialog boxes from which the user can navigate through the file systems and select files for loading or saving.

Chapter Review

1. Which streams must always be used to process external files?

2. What type of data is read or written by `InputStream` and `OutputStream`? Can you use `read()` or `write(byte b)` in those streams?

3. `InputStream` reads bytes. Why does the `read()` method return an `int` instead of a byte?

4. What type of data is read or written by `Reader` and `Writer`? Can you use `read()` or `write(char c)` in those streams?

5. What are the differences between byte streams and character streams?

6. What type of data is read or written by file streams? Can you use `read()` or `write(byte b)` in file streams?

7. How are the data input and output streams used to read and write data?

8. What are the differences between `DataOutputStream` and `PrintStream`?

9. Answer the following questions regarding `StreamTokenizer`:

   ■ When do you use `StreamTokenizer`?

   ■ How do you read data using `StreamTokenizer`?

   ■ Where is the token stored when you are using the `nextToken()` method?

   ■ How do you find the data type of the token?

10. Can you close a `StreamTokenizer`?

11. Can RandomAccessFile streams read a data file that is created by `DataOutputStream`?

12. Create a `RandomAccessFile` stream for the file **student.dat** to allow the updating of student information in the file. Create a `DataOutputStream` for the file **student.dat**. Describe the differences between these two statements.

13. What are the data types for `System.in`, `System.out`, and `System.err`?

Programming Exercises

1. Rewrite Example 14.1 using `FileReader` and `FileWriter` streams. Write another program with buffered streams to boost performance. Test the performance of these two programs (one with buffered streams and the other without using buffered streams), as shown in Figure 14.20.

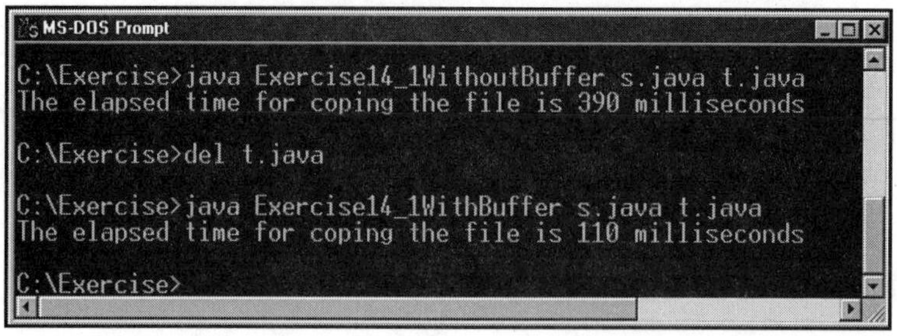

Figure 14.20   *The buffered streams can boost performance significantly.*

2. Write a program that will count the number of characters including blanks, words, and lines in a file. The filename should be passed as a command-line argument, as shown in Figure 14.21.

Figure 14.21   *The program displays the number of characters, words, and lines in the given file.*

3. Use `StreamTokenizer` to write a program that will add all the integers in a data file. Suppose that the integers are delimited by spaces. Display the result on the console. Rewrite the program, assuming this time that the numbers are `double`.

4. Rewrite Example 14.5 so that it reads a line as a string in a `BufferedReader` stream and then use `StringTokenizer` to extract the fields.

5. Rewrite Example 14.4 to enable the user to view the file by opening it from a file open dialog box. A file open dialog box is displayed when the Browse button is clicked. The file is displayed in the text area when the OK button is clicked in the file open dialog box, as shown in Figure 14.22.

6. Write a Java application that will display a stock index ticker, as shown in Figure 12.13 for the sixth exercise in the "Programming Exercises" section at the end of Chapter 12, "Multithreading." In that exercise, the stock index information is passed from the <param> tag in the HTML file.

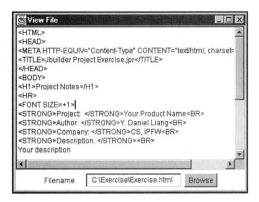

Figure 14.22 *The program enables the user to view a file by selecting it from a file open dialog box.*

Your program will get index information from an external text file. The first line in the file contains an integer, which indicates the number of stock indices given in the file. Each subsequent line should consist of four fields: **Index Name**, **Current Time**, **Previous Day Index**, and **Index Change**. The fields are separated by the pound sign (#). The file could contain two lines, such as the following:

```
2
"S&P 500"#15:54#919.01#4.54
"NIKKEI"#04:03#1865.17#-7.00
```

Use the double-buffering technique that you learned in Chapter 13, "Multimedia," to reduce flickering in the display.

7. Write a program that will display a histogram on a canvas. The histogram should show the occurrence of each letter in a text file, as shown in Figure 14.23. Assume the letters are not case sensitive.

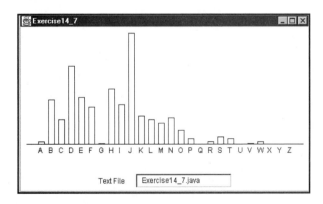

Figure 14.23 *The program displays a histogram that shows the occurrence of each letter in the file.*

1. Place a canvas that will display your results in the center of the frame.

2. Place a label and a text field in a panel and put the panel in the south side of the frame. The text file will be entered from this text field.

3. Clicking the Enter key on the text field causes the program to count the occurrence of each letter and display that count in a histogram.

NETWORKING

Objectives

- Comprehend socket-based communication in Java.
- Understand client/server computing.
- Implement Java networking programs.
- Produce servers for multiple clients.
- Create applets that connect to servers.
- Write programs that will work with Web servers.

Introduction

Network programming is tightly integrated in Java. Java provides *socket-based communication*, which enables programs to communicate through designated sockets. A *socket* is an abstraction that facilitates communication between a server and a client. Java treats socket communication much like it treats I/O operations: A program can read from or write to a socket as easily as reading from or writing to a file.

Java supports *stream socket* and *datagram socket*. Stream socket uses the TCP (Transmission Control Protocol) for data transmission, and datagram socket uses the UDP (User Datagram Protocol). The TCP can detect a lost transmission and resubmit it. Therefore, the transmission is lossless and reliable. However, the UDP cannot guarantee lossless transmission. Thus, stream sockets are used in the majority of Java programming. The discussion in this chapter is based on stream sockets.

Client/Server Computing

Network programming usually involves a server and one or more clients. The client sends requests to the server, and the server responds to the requests. The client first attempts to establish a connection to the server. The server can accept or deny the connection. After the connection is established, the client and server communicate through sockets.

The server must be running when a client starts. The server waits for a connection request from a client. The statements that are needed to create a server and a client and to exchange data between them are shown in Figure 15.1.

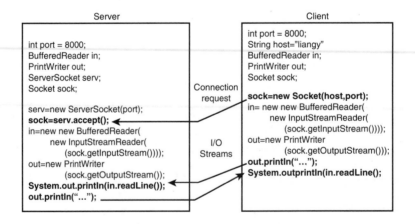

Figure 15.1   *The server uses I/O streams to establish a server socket that facilitates communication between the server and the client.*

To establish a server, you need to create a server socket and attach it to a port, which is where the server listens for connections. The port identifies the TCP service on the socket. Port numbers between 0 and 1023 are reserved for privileged processes.

For instance, the email server runs on port 25, and the Web server usually runs on port 80. You can choose any port number that is not currently used by any other process. The following statement creates a server socket s:

```
ServerSocket s = new ServerSocket(port);
```

NOTE

Attempting to create a server socket on a port already in use would cause the `java.net.BindException` runtime error.

After a server socket is created, the server can use the following statement to listen for connections:

```
Socket connectToClient = s.accept();
```

This statement waits until a client connects to the server socket. The client issues the following statement to request a connection to a server:

```
Socket connectToServer = new Socket(ServerName, port);
```

This statement opens a socket so that the client program can communicate with the server. *ServerName* is the server's Internet hostname or its IP address. For example, the following statement creates a socket at port 8000 on the client machine to connect to the host `liangy.ipfw.edu`:

```
Socket connectToServer = new Socket("liangy.ipfw.edu", 8000);
```

Alternatively, you can use the IP address to create a socket, as follows:

```
Socket connectToServer = new Socket("149.164.29.27", 8000)
```

An IP address, such as `149.164.29.27`, is a unique identity of a computer on the Internet, consisting of four dotted decimal numbers, each between 0 and 255. Because it is not easy to remember numbers like this, these numbers are often mapped to meaningful names called *hostnames*, such as `liangy.ipfw.edu`.

NOTE

There are special servers on the Internet to translate the hostnames into the IP addresses. These servers are called Domain Name Servers (or DNS). The translation is done behind the scene. When you create a socket with the hostname, the Java Runtime System requests the DNS to translate the hostname into the IP address.

After the server accepts the connection, the communication between the server and the client is conducted just as it is for I/O streams. To get an input stream and an output stream, use the `getInputStream()` and `getOutputStream()` methods on a socket object. For example, the following statements create an `InputStream` stream, `isFromServer`, and an `OutputStream` stream, `osToServer`, from the socket `connectToServer`:

```
InputStream isFromServer = connectToServer.getInputStream();
OutputStream osToServer = connectToServer.getOutputStream();
```

The `InputStream` and `OutputStream` streams are used to read or write bytes. You can use `DataInputStream`, `DataOutputStream`, `BufferedReader`, and `PrintWriter` to wrap on the `InputStream` and `OutputStream` to read or write values of data, such as `int`, `double`, or `String`. For example, the following statements create a `BufferedReader` stream, `isFromClient`, and a `PrintWriter` stream, `osToClient`, for reading and writing primitive data values:

```
BufferedReader isFromClient = new BufferedReader(
  new InputStreamReader(connectToClient.getInputStream()));
PrintWriter osToClient = new PrintWriter(
  connectToClient.getOutputStream(), true);
```

The Boolean `true` is for auto flush, and the `print()` methods flush the output buffer. The server can use `isFromClient.read()` to receive data from the client and `osToClient.write()` to send data to the client.

Example 15.1   A Client/Server Example

This example presents a client program and a server program. The client sends data to a server. The server receives the data, uses it to produce a result, and then sends the result back to the client. The client displays the result on the console. In this example, the data sent from the client is the radius of a circle, and the result produced by the server is the area of the circle (see Figure 15.2).

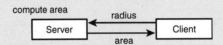

Figure 15.2 *The client sends the radius to the server; then, the server computes the area and sends it to the client.*

The server program follows. A sample run of the program is shown in Figure 15.3.

```java
import java.io.*;
import java.net.*;
import java.util.*;

public class Server
{
  public static void main(String[] args)
  {
    try
    {
      //create a server socket
      ServerSocket serverSocket = new ServerSocket(8000);

      //start listening for connections on the server socket
      Socket connectToClient = serverSocket.accept();

      //create a buffer reader stream to get data from the client
      BufferedReader isFromClient = new BufferedReader(new
        InputStreamReader(connectToClient.getInputStream()));
```

```java
        //create a buffer writer stream to send data to the client
        PrintWriter osToClient new PrintWriter(
          connectToClient.getOutputStream(), true);

        /*continuously read from the client and process it,
          and send result back to the client
        */
        while (true)
        {
          //read a line and create a string tokenizer
          StringTokenizer st = new StringTokenizer
            (isFromClient.readLine());

          //convert string to double
          double radius = new Double(st.nextToken()).doubleValue();

          //display radius on console
          System.out.println("radius received from client: "
            +radius);

          //compute area
          double area = radius*radius*Math.PI;

          //send the result to the client
          osToClient.println(area);

          //print the result to the console
          System.out.println("Area found: "+area);
        }
      }
      catch(IOException ex)
      {
        System.err.println(ex);
      }
    }
}
```

The client program follows. A sample run of the program is shown in Figure 15.4.

```java
import java.io.*;
import java.net.*;
import java.util.*;

public class Client
{
  public static void main(String[] args)
  {
    try
    {
      //create a socket to connect to the server
      Socket connectToServer = new Socket("localhost",8000);

      /*create a buffered input stream to receive data
        from the server
      */
      BufferedReader isFromServer = new BufferedReader(
        new InputStreamReader(connectToServer.getInputStream()));
```

continues

Example 15.1   continued

```
            //create a buffered output stream to send data to the server
            PrintWriter osToServer =
              new PrintWriter(connectToServer.getOutputStream(), true);

            /*continuously send radius and receive area
              from the server
            */
            while (true)
            {
              //read the radius from the keyboard
              System.out.print("Please enter a radius: ");
              double radius = MyInput.readDouble();

              //send the radius to the server
              osToServer.println(radius);

              //get area from the server
              StringTokenizer st = new StringTokenizer(
                isFromServer.readLine());

              //convert string to double
              double area = new Double(
                st.nextToken ()).doubleValue ();

              //print area on the console
              System.out.println("Area received from the server is "
                +area);
            }
          }
          catch (IOException ex)
          {
            System.err.println(ex);
          }
        }
      }
```

Figure 15.3   *The server receives a radius from the client, computes the area, and sends the area to the client.*

Figure 15.4   *The client sends the radius to the server and receives the area from the server.*

Example Review

You should start the server program first, then start the client program. The client program prompts the user to enter a radius, which is sent to the server. The server computes the area and sends it back to the client. This process is repeated until one of the two programs terminates. To terminate a program, press Ctrl+C on the console if running on Windows 95 or Windows NT, or kill the process if running on UNIX.

The networking classes are in the package `java.net`. This should be imported when writing Java network programs.

The `Server` class creates a `ServerSocket serverSocket` and attaches it to port 8000 using the following statement:

```
ServerSocket serverSocket = new ServerSocket(8000);
```

The server then starts to listen for connection requests using the following statement:

```
Socket connectToClient = serverSocket.accept();
```

The server waits until a client requests a connection. After it is connected, the server reads radius from the client through an input stream, computes area, and sends the result to the client through an output stream.

The `Client` class uses the following statement to create a socket that will request a connection to the server at port 8000.

```
Socket connectToServer = new Socket("localhost",8000);
```

The hostname `localhost` refers to the machine on which the client is running. If you run the server and the client on different machines, you need to replace `localhost` with the server machine's hostname or IP address. In this example, the server and the client are running on the same machine.

If the server is not running, the client program terminates with an `IOException`. After it is connected, the client gets input and output streams—which are wrapped by buffered reader and writer streams—in order to receive and send data to the server.

Serving Multiple Clients

It is quite common to have multiple clients that connect to a server at the same time. Typically, a server runs constantly on a server computer, and clients from all over the Internet may want to connect to it. You can use threads to handle the server's multiple clients simultaneously. Simply create a thread for each connection. The server should handle the establishment of a connection in the following way:

```
while (true)
{
  Socket connectToClient = serverSocket.accept();
```

```
        Thread t = new ThreadClass(connectToClient);
        t.start();
    }
```

The server socket can have many connections. Each iteration of the while loop creates a new connection. When the connection is established, a new thread is created to handle the communication between the server and this new client, which allows multiple connections to run at the same time.

Example 15.2   Serving Multiple Clients

This example shows how to serve multiple clients simultaneously. For each connection, the server starts a new thread. This thread continuously receives input (the radius of a circle) from a client and sends the result (the area of the circle) back to the client (see Figure 15.5).

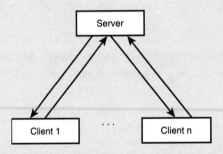

Figure 15.5   *Multithreading enables a server to handle multiple independent clients.*

The new server program follows. A sample run of the server is shown in Figure 15.6, and the sample runs of two clients are shown in Figures 15.7 and 15.8.

```java
import java.io.*;
import java.net.*;
import java.util.*;

public class MultiThreadsServer
{
  public static void main(String[] args)
  {
    try
    {
      //create a server socket
      ServerSocket serverSocket = new ServerSocket(8000);

      //to label a thread
      int i = 0;

      while (true)
      {
        //listen for a new connection request
        Socket connectToClient = serverSocket.accept();
```

```
                    //print the new connect number on the console
                    System.out.println("Starting thread "+i);

                    //create a new thread for the connection
                    ThreadHandler t = new ThreadHandler(connectToClient, i);

                    //start the new thread
                    t.start();

                    //increment i to label the next connection
                    i++;
                }
            }
            catch(IOException ex)
            {
                System.err.println(ex);
            }
        }
    }

    //define the thread class for handling new connection
    class ThreadHandler extends Thread
    {
        private Socket connectToClient; //a connected socket
        private int counter; //label for the connection

        public ThreadHandler(Socket socket, int i)
        {
            connectToClient = socket;
            counter = i;
        }

        public void run()
        {
            try
            {
                //create data input and print streams
                BufferedReader isFromClient = new BufferedReader(
                    new InputStreamReader(connectToClient.getInputStream()));
                PrintWriter osToClient =
                    new PrintWriter(connectToClient.getOutputStream(), true);

                //continuously serve the client
                while (true)
                {
                    //receive data from the client in string
                    StringTokenizer st = new StringTokenizer
                        (isFromClient.readLine());

                    //get radius
                    double radius = new Double(st.nextToken()).doubleValue();
                    System.out.println("radius received from client: "+radius);

                    //compute area
                    double area = radius*radius*Math.PI;

                    //send area back to the client
                    osToClient.println(area);
```

continues

Example 15.2   continued

```
          System.out.println("Area found: "+area);
      }
    }
    catch(IOException ex)
    {
      System.err.println(ex);
    }
  }
}
```

Figure 15.6   *The server spawns a thread in order to serve a client.*

Figure 15.7   *The first client communicates to the server on thread 0.*

Figure 15.8   *The second client communicates to the server on thread 1.*

Example Review

The server creates a server socket at port 8000. The server then waits for a connection. After the connection is established with a client, the server creates a new thread to handle communication with the client. It then waits for another connection.

The threads, which run independently of one another, communicate with designated clients. Each thread creates buffered reader and writer streams that receive and send data to the client.

This server accepts an unlimited number of clients. To limit the number of concurrent connections, you can use a thread group to monitor the number of active threads and modify the while loop, as follows:

```
ThreadGroup g = new ThreadGroup("serving clients");

while (g.activeCount() < maxThreadLimit)
{
  //listen for a new connection request
  Socket connectToClient = serverSocket.accept();

  //print the new connect number on the console
  System.out.println("Starting thread " + i);

  //create a new thread for the connection
  Thread t = new Thread(g, new ThreadHandler(connectToClient, i));

  //start the new thread
  t.start();

  //increment i to label the next connection
  i++;
}
```

Both Windows 95 and Windows NT have a Telnet utility. Telnet can be used to log onto another host and to communicate with other services on the host. Telnet can be used as a client to test the server. This is convenient if you don't have the client program in place.

You can enter the `telnet` command from the DOS prompt to display a Telnet window, as shown in Figure 15.9. In the Telnet window, choose Connect, Remote System to display the Connect dialog box. Enter the server's hostname and port number, and press Connect. You must have the server already running. Here is a sample run with a server running, as shown in Figure 15.10, and the Telnet session running, as shown in Figure 15.11.

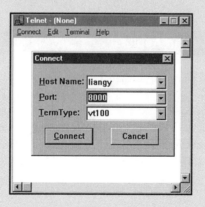

Figure 15.9   *A Telnet client connects to the server on port 8000.*

continues

Example 15.2   continued

Figure 15.10 *The server receives the radii 100, 30.5, and 40.5 from the Telnet client and sends the corresponding areas to the client.*

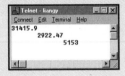

Figure 15.11 *The user enters the radius (not echo printed in the window). The Telnet client sends the radius to the server and receives the area that is displayed in the Telnet window.*

Applet Clients

Due to security constraints, applets can only connect to the host from which they were loaded. Therefore, the HTML file must be located on the machine on which the server is running. Following is an example of how to use an applet to connect to a server.

Example 15.3   Networking in Applets

This example, which is similar to that in Example 14.6, "Using Random Access Files," in Chapter 14, "Input and Output," shows how to register students using an applet. The client collects and sends registration information to the server. The server then appends that information to a data file using a random access file stream. The server program follows. A sample run of this program is shown in Figure 15.12.

```
import java.io.*;
import java.net.*;

public class RegServer
{
  public static void main(String[] args)
  {
    //declare a random access file
    RandomAccessFile raf = null;

    //open the local file on the server side
```

```
    try
    {
      //open the file if the file exists, create a new file
      //if the file does not exist
      raf = new RandomAccessFile("student.dat", "rw");
    }
    catch(IOException ex)
    {
      System.out.print("Error: " + ex);
      System.exit(0);
    }

    //establish server socket
    try
    {
      //create a server socket
      ServerSocket serverSocket = new ServerSocket(8000);
      int count = 1;

      while (true)
      {
        //connect to a client
        Socket socket = serverSocket.accept();
        //start a new thread to register a client
        new PutRegistration(raf, socket, count++).start();
      }
    }
    catch (IOException ex)
    {
      System.err.println(ex);
    }
  }
}

//define a thread to process the client registration
class PutRegistration extends Thread
{
  private Socket socket;  //the socket to serve a client
  //the file to store the records
  private RandomAccessFile raf = null;
  private int num; //the socket label
  //buffer reader to get input from the client
  private BufferedReader in;

  public PutRegistration(RandomAccessFile raf,
    Socket socket, int num)
  {
    this.raf = raf;
    this.socket = socket;
    this.num = num;

    System.out.println("Thread "+num+" running");

    //create an input stream to receive data from a client
    try
    {
      in = new BufferedReader
        (new InputStreamReader(socket.getInputStream()));
    }
    catch(IOException ex)
```

continues

519

Example 15.3   continued

```
      {
        System.out.println("Error "+ex);
      }
    }

    public void run()
    {
      String name;
      String street;
      String city;
      String state;
      String zip;
      try
      {
        //receive data from the client
        name = new String(in.readLine());
        street = new String(in.readLine());
        city = new String(in.readLine());
        state = new String(in.readLine());
        zip = new String(in.readLine());

        //display data received
        System.out.println(
          "The following data received from the client");
        System.out.println("name: "+name);
        System.out.println("street: "+street);
        System.out.println("city: "+city);
        System.out.println("state: "+state);
        System.out.println("zip: "+zip);

        //create a student instance
        Student s = new Student(name, street, city, state, zip);

        //append it to "student.dat"
        raf.seek(raf.length());
        s.writeStudent(raf);
      }
      catch (IOException ex)
      {
        System.err.println(ex);
      }
    }
  }
```

The applet client follows; its sample run is shown in Figure 15.13.

```
import java.io.*;
import java.net.*;
import java.awt.*;
import java.awt.event.*;
import java.applet.Applet;

public class RegClient extends Applet
  implements ActionListener
{
  private Button btRegister; //"Register" button

  //registration information panel
  private InformationPanel registerPanel;
```

```
        public void init()
        {
          setLayout(new BorderLayout());

          //add the panel and button to the applet
          add("Center", registerPanel = new InformationPanel());
          add("South", btRegister = new Button("Register"));

          //register listener
          btRegister.addActionListener(this);
        }

        //handling button action
        public void actionPerformed(ActionEvent e)
        {
          String actionCommand = e.getActionCommand();
          if (e.getSource() instanceof Button)
          {
            if ("Register".equals(actionCommand))
            {
              try
              {
                //establish connection with the server
                Socket socket = new Socket("localhost", 8000);

                //create an output stream to the server
                PrintWriter toServer =
                  new PrintWriter(socket.getOutputStream(), true);

                //get text field
                Student s = registerPanel.getStudent();

                //get data from text fields and send it to the server
                toServer.println(s.getName());
                toServer.println(s.getStreet());
                toServer.println(s.getCity());
                toServer.println(s.getState());
                toServer.println(s.getZip());
              }
              catch (IOException ex)
              {
                System.err.println(ex);
              }
            }
          }
        }
```

Figure 15.12   *The server receives information (name, street, city, state, and zip code) from the client and stores it in a file.*

continues

Example 15.3   continued

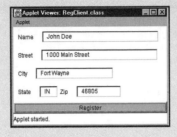

Figure 15.13   *The client gathers the name and address and sends it to the server.*

Example Review

The server handles multiple clients. It waits for a connection request from the client in the while loop. After the connection with a client is established, the server creates a thread to serve the client. The server then stays in the while loop to listen for the next connection request.

The server passes raf (random access file stream), socket (connection socket), and num (connection label) to the thread. The num argument is nonessential. It is only used for identifying the thread. The thread receives student information from the client through the BufferedReader stream and appends a student record to **student.dat** using the random access file stream raf.

The InformationPanel and Student classes are defined in Example 14.6. The following statement creates an instance of Student:

```
Student s = new Student(name, street, city, state, zip);
```

The following code writes the student record into the file:

```
s.writeStudent(raf);
```

The client is an applet. The data is entered into text fields (name, street, city, state, and zip). When the Register button is clicked, the data from the text fields is collected and sent to the server.

Viewing Web Pages

Given the URL of a page, a Web browser can view an HTML page, for example, **http://www.sun.com**. HTTP is the common standard used for communication between a Web server and the Internet. You can open a URL and view a Web page in a Java applet. A *URL* is a description of a resource location on the Internet. Java provides a class, java.net.URL, to manipulate URLs. The following code can be written to create a URL:

```
try
{
  URL location = new URL(URLString);
}
catch(MalFormedURLException ex)
{
}
```

For example, the following statement creates a Java URL object:

```
try
{
  URL location = new URL("http://www.sun.com");
}
catch(MalformedURLException ex)
{
}
```

A MalformedURLException is thrown if the URL string has a syntax error. For example, the URL string "http:/www.sun.com" would cause the MalformedURLException runtime error because two slashes (//) are required.

To actually view the contents of an HTML page, you would need to write the following code:

```
AppletContext context = getAppletContext();
context.showDocument(location);
```

The java.applet.AppletContext class provides the environment for displaying Web page contents. The showDocument() method displays the Web page in the environment.

Example 15.4 Viewing HTML Pages from Java

This example demonstrates an applet that views Web pages. The Web page's URL is entered, the Go button is clicked, and the Web page is displayed (see Figure 15.14 and Figure 15.15).

```
import java.net.*;
import java.awt.*;
import java.awt.event.*;
import java.applet.*;

public class TestAppletURL extends Applet
  implements ActionListener
{
  private Button btGo;
  private TextField tfUrl;

  public void init()
  {
    //add URL text field and Go button
    setLayout(new FlowLayout());
    add(new Label("URL"));
    tfUrl = new TextField(" ",20);
    add(tfUrl);
```

continues

Example 15.4   continued

```
                btGo = new Button("Go");
                add(btGo);

                //register listener
                btGo.addActionListener(this);
        }

        public void actionPerformed(ActionEvent evt)
        {
          String actionCommand = evt.getActionCommand();
          if (evt.getSource() instanceof Button)
            if ("Go".equals(actionCommand))
              try
              {
                AppletContext context = getAppletContext();
                //get the URL from text field
                URL url = new URL(tfUrl.getText());
                context.showDocument(url);
              }
              catch(Exception ex)
              {
                showStatus("Error "+ex);
              }
          }
        }
```

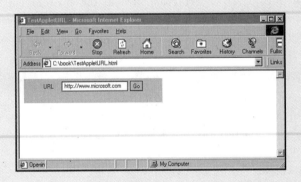

Figure 15.14   *Given a URL, the applet can display a Web page.*

Figure 15.15   *The Web page specified in the applet is displayed in the browser.*

Example Review

When the URL of a publicly available HTML file is entered and the Go button is clicked, a new HTML page is displayed. The page containing the applet becomes the previous page. A user could return to the previous page to enter a new URL and then view the new page.

Anyone using this program would have to run it from a Web browser instead of the Applet Viewer utility.

Retrieving Files from Web Servers

You can display an HTML page from an applet, as shown in the preceding section. But sometimes you need the Web server to give you access to the contents of a file. This access allows you to pass dynamic information from the server to the applets, as shown in Figure 15.16. The file stored on the server side can be a normal text file or a binary file that is created using DataOutput streams. To access the file, you would use the openStream() method defined in the URL class to open a stream to the file's URL.

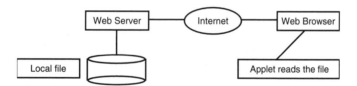

Figure 15.16 *The applet retrieves files from a Web server.*

The following method opens a connection to the file's URL and returns an InputStream so that you can read from that connection:

```
public final InputStream openStream() throws IOException
```

For example, the following statements open an input stream for the URL **http://www.ipfw.edu/kt2/liangy/web/java/in.dat** for the file **in.dat**, which is stored on the author's Web server.

```
try
{
  String urlString = "http://www.ipfw.edu/kt2/liangy/web/java/in.dat";
  url = new URL(urlString);
  InputStream is = url.openStream();
}
catch (MalformedURLException ex)
{
  System.out.println("Bad URL : "+url);
}
catch (IOException ex)
{
  System.out.println("IO Error : "+ex.getMessage());
}
```

Example 15.5 Retrieving Remote Data Files

This example, which is similar to Example 14.5, "Using StreamTokenizer" (see Chapter 14), demonstrates an applet that computes and displays student exam scores.

Rather than reading the file from the local system, this example reads the file from a Web server. The file contains student exam scores. Each record in the input file consists of a student name, two midterm exam scores, and a final exam score. The program reads the fields for each record, computes the total score, and displays the result in a text area. Figure 15.17 contains the output of a sample run of the program.

```java
import java.applet.Applet;
import java.awt.*;
import java.io.*;
import java.net.*;

public class RetrievingRemoteFile extends Applet
{
  //the author's Web site URL string for the input file
  private String urlString =
    "http://www.ipfw.edu/kt2/liangy/web/java/in.dat";

  //declare a Java URL object
  URL url;
  //the streamtokenizer for parsing input
  StreamTokenizer in;

  /*for input file fields: student name, midterm1,
    midterm2, and final exam score
  */
  String sname = null;
  double midterm1 = 0;
  double midterm2 = 0;
  double finalScore = 0;

  //for output file fields: total
  double total = 0;

  //text area for output display
  TextArea ta = new TextArea(5, 10);

  public void init()
  {
    try
    {
      url = new URL(urlString);  //create URL
      InputStream is = url.openStream();  //open stream

      //create streamtokenizer
      in = new StreamTokenizer(
              new BufferedReader(new InputStreamReader(is)));
    }
    catch (MalformedURLException ex)
    {
      System.out.println("Bad URL : "+url);
    }
    catch (IOException ex)
```

```
      {
        System.out.println("IO Error : "+ex.getMessage());
      }

      //add text area to the applet
      setLayout(new BorderLayout());
      add(ta);
      ta.setBackground(Color.yellow);

      try
      {
        //read first token
        in.nextToken();

        //process a record
        while (in.ttype != in.TT_EOF)
        {
          //get student name
          if (in.ttype == in.TT_WORD)
            sname = in.sval;
          else
            System.out.println("Bad file format");

          //get midterm1
          if (in.nextToken() == in.TT_NUMBER)
            midterm1 = in.nval;
          else
            System.out.println("Bad file format");

          //get midterm2
          if (in.nextToken() == in.TT_NUMBER)
            midterm2 = in.nval;
          else
            System.out.println("Bad file format");

          //get final score
          if (in.nextToken() == in.TT_NUMBER)
            finalScore = in.nval;

          //get total score
          total = midterm1*0.3 + midterm2*0.3 + finalScore*0.4;

          //display result
          ta.append(sname + " " +total + '\n');

          //get the next token
          in.nextToken();
        }
      }
      catch (IOException ex)
      {
        System.out.println("IO Errors "+ex.getMessage());
      }
    }
  }
```

continues

Example 15.5   continued

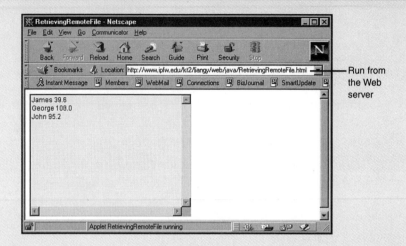

Figure 15.17   *The applet retrieves the file from the Web server and processes it.*

Example Review

For this program, a user would need to place three files on the Web server:

> **RetrievingRemoteFile.class**
>
> **RetrievingRemoteFile.html**
>
> **in.dat**

For convenience, the program assumes that these files are to be placed in one directory.

RetrievingRemoteFile.html can be browsed from any JDK 1.1–aware Web browser.

The `url = new URL(urlString)` statement creates a URL. The `InputStream is = url.openStream()` opens an input stream to read the remote file. After the input stream is established, reading data from the remote file is just like reading data locally.

The program uses `StreamTokenizer` to extract a student's name, two midterm exam scores, and the final exam score from the input stream; it computes the total score and displays it on the text area.

Chapter Summary

In this chapter, you learned how to write client/server applications and programs to work with the Web server. In client/server computing, the server must be running when a client starts. The server waits for a connection request from a client.

To create a server, you must first obtain a server socket using `new ServerSocket(port)`. After a server socket is created, the server can start to listen for connections using the `accept()` method on the server socket. The client requests a connection to a server by using `new socket(ServerName, port)` to create a client socket.

Stream socket communication is very much like input/output streams after the connection between a server and a client is established. The server and the client can communicate through input and output streams using `BufferedReader` and `PrintWriter`.

Often a server must work with multiple clients at the same time. You can use threads to handle the server's multiple clients simultaneously by simply creating a thread for each connection.

Applets are recommended for deploying multiple clients. They can be run anywhere with a single copy of the program. However, an applet client can only connect to the server where the applet is loaded, due to security restrictions.

To get the HTML pages through HTTP, Java programs can directly connect with a Web server. You can use the URL to view a Web page in a Java applet. To retrieve data files on the Web server from applets, you can open a stream on the file's URL on the Web server.

Chapter Review

1. How do you create a server socket? What port numbers can be used? What happens if a requested socket number is already in use? Can a port connect to multiple clients?

2. What are the differences between a server socket and a client socket?

3. How does a client program initiate a connection?

4. How does a server accept a connection?

5. How is data transferred between a client and a server?

6. How do you make a server serve multiple clients?

7. Can clients interfere with each other when multiple connections are served simultaneously?

Programming Exercises

1. Rewrite Example 15.2 using GUI for the server and the client rather than using console input and output. Display a message in the text area on the server side when the server receives a message from a client, as shown in Figure 15.18. On the client side, you can use a text field to enter the radius, as shown in Figure 15.19.

Figure 15.18   *The server receives a radius from a client, computes the area, and sends the area to the client.*

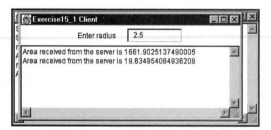

Figure 15.19   *The client sends the radius to the server and receives the area from the server.*

2. Write a client/server application. The client should retrieve a file from the server. The client can run as an application or an applet—similar to the one in Example 14.4, "Displaying a File in a Text Area"—that includes a text field in which to enter the filename, a text area in which to show the file, and a button that can be used to submit an action. Also, add a label at the bottom of the frame to indicate the status, such as File loaded successfully or Network connection problem. Figure 15.20 demonstrates an example of viewing the file **default.htm** located on Web server **http://www.ipfw.edu/kt2/liangy/default.htm**.

3. Modify Example 15.3 by adding the following features:

1. Add a View button to the user interface to allow the client to view a record for a specified name. The user will be able to enter a name in the Name field and click the View button to display the record for the student, as shown in Figure 15.21.

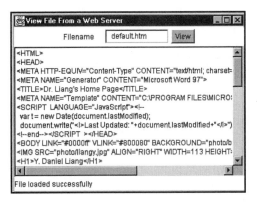

Figure 15.20 *The program displays the contents of a specified file on the Web server.*

2. Limit the concurrent connections to two clients.

3. Display the status of the submission (Successful or Failed) on a label.

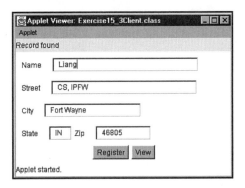

Figure 15.21 *You can view or register students in this applet.*

4. Write an applet that will display the stock index ticker—similar to the ones in the sixth exercise in the "Programming Exercises" section at the end of Chapter 14. Ensure that the applet gets the stock index from a file stored on the Web server.

5. Write an applet to show the number of visits made to a Web page. The count should be stored on the server side in a file. Every time the page is visited or reloaded, the applet should send a request to the server, and the server should increase the count and send that count to the applet. The applet should then display the count in a message, such as You are visitor number: 1000. The server can read or write to the file using a random file access stream.

APPENDIXES

The appendixes cover a mixed bag of topics. Appendix A lists Java keywords. Appendix B gives tables of ASCII characters and their associated codes in decimal and in hex. Appendix C shows the operator precedence. Appendix D summarizes Java modifiers and their usage. Appendix E introduces HTML basics. Appendix F contains information for using the companion CD-ROM. Finally, Appendix G provides a glossary of key terms and their definitions.

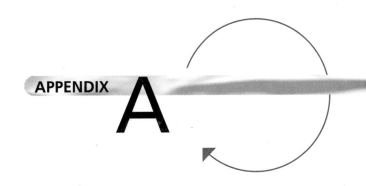

JAVA KEYWORDS

The following 47 keywords are reserved for use by the Java language:

abstract	finally	public
boolean	float	return
break	for	short
byte	goto	static
case	if	super
catch	implements	switch
char	import	synchronized
class	instanceof	this
const	int	throw
continue	interface	throws
default	long	transient
do	native	try
double	new	void
else	package	volatile
extends	private	while
final	protected	

The keywords goto and const are C++ keywords reserved in Java, even though they are not currently used in Java. This enables Java compilers to identify them and to produce better error messages if they appear in Java programs.

The Boolean literal values true and false are not keywords. Similarly, the null object value is not classified as a keyword. You cannot use them for other purposes, however.

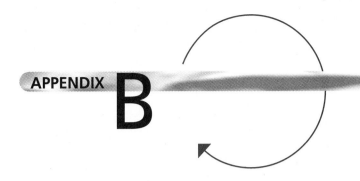

THE ASCII CHARACTER SET

Table B.1 and Table B.2 show ASCII characters and their respective decimal and hexadecimal codes. The decimal or hexadecimal code of a character is the combination of the row index and the column index. For example, in Table B.1, the letter A is at row 6 and column 5, so its decimal equivalent is 65; in Table B.2, letter A is at row 4 and column 1, so its hexadecimal equivalent is 41.

TABLE B.1   ASCII Character Set in the Decimal Index

	0	1	2	3	4	5	6	7	8	9
0	nul	soh	stx	etx	eot	enq	ack	bel	bs	ht
1	nl	vt	ff	cr	so	si	dle	dcl	dc2	dc3
2	dc4	nak	syn	etb	can	em	sub	esc	fs	gs
3	rs	us	sp	!	"	#	$	%	&	'
4	(	)	*	+	,	-	.	/	0	1
5	2	3	4	5	6	7	8	9	:	;
6	<	=	>	?	@	A	B	C	D	E
7	F	G	H	I	J	K	L	M	N	O
8	P	Q	R	S	T	U	V	W	X	Y
9	Z	[	\	]	^	_	`	a	b	c
10	d	e	f	g	h	i	j	k	l	m
11	n	o	p	q	r	s	t	u	v	w
12	x	y	z	{	|	}	~	del		

TABLE B.2   ASCII Character Set in the Hexadecimal Index

	0	1	2	3	4	5	6	7	8	9	A	B	C	D	E	F
0	nul	soh	stx	etx	eot	enq	ack	bel	bs	ht	nl	vt	ff	cr	so	si
1	dle	dc1	dc2	dc3	dc4	nak	syn	etb	can	em	sub	esc	fs	gs	rs	us
2	sp	!	"	#	$	%	&	'	(	)	*	+	,	-	.	/
3	0	1	2	3	4	5	6	7	8	9	:	;	<	=	>	?
4	@	A	B	C	D	E	F	G	H	I	J	K	L	M	N	O
5	P	Q	R	S	T	U	V	W	X	Y	Z	[	\	]	^	_
6	`	a	b	c	d	e	f	g	h	i	j	k	l	m	n	o
7	p	q	r	s	t	u	v	w	x	y	z	{	|	}	~	del

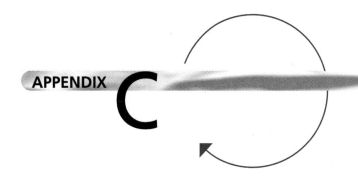

OPERATOR PRECEDENCE CHART

The operators are shown in decreasing order of precedence from top to bottom. Operators in the same group have the same precedence and are executed from left to right.

Operator	Type
()	Parentheses
()	Function call
[]	Array subscript
.	Object member access
++	Prefix increment
--	Prefix decrement
+	Unary plus
-	Unary minus
!	Unary logical negation
(type)	Unary casting
new	Creating object
*	Multiplication
/	Division
%	Integer remainder
+	Addition
-	Subtraction
<	Less than
<=	Less than or equal to
>	Greater than
>=	Greater than or equal to
instanceof	Checking object type
==	Equal comparison
!=	Not equal
&&	Boolean AND
||	Boolean OR
?:	Ternary condition

Operator	Type
=	Assignment
+=	Addition assignment
-=	Subtraction assignment
*=	Multiplication assignment
/=	Division assignment
%=	Integer remainder assignment

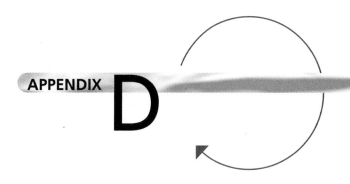

JAVA MODIFIERS

Modifiers are used on classes and class members (methods and data); however, the final modifier can also be used on local variables in a method. A modifier that can be applied to a class is called a *class modifier*. A modifier that can be applied to a method is called a *method modifier*. A modifier that can be applied to a data field is called a *data modifier*. Some modifiers can be applied to all three entities. The following table gives a summary of the modifiers covered in this book.

Modifier	Class	Method	Data	Explanation
(default)	✓	✓	✓	A class, method, or data field is visible in this package.
public	✓	✓	✓	A class, method, or data field is visible to all the programs in any packages.
private		✓	✓	A method or data field is only visible in this class.
protected		✓	✓	A method or data field is visible in this package and in subclasses of this class in any packages.
static		✓	✓	Define a class method or a class data field.
final	✓	✓	✓	A final class cannot be extended. A final method cannot be modified in a subclass. A final data field is a constant.
abstract	✓	✓		An abstract class must be extended. An abstract method must be overridden.
synchronized		✓		Only one thread can execute this method at a time.

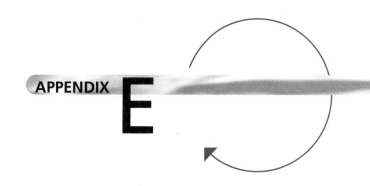

An HTML Tutorial

Java applets are embedded in HTML files. HTML (HyperText Markup Language) is a script language to design Web pages for creating and sharing multimedia-enabled, integrated electronic documents over the Internet. HTML allows documents on the Internet to be hyperlinked and presented using fonts and image and line justification appropriate for the systems on which they are displayed. The World Wide Web is a network of static and dynamic documents including texts, sound, and images. The Internet has been around for more than thirty years, but has only recently become popular. The Web is the major reason for its popularity.

The HTML documents are displayed by a program called a *Web browser*. When a document is coded in HTML, a Web browser can interpret the HTML to identify the elements of the document and to render it. The browser has control over the look and feel of a document. At present there is no absolute unifying HTML standard. Different vendors have rushed to introduce their own features interpretable by their proprietary browsers. However, the differences aren't significant. This tutorial introduces some frequently used HTML features that have been adopted by most of the browsers.

There are many easy-to-use authoring tools for creating Web pages. For example, you may create HTML files using Microsoft Word 97. The Internet Explorer and Netscape Navigator have simple authoring tools to let you create and edit HTML files. Microsoft FrontPage is a comprehensive and fully loaded tool that enables you to design more sophisticated Web pages. Authoring tools can greatly simplify the task of creating Web pages. However, the tools do not support all features of HTML. You will probably end up editing the source text produced by the tools. So, it is imperative to know the basic concept of HTML. In this tutorial, you will learn how to create your own Web pages using HTML.

Getting Started

Let us begin with an example to demonstrate the structure and the syntax of an HTML document.

Example E.1   An HTML Example

The following HTML document displays a message and a list of Web browsers: Netscape, Internet Explorer, and Mosaic. You may use any text editor, such as Microsoft NotePad on Windows, to create HTML documents, as long as it can save the file in ACSII text format.

```
<html>
<head>
<title>My First Web Page</title>
</head>
<body>
<i>Welcome to</i> <b>HTML</b>. Here is a list of popular Web
   browsers.
<ul>
  <li>Netscape
  <li>Internet Explorer
  <li>Mosaic
</ul>
<hr size=3>
Created by <A HREF=www.ipfw.edu/kt2/liangy>Y. Daniel Liang</A>.
</body>
</html>
```

Assume you have created a file named **ExampleE1.html** for this HTML document. You may use any Web browser to view the document. To view the document on Internet Explorer, start up your browser, choose Open from the File menu. A pop-up window opens to accept the filename. Type the full name of the file (including path), or click the Browser button to locate the file. Click OK to load and display the HTML file. Your document should be displayed as shown in Figure E.1.

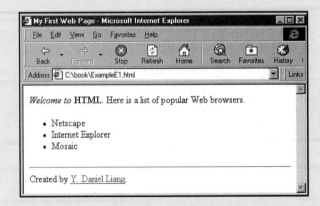

Figure E.1   *The HTML page is rendered by a Web browser.*

■ CAUTION

HTML filenames are case sensitive on UNIX and not case sensitive on other operating systems. The HTML files end with .html or .htm.

■ NOTE

The same document may be rendered differently subject to the capabilities of the Web browser. Regardless of the difference, the power of HTML is that your document can be viewed on a variety of browsers, on most platforms, and formatted to suit any reader. This tutorial uses Internet Explorer 4.0 for illustrations.

What makes *Welcome to* appear in italic in Figure E.1? What makes the document appear in the desired style? HTML is a document-layout and hyperlink-specification language; that is, it tells the Web browser how to display the contents of the document, including text, images, and other media, using instructions called *tags*. The browser interprets the tags and decides how to display or otherwise treat the subsequent contents of the HTML document. Tags are enclosed in brackets; <html>, <i>, <b>, and </html> are tags that appear in the preceding HTML example. The first word in a tag is called the *tag name*, which describes tag functions. Tags may have additional attributes, sometimes with values after an equal sign, which further define the tag's action. For example, in Example E.1, the attribute size in the tag <hr> defines the size of the bar to be 3.

Most tags have a *start tag* and a corresponding *end tag*. A tag has a specific effect on the region between the start tag and the end tag. For example, <b>text</b> advises the browser to display the word "text" in bold. <b> and </b> are the start and end tags for displaying boldface text. An end tag is always the start tag's name preceded by a forward slash (/). A few tags do not have end tags. For example, <hr>, a tag to draw a line, has no corresponding end tag.

A tag can be embedded inside another tag; for example, all tags are embedded within <html> and </html>. However, tags cannot overlap; for example, it would be wrong to use <b>bold and <i>italic</b></i>; the correct use should be <b><i>bold and italic</i></b>.

■ TIP

Tags are not case sensitive. However, it is good practice to use case consistently for clarity and readability. This tutorial uses lowercase for tags.

The following types of tags are introduced in the upcoming sections:

- **Structure tags**—Define the structure of the documents

- **Text appearance tags**—Define the appearance of text

- **Paragraph tags**—Define headings, paragraphs, and line breaks

- **Font tags**—Specify font sizes and colors

- **List tags**—Define ordered or unordered lists and definition lists

- **Table tags**—Define tables

- **Link tags**—Specify navigation links to other documents

- **Image tags**—Specify where to get images and how to display images

Structure Tags

An HTML document begins with the `<html>` tag, which declares that the document is written with HTML. Each document has two parts—*head* and *body*—defined by the `<head>` and `<body>` tags, respectively. The head part contains the document title (using the `<title>` tag) and other parameters the browser may use when rendering the document; the body part contains the actual contents of the document. An HTML document may have the following structure:

```
<html>
<head>
<title>My First Web Page</title>
</head>
<body>
<!-- document body-->
</body>
</html>
```

Here the special starting tag `<!--` and ending tag `-->` are used to enclose comments in the HTML documents. The comments are not displayed.

NOTE

Your documents may be displayed correctly even if you don't use the `<html>`, `<head>`, `<title>`, and `<body>` tags. However, use of these tags is strongly recommended because they communicate certain information about and properties of a document to the browser; the information they provide is helpful for the effective use of the document.

Text Appearance Tags

HTML provides many tags to advise the appearance of text. At present, some text tags have the same effect. For example, `<em>`, `<cite>`, and `<i>` will all display the text in italic. However, a future version of HTML may make these tags distinct. Text tag names are fairly descriptive. The text tags can be classified into two categories: *content-based tags* and *physical tags*.

Content-Based Tags

Content-based tags inform the browser to display the text based on semantic meaning, such as citation, program code, and emphasis. Here is a summary of content-based tags:

- **`<cite>`**—Indicates the enclosed text is a bibliographic citation, displayed in italic

- **`<code>`**—Indicates the enclosed text is a programming code, displayed in monospace font

- **`<em>`**—Indicates the enclosed text should be displayed with emphasis, displayed in italic

- **`<strong>`**—Indicates the enclosed text should be strongly emphasized, displayed in bold

- **`<var>`**—Indicates the enclosed text is a computer variable, displayed in italic

- **`<address>`**—Indicates the enclosed text is an address, displayed in italic

Table E.1 lists the content-based tags and provides examples of their use.

TABLE E.1   Using Content-Based Tags

Tag	Example	Display
`<cite>...</cite>`	`<cite>bibliographic </cite>`	*bibliographic*
`<code>...</code>`	`<code>source code </code>`	`source code`
`<em>...</em>`	`<em>emphasis</em>`	*emphasis*
`<strong>... </strong>`	`<strong>strongly emphasized</strong>`	**strongly emphasized**
`<var>...</var>`	`<var>programming variable</var>`	*programming variable*
`<address>... </address>`	`<address>Computer Dept</address>`	*Computer Dept*

Physical Tags

Physical tags explicitly ask the browser to display text in bold, italic, or other ways. Following are six commonly used physical tags:

- `<i>` (italic)

- `<b>` (bold)

- `<u>` (underline)

- `<tt>` (monospace)

- `<strike>` (strike-through text)

- `<blink>` (blink)

Table E.2 lists the physical tags and provides examples of their use.

TABLE E.2   Using Physical Tags

Tag	Example	Display
`<i>...</i>`	`<i>italic</i>`	*italic*
`<b>...</b>`	`<b>bold</b>`	**bold**
`<u>...</u>`	`<u>underline</u>`	underline
`<tt>...</tt>`	`<tt>monospace</tt>`	`monospace`
`<strike>...</strike>`	`<strike>strike</strike>`	~~strike~~
`<blink>...</blink>`	`<blink>blink</blink>`	blink (causes it to blink)

Paragraph Style Tags

There are many tags in HTML to deal with paragraph styles. There are six heading tags (`<h1>`, `<h2>`, `<h3>`, `<h4>`, `<h5>`, `<h6>`) for different size of headings, line break tag (`<br>`), paragraph start tag (`<p>`), preformat tag (`<pre>`), and block quote tag (`<blockquote>`).

The six heading tags indicate the highest (`<h1>`) and lowest (`<h6>`) precedence a heading may have in the document. The heading tags may be used with an align attribute to place the heading toward *left, center,* or *right.* The default alignment is left. For example, `<h3 align=right>Heading</h3>` tells the browser to right-align the heading.

The line break tag `<br>` tells the browser to start displaying from the next line. This tag has no end tag.

The paragraph start tag `<p>` signals the start of a paragraph. This tag has an optional end tag `</p>`.

The `<pre>` tag and its required end tag (`</pre>`) define the enclosed segment to be displayed in monospaced font by the browser.

The `<blockquote>` tag is used to contain text quoted from another source. The quote will be indented from both left and right.

Example E.2   HTML Source Code Using Structure Tags

The following HTML source code illustrates the use of paragraph tags. The text the code creates is displayed in Figure E.2.

```
<html>
<head>
<title>Demonstrating Paragraph Tags</title>
```

```
</head>
<body>
<!-- Example E.2 -->
<h1 align=right>h1: Heading 1</h1>
<h3 align=center>h3: Heading 3</h3>
<h6 align=left>h6: Heading 6</h6>
<p>
<pre>preformat tag</pre>
<blockquote>
block quote tag
<br>
and line break
</blockquote>
</body>
</html>
```

Figure E.2   *Paragraph tags specify heading styles, paragraph format, block quote, line break, and so on.*

Font, Size, and Color Tags

With HTML you can specify font size and colors using font tags. There are two font tags: `<basefont>` and `<font>`.

The `<basefont>` tag is typically placed in the head of an HTML document, where it sets the base font size for the entire document. However, it may appear anywhere in the document, and it may appear many times, each time with a new size attribute. Many browsers use a relative model for sizing fonts, ranging from 1 to 7; the default base font size is 3. Each successive size is 20 percent larger than its predecessor in the range.

The `<font>` tag allows you to specify the size and color of the enclosed text using size and color attributes. The size attribute is the same as the one for `<basefont>` tag. The color attribute sets the color for the enclosed text between `<font>` and

</font>. The value of the attribute is a six-digit hex number preceded by a pound sign (#). The first two digits are the red component, the next two digits are the green component, and the last two digits are the blue component. The digits are from 00 to FF. Alternatively, you may set the color using standard names such as red, yellow, blue, and orange.

Example E.3   Testing Font Tags

The following HTML source code illustrates the use of the `<basefont>` and `<font>` tags. The text it creates is displayed in Figure E.3.

```
<html>
<head>
<title>Demonstrating Fonts, Size and Color</title>
</head>
<basefont size=6>
<body bgcolor=white>
<!-- Example E.3 -->
basefont<br>
<font size=7 color=blue>blue7</font><br>
<font size=3 color=#FF0000>red3</font><br>
</body>
</html>
```

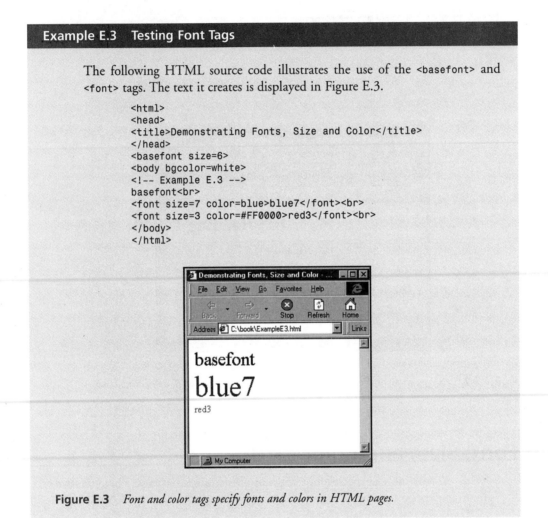

Figure E.3   *Font and color tags specify fonts and colors in HTML pages.*

List Tags

HTML allows you to define three kinds of lists: *ordered lists, unordered lists,* and *definition lists.* You can also build nested lists. Example E.1 contains an unordered list of three Web browsers.

Ordered Lists

Ordered lists label the items in them. The ordered list is used when the sequence of the listed items is important. For example, chapters are listed in order. An ordered list starts with the tag `<ol>` and ends with `</ol>`, and items are placed in between. Each item begins with an `<li>` tag. The browser automatically numbers list items starting from numeric 1. Instead of using the default numeric numbers for labeling, you may associate the tag `<ol>` with a type attribute. The value of the type determines the style of the label.

- Type value `A` for uppercase letter labels A, B, C, …
- Type value `a` for lowercase letter labels a, b, c, …
- Type value `I` for capital Roman numerals I, II, III, …
- Type value `i` for lowercase Roman numerals i, ii, iii, …
- Type value `1` for Arabic numerals 1, 2, 3, …

Unordered Lists

When the sequence of the listed items is not important, you may use an unordered list. For example, a list of Web browsers may be given in any order. An unordered list starts with the tag `<ul>` and ends with `</ul>`. Inside, you use `<li>` tags for items. By default, the browser uses bullets to mark each item. You may use `disc`, `circle`, or `square` as type values to indicate the use of markers other than bullets.

Definition Lists

The definition list is used to define terms. The list is enclosed between `<dl>` and `</dl>` tags. Inside the tags are the terms and their definition. The term and definition have leading tags `<dt>` and `<dd>`, respectively. Browsers typically render the term name at the left margin and render the definition below it and indented.

Example E.4   Using Various List Tags

This example illustrates the use of tags for ordered lists, unordered lists, definition lists, and nested lists. The output of the following code is displayed in Figure E.4.

```
<html>
<head>
<title>Demonstrating List Tags</title>
</head>
<body bgcolor=white>
<!-- Example E.4 List Tags -->
<center><b>List Tags</b></center>
```

continues

555

Example E.4   continued

```
An ordered List
<ol type=A>
  <li>Chapter 1: Introduction to Java
  <li>Chapter 2: Java Building Elements
  <li>Chapter 3: Control Structures
</ol>
An unordered List
<ul type=square>
  <li>Apples
  <li>Oranges
  <li>Peaches
</ul>
Definition List
<dl>
   <dt>What is Java?
   <dd>An Internet programming language.
</dl>
</body>
</html>
```

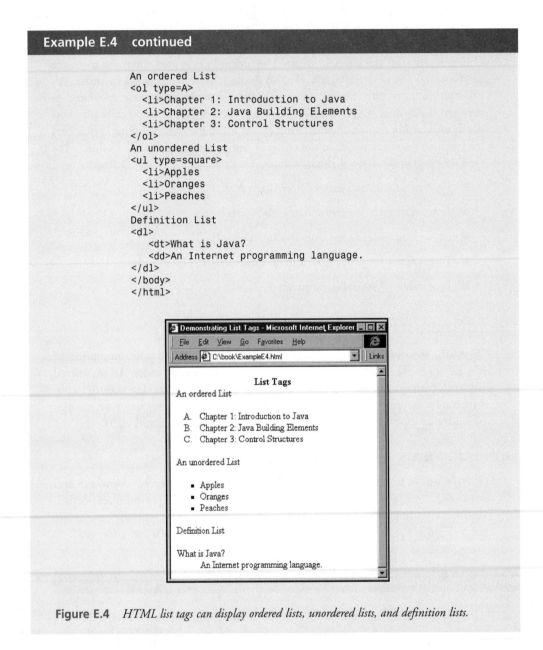

Figure E.4   *HTML list tags can display ordered lists, unordered lists, and definition lists.*

Table Tags

Tables are useful features supported by many browsers. Tables are collections of numbers and words arranged in rows and columns of cells. In HTML, table elements including data items, row and column headers, and captions are enclosed between `<table>` and `</table>` tags. Several table tags may be used to specify the layout of tables. Each row in the table is wrapped by `<tr>` and `</tr>`. Inside the row, data or words in a cell are enclosed by `<td>` and `</td>`. You may use `<caption>...</caption>` to display a caption for the table and use `<th>...</th>` to display column headers.

Table tags may be used with attributes to obtain special effects. Here are some useful attributes:

- **border**—Can appear in the <table> tag to specify that all cells are surrounded with a border.

- **align**—Can appear in the <caption>, <tr>, <th>, or <td> tags. If it appears in <caption>, it specifies whether the caption appears above or below the table using values top or bottom. The default is align=top. If it appears in <tr>, <th>, or <td>, align specifies whether the text is aligned to the left, the right, or centered inside the table cell(s).

- **valign**—Can appear in <tr>, <th> or <td>. The values of the attribute are top, middle, and bottom to specify whether text is aligned to the top, the bottom, or centered inside the table cell(s).

- **colspan**—Can appear in any table cell to specify how many columns of the table this cell should span. The default value is 1.

- **rowspan**—Can appear in any column to specify how many rows of the table this cell should span. The default value is 1.

Example E.5 Illustration of Table Tags

This example creates an HTML table. The output of the following code is displayed in Figure E.5.

```
<html>
<head>
<title>Demonstrating Table Tags</title>
</head>
<body bgcolor=white>
<!-- Example E.5 Table Tags -->
<center>Table Tags</center>
<br>
<table border=2>
<caption>This is a Table</caption>
<tr>
  <th>Table heading</th>
  <td>Table data</td>
</tr>
<tr>
  <th valign=bottom>Second row
  <td>Embedded Table
     <table border=3>
     <tr>
       <th>Table heading</th>
       <td align=right>Table data</td>
     </tr>
     </table>
  </td>
</tr>
</table>
</body>
</html>
```

continues

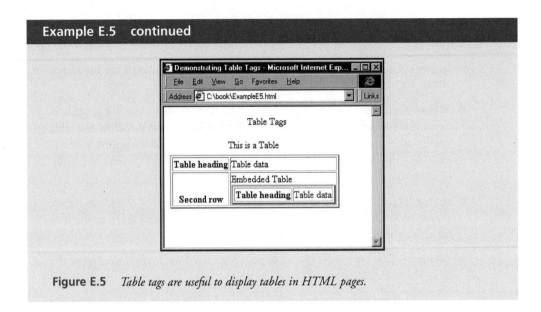

Example E.5   continued

Figure E.5   *Table tags are useful to display tables in HTML pages.*

Hyperlink Tags

The true power of HTML lies in its capability to join collections of documents together into a full electronic library of information, and to link documents with other documents over the Internet. This is called *hypertext linking*, which is the key character that makes the Web appealing and popular. By adding hypertext links, called *anchors*, to your HTML document, you can create a highly intuitive information flow and guide the users directly to the information they want. You can link documents on different computers, or on the same computer, or jump within the same document using anchor tags.

Linking Documents on Different Computers

Every document on the Web has a unique address, known as its *Uniform Resource Locator* (URL). To navigate from a source document to a target document, you need to reference the target's URL inside the anchor tags `<a>` and `</a>` using attribute `href`. The following example displays a list of database vendors:

```
<ul>
 <li><a href="http://www.oracle.com">Oracle</a>
 <li><a href="http://www.sybase.com">Sybase</a>
 <li><a href="http://www.informix.com">Informix</a>
</ul>
```

In this example, clicking on Oracle will display the Oracle home page. The URL of Oracle's home page Internet address is **http://www.oracle.com**. The general format of a URL is:

```
method://servername:port/pathname/fullfilename
```

method is the name of the operation that is performed to interpret this URL. The most common methods are `http`, `ftp`, and `file`.

- **http**—Accesses a page over the network using the HTTP protocol. For example, **http://www.microsoft.com** links to Microsoft's homepage. **http://** can be omitted.

- **ftp**—Downloads a file using anonymous FTP service from a server, for example: **ftp://hostname/directory/fullfilename**.

- **file**—Reads a file from the local disk. For example, `file://home/liangy/liangy.html` displays the file **liangy.html** from the directory `/home/liangy` on the local machine.

servername is the unique Internet name or Internet Protocol (IP) numerical address of the computer on the network. For example, **www.sun.com** is the hostname of Sun Microsystem's Web server. If a server name is not specified, it is assumed the file is on the same server.

port is the TCP port number that the Web server is running on. Most Web servers use port number 80 by default.

pathname is optional and indicates the directory under which the file is located.

fullfilename is optional and indicates the target filename. Web servers usually use **index.html** on UNIX and **default.htm** on Windows for a default filename. For example, `<a  href="http://www.oracle.com">Oracle</a>` is equivalent to `<a href="http://www.oracle.com/index.html">Oracle</a>`.

Linking Documents on the Same Computer

To link a document on the same computer, you should use the `file` method instead of the `http` method in the target URL. There are two types of links: *absolute link* and *relative link*.

When linking to a document on different machines, you must use an absolute link to identify the target document. An absolute link uses a URL to indicate the complete path to the target file.

When you are linking to a document on the same computer, it is better to use a relative link. A relative URL omits method and server name and directories. For instance, assume the source document is under directory `~liangy/teaching` on the server `sewrk01.ipfw.indiana.edu`. The URL

```
file://sewrk01.ipfw.indiana.edu/~liangy/teaching/teaching.html
```

is equivalent to

```
file://teaching.html
```

Here, `file://` can be omitted. An obvious advantage of using a relative URL is that you can move the entire set of documents to another directory or even another server and never have to change a single link.

Jumping Within the Same Document

HTML offers navigation within the same document. This is helpful to directly browse interesting segments of the document.

Example E.6   Navigation Within the Same Document

This example shows a document with three sections. The output of the following code is shown in Figure E.6. When the user clicks Section 1: Introduction on the list, the browser jumps to Section 1 in the document. The name attribute within the <a> tag labels the section. The label is used as a link to the section. This feature is also known as *using bookmarks*.

When you test this example, make the window small so that you can see the effects of jumping to each reference through the link tags.

```html
<html>
<head>
<title>Demonstrating Link Tags</title>
</head>
<body>
<ol>
  <li><a href="#introduction">Section 1: Introduction</a>
  <li><a href="#methodology">Section 2: Methodology</a>
  <li><a href="#summary">Section 3: Summary</a>
</ol>

<h3><a name="introduction"><b>Section 1</b>:
Introduction</a></h3>
an introductory paragraph

<h3><a name="methodology"><b>Section 2</b>:
Methodology</a></h3>
a paragraph on methodology

<h3><a name="summary"><b>Section 3</b>: Summary</a></h3>
a summary paragraph
</body>
</html>
```

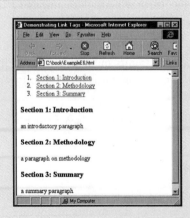

Figure E.6 *Hyperlink tags link documents.*

Embedding Graphics

One of most compelling features of the Web is its ability to embed graphics in a document. You may use graphics for icons, pictures, illustrations, drawings, and so on. Graphics bring a live dimension to your documents. You may use an image as a visual map of hyperlinks. This section introduces the use of *horizontal bar tags* and *image tags*.

Horizontal Bar Tags

The horizontal bar tag (`<hr>`) is used to display a rule. It is useful to separate sections of your document using horizontal rules. You may associate attributes `size`, `width`, and `align` to achieve the desired effect. You may thicken the rule using the `size` attribute with values in pixels. The `width` attribute specifies the length of the bar with values in either absolute number of pixels or percentage extension across the page. The `align` attribute specifies whether the bar is `left`, `centered`, or `right` aligned.

Example E.7   Illustration of Horizontal Bar Tags

This example illustrates the use of the `size`, `width`, and `align` attributes in horizontal bar tags. The output of the following code is shown in Figure E.7.

```
<html>
<head>
<title>Demonstrating Horizontal Rules</title>
</head>
<body bgcolor=white>
<!-- Example E.7 Horizontal Rule -->
<center>Horizontal Rules</center>
<hr size=3 width=80% align=left>
<hr size=2 width=20% align=right noshade>
<hr>
</body>
</html>
```

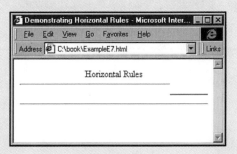

Figure E.7   *Horizontal bar tags are often used to separate contents in documents.*

561

Image Tags

The image tag, <img>, lets you reference and insert an image into the current text. The syntax for the tag is:

```
<img src=URL alt=text align = [top ¦ middle ¦ bottom ¦ texttop ]>
```

Most browsers support GIF and JPEG image format. Format is an encoding scheme to store images. The attribute src specifies the source of the image. The attribute alt specifies an alternate text message to be displayed in case the client's browser cannot display the image. The attribute alt is optional; if omitted, no message is displayed. The attribute align tells the browser where to place the image.

Example E.8   Illustration of Image Tags

This example creates a document with image tags. The output of the following code is shown in Figure E.8.

```
<html>
<head>
<title>Demonstrating Image Tags</title>
</head>
<body bgcolor=white>
<!-- Example E.7 Image Tags -->
<center>Image Tags</center>
<img name="Uconstruction" src="ipfwlogo.gif" align=middle>
</body>
</html>
```

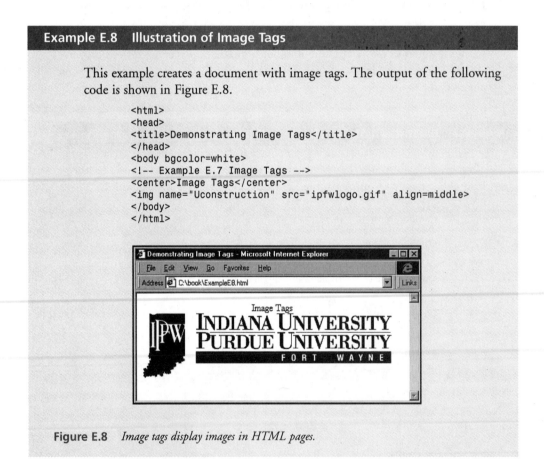

Figure E.8   *Image tags display images in HTML pages.*

More on HTML

This tutorial is not intended to be a complete reference manual on HTML. There are many interesting features, such as *forms* and *frames,* not mentioned in this tutorial. You may find dozens of books on HTML in your local bookstore. *Special Edition Using HTML* by Mark Brown and John Jung, published by Que, is a comprehensive reference on HTML; this complete book covers all the new HTML features supported by Netscape Navigator and Microsoft Internet Explorer. *HTML Quick Reference* by Robert Mullen, also published by Que, contains all the essential information you need to build Web pages with HTML in 100 pages. Please refer to these and other books for more information. You may also get information on line at the following Web sites:

- **www.ncsa.uiuc.edu/General/Internet/WWW/HTMLPrimer.html**

- **www.w3.org/pub/WWW/MarkUp/**

- **www.mcli.dist.maricopa.edu/tut/lessons.html**

- **www.netscape.com/assist/net_sites/frames.html**

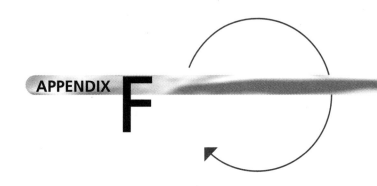

APPENDIX **F**

USING THE COMPANION CD-ROM

The companion CD contains the Java Development Kit 1.2 beta 4 for
Windows, JDK 1.2 documentation, and the source code in the text. The
JDK files are located in the jdk12 directory, the JDK documentation files are
located in the jdk12doc directory, and the source code is in the Book directory. This appendix covers installing JDK 1.2 and its documents on Windows
and introduces using source code from the text.

Installing JDK 1.2

The JDK files on the companion CD-ROM are only for installation on
Windows 95, Windows 98, or Windows NT. For using JDK 1.2 on a platform other than Windows, please refer to the Javasoft Web site at
www.javasoft.com. At the time of this writing, JDK 1.2 is also available on
Solaris/Sparc and Solaris/Intel.

To install JDK 1.2 on Windows, you need a 486/DX or faster processor, a
minimum of 32 megabytes of RAM, and at least 65 megabytes of disk space.
Here are the steps to install JDK 1.2 from the companion CD-ROM.

1. Insert the companion CD-ROM into your CD-ROM drive and
   double-click **jdk12-beta4-win32.exe** in the jdk12 directory to display
   a dialog box titled "InstallShield Self-extracting EXE," as shown in
   Figure F.1.

2. Click Yes to start extracting the files for installing JDK 1.2. The
   InstallShield wizard will guide you through the setup process. You will
   see the Welcome dialog box, as shown in Figure F.2.

3. Click Next to display the Software License Agreement dialog box, as
   shown in Figure F.3. Click Yes to accept the license. You will see the
   Select Components dialog box, as shown in Figure F.4.

Figure F.1 *The InstallShield Self-extracting EXE dialog box prompts you to start JDK installation.*

Figure F.2 *The Welcome dialog box reminds you to close all applications before installing JDK 1.2.*

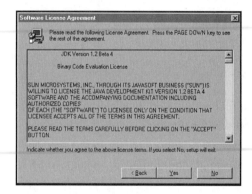

Figure F.3 *The Software License Agreement dialog box reveals license terms for using JDK 1.2.*

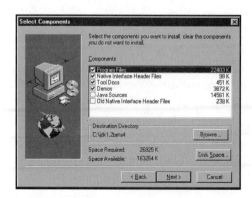

Figure F.4 *The Select Components dialog box lets you choose components for installation.*

4. Select the default components and use the default destination directory, as shown in Figure F.4, and click Next to display the dialog box titled "Start Copying Files."

5. Click Next to start copying files. You will then see a dialog box titled Plug-in installation, as shown in Figure F.5. If you click Yes, the Java Runtime Environment and plug-in will be installed. This feature is valuable for deployment. But for developing and testing Java code, you don't need the JRE and plug-in. Therefore, I recommend that you not install it in order to save some disk space.

Figure F.5 *The Plug-in Installation dialog box lets you choose whether to install the JRE and Plug-in.*

6. Click No to display the dialog box titled Setup Complete, as shown in Figure F.6. Click Finish to complete the setup.

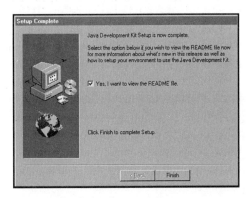

Figure F.6 *The Setup Complete dialog box indicates you have successfully completed JDK 1.2 installation.*

The preceding installation sets various registry entries to record installation information. You will need to perform some final configuration steps by hand. This consists primarily of adding c:\jdk1.2beta4\bin on the PATH variable and adding c:\jdk1.2beta4 on the CLASSPATH variable.

On Windows 95 or Windows 98, add the following two lines to the **autoexec.bat** file:

```
set PATH = c:\jdk1.2beta4\bin;%PATH%;
set CLASSPATH = .;c:\jdk1.2beta4\lib;%CLASSPATH%;
```

The period (.) indicates the current directory, which should always be in the CLASSPATH. %PATH% refers to the existing PATH and %CLASSPATH% refers to the existing CLASSPATH. These settings are automatically applied when you reboot—but *only* when you reboot.

On Windows NT, you need to add `c:\jdk1.2beta4\bin` in the PATH entry in the Environment tab of the System control panel and add `.;c:\jdk1.2beta4\lib` in the CLASSPATH entry of the same tab. These settings are stored permanently, and affect any new command-line windows, but not any existing command-line windows.

Installing and Browsing JDK 1.2 Online Documentation

The JDK 1.2 Help documents are archived into a compressed file in `\jdk12doc\jdk12-beta4-doc.zip` on the companion CD. You can unpack the files using an appropriate compressing/decompressing utility such as unzip, gunzip, pkunzip, or WinZip. Your utility must support long filenames. WinZip can be downloaded from **www.winzip.com**.

The files in the archive .zip file use path names that begin with `jdk1.2beta4\docs`. You should extract the files into the c:\ drive so that the Help documents will be stored in the `jdk1.2beta4\docs` subdirectory of the JDK installation directory, because you have already installed JDK in the `c:\jdk1.2beta4` directory. For instance, if installing the documents using WinZip, you should enter c:\ in the Extract to field of the Extract dialog box, as shown in Figure F.7.

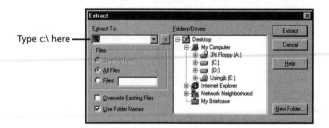

Figure F.7 *To preserve the hypertext links, you should install the JDK documents in the* `\jkd1.2beta4\docs` *directory.*

NOTE

The installation overwrites a number of existing JDK HTML files. This is deliberate. Overwriting these files changes hypertext links from **www.javasoft.com** to point to files in the local disk.

The Help documents are HTML files. You can start browsing your JDK documentation from the **index.html** file in the `jdk1.2beta4\docs` directory.

Using the Examples in the Book

The source code for the examples in the text can be found in the Book directory on the CD-ROM. For convenience, all the files are placed directly under the \Book directory. The files are named as follows:

1. If the example contains a single class, the class name is the filename. For instance, the class name in Example 1.1 is Welcome, thus the filename for this example is **Welcome.java**.

2. If the example is a Java application with multiple classes, the class that contains the main method determines the filename on the CD-ROM. For instance, the filename for Example 9.1 is **ButtonDemo.java,** because the main class is ButtonDemo.

3 If the example is a Java applet, the filename is the applet class name. For instance, the filename for Example 10.1 is **MortgageApplet.java,** because the applet class is MortgageApplet.

4. For each applet, the associated HTML file is also provided on the CD-ROM. The HTML file is named according to the applet name. For instance, the HTML filename for Example 10.1 is **MortgageApplet.html**, because the applet class is MortgageApplet.

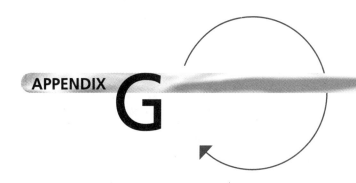

GLOSSARY

This glossary lists and defines the key terms used in *Introduction to Java Programming*.

abstract class When you are designing classes, a superclass should contain common features that are shared by subclasses. Sometimes the superclass is so abstract that it cannot have any specific instances. These classes are called *abstract classes* and are declared using the abstract modifier. Abstract classes are like regular classes with data and methods, but you cannot create instances of abstract classes using the new operator.

abstract method A method signature without implementation. Its implementation is provided by its subclasses. An abstract method is denoted with an abstract modifier and must be contained within an abstract class. In a nonabstract subclass extended from an abstract class, all abstract methods must be implemented, even if they are not used in the subclass.

Abstract Window Toolkit (AWT) A package (java.awt.*) that contains GUI components such as buttons, labels, text fields, text areas, check boxes, scrollbars, and menus. The AWT classes provide a platform-independent interface to develop visual programs and graphical user interfaces. For each platform on which Java runs, the AWT components are automatically mapped to the platform-specific components. This mapping enables the user applications to be consistent with other applications running on the specific platform.

abstraction A technique in software development that hides detailed implementation. Java supports method abstraction and class abstraction. *Method abstraction* is defined as separating the use of a method from the implementation of that method. The client can use a method without knowing how that method is implemented. If you decide to change the implementation, the client program will not be affected. Similarly, *class abstraction* hides the implementation of the class from the client.

actual parameter   The value passed to a method when the method is invoked. Actual parameters should match formal parameters in type, order, and number.

algorithm   Pseudocode that describes how a problem is solved in terms of the actions to be executed, and specifies the order in which these actions should be executed. Algorithms can help the programmer plan a program before writing it in a programming language.

applet   A special kind of Java program that can run directly from a Web browser or applet viewer. Various security restrictions are imposed on an applet. For example, an applet cannot perform input/output operations on a user's system and therefore cannot read or write files or transmit computer viruses.

application   A standalone program, such as any program written using a high-level language. Applications can be executed from any computer with a Java interpreter. Applications are not subject to the security restrictions imposed on Java applets. An application class must contain a main method.

argument   Same as actual parameter.

array   A container object that stores an indexed sequence of the same types of data. Typically, the individual elements are referenced by an index value. The index is an int value starting with 0 for the first element, 1 for the second, and so on.

assignment statement   A simple statement that assigns a value to a variable.

block   A sequence of statements enclosed in braces ({}).

bytecode   The result of compiling Java source code. The bytecode is machine independent and can run on any machine that has a Java running environment.

casting   The process of converting a primitive data type value into another primitive type or converting an object of one data type into another object type. For example, (int)3.5 is to convert 3.5 into an int value and (Cylinder)c is to convert an object c into the Cylinder type. In Java, an object of a class can be cast to an instance of another class as long as the latter is a subclass of the former, or if an interface, implements the former.

child class   Same as **subclass**.

class   An encapsulated collection of data and methods that operate on data. A class may be instantiated to create an object that is an instance of the class.

class hierarchy   A collection of classes organized in terms of superclasses and subclasses relationships.

class method   A method that can be invoked without creating an instance of the class. To define class methods, put the modifier static in the method declaration.

class variable   A data member declared using the static modifier. A class variable is global to a class and to all instances of that class. Class variables are used to communicate between different objects with the same class and for handling global states among these objects.

comments   Comments are for documenting what the program is and how the program is constructed. Comments are not programming statements and are ignored by the compiler. In Java, comments are preceded by two slashes (//) in a line, or enclosed between /* and */ in multiple lines.

compiler   A software program that translates Java source code into bytecode. You can use javac to invoke the compiler in JDK.

constant   A variable declared final in Java. A class constant is usually shared by all objects of the same class; therefore, a class constant is often declared static. A local constant is a constant declared inside a method.

constructor   A special method for initializing objects when creating objects using the new operator. The constructor has exactly the same name as the class it comes from. Constructors can be overloaded, making it easier to construct objects with different kinds of initial data values.

data type   Data type is used to define variables. Java supports primitive data types and object data types.

debugging   The process of finding and fixing errors in a program.

declaration   Defines variables, methods, and classes in a program.

default constructor   A constructor that has no parameters.

definition   Alternative term for a **declaration**.

design   To plan how a program can be structured and implemented by coding.

double buffering   A technique to reduce flickering in image animation in Java.

encapsulation   Combining of methods and data into a single data structure. In Java, this is known as a *class*.

event   A type of signal to the program that something has happened. The event is generated by external user actions such as mouse movements, mouse button clicks, and keystrokes; or by the operating system, such as a timer. The program can choose to respond or ignore the event.

event adaptor   A class that is used to filter event methods and handle only specified ones.

event delegation   In Java event-driven programming, the event is assigned to the listener object for processing. This is referred to as event delegation.

event-driven programming   Java graphics programming is event driven. In event-driven programming, the codes are executed upon activation of events, such as clicking a button or moving the mouse.

event handler   A method in the listener's object that is designed to do some specified processing when a particular event occurs.

event listener   The object that receives and handles the event.

event listener interface   An interface to be implemented by the listener class for handling the specified events.

event registration   To become a listener, the object must be registered as a listener by the source object. The source object maintains a list of listeners and notifies all the registered listeners when the event occurs.

event source   The object that generates the event.

exception   An unexpected event indicating that a program has failed in some way. Exceptions are represented by exception objects in Java. Exceptions can be handled in a try/catch block.

final   A modifier for classes, data, methods, and local variables. A final class cannot be extended, a final data or local variable is a constant, and a final method cannot be overridden in a subclass.

formal parameter   The parameters defined in the method signature.

getter method   For retrieving private data in a class.

graphical user interface (GUI)   An interface to a program that is implemented using AWT components such as frames, buttons, labels, text fields, and so on.

HTML (Hypertext Markup Language)   A script language to design Web pages for creating and sharing multimedia-enabled, integrated electronic documents over the Internet.

identifier   A name of a variable, method, class, interface, or package.

information hiding   A software engineering concept for hiding and protecting the internal features and structure of an object.

inheritance   With object-oriented programming, you can use the extends keyword to derive new classes from existing classes. This is called *inheritance.*

inner class   An inner class is a class embedded in another class. Inner classes enable you to define small auxiliary objects and pass units of behavior, thus making programs simple and concise.

instance   An object of a class.

instance method   A nonstatic method in a class. Instance methods belong to instances. These methods can only be invoked by the instances.

instance variable   A nonstatic data member of a class. A copy of an instance method exists in every instance of the class that is created.

instantiation   The process of creating an object of a class.

Integrated Development Environment (IDE)   Software to help programmers write code efficiently. Editing, compiling, building, debugging, and online help are integrated in one graphical user interface in an IDE tool.

interface   An interface is treated like a special class in Java. Each interface is compiled into a separate bytecode file, just like a regular class. You cannot create an instance for the interface. The structure of a Java interface is similar to that of an abstract class in that you can have data and methods. The data, however, must be constants, and the methods can have only declarations without implementation. Single inheritance is the Java restriction wherein a class can inherit from a single superclass. This restriction is eased by use of interface.

interpreter   Software for interpreting and running Java bytecode.

Java Development Kit (JDK)   Defines the Java API and contains a set of command-line utilities such as `javac` (compiler) and `java` (interpreter).

Just-in-Time compiler   Capable of compiling each bytecode once, and then reinvoking the compiled code repeatedly when the bytecode is executed.

keyword   A reserved word defined as part of Java language. (See Appendix A, "Java Keywords," for a full list of keywords.)

local variable   A variable defined inside a method definition.

main class   A class that contains a main method.

method   A collection of statements that are grouped together to perform an operation. (See **class method** and **instance method**.)

method overloading   Method overloading means that you can define the methods with the same name in a class as long as there is enough difference in their parameter profiles.

method overriding   Method overriding means that you can modify the method in a subclass that is originally defined in a superclass.

modifier   A Java keyword that specifies the properties of the data, methods, and classes and how they can be used. Examples of modifiers are `public`, `private`, and `static`.

multithreading   The capability of a program to perform several tasks simultaneously within a program.

object   Same as **instance**.

object-oriented programming (OOP)   An approach to programming that involves organizing objects and their behavior into classes of reusable components.

operator   Operations for primitive data type values. Examples of operators are +, -, *, /, and %.

operator precedence   Defines the order in which operators will be evaluated in an expression.

package   A collection of classes.

parent class   Same as **superclass**.

pass-by-reference   A term used when an object reference is passed as a method parameter. Any changes to the local object that occur inside the method body will affect the original object that was passed as the argument.

pass-by-value   A term used when a copy of a primitive data type variable is passed as a method parameter. The actual variable outside the method is not affected, regardless of the changes made to the formal parameter inside the method.

primitive data type   The primitive data types are `byte`, `short`, `int`, `long`, `float`, `double`, `boolean`, and `char`.

private   A modifier for members of a class. A private member can only be referenced inside the class.

protected   A modifier for members of a class. A protected member of a class can be used in the class in which it is declared or any subclasses derived from that class.

public   A modifier for classes, data, and methods that can be accessed by all programs.

recursive method   A method that invokes itself, directly or indirectly.

reserved word   Same as **keyword**.

setter method   For updating private data in a class.

signature   The combination of the name of a method and the list of its parameters.

socket   A term that describes the facilitation of communication between a server and a client.

statement   A unit of code that represents an action or a sequence of actions.

static method   Same as **class method**.

static variable   Same as **class variable**.

stream   A term that describes the continuous one-way flow of data between a sender and receiver.

subclass   A class that inherits from or extends a superclass.

superclass   A class that is inherited from a subclass.

tag   An HTML instruction that tells a Web browser how to display a document. Tags are enclosed in brackets such as `<html>`, `<i>`, `<b>`, and `</html>`.

thread   A flow of execution of a task, which has a beginning and an end, in a program.

Unicode   A code system for international characters managed by the Unicode Consortium. Java supports Unicode.

INDEX

EXAMPLE 7.2 (TESTING INHERITANCE)

EXAMPLE 7.3 (OVERRIDING THE METHODS IN THE SUPERCLASS)

M

V

W – Z